Shaping the Short Essay

Shaping the Short Essay

Ann Taylor
Salem State College

HarperCollins*Publishers*

Sponsoring Editor: Patricia Rossi
Project Editor: Steven Pisano
Art Direction and Cover Design: Jaye Zimet
Text Design: Glen M. Edelstein
Cover Photo: GABO, Naum. *Head of a Woman.* (c. 1917–20, after a work of 1916). Construction in celluloid and metal, 24 1/2 x 19 1/4 x 14″. Collection, The Museum of Modern Art, New York. Purchase. Photograph © 1990 The Museum of Modern Art, New York.
Production Administrator: Beth Maglione
Compositor: David E. Seham Associates, Inc.
Printer and Binder: R. R. Donnelley & Sons Company
Cover Printer: New England Book Components, Inc.

Shaping the Short Essay

Library of Congress Cataloging-in-Publication Data

Taylor, Ann M.
Shaping the short essay / Ann Taylor
p. cm.
Instructor's Edition: ISBN 0-673-52157-5
Student Edition: ISBN 0-673-39678-9
1. English language—Rhetoric. 2. College readers. 3. Essay.
I. Title.
PE1471.T39 1991
808′.0427—dc20 90-20429
CIP

91 92 93 94 9 8 7 6 5 4 3 2 1

to my mother

"The first principle of composition . . . is to foresee or determine the shape of what is to come, and pursue that shape."

E. B. White

Contents

Thematic Contents

Memories

Family Life

School Life

(NOTE: *In addition to the readings listed below, see the paragraphs on student housing in the "Working with . . ." introductions to sections.)*

Working

Sports

Entertainment and Media

Language and the Arts

Ideas and Values

For the Instructor

Like my earlier book, *Short Model Essays, Shaping the Shorter Essay* is primarily, although not exclusively, for writers who need to begin at the beginning and who need to develop some basic skills and some confidence while they are meeting the demands of writing in college. This book, however, is broader in scope, differing from the earlier book both in the organization and in the variety of pieces for analysis in Part I and in the detailed study of the process of writing in Part II.

Each chapter in Part I is organized generally around the basic modes of discourse—exposition, argumentation, description, and narration—and opens with a straightforward introduction, followed immediately by some practical advice called "Working with . . ." After each introduction is a set of examples, each opening with its own introduction, comments by the writer, and questions for thinking ahead. After each example is a vocabulary list; questions focusing on meaning, method, and variations; cross-references to other parts of the text; and suggestions for discussion and writing. These suggestions focus first on the mode of the chapter and then on related options. The readings within each chapter are arranged in the order of increasing complexity, thus illustrating the many possibilities within and among these various rhetorical modes.

In selecting these readings, I have chosen clear examples of particular modes so that students may see how they actually work and so that instructors may use them in whatever order they see fit. Although chapters work independently and may be easily rearranged, the plan reflects the usual order in my courses, beginning with exposition, moving through argument, and concluding with description and narration. In my experience, exposition, even on personal topics, "translates" more readily into the expository prose that students must write immediately in other courses. When they are more sure of how to identify purpose, of how to make a point in their writing, and of how to argue, I turn to the subtleties of description and narration. Once these are learned, the students seem more able to *use* these two modes for their own rhetorical purposes, not only as a "warm-up" for the "harder" exposition and argumentation yet to come.

Within the chapters, however, in the "Shifting Focus" questions and the "Exploring the Options" suggestions for discussion and writing, I also call attention to the problem of assigning certain pieces exclusively to certain modes, of fitting them into single categories. The purpose is to show that, while it remains true that some writing explains, some argues, some describes, and some tells stories, and while it remains essential to recognize these distinctions (particularly while writing), it is also important to recognize the frequent combinations and the deviations from the single track.

In the general introductions, the "Working with . . ." sections, the specific introductions, and the study questions, students first are asked to notice the specific focus of each chapter, and then they are encouraged to recognize such mergings: the narration in the service of argument; the description as an important part of exposition; the exposition as background for persuasion; and the description as the lifeblood of narration. And the suggestions for writing, while first focusing on pieces similar in rhetorical purpose to the ones in the book, also recognize the possibility of making other connections, and of trying other subjects, approaches, audiences, voices, or modes. Some suggestions, called "Exploring the Options," are, in fact, designed to highlight and encourage such possibilities, should instructors see fit. An alternative, thematic, table of contents allows for further experimentation.

One important factor is the selection of examples that are clearly organized and readable, mostly on topics that students may use as immediate inspirations for their own writing. I remain convinced that college freshmen, with serious writing assignments from other courses already stashed away in their gym bags, need to write as much as possible and as soon as possible. They need to write on subjects that are challenging but also *reasonable* within the time available. I prefer that in a writing course they concentrate immediately on clear, detailed, organized, and even polished prose, without the burden of extensive research or the irresponsible (and discouraging) glibness required by writing with too little information.

I also remain convinced that students learn from one another, that much as a beginning bird-watcher appreciates the simple annotated sketches of the *Peterson Field Guides,* they also appreciate clear, straightforward examples of what they are trying to comprehend. Student pieces are particularly valuable for showing up the "fieldmarks" that may so easily be obscured by showier plumage of the professional essay. And they are valuable for helping students to learn from professional writing, as discussed in later sections of each chapter and later in the book. Much of the focus, therefore, is on student writing: within each chapter of Part I through paragraphs, longer pieces, and comments from the writers themselves, and within each chapter of Part II through many of these same student pieces "in process," as they move toward final drafts. Students share their experience with other students.

Part II, a practical examination of the writing process, carries on with, and reflects back upon, the concerns of Part I. It focuses in detail on the major "steps" that writers take as they move from the earliest thoughts about writing to the final draft. It does not, however, present these steps as a military march—formal and inevitable—but, rather, as things that writers somehow get done, sometimes informally, often unpredictably. The chapters in Part II are broken down into general discussions, frequently based on drafts of student pieces found in Part I, followed by practice exercises, and some "For Your Own Paper" guidelines for whatever the students may be writing at the time.

Both Parts I and II stand independently and may be used in a variety of ways, but they may also be used simultaneously, thus focusing in some detail on both the process and the product. In the text, cross-references between Part I and Part II are regularly made, and in the *Instructor's Manual* there are further suggestions for coordinating the two parts.

Acknowledgements

I would like to acknowledge the help and support of the students—undergraduate and graduate—at Salem State College, plus colleagues and friends (Ellen Vellela, Tom Luddy, Phil DePalma, Frank Devlin, Bill Mahaney, Leon Jackson, Jim Stoll, David Vinopal, Tom and Leslie Moore, Gary Goshgarian, and Alicia Nitecki). I am grateful to Elaine Cruddas and Renee Meservey for their secretarial assistance and to my husband, Francis Blessington, and our children, Geoffrey and Julia, for their patience and resourcefulness. I would also like to thank the staffs of Scott, Foresman/Little, Brown and HarperCollins, particularly Joe Opiela, Ted Simpson, Byron Hopkins, David Munger, Guy Huff, Steven Pisano, and Tisha Rossi.

For the Student

This book is divided into two parts: Part I focuses on completed pieces, and Part II focuses on the process of how they got that way. Both parts are put together with you and your own writing in mind. They are meant to help you experience writing with less fear of the blank page, with more confidence as you work, and with more peace of mind as you turn in a paper.

In Part I are examples of finished prose, many of which were written by students and some of which were written by professional writers, but they all attempt to achieve a similar result: to give direction and shape to thoughts and to share them with readers. Each chapter focuses on a major, practical way of making writing work—explaining, arguing, describing, or telling a story—and considers how such purposes may be fulfilled. Specific introductions, comments from the writers themselves, and questions for thinking ahead help you to focus on the piece about to be read. The questions and the suggestions for discussion and writing concentrate on what has been done in the piece and on what *may* be done when the reader tries to become a writer.

Part II focuses on important steps taken by all writers as they move from the blank page to the final draft. These steps may or may not be taken in neat, predictable order, but they are always taken, sooner or later. All writers know this. Within these chapters are general discussions, concrete examples (many drawn from Part I) practices, and specific guidelines for the paper *you* are trying to write.

Ideally, you will be using both parts of this book simultaneously, each part supporting the insights of the other, as the need arises. Part I may, however, be used independently as a set of readings that may provide useful models for your own writing. Part II may also be read through separately, as a straightforward look at *how* papers are written.

Because writing is such a delightfully complex process and because it does not necessarily follow neat procedures or offer neat solutions, I always feel a need to tell my students everything all at once, at the beginning of the semester. My feelings are the same about this book. I would like you to know as much as possible as soon as possible. Follow your instructor's guidelines, but do not hesitate to read back and forth in the book as you work on your own writing. Don't wait. Writing isn't always neat, and neither is learning about it. Things you didn't understand in week one may become clear and useful in week three.

But, just as writing becomes better with greater knowledge of the entire process, so is learning to write well an ability to focus on the smaller details. None of this attention to detail can be rushed. Problems cannot be eliminated on the weekend near final grade time. Writing isn't that easy. As for any complex skill (e.g., hitting a backhand, playing the guitar, or doing a back handspring), accomplishment takes time, repetition, careful correction of errors, and, most of all, patience. The writer who fails to acknowledge problems, who fails to work at solutions, and who does not use new knowledge in writing a paper, will continue to write with exactly the same problems, no matter how many exercises are dashed off, no matter how many papers are scribbled out among the coffee cups in the cafeteria.

If you work on your writing—*all* aspects of your writing—that need attention, you may at first feel like a tripped-up beginner on a ski slope managing poles, skis, hips, shoulders, and knees all at the same time (while your new glove gets blown an insurmountable 3 feet away). Just remember that, with knowledge and practice, competent writing begins to feel more natural, just as does retrieving that glove. Things won't get away so easily.

It is also important to write as well as you can, every time you write, so you'll be learning new skills, not just repeating old, familiar errors. If you hear yourself saying things like, "Oh, yes, my teachers *always* say that. . . . I guess I'm just a wordy person," "I never *did* get those run-on sentences straight," or "What's a thesis?" be ready to work on just *those* problems, rather than to consign yourself to discouraging agreement with your teacher's criticisms. Give your next teacher something else, something more valuable, to focus on.

Inspiration goes only so far. As the English poet Alexander Pope warned, "True ease in writing comes from art, not chance,/ As those move easiest who have learn'd to dance."

Ann Taylor

PART 1

Shaping with a Purpose

PART I IS PRIMARILY A collection of examples, each one illustrating one of the major ways of adapting prose to the purpose at hand, such as explaining, arguing, describing, telling a story, or, as commonly happens, doing more than one of these at the same time. In each section, the paragraphs show briefly—and the longer pieces, more extensively—*how* these various tasks may be accomplished. In this way, the pieces may be studied closely and analyzed for technique.

These pieces, both short and long, may also be used as models or as inspirations for writing in ways that are similar to the original. It is possible to learn something about both manner and matter from them.

And, when read along with the discussions of composing in Part II, these pieces may also be seen as *results,* as final resolutions of real problems faced by real writers. It is thus possible to share with them the sometimes difficult, but often delightful, process of shaping words into essays.

Explaining Through Exposition

"To write about people you have to know people, to write about bloodhounds, you have to know bloodhounds, to write about the Loch Ness monster, you have to find out about it."

James Thurber

How many times in casual conversation do you hear questions like:

—"What's so bad about it?"
—"Is living in a condo like living in a house?"
—"Has he really changed that much?"
—"How do you do it?"
—"Why?"
—"What'll happen if I do?"
—"What is it?"

How many times in formal situations (as in examinations) are you asked to explain, to compare and contrast, to classify, to tell how, to give reasons why, to account for, to present results, or to define?

It would be difficult to make it through a day without having to explain something to someone who just doesn't "get it" or someone who wants to know if you get it.

Exposition, from the Latin *ex* and *ponere,* simply means "to place out" or "to set forth," and it gives the means to do just this. It gives us ways to explain, ways to make ourselves clear—by giving examples, by comparing and contrasting, by classifying, by describing a process, by examining causes and effects, or by defining. These are all ways of giving information straightforwardly to a reader, depending on what the subject demands. Exposition is the kind of writing most of us do most of the time.

Using Examples

When we give examples, we make concrete a more general statement. We put some substance behind our judgments. Consider the following:

1. Mr. Grumble is a terrible teacher, mostly because of the things he *doesn't* do:

   —Droning on from old, yellowed notes, he hasn't prepared a class in 20 years.
   —When he does give papers and tests, he doesn't pass them back until it's too late to drop the course.
   —Worst of all, he doesn't like students, responding most often with condescension and insults.

2. Thoreau's *Walden* offers several alternatives to life in the fast lane:

   —Dropping out of the race.
   —Enjoying the delights of freedom.
   —Appreciating simplicity.

3. I enjoyed several different kinds of books when I was a kid:

   —Adventure.
   —Mystery.
   —Science fiction.

4. Here are the things that make a part-time job worth the effort:

   —A reasonable boss.
   —Co-workers who do their fair share
   —Bearable responsibilities.
   —A paycheck that is appropriate for the work and the time put in.

5. A student searching out the best possibilities for housing during the school year has several friends who have chosen different living situations:

   —Kim (dorm, shared room).
   —Ryan (dorm, private room).
   —Jack (apartment).
   —Lisa (private home, babysitting).
   —Janice (own home).

Exemplification allows others to see what led the writer to make the general statement. The more detail there is, the better it is for the point being made and the greater the understanding and the interest of the reader.

Concerning the first example, I want to *hear* some of those old notes, I want to *feel* the frustration of getting an "F" test returned two days after the drop date, I want to *experience* Mr. Grumble's condescension, his insults. Whether or not I know who Mr. Grumble is, I want to share in enough of the writer's world to appreciate his reactions, to agree with the writer's assessment of the failure of a teacher. With Thoreau, I want to stroll along the shores of Walden Pond, appreciating the totally free delights of tracking a woodchuck or listening to the "hoo, hoo, hoo, hoorer, hoo" of the owls. With the student reader, I want to travel to the strange lands of her science fiction and benefit from her informed guidance. With the contented part-timer, I want to learn what is "bearable" about stocking coat racks in the storeroom of a big department store. Finally, I want to know what these living situations are really like for the student's friends.

WORKING WITH EXEMPLIFICATION

Consider topics for which you have several examples, drawn from personal experience (people), from specialized knowledge (bloodhounds), or from research (the Loch Ness Monster). Think of emotions you felt during times of important change in your life, jobs you have liked or disliked, your worst fault, your most exemplary trait, advertisements you find amusing or offensive, or relatives you admire. Think of daily experiences, frustrations, dreams, causes for anger or delight, books, things that you know about experts, such as hang-gliders, violin players, or stamp collectors, places that do or don't please you, things you'd change if you could, traits you admire, cars that should be taken off the road, bosses that should be fired, management approaches that should be taught, mistakes made by Louis XVI.

The interest for the reader will be in the examples that you pull together to illustrate and support a particular judgment, and in your reasons *why* you have made that judgment. The reader will be curious about what you have to say about each example. Your judgments, your connections will matter. The challenge is always to avoid making a simple list, a quick collection of thoughts about which you do not *write* enough. As soon as an example is suggested, it must receive enough attention to keep the reader reading.

Example

I know of a student who shared a dorm room, which ended up being a disastrous situation. My friend Kim shared her room for her first semester—for *most* of her first semester, that is. The room was just fine. It was big, clean, and close to the telephones in the hall. It also required that Kim be close to her roommate, Sally. Sally was a short, slim, studious type, with reading glasses always perched on the end of her nose and ink stains always on her fingertips. Sally had no use for roommates, only books. Least of all did she want a roommate like Kim, who was noisy, spoiled, and had the radio on all of the time and her desk littered with cosmetics, clothes, and *TV Guide* instead of books and notes. Her only notes were to her boyfriends. This dorm room was never really "shared," and Kim was delighted to move out by the fall break. Sally didn't look up long enough to say goodbye.

Warm-Up

In a journal (see pages 361–363) or in a free-writing exercise (see pages 355–361), write on one of the suggestions in the list of topics given (pages 362–363) and then try to rewrite it after you have studied the examples in this chapter.

Anger at First Sight

Lyn Capodanno (student)

In a short essay called "Freshman Feelings," this student gives examples of the emotional reactions she had at the beginning of her freshman year: loneliness because of separation from her family and friends; fear because of being in a new and bigger city with strangers in new classes; and anger. See notes for this paragraph on page 356 and a first draft on page 386. This paragraph, which is the climax (see page 377) of her paper, tells of this anger and reports in detail what made her want to call her parents and go home. Here is Lyn's comment: "I'm about to graduate now, and I have beginnings on my mind. I can still remember how awful I felt during those first days before I began to talk to the others in the dorm. I was amazed when they showed any interest in me. The details were easy for this one."

Thinking Ahead This student tries to give life to one example of her many feelings about entering college—anger. How does she proceed through her experience of this feeling in this paragraph? Can you remember your emotions as you entered college? What details do you recall most vividly from that time?

But lonely and afraid as I was, my strongest feeling was anger. I was upset with my parents for practically pushing me out of the car at Peabody Hall. Even though I had cried for most of the ride to school, they left me there anyway. As I stood by myself before the hazy, scratched plexiglass entranceway, I felt almost sick and asked myself, "How could *this* be home?" I was also angry at the students in the dorm, especially my roommates. They tried to talk to me, but I stayed sullenly on my side of the room. I didn't answer. I didn't even look at them. I knew *they'd* never be my friends. I had already lugged in crates full of pictures and cards from home, from the only friends I could ever want. I was also angry at myself for getting into this awful position. Who did I think I was? Who needed college anyway? As I sat at my bare desk writing letter after letter, I was most angry that I didn't have the nerve to get up and leave.

QUESTIONS

A. Discovering Meaning

1. Anger is one example of the author's many feelings about entering college. What were her other feelings at that time?
2. The author also develops this paragraph by giving examples of this feeling. What are these examples?

B. Examining Method

1. How does the author develop the example of anger beyond a simple word scratched out in an outline?
2. Which details contribute most to your understanding of the author's feeling?
3. This paragraph is the climax, the most forceful example of the author's feelings at that time. Do you see any attention to climax within this paragraph? Where?
4. Notice that some sentences are short and some are long (pages 426–428). How do they work in this paragraph? What would have been the effect if she had combined sentences, making the short ones long?
5. What is the effect of asking questions in this paragraph?

C. Shifting Focus

1. Sentences 2, 3, and 4 are actually a mini-narrative, a story of her arrival at school. How does the narrative work within this "example" paragraph?
2. Lyn chooses to give examples of early situations in which she felt angry. Do you see any other way in which she might have brought this feeling

to life? If you can, try writing an alternative paragraph expressing this same feeling but in a different way.

SUGGESTIONS FOR WRITING AND DISCUSSION

A. Using Examples

1. Write a paragraph focusing on one example of your emotional reactions as you began your college career. Use details to bring the emotion to life. How did you feel when you woke up that first day at school? How did you feel as you walked to your first class? How did the school look to you? What impression did the other students and the teachers make on you? How did you feel at the end of the day?
2. Write a longer paper in which you write about several examples of the dominant feeling you had as you entered college—nervousness in the dorm, in class, in the cafeteria, for example.
3. Write a paper in which you give examples of several reactions as you began college. If your reactions were mixed, say so in your thesis (page 364) and be sure to consider the order in which you discuss them, most effectively from least to most important (pages 377–378 on climax).
4. Write on your reactions to some other major change in your life: moving, losing a friend, experiencing the death of a relative, discovering a new interest, succeeding where you had always failed. (See the comment after suggestion 3.)
5. Write a longer paper giving examples of situations in which you experienced a particular feeling or attitude. I can think, for example, of several situations when I was traveling when fear almost made me take the next plane home.

B. Exploring the Options

1. Write two letters: one to Lyn's parents from Lyn, explaining in greater detail the problems of arriving at college, and another from the parents in answer to Lyn's letter. Be sure to consider tone (page 421), or your attitude, in this letter and the purpose of writing it. Does Lyn want simply to complain or to quit college? Are her parents sympathetic, forceful, or themselves angry? (You may also be able to adapt this suggestion to your own experience, in letter form.)

The Bowerbird

James Thurber

James Thurber (1894–1961) was born in Columbus, Ohio. He spent most of his professional career as a writer for the *New Yorker,* chiefly for the "Talk of the Town" column. Also well known as a cartoonist, teller of fables, and essayist, he published with E. B. White a volume, *Is Sex Necessary?* (1929), an autobiography, *My Life and Hard Times* (1933), and other works, including *The Middle-Aged Man on the Flying Trapeze* (1935), *Let Your Mind Alone* (1937), *Fables for Our Time* (1940), and *The Thirteen Clocks* (1950). The following paragraph is an example from the essay, "Courtship Through the Ages," in which, with characteristic humor and understatement, Thurber discusses the "sorrowful lengths to which all males must go to arouse the interest of a lady." He focuses on peacocks, a fly of the family Empidae, the fiddler crab, the web-spinning spider, the butterfly, the Argus pheasant, and the bowerbird. The passage about the bowerbird is included here. In an interview, Thurber said that he wrote as many as seven drafts for his essays: "For me it's mostly a question of re-writing. It's part of a constant attempt on my part to make the finished version smooth, to make it seem effortless."

Thinking Ahead The bowerbird is an example of what particular aspect of courtship? Thurber delights in exaggerating commonplace situations into absurdity. Where does he exaggerate here? What are some of the courtship rituals followed by humans—male or female?

> The bowerbird is another creature that spends so much time courting the female that he never gets any work done. If all the male bowerbirds became nervous wrecks within the next ten or fifteen years, it would not surprise me. The female bowerbird insists that a playground be built for her with a specially constructed bower at the entrance. This bower is much more elaborate than an ordinary nest and is harder to build; it costs a lot more, too. The female will not come to the playground until the male has filled it up with a great many gifts: silvery leaves, red leaves, rose petals, shells, beads, berries, bones, dice, buttons, cigar bands, Christmas seals, and the Lord knows what else. When the female finally condescends to visit the playground, she is in a coy and silly mood and has to be chased in and out of the bower and up and down the playground before she will quit giggling and stand still long enough even to shake hands. The male bird is, of course, pretty well done in before the chase starts, because he has worn himself out hunting for eyeglass lenses and begonia blossoms. I imagine that many a bowerbird, after chasing a female for two or three hours, says the hell with it and goes home to bed. Next day, of course, he telephones someone else and the same trying ritual is gone through with again. A male bowerbird is as exhausted as a night-club habitué before he is out of his twenties.

QUESTIONS

A. Discovering Meaning

1. This bird is one among many examples intended to support Thurber's thesis that males go through "sorrowful lengths" to "arouse the interest of a lady." How do the habits he describes here support this judgment?
2. Which side does Thurber take in this discussion?
3. Of what is the female's behavior an example?

B. Examining Method

1. This paragraph, itself an example of Thurber's larger point, contains many particular examples of the bowerbird's behavior *and* a list of examples of courtship gifts. What is the purpose of reporting this list in such detail (pages 400–403)?
2. What is the effect of the casual diction (pages 422–423): "nervous wrecks," "pretty well done," "the hell with it"?
3. What is Thurber's tone, his attitude toward his material (pages 421–422), in this paragraph?
4. How does humor work in this paragraph?
5. Does this paragraph seem "effortless," an effect Thurber said he worked to create?

C. Shifting Focus

1. "Personification" is the representation of animals, ideas, or inanimate objects as human. What examples of personification do you see in this paragraph? Why does Thurber describe the bird's behavior in human terms? What would happen to the paragraph if you removed all examples of personification and wrote it "straight"?

SUGGESTIONS FOR DISCUSSION AND WRITING

A. Using Examples

1. Write a paragraph giving one example, or a longer paper giving several examples, of courtship habits among human beings. In what places do

you have the best opportunity to observe such behavior? What is your attitude toward this behavior? How you feel about it will affect the tone (pages 421–422) of your essay, as it did Thurber's.

B. Exploring the Options

1. Must females, animal or human, also go to "sorrowful lengths" as part of the courtship ritual? Your paper may be simply expository, giving examples to support your conclusion, or it may attempt to argue a point, that such "sorrowful lengths" are unfortunate or demeaning, for example. You may want to read the sections on discovering a purpose (paged 368–371) and on argumentation (pages 180–183).
2. Write a paper reflecting on possible similarities between animal and human behavior. (See pages 33–35 for a discussion of comparison and contrast.)
3. Go to a place where people who are "courting" gather. Take notes on their behavior. Notice body language, gestures, facial expressions, approaches, and techniques for acceptance or rejection. Based on these experiences of behavior, write your conclusions. Remember to consider tone, your attitude toward the subject. (See pages 253–258 for a discussion of writing description and pages 364–366 for a discussion of the process of finding meaning in raw material.)

The Woes of a Waitress

Tien Truong (student)

In this essay, a student gives examples of the many things she didn't like about her job at a Chinese restuarant. Notice that her introduction begins with a list, a series of "pictures" that lead to her thesis. Also notice that she writes two paragraphs about her co-workers, who are a major source of her unhappiness.

Thinking Ahead What examples will Tien need to include if the reader is to understand her "woes"? Do you have examples of some things that make you woeful too?

In a deserted dining room, a fat, sourfaced headwaitress, dim lights, 1
a worn amber carpet, faded flowered wallpaper, dusty Chinese musical instruments, and ugly masks. In the kitchen, a greasy floor, cabbage and

peapods spread over the counter, a grinding dishwasher, and a constant clatter of pans. This was what I noticed on my first day. I'm not usually very hard to please, but things steadily got worse. In time, I came to hate almost everything about my job at this Chinese restaurant.

First, I hated the boredom. Every day, I had to wear the same thing: a 2
white blouse, black pants, and polished laced-up, white shoes. As soon as I got to work, my daily routine was to make and dilute gallons of tea, fill water pitchers, stack dishes, and put out duck sauce, pineapple chunks, and fortune cookies. After this, I got to fold more than a hundred table cloths and napkins, and if I wasn't careful, I also got to trim those peapods spread all over the counter. For variety after work, I had to help wash about thirty pu pu platters and candle warmers.

I thought the customers might improve things, but the daily routine 3
got even more boring when they came in. Many were "regulars," arriving at the same time on the same day every week and sitting in the same seats. But even if they weren't regulars, customers usually ordered the same old drinks—manhattans, martinis, or mai tai's—and the same old food—sweet and sour pork, chop suey (usually chicken), and fried rice. Sometimes they got daring and ordered a pu pu platter, and if they did, they always asked me to list the ingredients, even though they were all listed on the menu. I always felt like telling them to read what was in front of them, but my orders from the headwaitress were to smile and recite the list. I also hated smiling all the time. Even that can get boring. But there I was almost every day, smiling away as I recited for the two-thousandth time: "chicken wings, spare ribs, pork strips, and fried shrimp."

It wasn't just the boredom that bothered me, though. Unfortunately, I 4
also didn't like the people I worked with. The boss of the restaurant wasn't fair to his help. I sometimes had to do the work of other waitresses or stay extra hours, if I wanted to keep my job. (He knew I needed the money for tuition.) Unlike the boss, the bartender wasn't unfair; he was rude to everyone, especially the waitresses. He called us "Stupid!" in front of the customers if we made a mistake, and he wouldn't think of admitting his own mistakes. One day he kept a whole table waiting for drinks because he didn't pay attention to the order. Of course, I had to go out and face the customers. And don't forget old sourface, the headwaitress. My first impressions weren't wrong. She was a grouch and a gossip whose worst trait was criticizing other people behind their backs. If you didn't agree with her, she got mad, and she *never* learned how to smile.

But these weren't the worst people in the place. The worst were the 5
chefs. They spent most of their time telling dirty jokes, spreading rumors, and watching ball games. I don't know how anything got cooked, especially on Super Sunday. They barely listed to the waitresses and then blamed them if the orders were wrong. One day I called in an order, but they were too busy with the Bruins, and so the meals were still not ready fifteen minutes later when I came to pick them up. The head chef yelled, "What the hell do you want? You didn't order anything!" and began to

bang dishes, pots, and pans around: I was so upset, I almost quit, but I knew I couldn't afford to then.

I realize that no job is perfect, but this one had more than its share of 6
problems. The only good things were the paychecks, and they weren't very good, either. I don't even like Chinese food any more.

VOCABULARY

amber (1), dilute (2)

QUESTIONS

A. Discovering Meaning

1. Which examples of woes does Tina choose to write about?
2. What was the worst aspect of the job?
3. What is the purpose of the paper?

B. Examining Method

1. What does the series of images in the introduction contribute to the essay (see pages 394–397)?
2. Which details give you the best impression of the job? Why?
3. Why does the writer devote two paragraphs to her co-workers? How does she divide the topic up?
4. What is the writer's tone? Which words in the essay helped you to understand what the writer is like, not just what the job was like (see pages 421–422)?
5. How does the conclusion relate to the introduction and to the body of the essay? What does she do in the conclusion (see pages 435–439)?

C. Shifting Focus

1. Identify places where a brief story (narrative, pages 277–281) might add interest for the reader.

SUGGESTIONS FOR DISCUSSION AND WRITING

A. Using Examples

1. Write an essay about a job you have held. Was it a good, bad, or mixed experience? Base your paragraphs either on examples of feelings you had about the job or on the things you liked or disliked about it.
2. Write a paper giving examples of what makes a job good. Include details to illustrate your points.

B. Exploring the Options

1. Describe something that makes you angry now or did make you angry in the past. Be sure to include the details that made you feel that way. (You may want to read the section on narrative, pages 277–281.)
2. Assume you are the newly hired manager of the restaurant in which Tien Truong worked. What would you do to improve the situation? (This paper involves taking on the point of view of the manager (pages 368–373). It may also be based on examples of what you would do.
3. Write a paper in which you attempt to account for a strong feeling you have had about something or someone. Be sure to include enough detail for the reader to understand your reaction. (See pages 120–123 for a discussion of cause and effect.)

Seventh of the Litter

Sharyn Carbone (student)

In this short essay, a student gives examples of the disadvantages of being born last in a large family. Notice the tone and her mood (see page 421) as she discusses the things that go wrong for the last born. Here is Sharyn's comment: "This paper makes things sound a lot worse than they usually are, but I just wanted to get some of this out. It makes me feel a little guilty."

Thinking Ahead This is really a "complaint" paper, based on example. What kinds of examples do you anticipate? How do you feel about your birth position in your family? What is your biggest complaint about your situation in life at the moment?

I'm the youngest of seven children—two brothers and four sisters. It wasn't easy growing up with not only a mother and a father, but six other people telling me how to do it, when to do it, and who to do it with. They think I had it best being the baby. I don't. They just don't realize how difficult it can be. 1

At mealtime, for example, when we all lived at home, I barely ever got a complete one. When my mother put a full plate on the table, the food would disappear before she turned her back. I couldn't compete with the quicker speed and longer reach of the other six. With arms flying and mouths chomping, they devoured whole meals while I waited for my first bite. For survival, I soon learned to move fast, grabbing at whatever I could reach and devouring it immediately. I learned to eat fast so there'd be nothing left to steal. In fact, to this day, I inhale food without really enjoying it. My boyfriend, who is perfectly willing to let me have my fair share, describes my eating habits as "animalistic." 2

Another disadvantage is that I never got new clothes. Everything was a hand-me-down—too large, too long, or too worn out. Pants had patches over patches from the four sisters who ventured into the playgrounds before me. My sweaters were always stretched in at least six different directions and, it never failed, stained with a variety of substances. In Junior High, I was particularly ashamed of my ragged wardrobe and jealous of every pair of designer jeans and every sweater that fit. I didn't have the courage to refuse the hand-me-downs until High School. Then I could make enough money to buy my own new clothes. 3

Time with my mother and father was always limited, at least what they call "quality time," like during meals. My brothers and sisters claim that the baby got more time than they did, but they're wrong. And now that they're all gone from home and I'm the only one left, it's even worse. We don't have any seven-course sit-down dinners anymore. Now that I'm big enough to compete for my supper, I rarely see big platters of hot food. My busy parents serve cold cuts, microwave dinners, pizza, or take-out. My mother says there aren't enough people for a sit-down meal. So we don't hang around the table for a long chit-chat about the day. We watch T.V. I have supper with the Brady Bunch. Sometimes I read the paper, if I feel like reading. I can't imagine dinners without the T.V. blaring at the other end of the table, the way my brothers and sisters used to when they were all home. If my mother makes a real meal, I ask, "So what's the occasion?" 4

It isn't just during mealtimes, though, that I get ignored. My parents travel now. During the past several years, they have taken off to Hawaii, Bermuda, Florida, Atlantic City, New Orleans, and California. This year, they're heading off to Utah and Colorado for skiing vacations. I don't remember such extravagant trips when my brothers and sisters were home. I do remember traveling with them. But not these days. They go without kids, and I'm left at home for weeks at a time as a watchdog. (Most kids would take advantage of this situation, but my fear of breaking something in my parents' glass house keeps me on good behavior.) I 5 sometimes feel that I should pencil myself in for an appointment with my parents, especially if I have a problem or just a need for a talk.

Recently, I've felt even more this way—because I'm planning to be 6
married. My parents gave elaborate, elegant weddings to my sisters and my brothers. The guest lists were long, the meals were selected down to every last bread crumb, and only the best was considered for gowns and receptions. When I got engaged, there was no fuss, and very little excitement. When I tried to talk about my wedding plans, I got the feeling it was more a chore than anything else. A small wedding, "something inexpensive," they suggested. I was disappointed and angry, but I finally had to face where I really fit in the order of things in my family.

I had to realize that I'll never be a first, always a last. I'll never be able 7
to escape the birthing order that made me into the "baby." I'll have to live with my parents' "burn-out" as a result of raising six before me. I'll have to make the best of who I am. This is not to say that everything has been terrible. I have had much companionship and love in my family, and my wedding plans have turned out to be quite nice, though less expensive than the others' extravaganzas. I also have to admit that maybe my brothers and sisters are right, that maybe I exaggerate the effects of my "lowly" position in the family. But if you ever hear that the baby in the family has it made. Don't believe it. I'd much rather be the first.

QUESTIONS

A. Discovering Meaning

1. Which examples of disadvantages does Sharyn choose to write about?
2. What disadvantage bothers her the most?

B. Examining Method

1. What is the thesis (pages 364–366)?
2. In what order (see page 377 for discussion of climax) are these examples arranged? Why? Are they in the best order for maintaining interest?
3. What details (see pages 400–403) contribute most to your understanding of the difficulty of being the last born?
4. What is the effect of the conclusion (see pages 435–439)? Write a different, more angry one.
5. Consider the order of topics within the paragraphs. Are they arranged in the best order for maintaining interest (pages 374–378)?

C. Shifting Focus

1. How would you describe the tone, the mood of this essay (pages 421–422)—angry, amused, resentful, resigned? Why?
2. Do you have any difficulty determining how she really feels (page 364)?
3. Is the attitude of the conclusion consistent with the rest of the essay? Explain.

SUGGESTIONS FOR DISCUSSION AND WRITING

A. Using Examples

1. Write a paper on the disadvantages or advantages of being ________ . Give detailed examples of the situation.
2. Write a paper on a less personal topic, like the advantages or disadvantages of going to a small college, or choosing accounting as a major, or taking a year off to backpack through Europe.
3. Consider your own position in a family or other group. What are the effects of being in this position? (See 120–123 for a discussion of cause and effect.)
4. Write a complaint of your own, based on examples. Be sure to think of the purpose of your complaint, of what your goal is—to set things straight, to vent anger, to explore your own feelings, and so on. (See pages 368–371 for a discussion of discovering purpose.)

B. Exploring the Options

1. Write a response to Sharyn from her parents or her older brothers and sisters. Be sure to consider purpose and tone. What is the goal of their response, and how do they feel about the subject? (See pages 368–371 for a discussion of purpose and pages 421–422 for a discussion of tone.)
2. Rewrite this paper with a different tone—truly angry, for example, or happy with the experience of being the last born. You may want to try writing with irony, that is, saying one thing and meaning another. (See page 421 for a discussion of irony.)

Same Train, Different Time

David Vinopal

David Vinopal teaches English at Paul Smiths College in Saranac Lake, New York. A mandolin player, he has had a long-standing interest in bluegrass and country music and is the author of a book, *So You Think You Know: Country Music.* For this piece, Professor Vinopal wrote several drafts, the first of which focused on the love of country music in his childhood town, the second of which focused on the reasons for this affection, and the third of which, this draft, focused on the examples of singers who choose timeless, real-life themes for their songs.

Thinking Ahead Can you think of any examples of themes in country music or examples of specific country music songs that express certain themes? When you think of country music, what is your first reaction? Is it based on knowledge or preconception? What themes show up repeatedly in, say, rock music or opera? Which performers are important in perpetuating them?

American country music presents itself as facts-of-life music, bare-bones stuff, life's common ground. It likes to be autobiography sung, and country music fans like to believe that their stars know what they're singing about. They want their Dollys and Lorettas and Waylons and Willies to have worn coats of many colors, to have been coal miners' daughters or sons, or to have been rebels (if not actual outlaws) musically or in other ways. And these true-to-life themes have changed little over the years. 1

Take Jimmie Rodgers, for example, the 1920's star, often called the father of country music, and for good reason. He's the one who lived through and introduced to country music many of the subjects and sentiments still sung about today. Jimmy's mother died when he was four, so much of his childhood was spent in the world of roaring trains and lonesome whistles of his father, a section foreman for a Mississippi railroad. From age fourteen on, he too worked at railroading jobs, but always accompanied by his banjo or guitar, and always alert for the stories and songs around him. He was living what they were singing. 2

When he was twenty-six, his six-month-old daughter died and he left for work in Utah, where his increasingly serious tuberculosis kept him from earning money and frequently drove him to charity hospitals. At age twenty-nine, he won an audition for hillbilly talent and from then on became well known enough to earn some money and take care of his wife and remaining daughter. He didn't have long to enjoy his success, however. The T.B. grew steadily worse, and in 1933, he made his final recordings—twelve songs in seven days—but two days later he died of the disease he had already sung about in his "T.B. Blues." 3

Maybe Jimmie didn't invent country music, but he became a model for all subsequent country stars, just as his songs—happy and sad, rowdy and subdued, risqué and religious—provided the basic themes. His compositions include songs with a veneer of optimism, most of them about friendship, fidelity, and family—beneath the surface of which lurk the cold realities. Jimmie acknowledged life's successes, but portrayed thoroughly the failures, the disappointments and the losses, because he saw so many more of them. 4

It is Jimmie's attitudes, Jimmie's subjects—family, home, trains, rambling and gambling, hard times, good love and bad love, driving, jobs, jails, isolation, optimism, death, and God—that find their way into so much of the country music that follows. Examples are difficult to avoid. 5

Hank Williams, whose hard life and colossal successes are the equal of Rodgers', was born into poverty in a two-room cabin in Alabama. At age twenty-five, he sang "Lovesick Blues" (and six encores) in his first appearance on the Grand Old Opry. Taking drugs to relieve pain in his spine caused by an earlier rodeo accident and suffering the breakup of his marriage, he sang of loneliness, "Alone and forsaken by fate and by man/Oh, Lord, if you hear me, please hold to my hand . . .," rambling, broken love, and early death as in "Six More Miles to the Graveyard." He became the biggest star in country music history, but they had to fire him for chronic drunkenness. On New Year's Day, 1953, he died of a heart attack brought on by years of fast living and heavy drinking. 6

Loretta Lynn—married at thirteen, mother of four before the age eighteen, washed clothes and picked fruit to help support her family. She taught herself to play the guitar and wrote her own composition, "I'm a Honky-Tonk Girl," which she later promoted herself by traveling from radio station to radio station. Singing of the simple country life and of domestic problems, "Your Squaw Is on the Warpath," or, "Don't Come Home a Drinkin' (with Lovin' on Your Mind)," she too became a superstar. 7

Johnny Cash—of Cherokee Indian ancestry, was born to a poverty-stricken cotton farmer in Arkansas, worked in a Detroit body shop, swept floors in a margarine factory, sold products door-to-door, and started taking Dexedrine and then tranquilizers. Suffering blackouts, he missed show dates due to drugs, and his wife divorced him, before a policeman found him in a little Georgia town, deathly ill. With this, he reformed, remarried, and set out on a long and successful career singing of his many experiences—"I Walk the Line," "Ring of Fire," "Bitter Tears," "At Folsom Prison," "Junkie and Juicehead Minus Me." 8

Merle Haggard—after being forced out of the Oklahoma dustbowl, quitting school in the eighth grade, living in a series of reform schools and prisons, was arrested at age twenty for attempted burglary and sentenced to San Quentin. On his release, he moved back with his mother who had been taking care of his children in the converted boxcar in which Merle had grown up. His second recorded song, "Sing a Sad Song," 9 was a hit, followed by the many others that made him too a superstar: "I'm a Lonesome Fugitive," "Okie from Muskogee," "Mama Tried," "The Bottle Let Me Down," "The Fighting Side of Me," and "Branded Man."

It is these kinds of lives, these themes, that remain constant in country 10
music and that continue to entertain a faithful audience. The Urban Cowboy scare of the early 80's made some attempts at making a $300.00 pair of cowboy boots necessary for pounding the prairies of Manhattan country, and "country pop" (also known as "countrypolitan" and "Nash trash") asked its audience to take the glitz of the self-serving award ceremonies as the real thing, but it's still unlikely that country will ever get to singing of fuel injection problems in the BMW.

Today's young stars—Ricky Skaggs, Hank Williams, Jr., Reba McEntire, 11
George Strait, Patty Loveless, Randy Travis, and Dwight Yoakam—musically have less in common with their pop contemporaries than with the country singers of fifty years ago. Train songs may have whistled into Nashville history, but caravans of trucks and trucking songs now hog the road. TV, having decreased the isolation of the backwoods, leaves emotional isolation as a subject. And women now have the same rights as men in country songs; they too can drink, cheat, ramble, and complain about their tedious jobs, while praising the few joys that come their way. The specifics may be modern, but the music remains part of a long tradition. Same train, different time.

QUESTIONS

A. Discovering Meaning

1. This piece is based on examples, but examples of what?
2. Who is the major source for many of the traditional country themes?
3. What is happening to these themes now in country music?

B. Examining Method

1. What is the purpose of the long discussion of Jimmie Rodgers? What would be the effect of removing that biographical information?
2. Why are so many song titles mentioned? Would the piece work without them? (See pages 400–403 for a discussion of details.)
3. What is the purpose of paragraph 5? (See pages 415–418 for a discussion of transition.)
4. What is the purpose of the reference to the "Urban Cowboy"?

5. What is the tone of this piece, the attitude of the writer toward the material?

6. What is the connection between the introduction and the conclusion (see pages 435–436)?

C. Shifting Focus

1. How could similar material be used by someone who does not admire country music? (See pages 368–371 for a discussion of purpose.)

2. Could this paper also be described as argumentative (see pages 180–183)?

SUGGESTIONS FOR DISCUSSION AND WRITING

A. Using Examples

1. Analyze and give examples of typical themes and subjects in any particular kind of music that you choose. Be sure to consider your own tone.

2. Write a paper analyzing the themes of major performers in a particular kind of music.

3. Drawn from some specialized knowledge—of cars, musical instruments, boats, customs, or coins, for example—give examples to back up a judgment you feel able to make.

B. Exploring the Options

1. Write your own critical response to country music (or some other kind of music). Be sure to consider the stance you are able to take. Do you know this music well? Are you basically uninformed but strong in your prejudices? Whatever your stance is, let your readers know. Consider how far you can press your judgments and what audience is likely to be impressed with what you have to say. (See pages 368–369 for a discussion of playing the "expert" and pages 370–371 for a discussion of audience.)

2. Based on personal experience, write a critical review of a musical performance. (See pages 314–316 for Joseph Wood Krutch's discussion of reviewing.)

Early Impressions

Michiko Kakutani

Michiko Kakutani was born in 1955 in New Haven, Conecticut, and graduated from Yale University in 1976. She has worked at the *Washington Post* and *Time* magazine, and joined the *New York Times* in 1979 as a reporter covering cultural news. By listing examples of books read in childhood, Kakutani states the thesis clearly in the first paragraph and then illustrates how the books are "eclectic reminders" of what she "once imagined the world to be." In each paragraph she makes a connection between books and their ability to remind her of her past.

Thinking Ahead What kinds of examples of her "early impressions" does Kakutani select? What books do you remember from your childhood?

"There are some books one needs maturity to enjoy," the late poet and humorist Phyllis McGinley once said, "just as there are books an adult can come upon too late to savor." It's funny how the books we read as children and teen-agers somehow lodge in the attics of our memories, dusty and occasionally outgrown, but never really misplaced—eclectic reminders of what we once imagined the world to be. 1

I was never able to throw out anything, and there my old books sit in my parents' house, stacked sideways on the shelves, along with a ring binder of social studies papers, typed instructions on how to tie-dye shirts and a plaque from the 4-H club for animal husbandry. There are Arrow Book Club editions of *The Silent Spring,*[1] *I Never Promised You a Rose Garden*[2] and *To Kill a Mockingbird,*[3] a boxed set of *The Lord of the Rings*[4] and Signet editions of *The Merchant of Venice* and *Macbeth.*[5] 2

They're all paperbacks, these books. It was better that way: You didn't have to worry about breaking the spines—it was a sin to do that to a hard-cover book, my father used to say—and you could underline passages you liked to your heart's content. In fact there are entire pages in my Scribner Library editions of *The Great Gatsby*[6] and *The Sun Also Rises*[7] colored yellow by my zealous wielding of a Hi-Liter pen. 3

Books were how I learned about the world in those days. For years I believed that Long Island actually had communities named East Egg and 4

---

[1]*The Silent Spring,* by Rachel Carson (1907–1964).

[2]*I Never Promised You a Rose Garden,* by Joanne Greenberg (b. 1932).

[3]*To Kill a Mockingbird,* by Harper Lee (b. 1926).

[4]*The Lord of the Rings,* by J. R. R. Tolkien (1892–1973).

[5]*The Merchant of Venice* and *Macbeth:* Shakespearean tragedies.

[6]*The Great Gatsby,* by F. Scott Fitzgerald (1896–1940).

[7]*The Sun Also Rises,* by Ernest Hemingway (1899–1961).

West Egg;[8] that all Englishmen retained servants like Jeeves,[9] and that all romances ended happily or at least conclusively. And I remember checking off all the novels I'd read in the Scribner series, as though reading the complete list (thoughtfully provided on the inside cover) would confer knowledge or at least sophistication: *Tender Is the Night,*[10] *A Farewell to Arms, The Old Man and the Sea,*[11] *Look Homeward, Angel,*[12] *Haircut and Other Stories,*[13] *The Yearling,*[14] *Ethan Frome, The House of Mirth*[15] and *Cry, the Beloved Country.*[16] Were it not for all those novels by C.P. Snow,[17] I would have done rather well.

In retrospect, those Scribner editions—thick oversized books, bound 5 in gray—formed my earliest notion of what it meant to be an author. It meant writing a novel that was important enough to be included in a series or short stories memorable enough to be collected in an omnibus volume. It also meant having your picture on the book's back cover, set off by a paragraph telling the story of your life.

Actually, a lot of my time wasn't spent reading such classics. The first 6 complete *oeuvre* of any writer I read was that of Albert Payson Terhune, the author of the *Lad: A Dog* books, followed by that of Carolyn Keene, the creator of Nancy Drew. I must have ben about 9 at the time, and Nancy seemed the perfect heroine: She was smart and pretty and brave, and she had a nice boyfriend named Ned. She could fix a stalled outboard motor with a bobby pin, shoot a lynx at 100 yards, and she could even do credible impersonations of old movie stars. I wanted a life like hers.

Some years later *A Separate Peace*[18] and *The Catcher in the Rye*[19] 7 would create a similar identification. These were books, after all, about kids—kids who went to school but seemed to have more important things to worry about than whether they'd have to share a Bunsen burner in lab. For those of us enrolled in suburban public schools, the lives of Phineas and Holden, spent at private boarding schools, seemed ineffably glamorous. And the fact that Holden was kicked out of prep school and had to talk to a psychoanalyst—you learned that, I remember, on the second to last page of the book—made it even more romantic.

---

[8]East Egg and West Egg: Long Island towns in *The Great Gatsby.*
[9]Jeeves: butler in novels by P. G. Wodchouse (1881–1975).
[10]*Tender Is the Night,* by F. Scott Fitzgerald.
[11]*A Farewell to Arms, The Old Man and the Sea,* by Ernest Hemingway.
[12]*Look Homeward, Angel,* by Thomas Wolfe (1900–1938).
[13]*Haircut and Other Stories,* by Ring Lardner (1885–1933).
[14]*The Yearling,* by Majorie Rawlings (1896–1953).
[15]*Ethan Frome, The House of Mirth,* by Edith Wharton (1862–1932).
[16]*Cry, the Beloved Country,* by Alan Paton (1903–1988).
[17]C. P. Snow (1905–1980): English physicist and novelist, author of *The Two Cultures.*
[18]*A Separate Peace,* by John Knowles (b. 1926).
[19]*The Catcher in the Rye,* by J. D. Salinger (b. 1919).

Madness, in fact, fascinated us: *The Bell Jar,* with all its lurid details 8
about how Sylvia Plath tried to die,[20] and *One Flew Over the Cuckoo's Nest,*[21] with its scenes of shock treatment, exerted a strange hold over our imaginations. It was almost as good as reading the last few pages of "A Perfect Day for Bananafish,[22] where the guy sits down on the bed, pulls an automatic out of his suitcase and puts a bullet through his head. No doubt *Lord of the Flies,*[23] *The Collector*[24] and *The Lottery*[25] made a similar appeal to our callow appreciation for the perverse.

The rest of the time, I guess, we—or our teachers—tried pretty hard 9
to be relevant. *Black Like Me*[26] was already passé by the late 60's; we were into "harder" stuff—like *Soul on Ice*[27] and *Manchild in the Promised Land.*[28] Those were the days teach-ins had become as regular an after-school activity as cheerleading practice, and the P.T.A. seemed to worry less about our reading "subversive" books like *Catch-22*[29] or *Slaughterhouse Five*[30] than "dirty" ones like *Tropic of Cancer.*[31]

When we moved away to college and new lives, we abandoned many 10
of these books like so many sentimental reminders of our youth, and we sold them in bulk to secondhand bookstores, where customers perhaps puzzled over the annotations spelled out in neat, childish script. But some of the books we go back to. We may buy new copies—pristine hardbacks in uniform editions to fill our built-in bookcases—but somewhere, in our childhood rooms, their predecessors remain: soft paperbacks, broken of spine, bloated and dog-eared from all those early years of reading.

VOCABULARY

eclectic (1), zealous (3), retrospect (5), oeuvre (6), ineffably (7), lurid (8), callow (8), perverse (8), subversive (9), annotations (10), pristine (10), predecessors (10), dog-eared (10)

---

[20]Sylvia Plath (1932–1963).
[21]*One Flew Over the Cuckoo's Nest,* by Ken Kesey (b. 1935).
[22]"A Perfect Day for Bananafish," by J. D. Salinger (b. 1919).
[23]*Lord of the Flies,* by William Golding (b. 1911).
[24]*The Collector,* by John Fowles (b. 1926).
[25]*The Lottery,* by Shirley Jackson (1919–1965).
[26]*Black Like Me,* by John Howard Griffin 1900–1980)
[27]*Soul on Ice,* by Eldridge Cleaver (b. 1935).
[28]*Manchild in the promised Land,* by Claud Brown (1937).
[29]*Cath-22,* by Joseph Heller (b. 1923).
[30]*Slaughterhouse Five,* by Kurt Vonnegut (b. 1922).
[31]*Tropic of Cancer,* by Henry Miller (b. 1891).

QUESTIONS

A. Discovering Meaning

1. What early impressions were made by the various examples Kakutani discusses here?
2. What is the difference between the examples discussed in paragraphs 1–5 and those in paragraphs 6–9?

B. Examining Method

1. How does the author open the essay? Why does she use a quotation? (See pages 394–398 for a discussion of introductions.)
2. How does paragraph 2 relate to the thesis?
3. How does Kakutani move from one paragraph to another? Discuss the transitions (see pages 415–418).
4. What is the purpose of paragraph 5?
5. What does the mentioning of so many titles contribute to her essay? (See pages 400–403 for a discussion of details.)
6. Why does Kakutani list some of Nancy Drew's many achievements in paragraph 6?
7. How does the conclusion relate to the body of the essay and to the introduction? Why does she mention the "new copies" see pages 435–439)?

C. Shifting Focus

1. What makes this essay personal, more than just bibliographical?
2. If you were to make this piece longer, how could you extend it?

SUGGESTIONS FOR DISCUSSION AND WRITING

A. Using Examples

1. Discuss examples of reading that were important to you as a child. Mention specific titles and what they meant to you at the time. (Reading does not necessarily have to be "learned" or serious to be important in your background.)

2. Trace your reading habits from childhood to the present. Choose memorable examples and consider what they meant to you along the way.
3. What are the forces working both for and against developing the habit of reading in childhood? Give specific examples.

B. Exploring the Options

1. Discuss the beginning stages of an activity that has since become part of your adult life. (You may want to read about process, pages 92–95.)
2. Is reading being replaced by other means of mass communication? How do you feel about this possibility?
3. What might be done to encourage a childhood interest in reading?

Three Boys

John Updike

John Updike, short-story writer, essayist, novelist, was born in Shillington, Pennsylvania in 1932 and graduated from Harvard in 1954. He then attended the Ruskin School of Drawing and Fine Art in Oxford, England and later began writing for *The New Yorker,* where his work still appears regularly. He is the author of some 36 books, including 13 novels and 5 collections of verse. About writing, Updike says, "A writer hang-glides all the time, out over that terrible whiteness. The abyss is you, your own life, your mind."

Thinking Ahead Here Updike uses three boys he knew in his childhood as examples of certain kinds of relationships. Notice how many kinds of things the author tells about these boys. How does he tell what they *meant,* not just what they were? Have you had friends who could serve as examples of certain kinds of relationships?

A, B, and *C,* I'll say, in case they care. *A* lived next door, he *loomed* 1
next door, rather. He seemed immense—a great wallowing fatso stuffed with possessions; he was the son of a full-fashioned knitter. He seemed to have a beer-belly; after several generations beer-bellies may become congenital. Also his face had no features. It was just a blank ball on his shoulders. He used to call me "Ostrich," after Disney's Ollie Ostrich. My neck was not very long, the name seemed horribly unfair; it was its injustice that made me cry. But nothing I could say, or scream, would make him stop. And I still, now and then—in reading, say, a book review by one of the apple-cheeked savants of the quarterlies or one of the pious

gremlins who manufacture puns for *Time*—get the old sensations: my ears close up, my eyes go warm, my chest feels thin as an eggshell, my voice churns silently in my stomach. From *A* I received my first impression of the smug, chinkless, irresistible *power* of stupidity; it is the most powerful force on earth. It says "Ostrich" often enough, and the universe crumbles.

A was more than a boy, he was a force-field that could manifest itself 2
in many forms, that could take the wiry, disconsolate shape of wide-mouthed, tiny-eared boys who would now and then beat me up on the way back from school. I did not greatly mind being beaten up, though I resisted it. For one thing, it firmly involved me, at least during the beating, with the circumambient humanity that so often seemed evasive. Also, the boys who applied the beating were misfits, periodic flunkers, who wore corduroy knickers with threadbare knees and men's shirts with the top button buttoned—this last an infallible sign of deep poverty. So that I felt there was some justice, some condonable revenge, being applied with their fists to this little teacher's son. And then there was the delicious alarm of my mother and grandmother when I returned home bloody, bruised, and torn. My father took the attitude that it was making a boy of me, an attitude I dimly shared. He and I both were afraid of me becoming a sissy—he perhaps more afraid than I.

When I was eleven or so I met *B*. It was summer and I was down at 3
the playground. He was pushing a little tank with moving rubber treads up and down the hills in the sandbox. It was a fine little toy, mottled with camouflage green; patriotic manufacturers produced throughout the war millions of such authentic miniatures which we maneuvered with authentic, if miniature, militance. Attracted by the toy, I spoke to him; though taller and a little older than I, he had my dull straight brown hair and a look of being also alone. We became fast friends. He lived just up the street—toward the poorhouse, the east part of the street, from which the little winds of tragedy blew. He had just moved from the Midwest, and his mother was a widow. Beside wage war, we did many things together. We played marbles for days at a time, until one of us had won the other's entire coffee-canful. With jigsaws we cut out of plywood animals copied from comic books. We made movies by tearing the pages from Big Little Books and coloring the drawings and pasting them in a strip, and winding them on toilet-paper spools, and making a cardboard carton a theatre. We rigged up telephones, and racing wagons, and cities of the future, using orange crates and cigar boxes and peanut-butter jars and such potent debris. We loved Smokey Stover and were always saying "Foo."[1] We had an intense spell of Monopoly. He called me "Uppy"—the only person who ever did. I remember once, knowing he was coming down that after-

[1]Smokey Stover: comic-strip character of the 1930s and 1940s.

noon to my house to play Monopoly, in order to show my joy I set up the board elaborately, with the Chance and Community Chest cards fanned painstakingly, like spiral staircases. He came into the room, groaned, "Uppy, what are you doing?" and impatiently scrabbled the cards together in a sensible pile. The older we got, the more the year between us told, and the more my friendship embarrassed him. We fought. Once, to my horror, I heard myself taunting him with the fact that he had no father. The unmentionable, the unforgivable. I suppose we patched things up, children do, but the fabric had been torn. He had a long, pale, serious face, with buck-teeth, and is probably an electronics engineer somewhere now, doing secret government work.

So through *B* I first experienced the pattern of friendship. There are 4
three stages. First, acquaintance: we are new to each other, make each other laugh in surprise, and demand nothing beyond politeness. The death of the one would startle the other, no more. It is a pleasant stage, a stable stage; on austere rations of exposure it can live a lifetime, and the two parties to it always feel a slight gratification upon meeting, will feel vaguely confirmed in their human state. Then comes intimacy: now we laugh before two words of the joke are out of the other's mouth, because we know what he will say. Our two beings seem marvellously joined, from our toes to our heads, along tingling points of agreement; everything we venture is right, everything we put forth lodges in a corresponding socket in the frame of the other. The death of one would grieve the other. To be together is to enjoy a mounting excitement, a constant echo and amplification. It is an ecstatic and unstable stage, bound of its own agitation to tip into the third: revulsion. One or the other makes a misjudgment; presumes; puts forth that which does not meet agreement. Sometimes there is an explosion; more often the moment is swallowed in silence, and months pass before its nature dawns. Instead of dissolving, it grows. The mind, the throat, are clogged; forgiveness, forgetfulness, that have arrived so often, fail. Now everything jars and is distasteful. The betrayal, perhaps a tiny fraction in itself, has inverted the tingling column of agreement, made all pluses minuses. Everything about the other is hateful, despicable; yet he cannot be dismissed. We have confided in him too many minutes, too many words; he has those minutes and words as hostages, and his confidences are embedded in us where they cannot be scraped away, and even rivers of time cannot erode them completely, for there are indelible stains. Now—though the friends may continue to meet, and smile, as if they had never trespassed beyond acquaintance—the death of the one would please the other.

An unhappy pattern to which *C* is an exception. He was my friend 5
before kindergarten, he is my friend still. I go to his home now, and he and his wife serve me and my wife with alcoholic drinks and slices of excellent cheese on crisp crackers, just as twenty years ago he served me with treats from his mother's refrigerator. He was a born host, and I a born guest. Also he was intelligent. If my childhood's brain, when I look back at it, seems a primitive mammal, a lemur or shrew, his brain was an

angel whose visitation was widely hailed as wonderful. When in school he stood to recite, his cool rectangular forehead glowed. He tucked his right hand into his left armpit and with his left hand mechanically tapped a pencil against his thigh. His answers were always correct. He beat me at spelling bees and, in another sort of competition, when we both collected Big Little Books, he outbid me for my supreme find (in the attic of a third boy), the first Mickey Mouse. I can still see that book, I wanted it so badly, its paper tan with age and its drawings done in Disney's primitive style, when Mickey's black chest is naked like a child's and his eyes are two nicked oblongs. Losing it was perhaps a lucky blow; it helped wean me away from hope of ever having possessions.

C was fearless. He deliberately set fields on fire. He engaged in rock- 6
throwing duels with tough boys. One afternoon he persisted in playing quoits with me although—as the hospital discovered that night—his appendix was nearly bursting. He was enterprising. He peddled magazine subscriptions door-to-door; he mowed neighbors' lawns; he struck financial bargains with his father. He collected stamps so well his collection blossomed into a stamp company that filled his room with steel cabinets and mimeograph machinery. He collected money—every time I went over to his house he would get out a little tin box and count the money in it for me: $27.50 one week, $29.50 the next, $30.90 the next—all changed into new bills nicely folded together. It was a strange ritual, whose meaning for me was: since he was doing it, I didn't have to. His money made me richer. We read Ellery Queen[2] and played chess and invented board games and discussed infinity together. In later adolescence, he collected records. He liked the Goodman[3] quintets but loved Fats Waller.[4] Sitting there in that room so familiar to me, where the machinery of the Shilco Stamp Company still crowded the walls and for that matter the tin box of money might still be stashed, while my thin friend grunted softly along with that dead dark angel on "Your'e Not the Only Oyster in the Stew," I felt, in the best sense, patronized: the perfect guest of the perfect host. What made it perfect was that we had both spent our entire lives in Shillington.

VOCABULARY

loomed (1), congenital (1), savants (1), gremlins (1), disconsolate (2), circumambient (2), knickers (2), infallible (2), condonable (2), mottled (3), camouflage (3), maneuvered (3), taunting (3), austere (4), revulsion (4), despicable (4), indelible (4), lemur (5), shrew (5), quoits (6), infinity (6), patronized (6)

[2]Ellery Queen: hero of twentieth-century mystery and and detective novels.
[3]Benny Goodman (1909–1986): American jazz clarinetist and bandleader.
[4]Fats Waller (1904–1943): American jazz pianist.

QUESTIONS

A. Discovering Meaning

1. Of what kinds of relationships are *A, B,* and *C* examples?
2. What did Updike learn from each relationship?

B. Examining Method

1. How does Updike help the reader to understand *A*'s personality?
2. What vocabulary words in paragraph 1 best convey Updike's feelings about him?
3. One of the most important qualities of good writing is honesty, even when it may be painful for the writer. What examples of the writer's honesty do you see in this essay (see pages 365–366)?
4. How does Updike characterize *B?* What ***kinds*** of things does he tell about him?
5. What is the connection between paragraph 4 and paragraph 5?
6. What kinds of things does he tell us about *C?*
7. Why does he include the story about Monopoly in paragraph 3 and the one about Mickey Mouse in paragraph 5?
8. Which details were most interesting to you? Why?

C. Shifting Focus

1. Notice that Updike makes each boy represent not only himself but also a fact about life itself. What does each boy mean to Updike? How does he broaden his personal examples to make a more universal application?
2. Why does Updike end the piece with the discussion of *C,* rather than with a separate conclusion (see pages 435–439)?

SUGGESTIONS FOR DISCUSSION AND WRITING

A. Using Examples

1. Write your own account of three relationships you had in childhood and of what they exemplified in your life.

2. In a friendship, what are the most important things to you? Give examples.

3. Characterize three other figures in a particular category from your life and what each meant to you—three teachers, three aunts, or three babysitters, for example.

B. Exploring the Options

1. Consider the friends you have now and why you have chosen them. (See pages 120–123 for a discussion of cause and effect.)

2. Do you see any similarities or differences in the friendships of males and females? (See pages 33–35 for a discussion of comparison and contrast.)

Comparing and Contrasting

When we look for the similarities between one thing and another or when we show how one differs from the other, we are calling attention to the peculiar characteristics of each. Is it bigger than, better than, the same as, a lot like, amazingly different from? The daily process of comparing and contrasting helps us to make judgments and especially to make selections. The only comparisons worth making, however, are between things that actually *can* be compared—for example, two schools, two basketball teams, two brands of basketballs. To compare a school to a basketball team or a basketball team to the basketball itself (unless for an intentionally dramatic effect) would probably yield little of value. Consider the following:

1. For better or for worse, my cousin Bill is a lot like my oldest brother John in:

TOPIC 1 TOPIC 2 —Generosity. (They're both generous.)

TOPIC 1 TOPIC 2 —Athletics. (They're both successful athletes.)

TOPIC 1 TOPIC 2 —Lack of scholarship. (Neither one does very well in school.)

TOPIC 1 TOPIC 2 —Lack of humor. (Unfortunately, neither one has much of a sense of humor.)

2. In comparison to Portuguese restaurants in general, Lisbon's Sunrise Restaurant is worse in practically every way.

TOPIC 1 GENERAL
—Usually the service is polite and low-keyed.
—The atmosphere is warm and relaxing.
—The bills are exactly as expected.

TOPIC 2 SUNRISE
—However, the irritating service begins with the hustling at the door.
—The interior is stark and unpleasant.
—Finally, the billing is deceptive.

3. The King Arthur of Tennyson's *Idylls of the King* and Twain's Arthur in *A Connecticut Yankee in King Arthur's Court,* though both from the nineteenth century, have little in common.

TOPIC 1 TENNYSON'S —Tennyson's King Arthur inspires noble actions in his worthy court.

ARTHUR —Tennyson's King Arthur takes part in the action, performing courageous deeds, both physically and spiritually.
—Tennyson's King Arthur is decidedly "Victorian"—"Lo! I forgive thee, as Eternal God/Forgives."

TOPIC 2 TWAIN'S ARTHUR —Twain's King Arthur presides over a court of fools.
—Twain's King Arthur is a buffoon—"His head was an hourglass; it could stow an idea, but it had to do it a grain at a time, not the whole idea at once."
—Twain's satiric strokes paint anything but a "Victorian" King Arthur.

4. On-campus and off-campus housing are different from one another in three important ways:

TOPIC 1 —Expenses (on-campus).

TOPIC 2 —Expenses (off-campus).

TOPIC 1 —Living arrangements: food, room, services (on-campus).

TOPIC 2 —Living arrangements: food, room, services (off-campus).

TOPIC 1 —Social life: privacy, companionship, freedom (on-campus).

TOPIC 2 —Social life: privacy, companionship, freedom (off-campus).

As you can see from these examples, it is possible to compare in a "see-saw" or point-by-point style (1 and 4) one point on one topic, immediately followed by a point of comparison or contrast on another topic. It is a way of organizing that allows for immediate comparisons as each topic is discussed. It strikes while the subject is "hot." The other way to organize comparisons could be described as more "50–50," or subject-by-subject (2 and 3), with the first section of the essay focusing exclusively on one topic and the second, mostly on another topic. It provides one part of the comparison completely and assumes that the main points will carry over from the first to the second parts. The second method requires making connections, referring back to the earlier part, and recalling for the reader where you've been.

WORKING WITH COMPARISON AND CONTRAST

Consider *personal* situations, conversations, or journal entries in which you make comparative judgments—about clothing, appearances, people, animals, books, houses, teams, clubs, or cars. Also think about more *specialized* subjects for which you have the necessary information to make some comparisons—places of employment, schools, types of cars, or radio stations. Consider also subjects that would likely require *research*—treatments for alcoholism, the successes or failures of vice-presidents who have inherited office from the president, methods for responding to the savings and loan debts, ways of dispensing with nuclear waste.

As in writing by example, the interest in comparison and contrast is also in the writer's judgment about the subject and in the selection of specific topics to discuss. Comparisons, however, require assessing *relative* meaning and value. The writer asks the reader to think about the relationships among the topics, to weigh and consider them. The challenge is in choosing the most interesting and convincing details in order to make the distinctions and in making distinctions that are worth making.

Example

> On-campus living arrangements are quite different from off-campus ones. In a dorm, the supervision is usually greater; it is more an extension of the watchfulness of parents, with other people noticing your comings and goings, establishing fixed eating times, sometimes restricting guests. Living on campus also means sharing with many other students, not only a room but also meals, showers, telephones, and soap operas. Privacy and dorm living are mutually exclusive, but loneliness is unlikely. Off-campus housing, on the other hand, allows much more personal freedom. Whether or not you go out or come home is up to you. Eating or starving is up to you. Privacy is a constant option, but also the enforced privacy of loneliness is more possible. Off campus, you really notice when there's nothing to do.

Warm-Up

Possibly in a journal, write one of the suggested comparisons mentioned above (page 34) and then try to rewrite it after you have studied the following examples. Or write a comparison of the three automobile advertisements on pages 88–90.

Playing with the Bleacher Bums

(paragraph)

Don Paskowski (student)

This paragraph is from a longer paper, in which this student describes the behavior of two "box-seaters" who have made the mistake of taking seats among the "bleacher bums" at Boston's Fenway Park. In other paragraphs, he focuses on general appearance and knowledge of the players and the game, leading up to this look at their reactions to the bleacher entertainments. Here is Don's comment: "I have enjoyed writing since the third grade, when I read a story to my homeroom called 'The Great Escape.' Since then I've learned how much rewriting is necessary to write something good."

Thinking Ahead In this paragraph, Don compares "outsiders" with "insiders." Of which group is he a member? Have you ever been the outsider among a group of insiders? Were you conscious of the differences between your own behavior and theirs? Have you ever closely observed the behavior of an outsider among a group of insiders?

> It's not only Biff and Muffy's yuppie attire that causes them to stick out, but also their reaction when the Bums entertain themselves during lulls. It's the Bums who initiate "the wave," for example, when everybody (almost everybody) in the section and the stadium stands in sequence, raising and lowering their arms to a roaring chant, then sitting down until the next round. But Biff and Muffy hold back. Biff barely stands six inches, flailing a rubbery arm overhead, and saying nothing, while Muffy pretends to ignore the whole thing, searching her purse or fiddling with her watch strap. Nor do they take part in the "Tastes Great" vs. "Less Filling" Lite Beer Chant (and its sometimes obscene variations). They merely listen. They can't help listening. But they look uneasy, whispering to one another. As for the Bums' favorite pastime—beachball bouncing—they seem for a moment drawn in. The game is more like rugby than volleyball, everyone trying to hit the ball at once, lots of bumping and bruising. Muffy looks up at the striped ball descending just above Biff's head. He waits politely (a mistake), then makes a lunge at it too late to hit it. He's the one that gets hit before he ever gets a fingertip on the ball. He bounces off balance on a fat man's shoulder, then ricochets his cheekbone off a stocky kid's chest. He looks like the wounded bear in that old time arcade game. He wants to sit down, but the ball is still floating dangerously near, and the kid is standing on his seat. As the fat man sends the ball wobbling away to the right, Biff's seat reappears and he slumps down deflated. Muffy checks her watch. No, they are not happy here.

QUESTIONS

A. Discovering Meaning

1. What are the main differences between the "box-seaters" and the "bleacher bums"?
2. What do the "box-seaters" have in common?
3. What do Biff and Muffy have in common?

B. Examining Method

1. What is the attitude of the writer toward the "box-seaters"? What are the clues?
2. What is his attitude toward the "bums"? What are the clues?
3. Why does he name the "box-seaters" Biff and Muffy?
4. Which details contribute most to the contrast between the two types of baseball fans?
5. Why do you think the writer used a point-by-point comparison rather than a "50-50" pattern? (See pages 33–34 for discussion of these two styles.)

C. Shifting Focus

1. How did you feel as you read this comparison?
2. Do you share the attitude of the writer?
3. If you were to visit Fenway Park, would you want to sit in the bleachers? Why?

SUGGESTIONS FOR DISCUSSION AND WRITING

A. Using Comparison and Contrast

1. Observe closely the behavior of any two individuals or two groups of people and compare their reactions to a set of circumstances—two people at a party, at a concert, in the library, or possibly two types of people in class, at a political rally, at the beach. Write a paper in which you compare the two. Is your comparison objective observation, or is it slanted to a particular point that you are trying to make? (See pages 253–258 for a discussion of description and pages 368–371 for a discussion of purpose.)
2. Write a paper in which you compare your reaction in a specific situation to the reaction of others—for example, in a nightclub, at a concert, a meeting, a family gathering. In an essay called "Disconnection," for example, writer Carll Tucker compares his own distaste for Studio 54 to the delighted acceptance of it of those around him.*

**Saturday Review,* 1979.

B. Exploring the Options

1. Write a paper on the behavior of sports fans (or possibly some other category of fans), based primarily on your own experiences. Remember to consider purpose. Are you simply describing, or do you want to argue a point? (See pages 253–258 for a discussion of description, pages 180–183 for a discussion of argument, and pages 368–371 for a discussion of purpose.)
2. Rewrite the student's paragraph as if you were either Biff or Muffy.

A House or a Condo? A.M.

(paragraph)

Joseph Hession (student)

In a longer paper entitled, "Making a Choice—Single Family or Condo?" this adult student compares many aspects of owning a house with owning a condominium, all based on personal experience. He discusses the costs, privacy, prestige, and, here, an aspect sometimes omitted from the comparisons—snow shoveling. About this paper Joseph says, "Since we sold our family home, this comparison has been ever-present on my mind. I wanted to make a case for condos at a certain stage in life. The original draft was heavy on historical and philosophical justification, but I finally had to advise myself not to try to impress my audience, just to stick to my subject that I knew quite well. Snow I knew."

Thinking Ahead What are the main points of comparison in this paragraph? For what audience might this be written? Where could it be printed? Do you have strong preferences for where you would *like* to live?

> It is a cold day in January. There was a foot-deep snowfall at our house last night, and I must shovel our driveway to get to work this morning. The temperature is 10 degrees. At 6 A.M., I bundle up in my galoshes, scarf, mackinaw, gloves, and hat with the tie-down ear flaps. I can barely move in all of these clothes, but I select the best of the four bent and rusted show shovels from my wall of tools and grimly attack the three-foot drifts in front of my garage door and the four-foot ridge of hard-pack left across the driveway by the town plow. I realize the plow only meant to help, but it has doubled my work. I know I have a heart problem, but I also have a snow problem. I am expected at work, come hell or high snow. So I shovel, and shovel. Or, as now, I awake at 6 A.M. to the roaring and scraping of the plow in my condominium's driveway. I smile, pull my soft, warm comforter up under my chin, forget the galoshes and the

ear-flaps, and go back to sleep for another hour. When it's time for me to leave for work, my path will be clear. I'll stroll down my walk, out to the sidewalk, and up my driveway . I'll back the car out and take an easy road to work. I don't own a snow shovel.

QUESTIONS

A. Discovering Meaning

1. What aspects of snow-shoveling does the writer compare?
2. Which experience does he prefer—living in a house or in a condo?

B. Examining Method

1. How is this comparison structured? Does the plan affect the discussion?
2. What details contribute most to your understanding of the writer's preference?
3. What is the effect of mentioning the "tie-down ear flaps?"
4. The writer uses the "I" pronoun constantly throughout the paragraph. What effect does it have on his evaluation of the two living situations?
5. Why do you think this writer decided to focus on this particular aspect of living in a house or a condo?

C. Shifting Focus

1. How does narrative, storytelling (pages 277–281), work in this paragraph? Notice that the writer tells two stories to back up the point of his comparison.
2. Could this same information be presented outside the framework of a story? How?

SUGGESTIONS FOR DISCUSSION AND WRITING

A. Using Comparison and Contrast

1. Write an evaluation of two situations with which you are familiar—for example, attending a private or a public school, living at home or in a dormitory, playing baseball or football.

2. Write a comparison in which you tell two brief stories to illustrate your point.
3. Write a comparative paper in which you examine several pieces from this book that focus on housing.

B. Exploring the Options

1. What would be important to you if you were selecting a place to live? Consider order of priority and comparative merits of whatever selection you might make.
2. Rewrite the paragraph, using a point-by-point organization.

The Joys of Commuting

Deborah Pennimpede (student)

After some experience as a commuter, this student compares what people say about commuting with what she knows about it. She attempts to correct a false idea. Notice that the introduction begins with a common idea and then narrows to the opposing thesis. Also notice the many details she uses to make the commuter's real experience understandable to the reader.

Thinking Ahead What are the two main aspects of the comparison in this piece? What kind of details will she need for her comparison of fact with fantasy? Do you have the "insider's word" on a certain subject?

Commuter students live charmed lives. They get hot meals and quiet places to study, they enjoy the freedom that comes with owning a car, and at the same time they get the pleasures of campus life. Right? If only this rosy picture were true, commuter students would indeed lead charmed lives, but unfortunately they have more problems than charm in their lives. 1

Now, take the hot meal and the quiet place to study. More often than not, commuters hold part-time jobs that require them to work through the family dinner at least three or four nights a week. On these nights, if dinner doesn't come from a can or from under a pair of golden arches, it doesn't come at all. Last week I went four days straight eating only meals that began with "Mc." And even if commuters do find time to be home for supper, they often find it far from quiet when they try to study. A washing machine, a blaring television set, and squabbling brothers and sisters do little for concentration. At my house, my closed door seems to be an invitation for my little brother to enter and ask, "Whatchya'doin?" after which he proceeds to summarize his day or demonstrate the neat 2 noise he can make with his hands. One of my friends put a padlock on his bedroom door because his mother kept entering to tell him to turn off the stereo, turn on more lights, and sit at his desk, not on his bed. The other problem with "at-home" nights is the errands. There's no way to get out of these, especially with the reminder that it's important to take a break once in a while and only reasonable to help the family on occasion. So much for the household comfort.

What of the joys of owning a car? Due to finances, the average student's 3
car is 7 to 20 years old and gets anywhere from 14 m.p.g. to "don't-you-mean-gallons-per-mile?" This makes filling the tank traumatic because the dollars add up to half a paycheck. The other half should be put in the bank for the next fill-up—tomorrow? That is, unless it is one of the many months when the clunker needs its hundred dollars' worth of repairs. If any job costs less than thirty dollars, the car will continually break down till the total amount reaches $100. Clunkers are not to be shortchanged. One of my friends thought my $113 brake job was hilarious, especially because they were expected to last only a few months. I got the next few laughs, though, during the following weeks when he had a muffler fall off, a tire blow out, and a switch in his ignition wear out. His repairs? $142. Somehow, the commuters never quite enjoy owning a car.

And the best of both worlds? Maybe, if commuters didn't spend so 4
much time on the road between one world and another. How much freedom is there sitting in a traffic jam moving only a hundred yards in twenty minutes, listening to repeats of old news or to supermarket music on a radio that blacks out all the good stations? "Moon River" is not my favorite song. Most commuters spend a lot of time trapped, not free on the road, and when we are free, we're free possibly to get into an accident. If a pickup truck doesn't try to pass me at the blind corner at Maple Street and if I avoid the drivers who want to play bumper cars on the Salem Dodgem Rotary, I stand a chance of making it to school. So far I've been lucky. Making it to school does not, however, mean making it to "campus life" because the car still has to be parked—maybe in the lot that has enough spaces only at dawn, or maybe beside a no parking sign on the street if there's still a spot. Tickets and towing costs should be added to the commuter's monthly budget.

Oh yes, usually we do get to classes and sometimes we get to a dance 5
or a play after school. But we aren't charmed. It's impossible to live two lives; at least it's impossible for this commuter student, who would gladly exchange her clunker for a dorm student's room. I'd even leave the aspirin and the earplugs in the glove compartment for her.

VOCABULARY

squabbling (2), traumatic (3)

QUESTIONS

A. Discovering Meaning

1. To what does the writer compare the life of the commuter student?
2. What is her main point about commuting?

B. Examining Method

1. The controlling idea suggests that in each paragraph the writer will discuss a commuter's problem. How does the earlier part of the introduction influence the arrangement of the other paragraphs? How does she "echo" her thesis (see pages 374–378)?
2. Which paragraph sets forth the commuter student's predicament most convincingly? How?
3. Why does she mention the actual cost of repair bills rather than simply say that they are "expensive"?
4. Why does she mention the experience of other commuters as well as her own?
5. Where does this student use exaggeration to make her points more convincing? Do you think it is a good idea for her to do this? When might it be a fault in writing?

C. Shifting Focus

1. Write a one-sentence definition (see pages 152–156) of what this writer considers a commuter student to be.
2. How important is comparison to the message of the piece? Could it be written without comparison?

SUGGESTIONS FOR DISCUSSION AND WRITING

A. Using Comparison and Contrast

1. Write an essay in which you compare a popular representation of a subject with the reality about which you are informed—for example, the advertisement of apartments for rent versus the actual apartments, the

representation of cars or other products for sale versus the quality of them after the purchase.

2. Write an essay in which you attempt to correct a common misconception about something. What does it really mean to be a cheerleader, a popular person, a good athlete, rich?

B. Exploring the Options

1. Write a letter of response to Deborah—for example, about living in the dormitory or about your own ideas on commuting.

2. Write an essay on what it is to be a specific type of student—dormitory, international, adult, advanced-placement, handicapped, evening, married, and so on.

3. In an essay called "On Running after One's Hat," G.K. Chesterton suggests that it is better to enjoy life's difficulties (waiting in a train station, trying to open a stuck drawer, chasing a hat blown in the wind) than to grumble about them. Write an essay in which you suggest possible ways of "enjoying" the difficulties you face as a student (or ways of "enjoying" other inconveniences or difficulties in your life).

4. Write an essay on Chesterton's comment, "An adventure is only an inconvenience rightly considered. An inconvenience is only an adventure wrongly considered."

Little Boy Lost

Pat Hourihan (student)

In this piece, an adult student compares her "little boy" to the "jamoke" who has recently invaded her house. In a point-by-point comparison, she portrays the child that he once was with the teenager that he has become. Consider tone, the mother's attitude toward her son, and her experiences with him. Pat explains that the first draft of this piece was "handwritten at 2 A.M. after an argument with my son" and that the second, third, and fourth drafts were done more slowly on the word processor. She changed the order of the paragraphs and added detail, but the feelings have remained the same.

Thinking Ahead What are the two things being compared in this piece? What is the attitude suggested by the title? What are some methods she could use to bring the child and the teenager to life? Have you ever felt that "body snatchers" have invaded a world or a person once familiar to you?

It's the "Invasion of the Body Snatchers" all over again. The wonderful little boy whose laughter sang in my kitchen has disappeared. I think a switch has been made , but I'm not sure when. The change has been gradual. But I was looking at some of my little boy's pictures and I realized that I'm living with an imposter. I had my suspicions anyway, and now all of the puzzle pieces fit. 1

My child's twinkling smile seldom lights up this intruder's face. The copy I'm dealing with becomes more surly and critical by the minute, slamming things around the house. He sees only the dark side of the moon. And worst of all, he can't even fathom what gives me the right to guide him. "Welcome to the eighties, Mom," he says condescendingly when I share my extensive experience with him. He does not believe every word I say, nor does he think I'm the most beautiful woman alive. I don't know this child. He is not my son. 2

My little boy doesn't pay any attention to how he looks. Disgracefully dirty half the time, he concentrates on his trucks and his Lego. He's oblivious to everything else in the world. The gangling stranger in my house is a denizen of the shower and refers to one miniscule eruption as a case of acne. 3

As in the movie, the resemblance is remarkable. But I know *my* son and he would never say, "It's my fight, Mom. Mind your own business and stay out of it." *My* son would say, "Can you hit this kid for me, Mom?" knowing I'd say no, he'd have to do it for himself. My son would never say, "Ma, can I have five bucks for school today?" He'd walk around broke unless I made him take some money. He'd forget how dangerous it is to go without money. My son would never yell, "Can't you shut that radio off! I'm trying to study!" If this were my son, I'd have to cajole him from the T.V. and toward his books. And he would never, never raise his voice to me. 4

I knew definitely I was dealing with an outsider when I offered to help him with his homework. He said, "You don't know algebra, Mom." In response to my disappointed sigh, he said, "Mom, nobody knows everything, not even you." This can't be my kid because my kid thinks I know everything, even though I tell him that I don't. 5

I know my son. He's also not a joiner. I practically had to force him to join Cub Scouts. And I was the leader. This imposter has me driving pick-up and delivery to all the hot spots with a car full of blaring teenagers, many unknown to me. The kid I'm used to may not have many friends, but I always get to meet the ones he does have. He *always* drags them over to meet me. He wants us to live like one another. This jamoke says, "Mom, please! You're embarrassing me," whenever I try to speak to him anywhere near his friends. I've seen the hostile expression and heard the hissing voice before. In the movies. 6

I'm very understanding, but this changeling tells me I don't understand him at all. If he were my son, I'd understand him. And he'd know it. He always knew it. 7

So I've looked around the house, under and behind everything, to find the pod this stranger hatched from. But I can't find it. I've spoken to 8 others about my problem and outside opinions vary. His friends' mothers understand best and search daily for empty pods under their own sofas. My elders tell me not to worry. Everything will work out, they say. It's just growing pains, they say. I think they may be right. Mine.

QUESTIONS

A. Discovering Meaning

1. In what ways does the older child compare to his younger self?
2. Which child does the writer prefer? Why?

B. Examining Method

1. What details contribute most to our understanding of this mother's present relationship with her son? (See pages 400–403 for a discussion of details.)
2. What is the writer's tone in this comparison (see pages 421–422)?
3. What does the reference to the "Invasion of the Body Snatchers" contribute to the piece?
4. Why does the writer quote her son so often?
5. What is the overall purpose of the piece (see pages 368–371)?
6. Evaluate the introduction and the conclusion and the connections between them. (See pages 435–439.)

C. Shifting Focus

1. How does paragraph 5 contribute to the writer's characterization of her son?
2. In the conclusion, why does the writer use the word "they" three times within eleven words?

SUGGESTIONS FOR DISCUSSION AND WRITING

A. Using Comparison and Constrast

1. Write a piece in which you compare aspects of the same person (yourself?) at two different times in his or her life. Consider your attitude toward these changes.

2. You might also compare not just people but also other subjects at different times—for example, Sundays during childhood and now, trips to the country in the past and now, attitudes toward snow then and now.

3. Compare the method of characterization used in this piece to that used by Kafka in his account of his father.

B. Exploring the Options

1. Write a letter from the son to the mother as if it were composed at 2 A.M. after an argument.

2. Do some research on adolescent behavior and discuss the experience described in this paper. Place it in a larger context or among other examples, if necessary.

Football Red and Baseball Green

Murray Ross

Murray Ross, born in 1942, was educated at Williams College and the University of California at Berkeley. He now teaches English at the University of Colorado, where he directs the theater company. In this essay, Ross gives a "personality" to each of the sports he discusses—at first independently and then in comparison to one another.

Thinking Ahead What are the major differences between football and baseball? What is "red" about football and "green" about baseball? Can you assign two colors to describe two people in your life or possibly two other sports with which you are familiar?

Every Superbowl played in the 1970s rates among the top television 1
draws of the decade—pro football's championship game is right up there on the charts with blockbusters like *Rocky, Roots, Jaws,* and *Gone with the Wind.* This revelation is one way of indicating just how popular spectator sports are in this country. Americans, or American men anyway, seem to care about the games they watch as much as the Elizabethans cared about their plays, and I suspect for some of the same reasons. There

is, in sport, some of the rudimentary drama found in popular theater: familiar plots, type characters, heroic and comic action spiced with new and unpredictable variations. And common to watching both activities is the sense of participation in shared tradition and in shared fantasies. If sport exploits these fantasies without significantly transcending them, it seems no less satisfying for all that.

It is my guess that sport spectating involves something more than the 2
vicarious pleasures of identifying with athletic prowess. I suspect that each sport contains a fundamental myth which it elaborates for its fans, and that our pleasure in watching such games derives in part from belonging briefly to the mythical world which the game and its players bring to life. I am especially interested in baseball and football because they are so popular and so uniquely *American;* they began here and unlike basketball they have not been widely exported. Thus whatever can be said, mythically, about these games would seem to apply to our culture.

Baseball's myth may be the easier to identify since we have a greater 3
historical perspective on the game. It was an instant success during the Industrialization, and most probably it was a reaction to the squalor, the faster pace and the dreariness of the new conditions. Baseball was old-fashioned right from the start; it seems conceived in nostalgia, in the resuscitation of the Jeffersonian dream. It established an artificial rural environment, one removed from the toil of an urban life, which spectators could be admitted to and temporarily breathe in. Baseball is a *pastoral* sport, and I think the game can be best understood as this kind of art. For baseball does what all good pastoral does—it creates an atmosphere in which everything exists in harmony.

Consider, for instance, the spatial organization of the game. A kind of 4
controlled openness is created by having everything fan out from home plate, and the crowd sees the game through an arranged perspective that is rarely violated. Visually this means that the game is always seen as a constant, rather calm whole, and that the players and the playing field are viewed in relationship to each other. Each player has a certain position, a special area to tend, and the game often seems to be as much a dialogue between the fielders and the field as it is a contest between the players themselves: will that ball get through the hole? Can that outfielder run under that fly? As a moral genre, pastorals asserts the virtue of communion with nature. As a competitive game, baseball asserts that the team which best relates to the playing field (by hitting the ball in the right places) will win.

I suspect baseball's space has a subliminal function too, for topographi- 5
cally it is a sentimental mirror of older America. Most of the game is played between the pitcher and the hitter in the extreme corner of the playing area. This is the busiest, most sophisticated part of the ball park, where something is always happening, and from which all subsequent action originates. From this urban corner we move to a supporting in-

field, active but a little less crowded, and from there we come to the vast stretches of the outfield. As is traditional in American lore, danger increases with distance, and the outfield action is often the most spectacular in the game. The long throw, the double off the wall, the leaping catch—these plays take place in remote territory, and they belong, like most legendary feats, to the frontier.

Having established its landscape, pastoral art operates to eliminate any 6
reference to that bigger, more disturbing, more real world it has left behind. All games are to some extent insulated from the outside by having their own rules, but baseball has a circular structure as well which furthers its comfortable feeling of self-sufficiency. By this I mean that every motion of extension is also one of return—a ball hit outside is a *home* run, a full circle. Home—familiar, peaceful, secure—it is the beginning and end. You must go out but you must come back; only the completed movement is registered.

Time is a serious threat to any form of pastoral. The genre poses a 7
timeless world of perpetual spring, and it does its best to silence the ticking of clocks which remind us that in time the green world fades into winter. One's sense of time is directly related to what happens in it, and baseball is so structured as to stretch out and ritualize whatever action it contains. Dramatic moments are few, and they are almost always isolated by the routine texture of normal play. It is certainly a game of climax and drama, but it is perhaps more a game of repeated and predictable action: the foul balls, the walks, the pitcher fussing around on the mound, the lazy fly ball to center field. This is, I think, as it should be, for baseball exists as an alternative to a world of too much action, struggle and change. It is a merciful release from a more grinding and insistent tempo, and its time, as William Carlos Williams suggests, makes a virtue out of idleness simply by providing it:

> The crowd at the ball game
> is moved uniformly
> by a spirit of uselessness
> Which delights them. . . .

Within this expanded and idle time the baseball fan is at liberty to 8
become a ceremonial participant and a lover of style. Because the action is normalized, how something is done becomes as important as the action itself. Thus baseball's most delicate and detailed aspects are often, to the spectator, the most interesting. The pitcher's windup, the anticipatory crouch of the infielders, the quick waggle of the bat as it poises for the pitch—these subtle miniature movements are as meaningful as the home runs and the strikeouts. It somehow matters in baseball that all the tiny rituals are observed: the shortstop must kick the dirt and the umpire must brush the plate with his pocket broom. In a sense baseball is largely a continuous series of small gestures, and I think it characteristic that the

game's most treasured moment came when Babe Ruth pointed to where he subsequently hit a home run.

Baseball is a game where the little things mean a lot, and this, together with its clean serenity, its open space, and its ritualized action is enough to place it in a world of yesterday. Baseball evokes for us a past which may never have been ours, but which we believe was, and certainly that is enough. In the Second World War, supposedly, we fought for "Baseball, Mom and Apple Pie," and considering what baseball means, that phrase is a good one. We fought then for the right to believe in a green world of tranquility and uninterrupted contentment, where the little things would count. But now the possibilities of such a world are more remote, and it seems that while the entertainment of such a dream has an enduring appeal, it is no longer sufficient for our preeminent national pastime, and why its myth is being replaced by another more appropriate to the new realities (and fantasies) of our time. 9

Football, especially professional football, is the embodiment of a newer myth, one which in many respects is opposed to baseball's. The fundamental difference is that football is not a pastoral game; it is a heroic one. One way of seeing the difference between the two is by the juxtaposition of Babe Ruth and Jim Brown, both legendary players in their separate genres. Ruth, baseball's most powerful hitter, was a hero maternalized (his name), an epic figure destined for a second immortality as a candy bar. His image was impressive but comfortable and altogether human: round, dressed in a baggy uniform, with a schoolboy's cap and a bat which looked tiny next to him. His spindly legs supported a Santa-sized torso, and this comic disproportion would increase when he was in motion. He ran delicately, with quick, very short steps, since he felt that stretching your stride slowed you down. This sort of superstition is typical of baseball players, and typical too is the way in which a personal quirk or mannerism mitigates their awesome skill and makes them poignant and vulnerable. 10

There was nothing funny about Jim Brown. His muscular and almost perfect physique was emphasized further by the uniform which armored him. Babe Ruth's face was sensual and tough, yet also boyish and innocent; Brown's was an expressionless mask under the helmet. In action he seemed invincible, the embodiment of speed and power in an inflated human shape. One can describe Brown accurately only with superlatives, for as a player he was a kind of Superman, undisguised. 11

Brown and Ruth are caricatures, yet they represent their games. Baseball is part of a comic tradition which insists that its participants be above all human; while football, in the heroic mode, asks that its players be more than that. Football wants to convert men into gods; it suggests that magnificence and glory are as desirable as happiness. Football is designed, therefore, to impress its audience rather differently than baseball. 12

As a pastoral game, baseball attempts to close the gap between the players and the crowd. It creates the illusion, for instance, that with a lot of hard work, a little luck, and possibly some extra talent, the average 13 spectator might well be playing, not watching. For most of us can do a few of the things the ball players do: catch a pop-up, field a ground ball, and maybe get a hit once in a while. Chance is allotted a good deal of play in the game. There is no guarantee, for instance, that a good pitch will not be looped over the infield, or that a solidly batted ball will not turn into a double play. In addition to all of this, almost every fan feels he can make the manager's decision for him, and not entirely without reason. Baseball's statistics are easily calculated and rather meaningful; and the game itself, though a subtle one, is relatively lucid and comprehendible.

As a heroic game, football is not concerned with a shared community 14
of near-equals. It seeks almost the opposite relationship between its spectators and players, one which stresses the distance between them. We are not allowed to identify directly with Jim Brown any more than we are with Zeus, because to do so would undercut his stature as something more than human. Pittsburgh's Mean Joe Green, in the now classic commercial, walks off the battlefield like Achilles, clouded by combat. A little boy offers him a Coke, reluctantly accepted but enthusiastically drunk, and Green tosses the boy his jersey afterwards—the token of a generous god. Football encourages us to see its players much as the little boy sees Mean Joe: we look up to them with something approaching awe. For most of us could not begin to imagine ourselves playing their game without risking imminent humiliation. The players are all much bigger and much faster and much stronger than we are, and even as fans we have trouble enough just figuring out what's going on. In baseball what happens is what meets the eye, but in football each play means eleven men acting against eleven other men: it's too much for a single set of eyes to follow. We now are provided with several television commentators to explain the action to us, with the help of the ubiquitous slow-motion instant replay. Even the coaches need their spotters in the stands and their long postgame film analyses to arrive at something like full comprehension of the game they direct and manage.

If football is distanced from its fans by its intricacy and its "superhu- 15
man" play, it nonetheless remains an intense spectacle. Baseball, as I have implied, dissolves time and urgency in a green expanse, thereby creating a luxurious and peaceful sense of leisure. As is appropriate to a heroic enterprise, football reverses this procedure and converts space into time. The game is ideally played in an oval stadium, not in a "park," and the difference is the elimination of perspective. This makes football a perfect television game, because even at first hand it offers a flat, perpetually moving foreground (wherever the ball is). The eye in baseball viewing opens up; in football it zeroes in. There is no democratic vista in football, and spectators are not asked to relax, but to concentrate. You are encouraged to watch the drama not a medley of ubiquitous gestures, and you are constantly reminded that this event is taking place in time. The third element in baseball is the field; in football this element is the clock. Tradi-

tionally heroes do reckon with time, and football players are no exceptions. Time in football is wound up inexorably until it reaches the breaking point in the last minutes of a close game. More often than not it is the clock which emerges as the real enemy, and it is the sense of time running out that regularly produces a pitch of tension uncommon in baseball.

A further reason for football's intensity is that the game is played like a war. The idea is to win by going through, around or over the opposing team and the battle lines, quite literally, are drawn on every play. Violence is somewhere at the heart of the game, and the combat quality is reflected in football's army language ("blitz," "trap," "zone," "bomb," "trenches," etc.). Coaches often sound like generals when they discuss their strategy. Woody Hayes of Ohio State, for instance, explained his quarterback option play as if it had been conceived in the Pentagon: "You know," he said, "the most effective kind of warfare is siege. You have to attack on broad fronts. And that's all the option is—attacking on a broad front. You know General Sherman ran an option through the south." 16

Football like war is an arena for action, and like war football leaves little room for personal style. It seems to be a game which projects "character" more than personality, and for the most part football heroes, publicly, are a rather similar lot. They tend to become personifications rather than individuals, and, with certain exceptions, they are easily read emblematically as embodiments of heroic qualities such as "strength," "confidence," "grace," etc.—clichés really, but forceful enough when represented by the play of an Earl Campbell, a Terry Bradshaw, or a Lynn Sawnn. Perhaps this simplification of personality results in part from the heroes' total identification with their mission, to the extent that they become more characterized by what they do than by what they intrinsically "are." At any rate football does not make as many allowances for the idiosyncrasies that baseball actually seems to encourage, and as a result there have been few football players as uniquely crazy or humans as, say; Casey Stengel or Dizzy Dean. 17

A further reason for the underdeveloped qualities of football personalities, and one which gets us to the heart of the game's modernity, is that football is very much a game of modern technology. Football;s action is largely interaction, and the game's complexity requires that its players mold themselves into a perfectly coordinated unit. Jerry Kramer, formerly pro guard of the Green Bay Packers, explains how Lombardi would work to develop such integration: 18

> He makes us execute the same plays over and over, a hundred times, two hundred times, until we do every little thing automatically. He works to make the kickoff-team perfect, the punt-return team perfect, the field-goal team perfect. He ignores nothing. Technique, technique, technique, over and over and over, until we feel like we're going crazy. But we win.

Mike Garrett, the halfback, gives the player's version:

> After a while you train your mind like a computer—put the ideas in, and the body acts accordingly.

As the quotations imply, pro football is insatiably preoccupied with the smoothness and precision of play execution, and most coaches believe that the team which makes the fewest mistakes will be the team that wins. Individual identity thus comes to be associated with the team or unit that one plays for to a much greater extent than in baseball. To use a reductive analogy, it is the difference between *Bonanza* and *Mission Impossible.* Reggie Jackson is mostly Reggie Jackson, but Franco Harris is mostly the Pittsburgh Steelers. The latter metaphor is a precise one, since football heroes stand out not only because of purely individual acts, but also because they epitomize the action and style of the groups they are connected to. Kramer cites the obvious if somewhat self-glorifying historical precedent: "Perhaps," he writes, "we're living in Camelot." Ideally a football team should be what Camelot was supposed to have been, a group of men who function as equal parts of a larger whole, dependent on each other for total meaning. 19

The humanized machine as hero is something very new in sport, for in baseball anything approaching a machine has always been suspect. The famous Yankee teams of the fifties were almost flawlessly perfect, yet they never were especially popular. Their admirers took pains to romanticize their precision into something more natural than plain mechanics—Joe DiMaggio, for instance, became the "Yankee Clipper." Even so, most people seemed to want the Brooklyn Dodgers (the "bums") to thrash them in the World Series. Perhaps the most memorable triumph in recent years—the victory of the Amazin' Mets in 1969—was memorable precisely because it was the triumph of a random collection of inspired rejects over the superbly skilled, fully integrated and almost homogenized Baltimore Orioles. Similarly in the seventies, many fans watched with pleasure as the cantankerous Oakland A's went to work dismantling Cincinnati's self-styled "Big Red Machine." In baseball, machinery seems tantamount to villainy, whereas in football this smooth perfection is part of the unexpected integration a championship team must attain. 20

It is not surprising, really, that we should have a game which asserts the heroic function of a mechanized group, since we have become a country where collective identity is a reality. Football as a game of groups is appealing to us as a people of groups, and for this reason football is very much an "establishment" game—since it is in the corporate business and governmental structures that group America is most developed. The game comments on the culture, and vice versa: 21

> President Nixon, an ardent football fan, got a football team picture as an inaugural anniversary present from his cabinet....
>
> Superimposed on the faces of real gridiron players were the faces of cabinet members.(A.P.)

In one of the Vietnam war demonstrations, I remember seeing a sign that read, "49er fans against War, Poverty, and the Baltimore Colts." The notion of a team identity appeals to us all, whether or not we choose establishment colors.

Football's collective pattern is only one aspect of the way in which it 22
seems to echo our contemporary environment. The game, like our society, can be thought of as a cluster of people living under great tension in a state of perpetual flux. The potential for sudden disaster or triumph is as great in football as it is in our own age, and although there is something ludicrous in equating interceptions with assassinations and long passes with moonshots, there is also something valid and appealing in the analogies. It seems to me that football does successfully reflect those salient and common conditions which affect us all, and it does so with the end of making us feel better about them and our lot. For one thing, it makes us feel that something can be released and connected in all this chaos; out of the accumulated pile of bodies something can emerge—a runner breaks into the clear or a pass finds its way to a receiver. To the spectator, plays such as these are human and dazzling. They suggest to the audience what it has hoped for (and been told) all along, that technology is still a tool and not a master. Fans get living proof of this every time a long pass is completed; they appreciate that it is the result of careful planning, perfect integration and an effective "pattern," but they see too that it is human and that what counts as well is man, his desire, his natural skill and his "grace under pressure." Football metaphysically yokes heroic action and technology by violence to suggest that they are mutually supportive. It's a doubtful proposition, but given how we live, it has its attractions.

Football, like the space program, is a game in the grand manner, and it 23
is a relatively sober sport too—at least when set against the comic pastoral vision baseball regularly unfurls. Heroic action is serious business, and in the late fall and winter, when it is getting cold and miserable and brutal outside, football merely becomes more heroic, though sometimes the spectacle seems just absurd. I remember seeing the Detroit Lions and the Minnesota Vikings play one Thanksgiving in a blinding snowstorm, where—except for the small flags in the corners of the end zones—the field was totally obscured. Even with magnified television lenses, you could see only huge shapes come out of the gloom, thump against each other and fall in a heap, while occasionally, in desperation, the camera would switch to show us a cheerleader fluttering her pompoms in the cold and silent stadium. For the most part this game was the kind of theater of oblivion, and it's not hard to understand why some people find football pointless, a gladiatorial activity engaged in by moronic monsters. Yet these bleak conditions are also the stuff of which heroic legends are made. It was appropriate, I think, that what many regard as the greatest game of all time (the 1967 championship between the Packers and the Cowboys, won when the Arthurian Bart Starr plunged over the goal line in the final seconds behind Jerry Kramer's block) happened to be played when the temperature was a cool thirteen degrees below zero, the cold-

est December day in Green Bay history. These guys from Camelot had to beat the Cowboys, the clock and the weather too, so it's no wonder that Kramer waxed so ecstatically about his team. In the game I have just described, the pathetic monotony of the action was suddenly relieved when Jim Marshall, a veteran defensive end, intercepted a pass deep in his own territory. Marshall's off-season hobby is bobsledding, and he put his skills to good use here, rumbling upfield with a clumsy but determined authority through the mud, the snow, and the opposing team—then lateraling at the last moment at a teammate who scored the winning touchdown. It was a funny play, but it had something epic about it, and it was doubtless hailed in the bars of Minnesota with the same kind of rowdy applause that a good story once earned in the legendary halls of warrior kings.

Games like these get rarer and rarer, mostly because baseball and football have become so much more businesslike. It doesn't make good business sense to play outside where it might rain and snow and do terrible things; it isn't really prudent to play on a natural field that can be destroyed in a single afternoon; and why build a whole stadium or park that's good for only one game? More and more, both baseball and football are being played indoors on rugs in multipurpose spaces. The fans at these games are constantly diverted by huge whiz-bang scoreboards that dominate and describe the action, while the fans at home are constantly being reminded by at least three lively sportscasters of the other games, the other sports and the other shows that are coming up later on the same stations. Both pro football and pro baseball now play vastly extended seasons, so that the World Series now takes place on chilly October nights and football is well under way before the summer ends. From my point of view all this is regrettable, because these changes tend to remove the games from their intangible but palpable mythic contexts. No longer clearly set in nature, no longer given the chance to breathe and steep in their own special atmospheres, both baseball and football risk becoming demythologized. As fans we seem to participate a little less in mythic ritual these days, while being subjected even more to the statistics, the hype and the salary disputes that proceed from a jazzed-up, inflated, yet somehow flattened sporting world—a world that looks too much like the one we live in all the time. 24

Still, there is much to be thankful for, and every season seems to bring its own contribution to mythic lore. Some people will think this nonsense, and I must admit there are good reasons for finding both games simply varieties of decadence. 25

In its preoccupation with mechanization, and in its open display of violence, football is the more obvious target for social moralists, but I wonder if this is finally more "corrupt" than the seductive picture of sanctuary and tranquility that baseball has so artfully drawn for us. Almost all sport is vulnerable to such criticism because it is not strictly ethical in intent, and for this reason there will always be room for puritans like the Elizabethan John Stubbes who howled at the "wanton fruits which these cursed pastimes bring forth." As a long-time dedicated fan of almost 26 anything athletic, I confess myself out of sympathy with most of this; which is to say, I guess, that I am vulnerable to those fantasies which these games support, and that I find happiness in the company of people who feel as I do.

A final note. It is interesting that the heroic and pastoral conventions which underlie our most popular sports are almost classically opposed. The contrasts are familiar: city versus country, aspirations versus contentment, activity versus peace and so on. Judging from the rise of professional football, we seem to be slowly relinquishing that unfettered rural vision of ourselves that baseball so beautifully mirrors, and we have come to cast ourselves in a genre more reflective of a nation confronted by constant and unavoidable challenges. Right now, like the Elizabethans, we seem to share both heroic and pastoral yearnings, and we reach out to both. Perhaps these divided needs account in part of the enormous attention we as a nation now give to spectator sports. For sport provides one place where we can have our football and our baseball too. 27

VOCABULARY

rudimentary (1), vicarious (2), subliminal (5), anticipatory (8), juxtaposition (10), poignant (10), vulnerable (10), caricatures (12), imminent (14), ubiquitous (14), medley (15), inexorably (15), intrinsically (17), integration (18), insatiably (19), reductive (19), tantamount (20), ludicrous (22), salient (22), intangible (24), palpable (24), decadence (25)

QUESTIONS

A. Discovering Meaning

1. What is the thesis of the piece?
2. What are the major contrasts between baseball and football?
3. This essay contains comparisons within the larger comparison. Why is one sport "red" and the other "green"; one "heroic" and the other "pastoral"?
4. How does Ross account for the fact that Americans take pleasure in watching two sports that are so different from one another?

B. Examining Method

1. What kind of introduction does Ross use? (See pages 394–398 for a discussion of various types.)

2. What is the major comparison that is made in paragraph 5? Does it work?
3. What is the effect of the comparison made in paragraph 16?
4. What kind of conclusion does he use? (See pages 435–439 for a discussion of types.)
5. What is the overall purpose of the piece?

C. Shifting Focus

1. In paragraph 19, Ross calls attention to his own use of comparison. Why?
2. What is the effect of the extended example in paragraph 23?
3. Is there any way to make football "green" and baseball "red"?

SUGGESTIONS FOR DISCUSSION AND WRITING

A. Using Comparison and Contrast

1. Write a comparison and contrast of two sports, as Ross does. Remember that you are interested in meaning as well as in points of comparison. Consider possible colors to associate with them.
2. Write a comparative paper using colors as the major aspect of the characterization.

B. Exploring the Options

1. Write a characterization of some other sport: baseball, hockey, soccer, and so on. Consider important aspects of the game and what they represent to a particular audience.
2. Ross extends his judgments about the games to broader comments about American life. What connections does he make? Do they still seem valid?
3. Write a characterization of an athlete (or a comparison between two athletes, as Ross does in paragraphs 10–12).
4. Write a characterization of baseball or football, or both, from the point of view of the nonfan. What colors might apply?
5. Read Paul Grasso's narrative on the use of steroids (page 292). Does it seem consistent with the judgments made here?
6. In a column on the late commissioner of baseball, A. Bartlett Giamatti, a speechwriter makes the following comment:

He knew that while other sports were enjoyable—basketball for its sleekness; football, its force—baseball was the only sport one could love. Football was a mastiff—hulking, imperious. Baseball was a cocker spaniel—precious and unaffected—that one clasped, forever, as an heirloom of the heart.

Write a response to all or any one of these judgments.

Three Pictures of Death

On the following pages are three artistic representations of death—the famous Roman statue, *Dying Gaul,* the medieval painting, *Landscape with the Fall of Icarus* (see the discussion of Icarus on page 60), and the modern painting, *Death on a Pale Horse.*

Dying Gaul. About 240–200 B.C., Roman copy of original sculpture. Capitoline Museum, Rome.

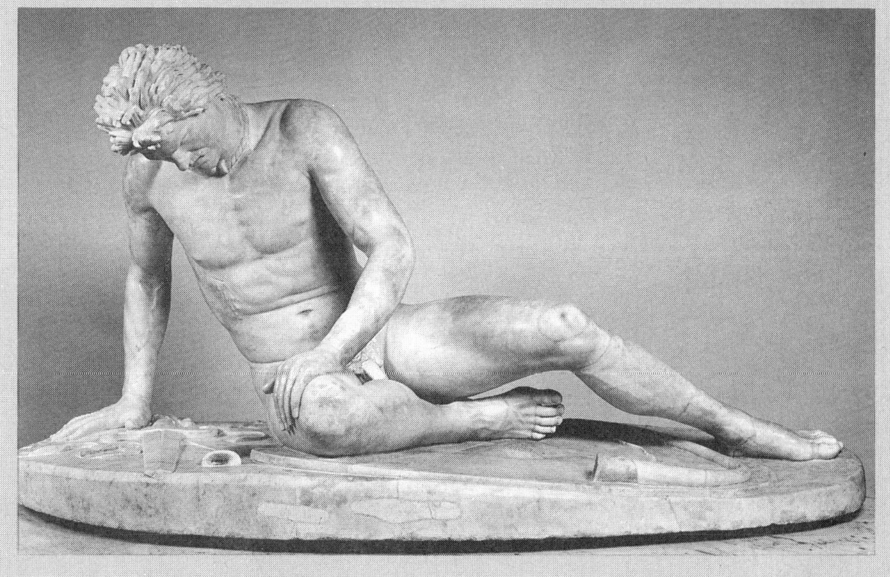

Albert Pinkham Ryder. *Death on a Pale Horse (The Race Track)*. c. 1910. The Cleveland Museum of Art. Purchase, J. H. Wade Fund.

Pieter Brueghel the Elder. *Landscape with the Fall of Icarus* (1525–1569). Museum of Fine Arts, Brussels.

SUGGESTIONS FOR WRITING

A. Using Comparison and Contrast

1. Study all representations carefully and compare them to one another. Notice details that distinguish them from one another and attempt to characterize the attitude toward death in each one. The reader should be able to visualize important aspects of each example, even without benefit of the printed illustrations.

3. Exploring the Options

2. Read W. H. Auden's poem, "Musée des Beaux Arts" and discuss his interpretation of the painting of the fall of Icarus by Brueghel.

3. Discuss the interpretation of Brueghel's painting in William Carlos Williams' "Landscape with the Fall of Icarus" (page 60). Compare it to Auden's poem, if it will make your discussion more complete.

Musée des Beaux Arts[1]

(poem)

W. H. Auden[2]

About suffering they were never wrong
The Old Masters: how well they understood
Its human position; how it takes place
While someone else is eating or opening a window or just walking
  dully along;
How, when the aged are reverently, passionately waiting
For the miraculous birth, there always must be
Children who did not specially want it to happen, skating
On a pond at the edge of the wood:
They never forgot

[1]The Museum of Fine Arts, Brussels, where the painting, *Landscape with the Fall of Icarus,* by Pieter Brueghel the Elder is located.

[2]Auden (1907–1973): English poet.

That even the dreadful martyrdom must run its course
Anyhow in a corner, some untidy spot
Where the dogs go on with their doggy life and the torturer's horse
Scratches its innocent behind on a tree.

In Brueghel's *Icarus,*[3] for instance: how everything turns away
Quite leisurely from the disaster; the plowman may
Have heard the splash, the forsaken cry,
But for him it was not an important failure; the sun shone
As it had to on the white legs disappearing into the green
Water; and the expensive delicate ship that must have seen
Something amazing, a boy falling out of the sky,
Had somewhere to get to and sailed calmly on.

Landscape with the Fall of Icarus

(poem)

William Carlos Williams

According to Brueghel
when Icarus fell
it was spring

a farmer was plowing
his field
the whole pageantry

of the year was
awake tingling
near

the edge of the sea
concerned
with itself

[3]In the Greek myth, the artificer, Daedalus, for an escape from Crete, makes wings for himself and his son, Icarus, and attaches them with wax. Against his father's advice, Icarus flies too close to the sun causing the wax to melt, and he drowns.

sweating in the sun
that melted
the wing's wax

unsignificantly
off the coast
there was

a splash quite unnoticed
this was
Icarus drowning

Classifying

The details of life are many and complex. Experiencing and evaluating each one independently—each human being, each town, each car, each animal, each thought, each job, each bite of food—would be a tedious and impossible task. We need ways to get through this maze of detail. We need to free ourselves so that we may concentrate on what is important to us.

One way to do this is to put the details of life into categories, to classify them into groups. *Human beings* may be grouped into relatives, friends, acquaintances, or strangers; male or female; child, adolescent, middle-aged, or elderly; dead or alive; historical or contemporary; fat, thin, or pleasingly plump—each category suggesting something shared by the members of that particular group. *Human beings* may also be nonstudents or students, and these students, in turn, may be sociology majors, English majors, or as yet undecided. *Food* may be divided into meat, fish, and dairy products or into groups for storage, for distribution at shelters, for purchase by restaurants. Think of a library or a video store without classification.

Classification is a way of organizing, of allowing a logical arrangement of the often chaotic details of life. It allows us to think about things logically, to see connections and distinctions that may not at first be obvious. It is the product of observation, of judgment, not simply a passing thought as we wade through the complexities of daily existence. In writing, it allows us to share these thought-out connections, to explain at a level based upon, but not submerged in, the all-too-numerous particulars.

Consider, for example, the following.

1. I have yet to meet the simpleton "cliché bird-watcher," but I have come across several other noteworthy types:

   —The devoted elders.
   —The experts.
   —The competitors.
   —The insecure ones, like me.

2. Certain types of females often appear in television commercials:

   —The yuppie businesswoman.
   —The superwoman.
   —The frazzled homemaker.
   —The femme fatale.
   —The frazzled fatale (frazzled by day, fatale by night).

3. While Thoreau was living the simple life at Walden Pond, he was concerned with several important aspects of his life:

   —The economic.
   —The social.
   —The political.
   —The intellectual.

4. Both on-campus and off-campus housing may be divided into several different categories:

   —On campus

   a. Dorm room, private.

   b. Dorm room, shared.

   c. Residence house, semiprivate.

   —Off campus.

   a. Apartment, private.

   b. Apartment, shared.

   c. Home, with host family.

   d. Home, private.

   e. Home, own family.

It is also possible to make some distinctions between classification and division, classification being the process of placing several individual examples into larger categories (as in examples 1 and 2) and division being the process of breaking down a larger category into its component parts (as in examples 3 and 4). What is important, however, in either procedure, is that the principle of selection is consistent and that the groups are related to one another, not, for example, several paragraphs on types of bird-watchers and one random one on binoculars, or paragraphs on women in commercials merged casually with other paragraphs on detergents and washing machines. Other approaches, other categories may yield interesting thoughts about bird-watching or about advertising, but to mix the categories is to start on the road back to the undifferentiated confusion of daily life. Classification ultimately simplifies, if only for a moment.

WORKING WITH CLASSIFICATION

Think about how often you put personal experience into categories—teachers, schools, friends, parents, clubs, teams, books, gifts, towns. On a more specialized level, you might be able to classify types of figure-skating judges, types of patrons at a local library, types of farms that supply the produce department where you work. With research, classification becomes even more sophisticated—types of tax breaks for small businesses, types of rhetorical figures used by Chaucer in *The Canterbury Tales*.

The interest in classification comes from the order you impose on separate pieces of information and from your ability to make convincing connections and distinctions. Readers appreciate order. Classification by its very nature involves comparisons. The challenge is in avoiding the superficial or commonly shared classifications (the types of people I like, for example, friendly, generous, kind) and in giving enough significant detail to keep the reader interested.

Example

An essay on student housing may include the following paragraph on "dorm room, private":

> Among the possibilities in the "on-campus category" is a private dorm room. The word *private*, however, should be written with a capital *P*, because private dorm rooms, especially for freshmen, are precious few. This particularly desirable arrangement, unlike the shared dorm rooms, offers some of the advantages of off-campus housing, without the extra expense and without too much isolation. Company is always just down the hall, but still, it's easier to close the door of "your own room" and to relax with some degree of peace. It's easier to keep track of your own things and to clean up your own mess. It's easier to have your own company and to concentrate on studying without a roommate's soap operas or stereo, and it's a lot easier to sleep. If they could, many students would choose this type of on-campus housing, but in many schools, this privilege is saved for those in the honors programs.

Warm-Up

Write a paragraph in which you classify a subject for discussion and, after you have studied the following examples, try to rewrite your paragraph.

Consider, for example, types of teachers you find most helpful; types of breakfast cereals you prefer not to eat; types of parties in which drinking is likely to get out of control.

The Dairy Group
(paragraph)
Linda Erickson (student)

In a classification paper called "The Discriminatory Eater," this student tells of her very cautious approach to various types of food—to those, like popsicles and hamburgers, associated in her mind with miserable occasions; to those with evil connotations, like "deviled ham" or "head cheese"; and to all dairy products, as discussed in this paragraph. Here is Linda's comment: "Because I approach foods seriously, it was easy to break it down into categories." Advice? "Do unto others, never say never, button up your overcoat, spare the rod, write from the heart."

Thinking Ahead What do the items in this category have in common for Linda? Linda takes food seriously, but what is her attitude toward *writing* about it? What clues does she give you about her attitude toward herself? Do you place food into special categories?

> I have the most difficulty with the dairy group. The expiration date on a milk carton is no light matter. I toss all milk by midnight, prior to the date of spoilage, that is unless it has become suspicious in the meantime. When I visit friends, I am compelled to sneak a peek at the milk date while they are pouring my tea. I refuse any milk that comes out of a little pitcher because I can't tell how long it's been there; I also know that it has been openly exposed to other dangerous elements in the refrigerator. I sniff cheese daily (sometimes hourly) and do regular checks for discoloration. Mold is not a sign of maturity and good taste for me. Butter must also be all one color. Golden yellow edges are absolutely out. Whipped cream that has taken on a pink hue atop a chocolate cream pie is enough to make me cry. And no matter what color they are, products such as cottage cheese and yogurt always make me uneasy. How, after all, can I determine if they have gone bad when they taste so rotten to begin with?

A. Discovering Meaning

1. What are the writer's problems with this type of food?
2. What does she look for, in particular, in this category?

B. Examining Method

1. Notice the verbs in this paragraph. What do they suggest about the writer's attitude toward this kind of food (see pages 421–423)?
2. What is the effect of adding a new detail in every sentence (see page 400)?
3. What is the tone, the attitude of the writer toward the subject (see pages 421–422)?

C. Shifting Focus

1. Study the diction, the choice of words in this paragraph. Which words contribute most to your understanding of how she feels about dairy products (see pages 422–423)?
2. Does the hyperbole, the deliberate exaggeration, of sniffing cheese "sometimes hourly," work in this paragraph?

SUGGESTIONS FOR DISCUSSION AND WRITING

A. Using Classification

1. Consider your own reactions to certain types of food. Do you place food into special categories?
2. Write a piece in which you categorize some other aspects of your daily life—for example, types of clothing, types of friends, types of entertainments, types of music. Remember that the task is not just to identify the groups but to share some insights about these groups and to make what you have to say interesting to readers.
3. Rewrite this paragraph as if dairy products were the writer's favorite food.

B. Exploring the Options

1. Compare the tone of this piece to that of Thurber (page 10) or Brown (page 131). (See pages 33–35 for a discussion of comparison and pages 421–422 for a discussion of tone.)

2. Write a discussion or a defense of a particular attitude toward food. (One student, a vegetarian, wrote a parody of Thanksgiving dinner, during which the turkey family ate humans and passed the "people slaw" to one another.)

Gifts in My Drawer
(paragraph)
Phillip Lopate

Phillip Lopate, born in 1943, has written two novels, *The Rug Merchant* and *Confessions of Summer,* two books of poems, *The Daily Round* and *The Eyes Don't Always Want to Stay Open,* two collections of personal essays, *Bachelorhood,* and *Against Joie de Vivre,* and a nonfiction book, *Being with Children.* He teaches one semester at the University of Houston, Texas, and lives the rest of the year in New York City. This paragraph is a selection that has been taken from a longer piece, "My Drawer," in which Lopate discusses the top drawer of his bureau, "a *way station* in which I keep the miscellanea that I cannot bear to throw away just yet." After shuffling through a variety of items, he concludes that classification may be the best approach: "But before I go on, shouldn't I try to approach this mess more systematically—to categorize, to make generalizations?" He then goes on to discuss several types of objects: jewelry, things to be "on the safe side," and, discussed here, gifts he doesn't like.

Thinking Ahead What generalizations does Lopate make about this category of gifts? How do you expect this paragraph to be organized? Think of a catch-all place in your life and the types of things contained there. What gifts do you receive that you would prefer not to get?

One category that suggests itself is gifts I have no particular affection for, but am too superstitious to chuck out. (If you throw away a gift, something terrible will happen: the wastebasket will explode, or you'll never get another.) They include this pair of cloth finger puppets that I suppose were meant to give me endless hours of delight while sitting on my bed pretending to be Punch and Judy with myself. Because I work with children, people keep bringing me juvenile toys—magic sets, mazes with ball bearings, paddleballs—confusing the profession with the profession's clients. Over the years I have been given a whole collection of oddities that do not really amuse me or match my sense of perversity. Nothing is trickier than bringing someone a novelty gift, since each person's definition of cute or campy is such a private affair.

QUESTIONS

A. Discovering Meaning

1. What category of gifts does Lopate discuss in this paragraph?
2. What specific gifts are included in this category?

B. Examining Method

1. How does he develop the discussion of these gifts?
2. What is the effect of the term "chuck out" in line 1?
3. Why does he include the parenthetical expression about throwing away a gift?
4. What does he do beyond simply listing the particular unwanted gifts? (See pages 400–403 for a discussion of development of paragraphs.)
5. What is the tone? (See pages 421–422 for a discussion of tone.)
6. What does the concluding sentence contribute to the paragraph? (See pages 435–439 for a discussion of conclusion.)

C. Shifting Focus

1. How does exemplification relate to Lopate's purpose of approaching "this mess more systematically." (See pages 5–7 for a discussion of exemplification.)

SUGGESTIONS FOR DISCUSSION AND WRITING

A. Using Classification

1. Write your own piece on miscellanea that you have collected. Remember to place these things into categories and to be concerned with meaning and interest, as well as with naming the objects. (One writer discussed gifts as representations of various friends at various stages of her life; another looked at the "oddities" he had saved over the years and tried to explain their meaning.)
2. Do you have a collection of gifts that fit into the category of "unamusing" or of not matching your own sense of yourself? Try to account, as Lopate does, for their being given to you. Could the reasons be put into categories?

B. Exploring the Options

1. Assume that you are the giver of the cloth finger puppets and have just read this paragraph. Write a letter to Lopate.
2. Look at the place where you are writing. What have you collected there or nearby? What do they say about you? What is your attitude toward them?
3. In an essay called "Possessions," E. V. Lucas tells of a grandfather "who, after he had reached a certain age, used birthdays as occasions on which to give away rather than receive presents," and argues that possessions "encumber and retard" our progress through life. Discuss this point of view.

What Makes a Being Super?

Roger Froilan (student)

In this piece, a student who has been a long-time reader of comic books and who occasionally writes his own analyzes the sources of the exceptional strength of certain types of superheroes. This paper grows out of more specialized knowledge, the kind provided by jobs, hobbies, and frequent pastimes. About writing this, Roger says, "The facts came easy for this paper, too easy. In my early drafts, I included so much detail the reader couldn't follow what I was saying. I had to cut words and put in transitions to make it work" (see page 418, Practice 3).

Thinking Ahead When you think of comic books or superheroes, what types come to mind? Do you expect to be interested in this subject? What kind of information will Roger be required to give on each subject? Do you have a hobby that you might be able to write about in an essay?

"With great power comes great responsibility." Peter Parker, a.k.a. "The Amazing Spiderman," learned this the hard way. By failing to use his special spiderlike powers to stop a thief, that very same thief later killed his Uncle Ben. After this loss, he decided not to waste his superpower, but to use it to fight for justice. Just how did he get this power in the first place? How do Superbeings in general get their powers? In "Sequential Art," more commonly referred to as "Comic Book Art," these questions are often addressed in great detail. Actually, Superbeings get their powers in many different ways, ways that are possible to categorize. 1

"The Mutant," for example, is a person born of normal or sometimes mutant parents, but with a special gift, like the ability to fly, to be trans- 2 ported through thought (teleportation), to move things simply by thinking (telekinesis), or to read and send thoughts (telepathy). They may also have enhanced senses and abnormally high intelligence. Usually surfacing during adolescence, these powers are the result of high background radiation in the Earth. The two major comic book companies, Marvel and DC, explain their mutants in slightly different ways. Marvel attributes their powers to an "X-factor" present in the DNA of everyone, but activated in Mutants. DC attributes their powers to a "Meta-gene." In Marvel's "X-Men" (a group of mutant superheroes), Nightcrawler, for example, has the ability to teleport while in DC's "Titans," Jericho can enter other people's bodies and control them if he looks them straight in the eye.

Mutants, part of a separate race called "Homo Superior," are often regarded as highly dangerous and are therefore subject to racial discrimination. As a result, many of them get together to fight evil. In doing so, many lose their lives, but mutants continue to hope for peaceful coexistence with normal humans. 3

The second major category, "The Mutate," also lives with an "X-factor" or a "Meta-gene," but this type needs a special catalyst to induce the powers. These beings are like blank slates; they need something to fill in. A good example of this would be DC's "Flash." As a boy, Wally West stood next to a shelf of chemicals that was struck by lightning. They spilled all over him and he found that he had gained the power of superspeed, and thus became "Flash." Dr. David Banner was belted by Gamma rays while trying to save a boy from an exploding Gamma Bomb and thus became "The Incredible Hulk," and young Matt Murdock lost his sight, but acquired superhuman hearing, taste, touch, and smell when a cannister of toxic waste crashed in front of him. His special radar sense enables him to "see" with his mind. One of the most popular of the Mutates is Marvel's "Spiderman." Bitten by a radioactive spider, Peter Parker gained the proportionate strength, speed, and agility of that spider, although someone without the "X-factor" would probably have died. 4

Very different from both the Mutant and the Mutate, is "The Sorcerer," one who uses magic as a tool for healing the sick, exorcising evil spirits, warding off evil beings, and even defending the earth from invasion. Marvel's Dr. Stephan Strange is the earth's sorcerer supreme, creating, for example, a spell to rid the world of vampires. At DC, Dr. Fate, given magic powers by the Lords of Order, is in constant battle with the Lords of Chaos—a seemingly never-ending battle. These magic spells are far more powerful than any used by so-called "witches," and could be potentially dangerous if the sorcerers were evil. But those like Dr. Strange and Dr. Fate use their powers only for good. They help in the fight against wielders of evil magic. 5

A being who is neither a Mutant, nor a Mutate, nor a Sorcerer may use technology to gain superpowers: "The "Hi-Tech Superbeing." Marvel's Tony Stark, or "Iron Man," for example, although crippled, uses microcircuitry, aeronautics, and modern weapons technology to create a powerful suit of armor. Dressed in this suit, he can walk, fly, project forcefields, 6 fire repulsor rays, and use radar, to name only a few of the armor's capabilities. Hawkeye uses High-Tech archery gear, his arrows including grappling hooks, nets, and concussion blasts. Green Lantern's alien ring is an extension of his own will-power and can make fists or hammers or even a vehicle. DC's Bruce Wayne, or "Batman," also often uses gadgets to get out of traps—advanced lockpicks, grappling hooks, or souped-up cars. But even though he has the incredible skills to create such Hi-Tech devices, he mostly relies on thinking. His detective skills are compared to those of Sherlock Holmes. Using this intelligence, he employs certain principles of technology for out-thinking his enemies, but for him the most advanced piece of technology is really his own mind.

The Multiverse is filled with Superbeings, from aliens to gods, but in 7
the comics, the Earth has the most variety in the development of these beings. Like Superman, they may be outsiders who land on Earth, or like Wonder Woman, they may get their powers as a direct gift from the gods, but the vast majority of the earth's Superbeings are mutants, mutates, sorcerers, or managers of Hi-Tech. Some do use their powers for evil, but most, along with Peter Parker, believe that "With great power comes great responsibility."

QUESTIONS

A. Discovering Meaning

1. On what principle does the writer base his classification of Superbeings?
2. What are the various types of heroes discussed in this piece?

B. Examining Method

1. What kind of introduction does the writer use (see pages 394–398)?
2. What is the purpose of this piece (see pages 368–371)?
3. What is the thesis (see page 364)?
4. The writer says that he needed to add transitions in later drafts. How does he move from paragraph to paragraph in this final draft? How does he make connections within the paragraphs? (Take, for example, paragraph 2). (See pages 418–419.)
5. What is the effect of mentioning so many specific names (see pages 400–403)?
6. What is the tone of this piece (see pages 421–422)? What are the indications of the writer's attitude toward comic books?

C. Shifting Focus

1. Remove the proper names from paragraph 5. What is the effect?
2. In what other ways could these same heroes be classified?

SUGGESTIONS FOR DISCUSSION AND WRITING

A. Using Classification

1. Write a paper on one of your own hobbies or interests. Consider classifying aspects of your knowledge—types of sailboats, types of CB broadcasts and services, types of music. Make detailed knowledge the basis of your discussion.
2. Write a paper on the sources of various individuals' rise to success—athletes, musicians, artists, celebrities. From what did they receive *their* powers?

B. Exploring the Options

1. Write a detailed discussion of something often underestimated that you feel deserves greater respect.
2. Read some of these "superbeing" comic books mentioned by Roger and write your own reaction to them. (See sample movie reviews on pages 241–249 and a discussion of book reviews on page 315).

Who's Who at the Modern Health Club?

Robert Crouse (student)

In this essay, a student who spends considerable time at various health clubs puts the people he meets there into three major categories. He also gives examples of each type, thus making the groups more than just labels. He advises choosing a topic you know about and discussing it with others if you need further information.

Thinking Ahead What types of people go to health clubs? Do you have any special knowledge of or curiosity about who goes there? Could you do your own "who's who" about some particular location?

The sounds of squeaking pulleys, humming stationary bikes, and clapping steel plates permeate the climate-controlled air. Silk flowers are strategically placed along neon-lit, colorfully-carpeted walls. "Fitness center?" "Country club?" "Nightclub of the eighties?" Just how do the members of these health centers see these places? What kinds of people come to them in the first place? First of all, there *are* those who seriously visit with a goal of improved fitness; then there are those with ulterior motives, like an improved social life; and, finally, there are those who jump on the bandwagon because it just seemed like the right thing to do. 1

Susan, the "beautiful bod," would look good in a paper bag—and knows it. But she comes with workouts on her mind. She's not thrilled about exercise, but she's not there for a social life either. She knows that every man in the club is dying for her company, but she rejects even the most innocent hello's. 2

Phil, the "Brian Bosworth lookalike" is another serious member. He includes steroids in his daily diet and expects other members, even Susan, to drool over him. He has a pierced ear and wears physique-flattering clothes like a skimpy tank top and nylon shorts. Between exercises, he sometimes converses with the rest of the mere mortals. 3

A final example of the serious member is John, the "all-important-businessman." He thinks he's Donald Trump. At precisely 5:30 on Mondays, Wednesdays, and Fridays, he strides in with a formal air, as if he were walking into a board meeting. He wears glasses, his hair is neatly parted to the side, and his exercise attire (no matter what size) is always too tight. His extra baggage comes from sitting on his Gluteus Maximus at his desk. John likes to order the fitness instructors around and ignores everyone else. His time, after all, is more valuable than everyone else's. 4

Tom is a member with ulterior motives. This "desperate divorcee" doesn't really have fitness in mind when he struts into the club. For as long as possible, he wears a gray business suit with a pink dress shirt strategically opened at the collar to show off a thick gold chain and gaudy medallion. He spends little time exercising, preferring to lounge in the stretching area and making small talk to any girl unfortunate enough to get near him. His prey can usually be seen rolling her eyes in boredom while he brags about his prosperous business (selling whirlpools). He attends every club party, always on the lookout for a "scoop." 5

Kelly, the "bottle-blonde-bimbo," also has ulterior motives. She has over-processed hair with dark roots and wears form-fitting, shiny spandex outfits (complete with accessories). Her face is layered with makeup and her fingernails are too long to hold a dumb-bell. Kelly giggles and smiles at all of the men and desperately wants to hook up with Phil. 6

Among the jump-the-bandwagon types is Bob, the "kind, lonely widower," who has nothing better to do with his time. He does very little exercising and is obviously afraid of boring anyone who might be listening to him. He has tired eyes and a sweet smile, and he loves to reminisce. 7

Jane, the "obese housewife," has also jumped the bandwagon. She has curly hair, glasses, and is middle-aged. She wears bulky, pastel sweatsuits and hibernates in the ladies' gym. She is too self-conscious to exercise 8 co-ed. Jane chronically complains to the instructors because she works out "maybe once or twice a week," and can't understand why she hasn't lost any weight yet.

Susan, Phil, and John; Tom and Kelley; Bob and Jane are all examples 9
of their kind, the kind of people most often with a membership at a health club. Some of them get in better shape, some of them get companionship, some of them get less than they expect. But all of them find a motive for signing up.

QUESTIONS

A. Discovering Meaning

1. How does the writer classify the members of the club?
2. What is the source of information for this paper? What leads you to think so?

B. Examining Method

1. What kind of introduction does the writer use (see pages 394–398)?
2. Is it necessary to be familiar with the health club environment in order to understand this student's comments? Why?
3. What is the effect of naming these various members of the club (see pages 400–403)?
4. Which details seem to best characterize the members?
5. What is the tone, the attitude of the writer toward the subject (see pages 421–422)?
6. Do these three categories seem sufficient to describe the members of a health club?

C. Shifting Focus

1. Add some dialogue to any one of these paragraphs. Does it improve the characterization?
2. What does the use of specific examples contribute to the analysis? How does this piece differ from one based on examples? (See pages 5–7.)
3. Compare this introduction to Tien Truong's on page 12.

SUGGESTIONS FOR DISCUSSION AND WRITING

A. Using Classification

1. Write your own classification of members of a particular group. You might discuss the categories themselves, or you might, as this student did, give examples of the categories.
2. Classify members of a group according to their various reasons for joining it. Consider, for example, college students, professors, or members of a sports team.

B. Exploring the Options

1. Write a characterization of these same people from the point of view of one of the members. Include a reaction to Bob, the writer of this piece.
2. Write a letter of complaint to the management written by Susan about Tom or by Phil about Kelley.
3. Write some advertising copy for the "Gilded Crowne Health Spa" in order to get the Susans, the Toms, the Janes, and the writer of this piece to sign up for a year.

Homes Away from Home

Leslie S. Moore

Written by a former Peace Corps volunteer who has spent time in both Korea and Africa, this piece classifies the various houses she and her husband shared during a difficult stay in Mali. Notice the many details used to distinguish one house from another and also notice that the three African houses are compared, not only among themselves, but also with their home in New England. About writing this piece, Leslie explains, "The houses article pretty much wrote itself. Although I did refer to journals to refresh my memory, most of the images were still clear in my mind. We actually lived in more African houses than I mentioned, but I left them out because they didn't fit the types of homes I was discussing or the 'woe-are-we' tone I was trying to get."

Thinking Ahead What are some possible categories for distinguishing among houses? Think of various houses or apartments in which you have lived.

Does each one stir a certain kind of memory? Are you able to put the houses or the memories into categories?

Something in me likes to pack a suitcase and say goodbye. Far from feeling a sense of loss, I am enriched by each old place that I leave and by each new place that I visit. I also find that the farther I wander from comfort and familiarity, the deeper the details burn, and there they rest. A glow of fondness gradually surrounds them as I return to my more familiar life. Take my homes away from home in Africa. 1

When my husband and I left to teach English in Mali for the Peace Corps, we knew and loved what we were leaving. It was a modest New England house that Tom himself had built, tucked into a slice of woods not a mile from the center of town, yet too secluded to bother with curtains. Windows were its extravagance; a wealth of light reflected off white walls and wooden floors. We were comfortable there. But we were still excited about leaving. I remember admiring the brightness, the clean lines of our little house as we walked out, but I never considered turning around. 2

Two weeks later, in the village of Souban between the Niger River and the African bush, I had a chance to live a transformation. Stripped of our familiar surroundings like snakes that have sloughed off old skins, we faced this world feeling renewed, but tender. No electricity. No running water. No transportation but two feet, donkey carts, and bicycles. Our first "house" consisted of two rooms in a mud compound shared with Kognan Diarra and his family—his mother, two wives, a sister-in-law, eight children, a herd of goats, a flock of guinea fowl, a donkey, and a dog. 3

Yes, Peace Corps had "upgraded " our accommodations by replacing the thatched roof with corrugated metal, covering the dirt floors with concrete, slapping a thin coat of whitewash over the mud walls, and adding two tiny windows with screens. Unlike our house in the woods though, these rooms were dim and dusty, infested with termites and stifling in the heat. Peace Corps also provided the furnishings: a bamboo bed with mosquito netting, two metal trunks, two grass mats, two kerosene lanterns, two plastic buckets, and two matching scoops. The details linger. I remember wondering why I had felt so compelled to pack suitcases and leave my comfortable home. 4

But that night we made the best of it. We hung a Monet calendar on the wall, Tom typed a letter by smoking lantern light, and I tried to get some rest. Goats bleated, a child cried himself to sleep, and the guinea fowl scrabbled for footholds on the roof. The mosquito netting draped over me like a shroud. The lumpy cotton mattress sagged toward the middle, and when Tom came to bed, it got worse. His stomach steadily percolated the rice and peanut sauce he had for dinner. When I did finally get to sleep, I remember dreaming of smooth sheets stretched taut over firm mattresses. 5

The dream couldn't have lasted for long, because at 3 A.M. the wind woke us, a blowing gale that demanded all hands on deck—our landlord 6 battening down the shutters, Tom fumbling with their clasps, me holding the flashlight. The first fat drops hit the metal roofing like bullets, then multiplied into a bombardment. Next morning, the sun sat astride mango trees like a bloodied yolk. The compound looked shipwrecked. Guinea fowl stood knee-deep in water, mortars and pestles sank in mud, and the grass matting over the lean-to hung in tatters. A neighbor in his field bent double over his short-handled "daba," turning the red rain-soaked earth around fresh millet stalks. I picked my way through puddles to the bathroom—outside and uncovered, a mud-walled enclosure with a hole for a toilet, a flat stone for a tub. As I sat sluicing myself with murky river water, the donkey cut loose with a gusty he-hee-heee-heeee-haaaaaw! Thinking of my white porcelain sink, my polished fixtures, my hot water back home, I laughed with him.

After nine weeks of this, Tom and I had lost ten pounds each to dysen- 7
tery, our Monet calendar to termites, and much of our initial enthusiasm. We weren't really sure if we were being "enriched" by our adventure so far, but we weren't ready to give up. Having survived our initiation into Peace Corps Mali, we placed our hopes on our next residence—a house in the capital city, Bamako.

Unlike our "compound" house, our "city" house seemed luxurious at 8
first. There were tile floors and electric ceiling fans, plaster walls without termites, two sinks, a bathtub, a bidet, a sit-down toilet, a hot-water heater, and running water. We celebrated with a festival of housekeeping. I did a laundry, rubbing out the red mud of Souban; Tom jury-rigged a closet of bamboo, string, and duct tape; we plugged in our Peace Corps refrigerator, and made ice cubes. Taking cold showers, we sang. We slept well.

After living there for a few days, however, we stopped singing. Our 9
city house came to seem more a "rabbit-hutch"—two tiny rooms with very little that actually worked. The ceiling fan in the living room whirled so fast it was dangerous, the hot-water heater made no hot water, the toilet was missing its seat, and the refrigerator door barely had room to open. Every morning, at 5 A.M. the muezzin woke us up, chanting the first prayer over a loudspeaker from the local mosque. Mosquitoes clung to the netting around our bed, and a cock cleared its throat on the street just beneath our window.

Each morning, though, I also watched a neighbor sweeping. He was an 10
old man, tall and spare, dressed in a farmer's loose trousers, a skull cap on his grey head. He bent from the waist to whisk his clutch of dried millet stalks over the ground, gathering together the yellow blossoms the cassia trees had dropped during the night. He swept the bright petals into a pile and left them, a cache of gold in the dust. He was a delight to watch. I also enjoyed buying ripe fruit from a woman who carried a pyramid of green mangoes on a tray balanced on her head. She wrapped herself Madonna-like in her flowered "pagne" and offered a soft greeting—"Ah-ni-sogoma" ("You and your morning"), a shy smile, and both palms raised in benediction. These were the rare beauties of our city house, but not enough to make us want to stay.

When we got a chance for another residence in the suburbs, "une petite villa," it said in the contract, we left easily. Our landlord was the 70-year-old husband of three wives, the father of 21 children (the oldest was 50, the youngest 1 , and the grandfather and great-grandfather of more than he could remember. Even without the contributions of our landlord, the "villa" was the hub of a busy neighborhood, crowded with people just one step out of their villages. They drew water from the neighborhood tap, cooked food over wood fires, and kept sheep, goats, and chickens in their compounds. The villa turned out to be as dim, dusty, and stifling as the compound house, so we spent most of our time in the walled-in garden where the mango tree gave some relief from the heat. Both inside and out were incessantly noisy. 11

At this house too, the muezzin started his chant at five o'clock in the morning. But then, the dogs picked it up, and the roosters went on with it. The chanting, barking, and crowing was our alarm clock. Across the street, young girls gathered early at the municipal water faucet, sitting on the rims of their buckets as they awaited their turn. They chattered, without rest, then head-balanced their brimming buckets back home for the first wash. From the distance, the dull thud of a pestle pounding millet echoed off compound walls and just beneath our windows, shepherds herded flocks to the riverbanks, the ewes bawling at recalcitrant lambs. 12

By afternoon, when heat and heavy teaching loads made us long for naps, the children took over. Tom compared it to the middle of a playground at recess. They rapped on our metal shutters with sticks. They spun the shutter-holders in their sockets. They shouted "Toubaboo!" ("Whiteman!") through the slats. Then they jiggled the handle on our gate and ran away when we opened it. The night was no better for sleeping. Everyone stayed up late. The children kicked soccer balls and played hide-and-seek, women gossiped, and men clustered around tiny braziers to brew sweet mint tea. A beggar woman and her blind husband traversed the streets, singing a litany of woes back and forth, and rattling their alms in a tin can. The sheep came home. And until midnight, Bob Marley wailed reggae on a cassette tape. The insomnia of the entire neighborhood, and Tom's, kept me awake—night after night. 13

By Christmas, we knew we couldn't go on with it. For lots of reasons, including our problems with housing, our yearning for adventure away from home had given way to a yearning to return. We finished the school year and returned to New England in June. So today, I sit in my own study, surrounded by white walls and familiar books, a Monet print above my desk, soft carpet at my feet, a comfortable chair, and a good light. Outside, the leaves are changing. Chickadees crack sunflower seeds at the feeder. A red squirrel drops hickory nuts from a tree. Tom splits wood in the driveway. 14

It is here that I can reflect on all those uncomfortable houses, all those noisy children, all those long and sleepless nights. Yet a glow of fondness has begun to surround them. For it's also here that I can see all those African sunrises over mango trees, a smiling woman balancing a tray of fruit, and an old man gathering a clutch of gold petals in the dust. It's 15 these memories that will probably have me packing my suitcase again . . . before long.

QUESTIONS

A. Discovering Meaning

1. What were the three types of residences provided by the Peace Corps?
2. Into what large category do all of these homes fit?
3. What do they all have in common?
4. In what ways are they different from one another?

B. Examining Method

1. Which details contribute most to your understanding of the experience (see pages 400–403)?
2. What is the main purpose of this piece (see pages 368–371)?
3. What is the tone (see pages 421–422)?
4. Why did she include the more positive aspects of the experience?
5. What is the effect of the description of the old man who is sweeping in paragraph 10 (see pages 253–258)?
6. What is the connection of the introduction to the conclusion (see pages 435–439)?

C. Shifting Focus

1. What would the difference be between this piece and an official description of the difficulties with housing?
2. What does description contribute to the classification of the houses?

SUGGESTIONS FOR DISCUSSION AND WRITING

A. Using Classification

1. Classify two or three places in which you have lived. Use details to help the reader sense what they were like and what your feelings about them

were. Are they all examples of the same type, or does each one fit into a different category?

2. Write a paper on a certain category of experience—things that got easier with time, things that became increasingly more difficult, things you gradually learned to accept.

B. Exploring the Options

1. Trace a single experience that became increasingly difficult as time went on. Bring each stage of the difficulty to life by selecting significant detail. (See pages 92–95 for a discussion of process before you trace your experience in story form and pages 277–281 for a discussion of narrative.)
2. Write an official resignation letter to the Peace Corps in which concerns with housing are addressed.
3. Write a letter from the Peace Corps in response to your letter of resignation.
4. Read Vladimir Glezer's piece on his apartment in Russia (page 268) and compare it with this piece in tone, detail, and overall purpose.
5. Write a paper that illustrates the truth of some belief you hold about life or some pattern that seems to recur—for example, that bad experiences can take on a certain glow in one's memory, that honesty is the best policy, or that it's important to learn from our mistakes.

How to Detect Propaganda

Institute for Propaganda Analysis

The Institute for Propaganda Analysis was a nonprofit, educational corporation, with headquarters in New York City, which from 1938 through 1942 issued pamphlets and articles similar to the following one on how to detect propaganda. The discussion divides the general category of propaganda into seven major "devices," of which, in turn, there are many examples. Notice the detail used to make each device concrete. The categories may easily be related to modern political campaigns or to methods of advertising.

Thinking Ahead According to this essay, the propagandist is trying to "put something across" and often does not want "careful scrutiny and criticism." With what types of propaganda are you familiar? Can you think of any specific examples?

If American citizens are to have clear understanding of present-day 1
conditions and what to do about them, they must be able to recognize propaganda, to analyze it, and to appraise it.

But what is propaganda? 2

As generally understood, *propaganda is expression of opinion or action by individuals or groups deliberately designed to influence opin-* 3
ions or actions of other individuals or groups with reference to predetermined ends. Thus propaganda differs from scientific analysis. The propagandist is trying to "put something across," good or bad, whereas the scientist is trying to discover truth and fact. Often the propagandist does not want careful scrutiny and criticism; he wants to bring about a specific action. Because the action may be socially beneficial or socially harmful to millions of people, it is necessary to focus upon the propagandist and his activities the searchlight of scientific scrutiny. Socially desirable propaganda will not suffer from such examination, but the opposite type will be detected and revealed for what it is.

We are fooled by propaganda chiefly because we don't recognize it 4
when we see it. It may be fun to be fooled but, as the cigarette ads used to say, it is more fun to know. We can more easily recognize propaganda when we see it if we are familiar with the seven common propaganda devices. These are:

1. The Name Calling Device
2. The Glittering Generalities Device
3. The Transfer Device
4. The Testimonial Device
5. The Plain Folks Device
6. The Card Stacking Device
7. The Band Wagon Device

Why are we fooled by these devices? Because they appeal to our emo- 5
tions rather than to our reason. They make us believe and do something we would not believe or do if we thought about it calmly, dispassionately. In examining these devices, note that they work most effectively at those times when we are too lazy to think for ourselves; also, they tie into emotions which sway us to be "for" or "against" nations, races, religions, ideals, economic and political policies and practices, and so on through automobiles, cigarettes, radios, toothpastes, presidents, and wars. With our emotions stirred, it may be fun to be fooled by these propaganda devices, but it is more fun and infinitely more to our own interests to know how they work.

Lincoln must have had in mind citizens who could balance their emo- 6
tions with intelligence when he made his remark: ". . . but you can't fool all of the people all of the time."

Name Calling

"Name Calling" is a device to make us form a judgment without examining the evidence on which it should be based. Here the propagandist appeals to our hate and fear. He does this by giving "bad names" to those individuals, groups, nations, races, policies, practices, beliefs, and ideals which he would have us condemn and reject. For centuries the name "heretic" was bad. Thousands were oppressed, tortured, or put to death as heretics. Anybody who dissented from popular or group belief or practice was in danger of being called a heretic. In the light of today's knowledge, some heresies were bad and some were good. Many of the poineers of modern science were called heretics; witness the cases of Copernicus, Galileo, Bruno. Today's bad names include: Fascist, demagogue, dictator, Red, financial oligarchy, Communist, muckraker, alien, outside agitator, economic royalist, Utopian, rabble-rouser, troublemaker, Tory, Constitution wrecker. 7

"Al" Smith called Roosevelt a Communist by implication when he said in his Liberty League speech, "There can be only one capital, Washington or Moscow." When "Al" Smith was running for the presidency many called him a tool of the Pope, saying in effect, "We must choose between Washington and Rome." That implied that Mr. Smith, if elected President, would take his orders from the Pope. Likewise Mr. Justice Hugo Black has been associated with a bad name, Ku Klux Klan. In these cases some propagandists have tried to make us form judgments without examining essential evidence and implications. "Al Smith is a Catholic. He must never be President." "Roosevelt is a Red. Defeat his program." "Hugo Black is or was a Klansman. Take him out of the Supreme Court." 8

Use of "bad names" without presentation of their essential meaning, without all their pertinent implications, comprises perhaps the most common of all propaganda devices. Those who want to *maintain* the status quo apply bad names to those who would change it. . . . Those who want to *change* the status quo apply bad names to those who would maintain it. For example, the *Daily Worker* and the *American Guardian* apply bad names to conservative Republicans and Democrats. 9

Glittering Generalities

"Glittering Generalities" is a device by which the propagandist identifies his program with virtue by use of "virtue words." Here he appeals to our emotions of love, generosity, and brotherhood. He uses words like truth, freedom, honor, liberty, social justice, public service, the right to work, loyalty, progress, democracy, the American way, Constitution defender. These words suggest shining ideals. All persons of good will believe in these ideals. Hence the propagandist, by identifying his individual group, nation, race, policy, practice, or belief with such ideals, seeks to win us to his cause. As Name Calling is a device to make us form a judgment to *reject and condemn,* without examining the evidence. Glittering Generalities is a device to make us *accept and approve,* without examining the evidence. 10

For example, use of the phrases "the right to work" and "social justice" may be a device to make us accept programs for meeting labor-capital problems, which, if we examined them critically, we would not accept at all. 11

In the Name Calling and Glittering Generalities devices, words are used to stir up our emotions and to befog our thinking. In one device "bad words" are used to make us mad; in the other "good words" are used to make us glad. 12

The propagandist is most effective in the use of these devices when his words make us create devils to fight or gods to adore. By his use of the "bad words," we personify as a "devil" some nation, race, group, individual, policy, practice, or ideal; we are made fighting mad to destroy it. By use of "good words," we personify as a godlike idol some nation, race, group, etc. Words which are "bad" to some are "good" to others, or may be made so. Thus, to some the New Deal is "a prophecy of social salvation" while to others it is "an omen of social disaster." 13

From consideration of names, "bad" and "good," we pass to institutions and symbols, also "bad" and "good." We see these in the next device. 14

Transfer

"Transfer" is a device by which the propagandist carries over the authority, sanction, and prestige of something we respect and revere to something he would have us accept. For example, most of us respect and revere our church and our nation. If the propagandist succeeds in getting church or nation to approve a campaign in behalf of some program, he thereby transfers its authority, sanction, and prestige to that program. Thus we may accept something which otherwise we might reject. 15

In the Transfer device, symbols are constantly used. The cross represents the Christian Church. The flag represents the nation. Cartoons like Uncle Sam represent a consensus of public opinion. Those symbols stir emotions. At their very sight, with the speed of light, is aroused the whole complex of feelings we have with respect to church or nation. A cartoonist by having Uncle Sam disapprove a budget for unemployment relief would have us feel that the whole United States disapproves relief costs. By drawing an Uncle Sam who approves the same budget, the cartoonist would have us feel that the American people approve it. Thus the Transfer device is used both for and against causes and ideas. 16

Testimonial

The "Testimonial" is a device to make us accept anything from a patent medicine or a cigarette to a program of national policy. In this device the propagandist makes use of testimonials. "When I feel tired, I smoke a Camel and get the grandest 'lift.' " "We believe the John L. Lewis plan of labor organization is splendid; C.I.O. should be supported." This device works in reverse also; counter-testimonials may be employed. Seldom are these used against commercial products like patent medicines and 17 cigarettes, but they are constantly employed in social, economic, and political issues. "We believe that the John L. Lewis plan of labor organization is bad; C.I.O. should not be supported."

Plain Folks

"Plain Folks" is a device used by politicians, labor leaders, businessmen, and even by ministers and educators to win our confidence by appearing to be people like ourselves—"just plain folks among the neighbors." In lection years especially do candidates show their devotion to little children and the common, homey things of life. They have front porch campaigns. For the newspapermen they raid the kitchen cupboard, finding there some of the good wife's apple pie. They go to country picnics; they attend service at the old frame church; they pitch hay and go fishing; they show their belief in home and mother. In short, they would win our votes by showing that they're just as common as the rest of us—"just plain folks"—and, therefore, wise and good. Businessmen often are "plain folks" with the factory hands. Even distillers use the device. "It's our family's whiskey, neighbor; and neighbor, it's your price." 18

Card Stacking

Card Stacking" is a device in which the propagandist employs all the arts of deception to win our support for himself, his group, nation, race, policy, practice, belief, or ideal. He stacks the cards against the truth. He uses under-emphasis and over-emphasis to dodge issues and evade facts. He resorts to lies, censorship, and distortion. He omits facts. He offers false testimony. He creates a smoke screen of clamor by raising a new issue when he wants an embarrassing matter forgotten. He draws a red herring across the trail to confuse and divert those in quest of facts he does not want revealed. He makes the unreal appear real and the real appear unreal. He lets half-truth masquerade as truth. By the Card Stacking device, a mediocre candidate, through the "build-up" is made to appear an intellectual titan; an ordinary prize fighter, a probable world champion; a worthless patent medicine, a beneficent cure. By means of this device propagandists would convince us that a ruthless war of aggression is a crusade for righteousness. Some member nations of the Non-Intervention Committee send their troops to intervene in Spain. Card Stacking employs sham, hypocrisy, effrontery. 19

The Band Wagon

The "Band Wagon" is a device to make us follow the crowd, to accept the propagandist's program en masse. Here his theme is. "Everybody's doing it." His techniques range from those of medicine show to dramatic spectacle. He hires a hall, fills a great stadium, marches a million men in parade. He employs symbols, colors, music, movement, all the dramatic arts. He appeals to the desire, common to most of us, to "follow the 20 crowd." Because he wants us to "follow the crowd" in masses, he directs his appeal to groups held together by common ties of nationality, religion, race, environment, sex, vocation. Thus propagandists campaigning for or against a program will appeal to us as Catholics, Protestants, or Jews; as members of the Nordic race or as Negroes; as farmers or as school teachers; as housewives or as miners. All the artifices of flattery are used to harness the fears and hatreds, prejudices, and biases, convictions and ideals common to the group; thus emotion is made to push and pull the group on to the Band Wagon. In newspaper article and in the spoken word this device is also found. "Don't throw your vote away. Vote for our candidate. He's sure to win." Nearly every candidate wins in every election—before the votes are in. . . .

Observe that in all these devices our emotion is the stuff with which propagandists work. Without it they are helpless; with it, harnessing it to their purposes, they can make us glow with pride or burn with hatred, they can make us zealots in behalf of the program they espouse. As we said at the beginning, propaganda as generally understood is expression of opinion or action by individuals or groups with reference to predetermined ends. Without the appeal to our emotion—to our fears and to our courage, to our selfishness and unselfishness, to our loves and to our hates—propagandists would influence few opinions and few actions. 21

To say this is not to condemn emotion, an essential part of life, or to assert that all predetermined ends of propagandists are "bad." What we mean is that the intelligent citizen does not want propagandists to utilize his emotions, even to the attainment of "good" ends, without knowing what is going on. He does not want to be "used" in the attainment of ends he may later consider "bad." He does not want to be gullible. He does not want to be fooled. He does not want to be duped, even in a "good" cause. He wants to know the facts and among these is included the fact of the utilization of his emotions. 22

Keeping in mind the seven common propaganda devices, turn to today's newspapers and almost immediately you can spot examples of them all. At election time or during any campaign, Plain Folks and Band Wagon are common. Card Stacking is hardest to detect because it is adroitly executed or because we lack the information necessary to nail the lie. A little practice with the daily newspapers in detecting these propaganda devices soon enables us to detect them elsewhere—in radio, news-reel, books, magazines, and in expressions of labor unions, business groups, churches, schools, political parties. 23

VOCABULARY

scrutiny (3), heretic (7), demagogue (7), pertinent (9), personify (13), sanction (15), testimonial (17), gullible (22)

QUESTIONS

A. Discovering Meaning

1. What is propaganda?
2. What are the major categories of propaganda discussed in this piece?
3. What do all of these devices for propaganda have in common?
4. How do they differ from one another?

B. Examining Method

1. What is the purpose of dividing these devices into groups?
2. Why does each section contain examples of each grouping?
3. Written in 1937, some of the references in this piece may seem dated. What keeps this piece alive and still relevant to our own time?
4. Why did the Institute write this piece? (See pages 368–371 for a discussion of purpose, and pages 180–183 for a discussion of argument.)
5. What is the purpose of the introductory and concluding paragraphs, which frame the specific discussion of the devices for propaganda (see pages 435–439)?
6. What is the tone of this discussion (see pages 421–422)?

C. Shifting Focus

1. Does this piece also work as argument (see pages 180–183)?
2. Give some examples of current name-calling devices.
3. Give an example of a modern "good name to make us glad," discussed under the heading "Glittering Generalities."
4. Give a current example of "Transfer," the carrying over of respect for one thing to acceptance of something else.
5. Advertising is full of testimonials by individuals hired to sell certain products "by association." Give some examples.
6. Americans particularly like believing that their politicians, heroes, and heroines can also be "just regular people." Think of some examples.
7. Card stacking is identified as the "hardest to detect because it is adroitly executed or because we lack the information necessary to nail the lie." Can you think of any example of card stacking, possibly on campus or in local politics?

8. In the "Band Wagon" approach, people are encouraged to join the group, either one they are already in or one they aspire to join. Can you think of any such appeal made to you?

9. Identify the methods of the following:

   a. Candidate George Bush being photographed at a flag factory.

   b. Candidate Michael Dukakis being photographed in an army tank.

   c. "He's just a red-necked bumpkin."

   d. "He's a card-carrying liberal."

   e. "I am in favor of an armed citizenry."

   f. "Those gun-toting ninnies should be exiled."

   g. "The Soviet Union is the evil empire."

   h. "Willie Horton plans to vote for Dukakis."

   i. Bob Uecker drinks Miller Lite.

   j. A photograph of a well-dressed family checking the tires at a used car lot.

   k. A political postcard showing a picture of the candidate surrounded by his wife, two kids, a golden retriever, and two grandparents.

   l. "I am a firm advocate of the 'right to life.' "

   m. "I support the pro-choice movement."

   n. "Come and share Celtics pride day!"

   o. "I wonder about this change in our town tavern regulations. Well, you know that Senator Cognac has a drinking problem."

   p. "People in the know vote NO!"

   q. "The other brand thinks that 'passable' is good enough."

   r. "You are the only person I've talked to today who is willing to put her family at risk. Our home security system is sure to protect all those who are important to you. Frankly, I would be amazed if you refused our offer of a free estimate."

   s. This from a bank announcing an *increase* in the minimum balance from $1,000.00 to $3,000.00. "We've also added another option that makes it even easier for you to avoid your monthly service charges. If you keep just $3,000.00 in a savings account linked to your checking account, you pay *no* monthly service charges."

SUGGESTIONS FOR WRITING

A. Using Classification

1. Write an essay in which you provide current examples for the seven major categories listed in the essay. Consider possibly the techniques of advertisers, themselves propagandistic in their desire to influence through emotions.
2. What types of advertisements are used to appeal to particular audiences?
3. Choose a particular publication, analyze the types of advertising included there, and then place them into groups (of your own devising or the ones provided in this study).

B. Exploring the Options

1. Write and discuss your own list of devices used by one group to influence the behavior of another.
2. Select one advertisement from a magazine or possibly from radio or television and analyze the devices used to involve the potential buyer.
3. Do you agree with Lincoln that "... you can't fool all of the people all of the time?" or do you tend to side with the judgment of H. L. Mencken who said that "No one ever went broke underestimating the intelligence of the American public"?
4. Study the three advertisements for automobiles on the following pages and then discuss what distinguishes them from one another.

CRUISE IN QUIET. Nash's exclusive Super Shock-absorbers combine with Individual Front Wheel Springing to quietly smooth the roughest road. New Sealed Beam lights are glareless, yet 50% more powerful.

NEVER FEEL THE FROST or sudden changes in the weather. Nash's exclusive Weather Eye keeps "balanced" conditioned air comfort always in the car. Automatic. No dust or drafts.

You Won't be Home Tonight

YOU'LL see it pass like a ship in the night . . . a silent blur . . . a silver phantom. And you'll know by the sudden thump in your pulse—you've seen your first 1940 Nash!

You won't wait long.

But when you take the pilot's seat, hold on tight! For there's more power under this flashing hood than you've probably ever toed before.

At throttle touch, the country outside becomes a crazy-quilt. Then a Fourth Speed Forward seems to shoot you forward on the giant shoulder of a wave.

When a car looms up ahead, just *nudge* the throttle, and you'll *sprint* by, in Nash's new dazzling Automatic Overtake.

Exciting? Yes—but *wait!*

Head for a road that's full of bumps. Then watch the hood ahead. See if you can make it bobble—try to feel a rise in that airy seat beneath you.

With a baby's grip on the wheel, you feather around sharp curves . . . walk a chalk-line on loose gravel.

Outside, a frosty wind is stripping the trees—but you don't feel it. Nor will you ever know cold, dust, or stuffy air again —thanks to the Weather Eye.

You're having your first Arrow-Flight Ride.

And when it darkens, just pull up—beneath a scarlet tree—and turn into your Nash convertible bed.

As a thousand stars wheel above, you'll forget about business and politics, in learning what living on wheels may be like!

• • •

Five minutes in a new 1940 Nash is more fun than a lifetime in ordinary cars . . . yet a Nash is as easy to own as any. Big as it is, it's priced with the lowest, and a Gilmore-Yosemite economy winner.

Give your Nash dealer those five exciting minutes . . . today!

Memorable Days in a Knight

On school days, on shopping days, on Sundays, on all days of the calendar, season in and season out, the Willys-Knight Coupe-Sedan is keeping owners young and happy—a family car faithful to every trust, and as smart as Fifth Avenue!

This is the car that made folding seats as old-fashioned as haircloth furniture. Doors both *front* and *rear* let everybody enter and leave without climbing over seats or feet. A Wilson-built-Body — with the *capacity* of a sedan and the *sociability* of a coupe—finished in a beautiful color scheme of blue, black and nickel.

Coupe-Sedan
$1550
F·O·B TOLEDO

As fine as it looks, it is yet finer internally. The Willys-Knight sleeve-valve engine *actually improves with use*—supremely smooth and quiet. No valve-grinding. No bother with carbon. Owners report 50,000 miles and more without once having had a mechanic tinker with the engine.

There is a definite social distinction in owning a Willys-Knight . . . and everlasting satisfaction in its performance. The greater the mileage you drive the more you enjoy the driving—and the more value you attach to the car. Try a Knight on the road today!

Willys-Knight Models: 2-pass. Roadster $1175, 5-pass. Touring $1195, 7-pass. Touring $1325, 5-pass. Sedan $1695 (DeLuxe $1895), 7-pass. Sedan $1995; f.o.b. Toledo. We reserve the right to change prices and specifications without notice.

Willys-Overland, Inc., Toledo, Ohio · Willys-Overland Sales Co. Ltd., Toronto, Canada

WILLYS-KNIGHT

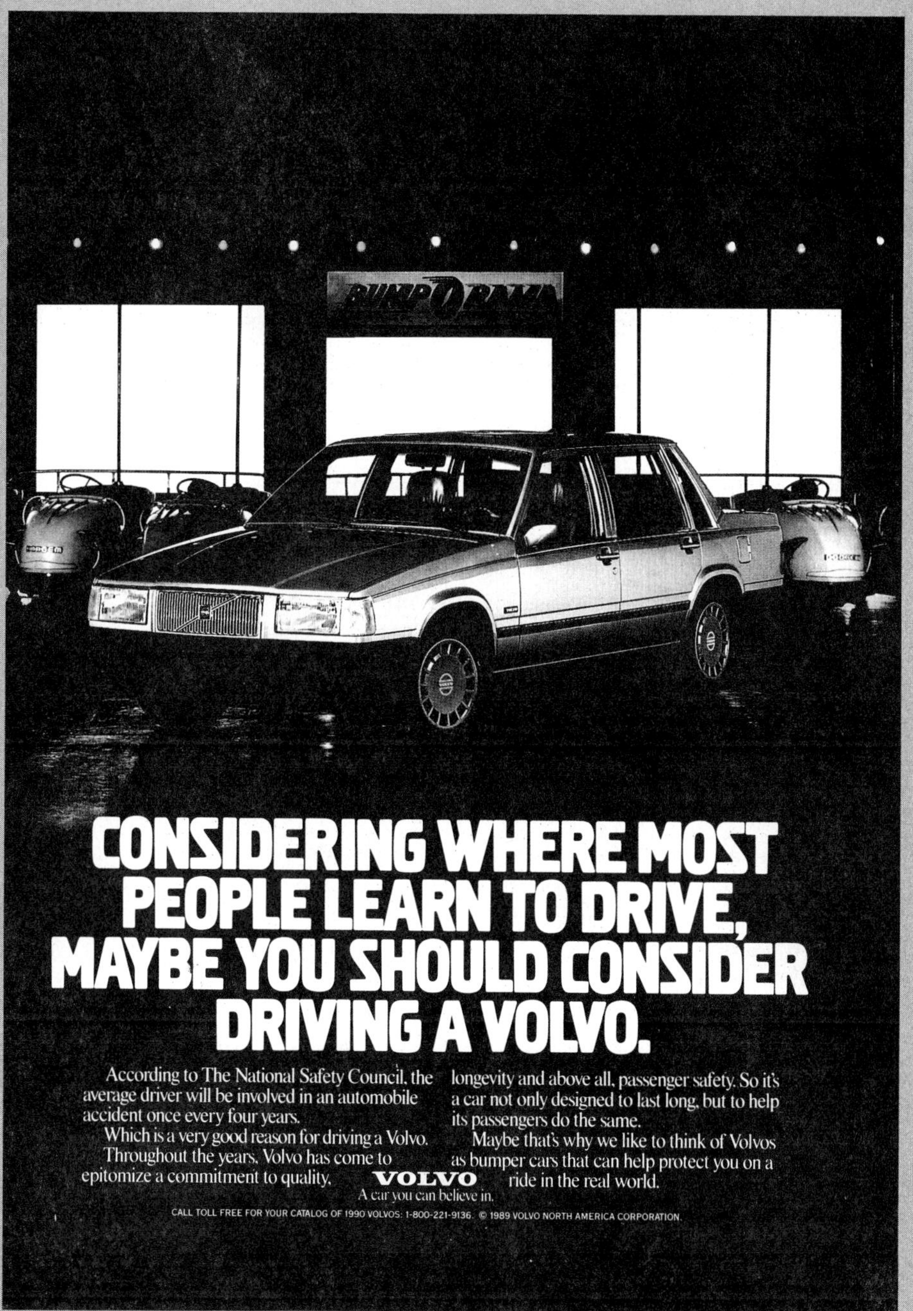
CONSIDERING WHERE MOST PEOPLE LEARN TO DRIVE, MAYBE YOU SHOULD CONSIDER DRIVING A VOLVO.
According to The National Safety Council, the average driver will be involved in an automobile accident once every four years.
Which is a very good reason for driving a Volvo.
Throughout the years, Volvo has come to epitomize a commitment to quality, longevity and above all, passenger safety. So it's a car not only designed to last long, but to help its passengers do the same.
Maybe that's why we like to think of Volvos as bumper cars that can help protect you on a ride in the real world.
VOLVO
A car you can believe in.
CALL TOLL FREE FOR YOUR CATALOG OF 1990 VOLVOS: 1-800-221-9136. © 1989 VOLVO NORTH AMERICA CORPORATION.

Describing a Process

Writing "process" essays may involve different types of activity: describing "how to" do something ("how to score on the SAT's," "how to win at golf") or describing the process of "how something happens or happened" ("how the vice-president is selected," "how electricity was discovered"). The first seeks to give instruction; the second has no intention of teaching the reader "how to."

Both types of "process" writing require moving through the stages of a procedure; both involve careful transitions from one stage to another so that the reader may step surely. Consider the instructions for putting together swing sets, bicycles and VCR's: "Turn screw A into socket B after turning screw C into socket B2. . . ." This is a particular kind of process writing that very often sends the reader stumbling over the unassembled pieces long before the last screw is turned. Essays may be equally befuddling if the writer is not always conscious of the reader's questions, distractions, and potential predicaments. The student studying for the SAT's or the duffer hoping for a better putt should both be performing with more assurance at the end of the "how to" essay.

Aside from the issue of clarity, there is the issue of interest in writing process papers. The harried father or mother on Christmas Eve needs little encouragement to get through the instructions and the bicycle, but most readers need to be engaged in reading through a process, particularly one that professes to show "how to." Cookbook recipes are probably the most straightforward examples of "process" writing, but they hardly consist of prose that will lure the reader to an easy chair for an evening's read. More unusual or specialized topics like "how to climb a tree," or "how to start your own beer can collection" require getting the reader interested in the first place. Most readers will be grateful for the personal experiences, the narratives, the details, the dialogue, the sharp verbs, the descriptions, or any of the other attention-getters included with the list of instructions.

What of familiar topics—the "how to make a peanut butter sandwich," "how to change a tire" topics? Here, too, the primary challenge is interest. Familiarity may well breed a yawn and an urge for that easy chair—to sleep in. The writer must think of some way, some original treatment, some personal quirk that may save such subjects from somnolence. Maybe the peanut butter sandwich could become a work of art, for example, a Pollack? Maybe the tire changer needs to become heroic, a modern warrior against all odds, or maybe just the opposite, a Walter Mitty losing the struggle for even a small portion of heroism. Here, too, the reader yearns for more than a list.

Consider the following subjects as they might be outlined for a process paper.

1. Choosing a place to live for the academic year requires taking several important steps:

   —Call or write for any information available on living arrangements.
   —Visit the campus early, well before the school year starts.
   —Talk to administrators who are responsible for student housing and gather detailed information on options and costs.
   —Visit locations on and off campus and interview those who may be living there.
   —Think carefully of the options and your own resources—personal and financial.
   —Only then, make a final decision.

2. Do you have an unexpected visitor coming? Here's how to do a quick cleaning.

   —Hide all dirty dishes in the dishwasher or in the cabinet under the sink.
   —Throw lumpy things in closets.
   —Sweep flat things under the rug.
   —Toss puffy comforters over unmade bedclothes.
   —Dust visible surfaces with the palm of your hand.
   —Brush your hair and look serene when the doorbell rings.

3. Taking good pictures involves several important steps.

   —Know your camera well and practice using it.
   —Pay attention to what's in the picture (observe background, leave out clutter, select a main subject).
   —Take many pictures to increase the potential for success.
   —Learn from successes and failures and keep at it.

4. Research has suggested that there are several ways to handle stress:

   —Relaxing by deep breathing and meditation.
   —Exercising.
   —Eating well.
   —Identifying causes of stress by keeping a journal or a log of stressful situations.
   —Talking with friends or, if necessary, counselors in therapy.

Process "instructions" need to be readable and clear, putting steps in the best order for imitation. Process "discussions" need to be interesting and informative, rising in interest; the reader does not have the extra enticement of learning how to *do* something independently.

WORKING WITH PROCESS

Think about things you know how to *do* well—how to slam a forehand, how to be a college student and a mother at the same time, how to respond to a schizophrenic patient. Or think about what you know about how something happened or happens—how Mayor Gonzalez got elected, how the ozone layer is monitored, how the United States became involved in the war in Vietnam.

The interest in reading process papers comes from various sources. Sometimes it arises directly from the reader's *need* to know how to do something (e.g., how to sleep better). The interest may therefore be almost purely practical. Interest may also, however, arise from the reader's curiosity about how something works or gets done, yet the reader has no intention of trying it. In response to this "idle curiosity," entire books are published on how things work. The challenge is in keeping the writing interesting. Some processes are all too familiar to maintain easy interest (how to do a laundry); some are so obscure that the writer must make an extra effort to provide what the reader needs to proceed (how to distinguish among Central American beetles). It is important to consider audience (pages 370–371) in process writing. There is also a certain predictability in step-by-step sequential writing. Most process papers are, by nature, "beginning-to-end" papers. The writer needs to think of ways to maintain interest—surprises, comparisons, stories, dialogue, repetitions. Close attention to the transitions (pages 415–418), to the connections among the parts of the piece, is particularly important.

Example

This was written by a student who was giving advice about housing:

> One important step, and I find, a usually rewarding one, is to talk to students already familiar with the housing situations both on and off campus. Nothing speaks like experience. These students are the ones who know best who has the leaky faucets, which rooms are too close to the exit doors, which roommates should be avoided. They also know which off-campus landlord refuses to return telephone calls and security deposits. Even a quick on-site visit to the dorms and the housing units, a glance at the rooms, and a few well-timed questions can help you make a more informed choice. Try for a little "hands on" research before signing any contracts.

Write a paragraph on at least one step in a process with which you are familiar, either from experience or research, for example, how to dunk a basketball, how to respond to a customer who has just thrown a slice of pizza at you, how to get a "crime-watch" group formed, how children cope with divorce, how the local papers handle reports on student activities, or how the campus judicial system works in cases of plagiarism. You may want to try reversing a process, as in W. S. Merwin's "Unchopping a Tree," in which he gradually rebuilds a tree that has been senselessly destroyed. You may want to try irony, for example, teaching someone how to fail or how to dress in the wrong clothing. Remember to think of your purpose, to make necessary connections, to do what you have to do to maintain interest. After you have studied the following examples, try to rewrite your paragraph.

How to Reef a Mainsail

(paragraph)

Erick Scheiderman (student)

Winner of the 1988 Snipe National Sailing competitions in San Francisco, this student is qualified to teach this particular skill. Erick had to consider carefully the potential readers of this information and ended up writing two different versions of this process essay: this one, for a more specialized audience interested in the details of the operation, and a second one, a narrative (printed on pages 281–282), for a general audience not seeking information on how to sail. Says Erick, "This was easy to imagine, but not so easy to write. I had to think about how much the readers would know. Definitions were also a problem, because they can make the writing boring."

Thinking Ahead How does the writer organize the process? Can you think of a topic about which you could write a "how to" paper?

In the dictionary, to "reef" means "to reduce the size of sail by tucking in a part." It sounds so simple, but it actually involves a series of sometimes tricky steps. First of all, you must decide if it is even worth the trouble. Improper reefing can result in disaster, like tearing the sail or even tipping the boat over, and reefing in a dangerous wind may be as unwise as staying with it. But if you do decide to reef, you must first head the boat up into the wind, thus allowing the air to spill out of the sail in a process called "luffing." Second, you lower the main halyard, or rope, to the grommets (holes) for the first or second reef on the sail, depending on the strength of the breeze. In the third step, after the sail is in control, you use short pieces of line, usually about three, to tie the grommets to the boom (the arm extending from the mast). And fourth, depending on the length of the boat's outhaul (that is, the hauling rope attached to the bottom of the sail), you take the outhaul off the old grommet and move it to the new one. In other words, you adjust the amount of sail. And finally, you tighten your main halyard so that the sail is no longer luffing. At this point, you could "fall off" and go sailing, or you could head safely to the dock.

QUESTIONS

A. Discovering Meaning

1. What are the main steps in this process?
2. Why is it important for a sailor to know how to reef?

B. Examining Method

1. For which readers is this paragraph written (see pages 370–371)?
2. What are the main clues that help the reader to move through the process?
3. What are the transitions in the paragraph? Why are they important (see pages 415–418)?
4. What is the effect of the specialized vocabulary? It is necessary (see pages 422–423)?
5. What is the purpose of the sentence, "In other words, you adjust the amount of sail."

C. Shifting Focus

1. Do you now understand the process of reefing? Explain.
2. In comparison to the paragraph on page 281, what distinguishes a process from a narrative (pages 277–281)?

SUGGESTIONS FOR DISCUSSION AND WRITING

A. Using Process

1. Teach a reader how to perform a special task with which you are very familiar. Consider the knowledge of the reader and what problems you may need to anticipate.
2. Write a "nonsense" paragraph in which you describe how to ______ a ______—for example, how to tie a fuddlebumper or how to release a gringe.

B. Exploring the Options

1. Do you see any way to make this description of a process better? Try it.

2. Write a version of this process paper for a very young, inexperienced sailor.

3. Where would such an account most likely be printed (see pages 456–459)?

Getting the Film Moving Again

(paragraph)

Tracy Bowen (student)

In this paragraph, a theater projectionist describes an "emergency process," the fixing of a torn film during a screening. This paragraph is part of a long account of the writer's job at a big-city movie house, a job she usually enjoys—except when the film tears. In this case, the customers thought she had robbed them of a large portion of the film and complained bitterly. Notice that this discussion of the process already hints that she has lost very little of the film and thus prepares the reader for her self-defense later in the paper. Tracy explains that her pride in a "job well done" becomes ironic as the story progresses. She thinks the process was just perfect; the crowd thinks otherwise.

Thinking Ahead Is this discussion of process intended to teach the reader how to fix a torn film? Have you ever carefully followed a process that was not appreciated by others?

Tonight, when a customer comes out of "sex, lies, and videotape" to say there's no picture, my reaction is the same as always. I feel a brief flash of panic and hope the problem is an easy one. Then I bolt for the booth. It *is* an easy one. The film has torn. The projector has done its job by automatically shutting off to keep loose film out of the gears. I quickly replace the almost-full bottom reel with an empty one. I rip off about three feet—roughly *three* seconds—of damaged film and secure the loose end in the new reel. Taking another four or five feet of film, I lace up the projector. In less than a minute, it's ready to go again. As always, I cross and uncross my fingers before pushing the button to start the film. Everything goes as it should: the engine whirrs on, the bulb snaps on in the lamphouse, the exciter bulb for the sound comes on, and the lights in the theater dim. A focused, nicely-framed image appears on the screen as the estranged wife joins her new love on his stoop and asks, "Do you think it will rain?" They smile, and the ending credits begin to roll. I congratulate myself on another crisis deftly handled.

QUESTIONS

A. Discovering Meaning

1. What is the process being described here?
2. What are the two parts to the process?
3. Why does she congratulate herself?

B. Examining Method

1. How does the writer feel about the process she is describing here?
2. Why does she make her feelings so clearly known?
3. Why does she mention that the projector turns off automatically and that she rips off about "*three* seconds" of film?
4. Are you convinced that the writer understands the process she is describing? Why?
5. What is the purpose of discussing this process?

C. Shifting Focus

1. Later in this story, the writer is confronted by "two hundred irate customers" who believe she has robbed them of at least ten minutes worth of the film. How would you handle this crowd?
2. Notice that this discussion of process is part of a larger narrative account of "my job." Within her narrative, she could simply say, "Then one day I fixed a film that had broken. The crowd got angry at me." Why does she stop for such a detailed discussion of the process?

SUGGESTIONS FOR DISCUSSION AND WRITING

A. Using Process

1. Describe a process that failed or one that did not appear the same to you as it did to others. (Italian novelist Primo Levi, for example, describes the process of psychological testing that did not proceed as the tester had planned.)

B. Exploring the Options

1. Describe a process within a larger paper of some other type, a narrative, for example, or possibly an argument. Remember to consider the purpose of describing the process. What does it have to do with the larger point of your essay? (One student, for example, described the slow process of therapy for a leg injury as part of a character sketch of an unusually determined person. As part of an argument against unnecessary chaos in tax regulations, a student/accountant described the tedious process of wading through the laws and the forms.)

Bradley's Shooting Practice

(paragraph)

John McPhee

John McPhee (b. 1931) was born in Princeton, New Jersey, where he graduated from college and still lives. His books, often explorations of the American wilderness, include such titles as *Coming into the Country* (1977) about Alaska and most recently, *The Control of Nature* (1989). *A Sense of Where You Are* (1965) is a book on Princeton's 1960s basketball superstar, Bill Bradley (later a forward for the Knickerbockers, a Rhodes Scholar at Oxford, and now U.S. Senator from New Jersey). This paragraph is an account of how Bradley practiced his set shots, hook shots, and jump shots. McPhee allowed Bill Bradley to read the manuscript of his book before McPhee turned it in: "He did the job quickly. He ran one finger down the middle of each page, reading, I would guess, ten or eleven pages a minute, completely ignoring all the passages about his personality and all the other things that ordinarily make it a poor idea to show an unpublished story to its subject. Picking out eight or ten technical flaws along the way, he caught all that there apparently were. Handing back the manuscript, he said he looked forward to reading it."

Thinking Ahead What would you use to describe the process of Bradley's practice? Have you ever watched an expert at practice or work? What details come to mind? If someone observed you practicing a favorite activity, what details might they notice?

When Bradley, working out alone, practices his set shots, hook shots, and jump shots, he moves systematically from one place to another around the basket, his distance from it being appropriate to the shot, and he does not permit himself to move on until he has made at least ten shots out of thirteen from each location. He applies this standard to every kind of shot, with either hand, from any distance. Many basketball players, including reasonably good ones, could spend five years in a gym and not make ten out of thirteen left-handed hook shots, but that is part of Bradley's daily routine. He talks to himself while he is shooting, usually reminding himself to concentrate but sometimes talking to himself the way every high-school j.v. basketball player has done since the dim twenties—more or less imitating a radio announcer, and saying, as he gathers himself up for a shot, "It's pandemonium in Dillon Gymnasium. The clock is running out. He's up with a jumper. Swish!"

QUESTIONS

A. Discovering Meaning

1. What does this process suggest about the subject, Bill Bradley?
2. What impresses you most about the process of Bradley's practice?

B. Examining Method

1. What is the main purpose of this process paragraph (see pages 368–371)?
2. What is McPhee's attitude toward Bradley's practice (see pages 421–422)?
3. Who is the intended audience (see pages 370–371)?
4. Why does McPhee mention the "ten out of thirteen" shots?
5. Does this paragraph build in interest? How? (See page 377.)

C. Shifting Focus

1. How does McPhee express his attitude without actually stating it?
2. How does he suggest Bradley's attitude?

SUGGESTIONS FOR DISCUSSION AND WRITING

A. Using Process

1. Write an account of how you or someone else gets ready for some activity—taking a test, going on a trip, reading a book, going to a basketball game.

2. Describe a process that has become routine for you, but remember to keep the details interesting.

3. Describe the process of someone else's practice or work. Select details that will help the reader to see the action and possibly to understand more about the person.

B. Exploring the Options

1. Rewrite McPhee's paragraph as if McPhee were bored by Bradley's routine.

2. In his book, *Learning by Teaching,* Donald Graves describes this one stage in the process of writing:

> The writing is going well. Everything is connecting. I need a word, and it is in my ear; I need a fact, and it flows out of my fingers; I need a more effective order, and my eye watches sentences as they rearrange themselves on the page. I think this is what writing should be like, and then I stop. I go for another mug of coffee, visit the bathroom, check the mail.
>
> I wonder about this compulsion to interrupt writing which is going well. I see my students do it in the writing workshop. It's so much of a pattern there must be a reason for it. Sometimes I think it is the workman's need to stand back to get distance; other times I think it is simple Calvinist distrust—when everything's going well something must be wrong.

Write your own description of at least one stage in your usual process of writing.

How to Correspond with the Stars

John Baron (student)

This piece is an account of how to become involved in a particular hobby: autograph collecting. Notice how much of the piece involves personal experiences, not just rules on how to go about the task. While rewriting certain sections of this piece, John wrote, "I'll have more ideas, I hope. I'm not a real demon for ideas. I might inquire at my parish rectory to find out if there is a patron saint for frustrated, would-be writers."

Thinking Ahead What are the major steps in the process of collecting autographs? What does the title suggest to you? Do you have a hobby or leisure-time activity that readers might enjoy learning about?

"I posed for a Boston sculptress to help my mother support my sister and me. This was long before I went into the theatre." Bette Davis sent me this note in March of 1983. At that time a small furor had erupted in the Boston area: apparently, someone strolling in a local park had noticed that several nude statues of women in the park bore a suspicious resemblance to the legendary film star. The local media wasted no time in reporting the scandal. Had Ms. Davis really taken it all off? A spokesperson for the actress revealed that yes, she had, and soon, hampered by the unspectacular truth, the incident was forgotten. 1

But I was curious. Why would a successful movie star do something as risqué as posing in the buff? I got up the courage to write Ms. Davis and ask that question. Her response told me three things I didn't read in the papers: that she posed for a sculptr*ess,* not a sculpt*or;* that it helped feed her family; and that it happened before she began her film career. This is autograph collecting at its best. It's a hobby that requires only a few stamped envelopes and a little imagination to make it fun and, perhaps, profitable. 2

It doesn't matter whom you write to as long as they're famous. Movie stars, celebrities, athletes, authors, military figures—anybody with notoriety is worth writing. But like most things, fame is fleeting and unpredictable. Who would have guessed two years ago that a State Department employee named Oliver North would become a national celebrity? A little insight helps. 3

As people become more famous the chance of getting a letter back becomes less likely. Try to get them early in their career. I recall a signed photo of Marilyn Monroe which sold at auction for $250.00. The bid rose that high because it was a very early picture of Marilyn signed *before* she made it big in Hollywood. It was just a shot of a strikingly pretty young woman; it didn't even look like Marilyn. Missing were the pouting lips, come-hither gaze, and peroxide-blonde hair common to photos of the older Marilyn. 4

Once you decide whom to write to, you must obviously find a mailing address. Most celebrities are reluctant to make their addresses known, but a few books can help. Many libraries carry *Who's Who,* a two volume set that lists notable people, their background, education, and achievements. Unfortunately, *Who's Who* is partial to lawyers, neurosurgeons, and insurance company vice-presidents. If *Who's Who* publishes a celebrity's biography, that person can decide whether to include an address. Some do, some don't. Some opt to write a few sentences explaining their philosophy of success; these are generally nauseating. 5

A better source is *Christensen's Ultimate Movie, T.V., and Rock Directory.* It's published by Cardiff-by-the-Sea Publishing Co., San Diego, CA. Somehow the compilers of this book have located the address of every- 6

RICHARD WILBUR

Cummington, 23 July

Dear Mr. Baron,

Thank you for your good letter. Unfortunately, I have no photographs on hand, but this is what I look like:

EXCELSIOR

With good wishes,

Richard Wilbur

4/16/84

— Dear John —

Hope you're having a good time in school. I looked for a photo, but the only ones I could find are ones where I look sort of stupid. Sorry —

Stephen King

body who is anybody in the entertainment business. Also, the Boston *Globe* periodically prints celebrity addresses in a part of its Ask the *Globe* column called "The Address Book." The *Globe* made an eerie mistake in timing in 1987. On the same day they printed the addresses of both Fred Astaire and Jackie Gleason; within days, both were dead. I've come to regard death in terms of autograph collecting: it's like moving to a new and permanent residence without leaving a forwarding address.

Imagination is important when writing. Try to learn something about 7 the celebrity's life or work first; then write and ask a pertinent question. End the letter by asking for a signed photo; that way, if the person hasn't the time or desire to answer your question, you might get just a signature anyway. Even a good question can fail miserably. I recall writing to General Maxwell D. Taylor, who was instrumental in getting the United States involved in Vietnam, and asking if he believed we could have won the war with the full support of Congress and the American people. Taylor wrote his answer in the margin of my letter, replying curtly: "Negative, with regret—M.D.T." The risk in writing soldiers is that you're likely to get a response in military shorthand.

Worse than celebrities fond of brevity are those who refuse to sign at 8 all. A story is told about an American collector, a fan of Rudyard Kipling, wrote the English author letter after letter with no result. In one he promised to donate the signature to a museum; another time he wrote that any response would go to an auction for homeless children. Finally the frustrated collector traveled to England and drove directly to Kipling's home, where he ran over the shrubs in the front yard. Kipling rushed out. The collector apologized for the "accident" and promised to reimburse the author if he would send him papers documenting the damage. Kipling agreed. The triumphant collector later wrote Kipling that it would have been much simpler had the author responded to one of his letters.

Be sure to send a self-addressed stamped envelope (SASE) along with 9 the letter. It's a courtesy that should increase the chances of getting a response. I buy two different sized envelopes at the stationery store—the smaller return envelope fits neatly into the bigger one. When asking for a photo, it's a good idea to add a piece of cardboard. I got an 8 × 10 glossy from Cheryl Tiegs one day. In the picture, Ms. Tiegs (every inch the woman) is standing on a beach somewhere—Malibu, presumably—sporting a golden tan, a mischievous smile, and not much else. Anyway, the mailman folded the envelope when he stuffed it in the mail box, cracking the celluloid surface of the photo and putting a jagged crease down Ms. Tieg's . . . uh, front. A sturdy piece of cardboard would have prevented this tragedy.

Unlike Ms. Tiegs, some celebrities refuse to sign photographs. Actress 10 Katharine Hepburn is perfectly willing to sign a letter, but will not sign or send photos. It is said that playwright George Bernard Shaw felt the same way, but once used his sharp sense of humor to spoil a request for an autographed photo. Shaw *did* sign the photo. However, he did so several times, and wrote only on that part of the picture that showed his face, in tiny, compact letters that concealed it entirely.

After building a collection of signatures you might want to sell some. 11
Put a small ad in the local paper, or the weekly *Bargain Hunter's Guide,* and list some of the more notable names you have. Determining how much to ask for them is difficult. It requires a familiarity with what most collectors will pay, and *that* requires experience. Besides, you may find that some autographs are like old friends.

I sold my first autograph to my high school history teacher, a military 12
buff. It was a letter from Captain Robert H. White, the only US Naval Commander to lead boarding parties on both German and Japanese submarines. I'll never forget the cold sense of betrayal I felt when, like some sort of epistolary Benedict Arnold, I handed the letter over in return for two dollars. It would be my first and last sale.

I once thought autograph collecting meant standing on the red plastic 13
seats of Fenway Park, waving a ballpoint and a mustard stained program at Wade Boggs, and calling his name out over and over. Now, after mailing about 200 letters, I have found a more dignified method. What's more, it's a challenge to get a celebrity to sign by virtue of a good letter. Mostly I get back what I expect, as with General Taylor. But sometimes, as with Bette Davis, I find that people aren't always what they seem, and that is a pleasant discovery.

QUESTIONS

A. Discovering Meaning

1. What are the major steps of the process of collecting autographs?
2. What are some of the major reasons for getting involved in this process in the first place?
3. What do you see as the most interesting response to the writer's inquiries?
4. What do you think of autograph collecting as a hobby? Why?

B. Examining Method

1. What is the major purpose of this piece (see pages 368–371)?
2. In what order are the steps of the process presented? Why? (See pages 374–378.)
3. What is the writer's attitude toward this hobby (see pages 421–422)?

4. What is the effect of the first sentence (see pages 394–398)?
5. Why is the history teacher mentioned (see pages 400–403)?

C. Shifting Focus

1. What does the writer add to the simple description of process? Where? How does it contribute to the effectiveness of the piece?
2. Why does he feel like "some epistolary Benedict Arnold"? What does this confession contribute to the piece?

SUGGESTIONS FOR DISCUSSION AND WRITING

A. Using Process

1. Write a paper on how to become involved with a certain activity or hobby. Try to have the reader feel some of the attraction that you feel for it.
2. Describe the process of collecting something—for example, stamps, books, souvenir spoons. Be sure to consider your attitude toward this process.

B. Exploring the Options

4. In a letter to *The Boston Globe* on March 1, 1989, Endicott Peabody complains: "I am disgusted with the appearance of Roger Clemens in Nashua for a day of autograph signing. Each kid was charged $8.50, and he took $30,000.00 out of this community. I understand he did the same in Worcester."

   Peabody then vows to boycott all professional sports until these "prima donnas" shape up. What do you think of the current professional methods for distributing autographs?
5. Change the point of view (see pages 368–373) and write a response to John and other autograph collectors as if it had been written by a "star." (See pages 180–183 for a discussion of argument.)
6. Why do people collect things in the first place, and more specifically, why do they collect things associated with famous people? (See pages 120–123 for a discussion of cause and effect.)

The Process of Writing 'Epiphany'

Don Paskowski (student)

This paper examines the process of writing the narrative essay, "Epiphany," printed on pages 296–300 of this collection. Please read that essay before you read this account of how it was written. Notice that this essay is a "how something was done" process paper, not a set of instructions on how a paper should be written. In writing this account of his own writing, Don was surprised to discover just how many times he revised certain parts of the original piece. He also found this process paper easier to write than the original narrative.

Thinking Ahead How would you describe the process reported here? Does it help you to appreciate what went into "Epiphany?" Think back to or check into your own journals for thoughts on writing one of your own recent pieces. See if you can retrace the steps.

Much of "Epiphany" resulted from at least a month's worth of "mental tinkering" prior to writing the first draft. The first week of class, I looked over the assignments and began mapping out tentative topics for each. However, when I saw the phrase: *Narration within essay/narration as essay,* I had no doubts that I would write about "operation day" in my most recent stay at the hospital because I'd been thinking of that day a lot at the semester's outset anyway, and the memories were rather vivid. I started to remember that day as a story, testing if it would work as a narrative, I realized it would. I began to prepare the assignment. 1

I started by "reliving" the day, not worrying about writing anything down, not worrying about detail, not worrying about anything. I simply wanted to reacquaint myself with the day. I became an observer. I became conscious of how I felt emotionally, of the surroundings, of the people around me, and so on. 2

Feeling confident that I had sorted out these things, I asked myself a basic question I've heard time and again since high school and which was often reiterated in this workshop class: What do you want to say in this piece? I wanted to say that I hadn't realized how much I missed my father until I went through a hospital stay without him. I also knew I didn't want to ruin the narrative by saying that too soon, or saying it directly because it's especially important in a narrative essay to keep readers interested in the story. It's important to entice readers, string them along, involve them. 3

Considerations equally important to me in planning the first draft were past versus present tense, pacing, and tone. I opted for present tense because it provides readers with a sense of immediacy. I wanted readers to be me, or at least be with me, on this day; letting readers know my 4 thoughts lends to this immediacy, too. Moreover, I planned a quick pace. I'd need to show nervousness through both short and long sentences and through passages packed with detail and a sense of quick motion; as for tone, I would allow wording, questions, thoughts, and other details to take care of that for me.

Since I'd mapped and shaped the "plot" and many of the details in my 5
head, I had little trouble writing a first draft. I made no outline, and wrote down vivid metaphors, images or verbs with verve that I'd thought of during the "mental tinkering" stage. Everything else in the preliminary draft came to me while writing, and about seventy percent of what appeared in the first draft appears here, which is more than I expected when I first showed it in workshop. There were certain sections of the first draft I knew couldn't be improved upon (except for a bit of wordiness). For example, the intro. down to "... never been through this before," and the passage dealing with the flashback.

This is not to say that I had no crises during revision. Most everyone 6
in workshop pointed out that I had not included why I had so many operations; others didn't understand some of my references such as "Gilda Radner doing Emily Latella" (but that's more of a "cultural literacy" thing); still others spotted a weak transition between the hall and "It's gone well here in Pre-Op."

But by far the most troublesome section of the essay had to do with 7
slowing down the pace to show the exact moment when the epiphany occurred. In the initial draft, I said this of my revelation: "Why did this operation day work me up so? When I came to in my room on the fourth floor ... I understood why." When it was brought to my attention, I realized I hadn't identified the most important moment of the piece.

Revising this section was painful. It pained me because it brought back 8
the sadness of my father's death and my loneliness during that operation, but also because it required a struggle to get those feelings across. I'd sometimes spend up to a half hour on a paragraph trying to find just the right words, the right sentences. I'd write something like "Finally I understand why I'm nervous," print the page and decide it'd be better if I said, "Finally I discover the truth behind today's nervousness." I'd change it and reprint the page. I easily went through thirty-odd sheets of paper recopying and reprinting pages three and four. Would it be better if the moment of the epiphany read like this: "... parents—his mother, his *father*—sitting on either side of his bed ..." Or like this: "... parents: his mother—

His *father,* sitting beside his bed. ..."? 9

I decided on the latter after numerous fits and starts, because it best 10
emphasized the epiphany. Although I noticed both parents, I concentrated on the father, and that's when I *knew* why I was nervous.

During revision I often debated such things as comma versus dash, 11
dash versus ellipses. As I said, I'd spend up to half an hour on a single paragraph, and I'd usually end up with nothing but a headache. I'd yell. I'd always second guess myself, thinking that there's a better way to say something. I'd become frustrated and block, in which case I'd curse the

day I ever thought that I wanted to write. I'd stress out, run my hand through my hair and watch the strands fall out. I'd bang doors, scream at my family, wrestle our little Jack Russell Terrier, and in general become a monster.

But then, having fought through insomnia, I'd awaken at two, three o'clock in the morning with a perfect sentence or passage and couldn't sleep again until I punched it out on the processor. For example, the passage that begins, "A pang of depression . . ." and ends, ". . . through gluey eyes," I thought up one morning at about four A.M. By six A.M. I had revised it six or seven times. 12

When I get into revising a piece, however, I tend to think about it more than I should. Maybe that's why I went berserk so often in dealing with this piece. I thought about it everywhere: in the shower, in the car (I'd pull over and write notes on the inside cover of textbooks), on walks. But I was at my most productive in revising "Epiphany" when I slipped the headphones on and cranked Clapton or Hendrix while pacing before my word processor. 13

QUESTIONS

A. Discovering Meaning

1. How did the writer begin to think about writing his essay, "Epiphany?"
2. How did he move through the stages of writing it?
3. What details occurred to him randomly?
4. How did the first draft of "Epiphany" get written?
5. Where does he himself seem to be most interested in the process of creating that piece?
6. What role did rewriting play in the creation of the final draft of "Epiphany"?
7. What did this process paper contribute to your reading of the original narrative?

B. Examining Method

1. Why does the writer use quotations frequently?
2. What is the purpose of the list in paragraph 11?
3. How does the writer feel about the process of writing "Epiphany?"

C. Shifting Focus

1. What is the purpose and possible value of writing a piece like this one?

2. By reading this writer's account, did you learn anything about the process of writing itself?
3. Did you learn anything about writing process papers?
4. The writer says that it was easier to describe the process of writing "Epiphany" than it was to write it. Can you think of any reasons why?
5. Do you see any evidence that these two pieces were written by the same person? (You might also look at the comparison on pages 33–35.)

SUGGESTIONS FOR DISCUSSION AND WRITING

A. Using Process

1. Write a discussion of the process of writing one of your own pieces. Be sure to focus on details, not just steps. Try keeping a record in a journal.
2. Write about the process of how you "created" something other than an essay—for example, a drawing, a meal prepared for company, a song. Remember to interest your reader.

B. Exploring the Options

1. Both the narrative, "Epiphany," and this process paper on writing it focus to some extent on the same subject matter. What do these two pieces have in common and in what important ways do they differ? (See pages 277–281 for a discussion of narrative, pages 368–371 for a discussion of discovering purpose, and the essay, "Think About It," by Frank Conroy (pages 310–314.)

It's Time to Play Final 'Jeopardy!'

Mark M. Lowenthal

Mark M. Lowenthal is a State Department employee who won the Jeopardy! 1988 Tournament of Champions. In this piece, he discusses the process of preparing for, and finally winning, the popular television quiz show.

Thinking Ahead What process do you think someone might follow to prepare for winning "Jeopardy!" or some other television quiz show? Try to recall your own preparations for, and experience of, a particular program, contest, game, or performance.

1 As a successful contestant on the television quiz show "Jeopardy!" I have heard three questions repeatedly: What is the host, Alex Trebek, like? What will you do with the money? Did you study?

2 Invariably, the answer that fascinates most is, "Yes, I studied." After all, the average prize for an undefeated five-game winner is $50,000; the season champion pockets another 1,000. It seemed worth several hours' work.

3 "Jeopardy!" players pride themselves on the fact that most of their knowledge is useful information, not trivia. Ah, but how do you learn it all?

4 In the "Jeopardy!" format, contestants are given answers in various categories for which they must provide the questions. If you watch the show for any length of time, you quickly recognize that certain categories recur frequently.

5 Thus, you have to master the Presidents (a: This future President received unanimous confirmation to a Supreme Court seat) and their elections (Note: the correct "questions" to this "answer" and the others in this article can be found at the end.) You must learn everything about the 50 states (b: The two "Sunshine States") and their capitals (c: The nation's southernmost); world geography (d: This country has the most bordering states); movies (e: These two films captured all four major Oscars); literature and prizes (f: This American author rejected a Pulitzer but accepted a Nobel four years later); and Shakespeare (g: The longest role).

6 As a former history major with an English minor, I was fortunate that most of these played to my strengths. I began to make refresher lists of necessary facts in these areas. But you also have to think about the things you don't know, and then put them in a digestible form.

7 I made lists of classical composers and their major opuses, orchestral, operatic and balletic (h: Both of these composers set "Don Quixote" to music).

8 I learned the books of the Bible and memorized the human skeleton and the chemical periodic table (i: Two people who have elements named after them). I tried valiantly to cope with sports records, noting that in basketball the answer is almost always Kareem Abdul-Jabbar or Wilt Chamberlain. I memorized the site of every Olympics since 1896.

9 I reviewed the fronts and backs of all United States currency (j: These three are the only non-Presidents on our bills). I went through almanacs for more esoteric items (k: This is Mickey Rooney's real name). I filled my notebook with lists about pop music (l: This group's album was No. 1 longest); animal groups (m: These birds flock in "parliaments"); television-show locales. I culled the "Guinness Book of World Records" for more facts (n: The world's largest employer).

10 Did it help? Well, first of all, it was fun. "Jeopardy!" players tend to be curious, and they like learning new facts, especially slightly offbeat ones. Yet, in truth, after nine games (five in the regular season and four in the championship) for a total of 540 questions, I can point to maybe 10 answers that I knew because I studied.

11 Then there was the physical training, a nightly regimen of watching "Jeopardy!" with a home-rigged buzzer in hand to test myself against the competition and to hone my timing. Players cannot answer until host Alex Trebek finishes reading the clue. Ring too fast and your system cuts out for two seconds; ring too late and someone else beats you to the punch. Also, you have to discipline yourself not to ring impulsively when you clearly don't know the answer—which tends to happen if you fall far behind. Sizing up my apponents, I would think of that old gunslinger's cliché from the westerns: "How fast are you, stranger?"

12 At the championship, there were three groups of players: those who admitted having studied, those who said they had not and those who denied it, but kept sneaking peeks at almanacs as they awaited their turn before the cameras. Some clutched reference books like talismans.

13 Most people assume that it was worth all the effort, given that I won. But there was more at stake than just winning. Like any public performance, a game show involves ego and risk, the willingness to put a special talent on the line for public review. Luciano goes for the high C and Doc looks for the high inside corner. "Jeopardy!" players try to cash in on their curiosity for that one extra fact.

14 The feeling when it was over was one of relief—not at having finished nor even at having won. No, as the television hummed in the background advertising some show I had never seen, I smiled at the realization that I didn't know anything about its actors, the plot or the setting—and I didn't have to! Even quiz show players like to hang it up at some point.

The correct questions are:

16 (a) Who was John Quincy Adams? (b) What are Florida and South Dakota? (c) What is Honolulu? (d) What is China? (e) What are "It Happened One Night" and "One Flew Over the Cuckoo's Nest?" (f) Who was Sinclair Lewis? (g) What is "Hamlet"? (h) Who are Strauss and Massenet? (i) Who are Einstein, Curie, Fermi, Nobel, Lawrence or Mendeleev? (j) Who are Alexander Hamilton ($10), Benjamin Franklin ($100) and Salmon Chase ($10,000)? (k) Who was Joel Yule? (l) Who were the Monkees? (m) What are owls? (n) What is the Indian Government Railway?

VOCABULARY

talisman (13)

QUESTIONS

A. Discovering Meaning

1. What kind of process is being described here?
2. What steps did the writer take in order to prepare for the final game of "Jeopardy!"?
3. How important was studying to the process of winning?
4. Does anything surprise you in this account?

B. Examining Method

1. What kind of introduction does the writer use (see pages 394–398)?
2. For what audience was this piece written? What assumptions does the writer make? (See pages 370–371.)
3. What is the purpose of the piece (see pages 368–371)?
4. Why does he so frequently give examples of questions (see pages 400–403)?
5. Why does he mention Luciano (Pavarotti) and Doc (Dr. J, Julius Erving)?
6. What kind of conclusion is it (see pages 435–439)?

C. Shifting Focus

1. What is the point of the comparison between the contestant with the buzzer and the gunslinger with the gun (see pages 431–433)?
2. If this piece were longer, what additional information would you enjoy reading about?

SUGGESTIONS FOR DISCUSSION AND WRITING

A. Using Process

1. Describe the process of preparing for and either winning or losing some event—for example, a game, a contest, a television quiz show, or a dance competition. Be sure to include some of your feelings about the process.

2. Write an informative piece in which you let the reader in on a process not apparent to an outsider—for example, how football players get "psyched" for a game, how dancers warm up, or how an engine is repaired.

B. Exploring the Options

1. Write a piece on the reasons why large audiences watch television quiz shows like "Jeopardy!" (See pages 120–123 for a discussion of cause and effect.)

2. Write a paper in which you analyze the format, the tone, the personalities, the props, and so forth, for the "Jeopardy!" program. Describe them, explain how they work and their purpose. Evaluate their success or failure. (Remember to consider what *kind* of piece you will be writing and to shape it accordingly. It could be straightforward exposition based on examples or it could concentrate on cause and effect, in which you account for what you observe, or possibly argument in which you make some judgment about what assumptions the producers make about the audience.)

How Children Learn Prejudice

Ian Stevenson, M.D.

Written by a physician, this piece analyzes the process by which children take on the prejudices of their elders.

Thinking Ahead What do you think are some of the most important ways of acquiring prejudice? Do you have any particular prejudice yourself? How did you acquire it?

The first important point about how children learn prejudice is that they do. They aren't born that way, though some people think prejudice is innate and like to quote the old saying, "You can't change human nature." But you can change it. We now know that very small children are free of prejudice. Studies of school children have shown that prejudice is slight or absent among children in the first and second grades. It increases thereafter, building to a peak usually among children in the fourth and fifth grades. After this, it may fall off again in adolescence. Other studies have shown that, on the average, young adults are much freer of prejudice than older ones. 1

In the early stages of picking up prejudice, children mix it with ignorance which, as I've said, should be distinguished from prejudice. A child, 2 as he begins to study the world around him, tries to organize his experiences. Doing this, he begins to classify things and people and begins to form connections—or what psychologists call associations. He needs to do this because he saves time and effort by putting things and people into categories. But unless he classifies correctly, his categories will mislead rather than guide him. For example, if a child learns that "all fires are hot and dangerous," fires have been put firmly into the category of things to be watched carefully—and thus he can save himself from harm. But if he learns a category like "Negroes are lazy" or "foreigners are fools," he's learned generalizations that mislead because they're unreliable. The thing is that, when we use categories, we need to remember the exceptions and differences, the individual variations that qualify the usefulness of all generalizations. Some fires, for example, are hotter and more dangerous than others. If people had avoided all fires as dangerous, we would never have had central heating.

More importantly, we can ill afford to treat people of any given group 3
as generally alike—even when it's possible to make some accurate generalizations about them. So when a child first begins to group things together, it's advisable that he learn differences as well as similarities. For example, basic among the distinctions he draws is the division into "good" and "bad"—which he makes largely on the grounds of what his parents do and say about things and people. Thus, he may learn that dirt is "bad" because his mother washes him every time he gets dirty. By extension, seeing a Negro child, he might point to him and say, "Bad child," for the Negro child's face is brown, hence unwashed and dirty, and so, "bad." We call this prelogical thinking, and all of us go through this phase before we learn to think more effectively.

But some people remain at this stage and never learn that things that 4
seem alike, such as dirt and brown pigment are really quite different. Whether a child graduates from this stage to correct thinking or to prejudicial thinking, depends to a great extent on his experiences with his parents and teachers.

Parents Play Role

Generally speaking, a child learns from his parents in two main ways. 5
Each of these may contribute to his development either as a prejudiced personality or a tolerant one. First, a child learns a good deal by direct imitation of his parent. If parents reveal prejudiced attitudes, children will tend to imitate those attitudes. If a mother or father, for example, tells a child, "I don't want you playing with any colored children," they foster in their child's growing mind the connection between "colored" and "bad"—and thus promote the growth of prejudice. If instead of saying "colored children," a mother says "nigger" in a derogatory tone of voice, this makes another harmful connection in a child's mind. Even

before he clearly knows to what the words Negro or "nigger" refer, he would know that these words mean something "bad" and hence indicate people for him to avoid. It may be that some colored children, like some white children, are unsuitable playmates. But the prohibition should be made on the grounds of the particular reasons for this unsuitability, not on the basis of skin pigment.

How parents actually behave towards members of other groups in the 6
presence of their children influences children as much or more than what parents say about such people. Still, parents can and do communicate prejudices in subtle ways, by subtle remarks. For example some parents take pride in belonging to a special group, lay stress on the child's membership in that group, and consequently lead him to believe that other people are inferior because they're outside this group. Sometimes parents are unaware that the pride they take in such membership in a special group can be an insidious form of prejudice against other groups. This isn't always so, because often pride in belonging can be related to the genuine accomplishments of a group. But just as often, pride stems simply from thinking of the group as special and superior because of its selectivity, not because of its accomplishments. However, this kind of direct transmission of prejudice from parents to children is the conforming type, and so can usually be modified by later experience if the child comes into contact with other unprejudiced people or if he has the opportunity to get to know members of the group toward which he has had prejudiced attitudes. For example, during the Second World War and the Korean War, many white soldiers of both North and South fought with Negro troops; knowing Negroes as people, they lost their old prejudices.

Unfortunately, however, parents tend to restrict their children's expe- 7
riences with different kinds of people, for fear that the children might be harmfully influenced. This naturally prevents the children from unlearning prejudices. Unfortunately these children who most need broadening and correcting experiences are often deprived of them.

Parents promote prejudice in a second, more subtle and harmful way 8
by their own treatment of their children. Studies of markedly prejudiced persons show that they usually come from families in which they were treated harshly, authoritatively, and unfairly—in other words, they were themselves the objects of prejudice. This parental behavior promotes prejudice in the children—apart from their imitation of it—in two ways. First, if parents treat a child harshly and punish him unfairly, they are relating to the child in terms of power instead of love. Treated as if he were always bad, the child will respond to his parents as if they were always dangerous. Growing skilled in the quick detection of threats or possible injury, he becomes sensitive to danger not only from parents but from other people as well. He makes quick judgments in order not to be caught unaware. Quick judgments are a facet of prejudiced thinking. An insecure and easily frightened person makes sweeping judgments about whole groups, finding it safer to treat the whole group as if it might be harmful to him. He thinks, often unconsciously and always incorrectly, that then he can never be hurt.

Secondly, when parents relate to a child in terms of power, when they punish him, say, with equal severity for accidentally knocking over a dish or for biting his baby brother, he not only thinks of his parents as dangerous people but he thinks of himself as dangerous, too. He must be bad, otherwise why would he be punished so often? Given this low opinion of himself, he will often try to raise it by putting the blame on others—using the old unconscious scapegoat mechanism. Here again, psychological studies have shown that people who are able to blame themselves when they're responsible for things going wrong tend to be much less prejudiced than people who blame others when things go wrong. But a child can only learn to accept blame fairly if his parents attribute blame fairly to him. If he is blamed for everything, he may—in his own defense—grow up unable to accept the blame for anything. If he cannot blame himself he has to blame others—he has to see them as more deficient and blameworthy than they are—which means making prejudiced judgments about them. 9

School Plays a Role

School can help undo the damage. Actual personal experience with children of other groups can show a child directly, immediately, and concretely that not all members of a group are blameworthy, stupid, dirty, or dishonest. In addition, unprejudiced teachers can instruct children in the ways of clear thinking that underlie tolerance. There is definite evidence that education reduces prejudices. It's been found, for example, that college graduates are less prejudiced on the whole than people with less education. Direct instruction about different groups and cultures, another study shows, reduced prejudice in those who were taught. 10

Fortunately, we seem today to be making progress in the direction of less prejudiced belief and behavior. Today, parents treat children with greater respect for them as individuals—in short, with less prejudice. This will continue to exert a healthy influence on the next generation. In fact, one survey has shown that it already has! College students of our generation, it demonstrates, are less prejudiced than college students of the last generation. 11

But since prejudice against members of a minority group or the peoples of other countries is a luxury we can increasingly ill afford—no parent should relax his vigilance in guarding against sowing the seeds of intolerance. 12

VOCABULARY

prejudice (1), innate (1), generalizations (3), pigment (4), derogatory (5), insidious (6), facet (8), scapegoat (9), attribute (9), deficient (9), tolerance (10), vigilance (12)

QUESTIONS

A. Discovering Meaning

1. What is prejudice?
2. What are some sources of prejudice in children?
3. How do parents contribute to the development of prejudice in children?
4. How might schools help to curb the development of prejudice?
5. What is the connection between ignorance and prejudice?

B. Examining Method

1. What is the thesis of this essay (see page 364)?
2. Why was it written (see pages 368–371)?
3. What kind of introduction does the writer use (see pages 394–398)?
4. What is the purpose of paragraph 4 (see pages 415–418)?
5. What is the main purpose of the conclusion (see pages 435–439)?

C. Shifting Focus

1. What is the value of studying *how* a trait like prejudice is acquired?
2. What are some common prejudices that you hear expressed? How do you feel about these judgments?

SUGGESTIONS FOR DISCUSSION AND WRITING

A. Using Process

1. Describe the process of learning one of the prejudices that you have acquired (and possibly the process of abandoning it).
2. Write an analysis of how children acquire some other trait—possibly a more positive one, like curiosity, open-mindedness, kindness, or possibly a negative one, like cruelty, violence, selfishness. Be sure to consider your audience and just how much you may responsibly say about the subject. Research may well be necessary.
3. Describe the process of learning to live with the prejudice of others.

B. Exploring the Options

1. In paragraph 8, Dr. Stevenson says, "Quick judgments are a facet of prejudiced thinking." Discuss this comment.

2. Do you feel that you are, or will be, less prejudiced than other people of your background, as Dr. Stevenson suggests?

Examining Cause-and-Effect Relationships

Cause-and-effect papers are concerned with explanations—with causes as they answer "why" and with effects as they consider "what happens if?"

"Why? Why? Why?" asks the child about almost every aspect of life. "Why do I have to brush my teeth?" "But why *can't* I go!" "Why do wolves howl?" "What will happen if I *do* go in over my head?" With time, we may become complacent about certain facts, so that they no longer seem worthy of inquiry—brushing our teeth, for example—and we may, unfortunately, lose some of our wide-eyed curiosity about things that no longer seem to matter—like wolves' howling—but we cannot fully outgrow the child's "why's."

We need to understand more and more about the world and how it operates. We need to understand how things got to where they are, and we need to anticipate things that are yet to come. In school, we learn the reasons why our forebears wisely wrote a constitution. At home, we learn the painful results of unwisely leaving roller skates on the attic stairs.

A continually moving reel, our life in the present quickly becomes our past, and our life in the future hurries into our present. Causes become effects that, in turn, may become causes themselves. Understanding both causes and effects helps us to step more surely through decisions and arguments (and down the attic stairs). It helps us to avoid the pratfalls, to play our parts with a more readable script, to prepare better for the next act. We know better where we came from and where we are going.

How might we answer the child's question about why teeth need to be brushed?

—Because you will have less chance for tooth decay
—Becuause your smile will look more attractive
—Because you will develop good habits for a lifetime

How might we answer the question about why wolves howl? According to the experts at Ontario's Algonquin Park, the answer would be:

—To stay in touch with other members of the pack
—To maintain social communication and comradeship, similar to humans' singing
—To declare territory and warn off possible competitors

—Among the pups, possibly to express loneliness while the adults are out hunting

For the student seeking housing, a knowledge of causes and effects may also prove valuable. Her friends may offer several reasons why it's better to live on campus:

—It's possible to take part more fully in campus life because you're always "on the scene."
—It's cheaper, because on-campus housing is not primarily a money-making business, as off-campus housing so often is.
—It's a chance to develop wider friendships, because you're living with a building full of students.

The college housing officer may, however, suggest some possible effects of living with a family off campus:

—You may be able to continue some aspects of family life.
—You may have less noise and fewer interruptions while you are studying.
—You may have more personal freedom without dorm rules and regulations.
—But you may miss out on some of the companionship that comes with sharing campus life, including sleeping quarters.

(The more aware this student is of both causes and effects, the better her decision will be when she signs the housing agreements.)

It is not always easy to identify causes and effects. Some causes are *immediate:* "I failed the test because I thought it was next Monday, not today!" Some slightly *less immediate:* "I failed the test because I was tired from the weekend." Some causes are *remote:* "I failed the test because I'm hoping for a job offer in California." Or even *more remote:* "I failed the test because my competitive and unsympathetic parents are pressuring me into school and I need some F's so I can flunk out."

The best analyses of causes and effects will go as deeply, as far back, or as far forward as the subject demands. It is unconvincing, and even silly, to account for the tragic chaos in Lebanon, for example, simply by focusing on a particular bombing, but it makes perfect sense to account for the shutting of a door by identifying the one shutting it as your roommate who just went out. Simple matters may be explained simply; complex matters call for complex explanations. Absolute and complete explanations are rare, but the writer must aim for the *best* that can be said.

Another matter for attention in cause-and-effect discussions is the relationship among events in time sequence. Not everything that happens *before* something is a *cause;* not everything that happens *after* something is an *effect.* The student may or may not have left school *because* her parents are overachievers. Sparse snow in the winter may or may not be a result of the "Greenhouse Effect." It may take research and some careful thinking to come to any conclusions about the causes of these events. Technically, the false assignment of causes based on time sequence, is a fault in logic known as *post hoc ergo propter hoc*—"after this, therefore because of this."

Some causes and effects are unlikely, some are possible, some are probable, and some are certain. It is the writer's responsibility to distinguish among these, if the explanations are to be convincing. Glibness, a hasty dismissal of complexity, is the major downfall of cause-and-effect writing. Don't oversimplify.

WORKING WITH CAUSE AND EFFECT

Consider explanations for events familiar to you—why you recently gained weight, why you react to someone the way you do, why you chose your major, the effects of spending time with a particular person. Things requiring more specialized knowledge of causes and effects may also provide good subjects—causes for the popularity of a recent film, fad, or song; effects of divorce on young children. Then there are the research subjects—the physical effects of using drugs, the causes for the stock market crash of 1987, the effects of stress on the heart, the recent discoveries on the formation of drumlins.

The interest is in your ability to discover and report explanations as they are experienced on the continuum of life—to recognize causes, to anticipate effects. You consider not only the "what" but the "why" and the "what if." The challenge is to make your connections, your identification of causes and effects, interesting and convincing. If they are too obvious, the reader will be bored. Nothing falls flatter than explanations that readers might discover better on their own, with very little thought. If the explanations are too quirky or too private, the reader will be unconvinced. Nothing is worse in cause-and-effect writing than the sense that the writer is naïve or bullying, forcing connections where there are none. Be careful of being a know-it-all, an "Oh, *I*-know-why-he-said-that" type, when you really *know* nothing of the sort. An effective writer of cause-and-effect analysis cannot leap to anything—to a subject, to connections among events, or to conclusions.

Example

One possible beneficial effect of living off campus with a family may be described in detail by a campus housing officer:

> With the right family off campus, your transfer from home family life to school life may not be quite so abrupt. In our files, for example, we have a family that prefers a student, preferably a woman, who is looking for a 'home away from home.' By providing a private room with a separate entrance and no regulations on coming and going, this family allows more freedom than parents might, but they also welcome personal involvement with them and their three children—ages 3, 5, and 8. You may also earn some extra money babysitting, although it is not required in the arrangement. I know these people well, two professors and their children, and, given your concerns about dorm life, I highly recommend your spending at least a semester with them.

Warm-Up

Check journals, recall conversations, observe those things in your life that make you curious. Think of reasons to change your major, why you should join the gymnastics team, what would happen if you went to an AA meeting, why others go to AA meetings, or why something or someone is important to you. Consider causes and effects of certain study habits; do research on why people procrastinate. Examine why people watch certain television programs or why a certain performer is popular. (With some simple research, one student examined why Beach Boy records are dusted off every summer; another tried to account for her desire to work with dolphins at the local aquarium; another researched the reasons why the "Bay of Pigs" invasion failed.)

Write a paragraph or a longer draft examining causes or effects, and then rewrite it after you have studied the examples in this chapter.

Nutella or Guess?

(paragraph)

Ellen McGinn (student)

This paragraph is part of a longer, humorous account of this student's slide into gluttony during her recent semester in France. Here she focuses on the reasons she was losing the battle. What is Ellen's advice about writing? Here is her answer: "I never thought I had anything to say, especially about personal experience subjects, but learning to look closely at what I actually *knew* was a big help."

Thinking Ahead What are the reasons for the writer's gain in weight? What is the major aspect of the humor in this paragraph? Do you have a fault that you are able to observe with some degree of humor?

> I knew I was getting into trouble every time I sat down to one of the Ernault's evening feasts. I wasn't sure how to say, "Sorry, but I think I'm going to blow up!" in French, and besides Mr. Ernault seemed to be miming that he wanted me to fatten up. He was succeeding. My Guess jeans, earned by long hours at the college weight room, were getting too tight to snap. I was downing hefty breakfasts, good-sized lunches, and six-course dinners. And practically every day, I'd buy a jar of Nutella for 13 francs, grab a spoon from the Ernault's kitchen, go to my room, and chow down. I was addicted to this chocolate spread, a fact that became evident one night when I was alone in my room. I searched for a spoon, but I couldn't find one. It was too late to go down to the kitchen. I was desperate. I grabbed the cleanest "Bic" pen I could find and dug into the jar of Nutella. After about three penfulls, I saw myself in the mirror eating with a pen and realized just how far I had sunk into gluttony. I knew then it had to be either Nutella or Guess. I slapped myself when I found I was actually contemplating which to give up.

QUESTIONS

A. Discovering Meaning

1. What is the writer exploring in this paragraph?
2. What causes does she identify here?

B. Examining Method

1. How does the writer organize the details in this paragraph (see pages 400–403)?
2. When you finish reading the preceding paragraph, put it down and try to recall specific details. Which ones come to mind? Why? (See pages 400–403 and pages 448–450.)
3. What is the effect of the short, direct sentences (see pages 426–428)?
4. What is the evidence for her attitude toward this experience (see pages 421–422)?

C. Shifting Focus

1. Rewrite this paragraph as if the writer were deeply concerned about her weight. (See pages 421–422 for a discussion of tone.)

SUGGESTIONS FOR DISCUSSION AND WRITING

A. Using Cause and Effect

1. Identify a physical or psychological condition of your present life—shapely, skinny, bored, happy, tired—and analyze it in great detail. Consider the order of the details in the paragraph and the relationships among them.
2. Write a humorous explanation for one of your failings—why you stay up too late, why your room is always uninhabitable.

B. Examining the Options

1. Compare this essay to the one by Tina Beecher (pages 186–188). (See pages 33–35 for a discussion of comparison and contrast.)
2. Rewrite this paragraph from Mr. Ernault's point of view (see pages 368–373).

Why a Muscle Car?

(paragraph)

Stutz Plaisted (student)

This paragraph, taken from a longer research paper on muscle cars, offers some *reasons* for their recent popularity. What is a muscle car? It is a car from the mid-1960s to early 1970s with a distinctive, racey look and sound. And, according to Jerry Heasley (*Guide to Muscle Cars,* February 1989), a muscle car "must be a two-door sedan with a heavy duty suspension and an engine that puts out at least three hundred horsepower. Most of these cars also have a showy name like Boss, Mustang, Charger, Goat, Roadrunner, or Hemi-Cuda.

They also have special added features like hood scoops, spoilers, and usually some kind of sporty striping." About writing on this topic, Stutz says, "This paper was enjoyable. My father owns a car dealership, so I have some interest in cars anyway. Reading about muscle cars was just an extension of this interest."

Thinking Ahead What are the reasons for the popularity of muscle cars? This paragraph is not entirely based on personal experience. What is the evidence of specialized knowledge or interest? Can you think of any popular trend or interest for which you might like to account (e.g., Batman, rap music, current fashion)?

> I was curious about why there was this sudden interest in muscle cars. Why would something that has been around for years and readily available to anyone all of a sudden become the hottest ticket in town? One dealer reminded me of the fast approaching "antique" status—25 years old. Their value is thus increasing, and as people seek them out for restoration, the price tag goes up. Muscle cars also have distinctive looks—often cherry red, impact blue, bumble-bee yellow, or orange roadrunner, most with chrome dressing, in contrast to today's gray and graphite dime-a-dozen cars. They have a work of art quality—expensive, but worth it. And it's the Baby Boomers and the Yuppies who can now afford one of these cars—a BMW in the parking lot at work, a '69 Pontiac G.T.O. being restored in the garage. They're not only restoring a car, they're bringing back something of their good old days when they roared around town in their Plymouth Hemi-Cuda with the radio blaring. For anyone with a muscle car, it's also a chance to join a certain kind of club, with members who meet at highway parking lots or annual muscle car events to show off their new rear quarter panel or their bumble-bee yellow restoration work.

QUESTIONS

A. Discovering Meaning

1. What are the main reasons for the popularity of these cars?
2. Which seems to be the most convincing cause of the rise in popularity?

B. Examining Method

1. How is this paragraph organized (see pages 374–378)?
2. Does the writer seem sufficiently informed to make these judgments (see pages 449–450)?

3. Notice the transitions from sentence to sentence. Specifically, how are the sentence linked (see pages 415–418)?

4. What is the effect of the specialized vocabularly in this paragraph?

C. Shifting Focus

1. In a longer paper, what else could be reported about these cars? How could this information be organized into a research paper on the topic? (See pages 374–378.)

2. What changes would be made if the writer thought the "muscle car trend" were a waste of time?

SUGGESTIONS FOR DISCUSSION AND WRITING

A. Using Cause and Effect

1. Consider a recent fashion or trend—in clothing, car styles, foods, entertainments, hobbies, for example—and try to account for its current popularity.

2. Write a research paper on the causes of public interest in a subject of the past—Pet Rocks, for example, or a famous murder case, like the murder of Kitty Genovese in New York. (One student wrote a paper suggesting some reasons for the great popularity of Senator Joseph McCarthy.)

3. Write a paper on the effects of public interest in a particular subject—Cabbage Patch Kids, for example.

4. Read the comments of de Tocqueville on pages 322–325 and analyze the popularity of muscle cars or some other "new" object of exceptional interest.

5. In an article on current trends in eating, "Is That a Menu or a Prescription?" columnist Ellen Goodman suggests that much of the pleasure in eating has been lost because of the single-minded search for health that has become so prevalent. She says, "But there is something missing in any cuisine that asks us to think of a banana as a portion of potassium . . . what I need, creature of comfort that I am, is a regular dose of chocolate truffles." Write a response to Goodman's analysis of current eating habits, or write your own reaction to another current fashion or trend. (You will probably be moving into argumentation or persuasion and may want to see the discussions on pages 180 and 214.)

Letter to My Father

(paragraph)

Franz Kafka

A member of a Czechoslovakian Jewish family, Franz Kafka was born in Prague in 1883. He earned a degree in law and then took a job with the Austrian government. Always ailing, he never married and spent much of his time in sanatoriums. In 1924, he died of tuberculosis in Austria. In such works as the short stories, "In the Penal Colony" and "Metamorphosis," and the novels, *The Trial* and *The Castle,* he often writes of the individual's vain struggles to contend with unseen forces that he never fully understands. Possibly some of this feeling of powerlessness derived from Kafka's unsatisfactory relationship with his father, a successful and remote dealer in wholesale fancy goods. In this paragraph, he focuses on just one among many of his reasons for fearing his father—the ordeal at the dinner table. About writing this, Kafka explains to his father, "You asked me recently why I maintain that I am afraid of you. As usual, I was unable to think of any answer to your question, partly because an explanation of the grounds for this fear would mean going into far more details than I could even approximately keep in mind while talking." Kafka needs to write what he cannot say.

Thinking Ahead In this paragraph, what happens at the dinner table that causes Kafka to fear his father? Think of someone to whom you have a strong emotional reactions and try to account for them. Imagine a scene in which these feelings typically emerge.

But that was what your whole method of upbringing was like. You have, I think, a gift for bringing up children; you could, I am sure, have been of use to a human being of your own kind with your methods; such a person would have seen the reasonableness of what you told him, would not have troubled about anything else, and would quietly have done things the way he was told. But for me as a child everything you shouted at me was positively a heavenly commandment, I never forgot it, it remained for me the most important means of forming a judgment of the world, above all of forming a judgment of you yourself, and there you failed entirely. Since as a child I was together with you chiefly at meals, your teaching was to a large extent teaching about proper behavior at table. What was brought to the table had to be eaten up, there could be no discussion of the goodness of the food—but you yourself often found the food uneatable, called it "this swill," said "that brute" (the cook) had ruined it. Because in accordance with your strong appetite and your particular habit you ate everything fast, hot and in big mouthfuls, the child had to hurry, there was a somber silence at table, interrupted by admonitions: "Eat first, talk afterwards," or "faster, faster, faster," or "there you are, you see, I finished ages ago." Bones mustn't be cracked with the teeth, but you could.... The main thing was that the bread should be cut straight. But it didn't matter that you did it with a knife dripping with gravy. One had to take care that no scraps fell on the floor. In the end it was under your chair that there were most scraps. At table one wasn't allowed to do anything but eat, but you cleaned and cut your fingernails, sharpened pencils, cleaned your ears with the toothpick. Please, Father, understand me rightly: these would in themselves have been utterly insignificant details, they only became depressing for me because you, the man who was so tremendously the measure of all things for me, yourself did not keep the commandments you imposed on me. Hence the world was for me divided into three parts: into one in which I, the slave, lived under laws that had been invented only for me and which I could, I did not know why, never completely comply with; then into a second world, which was infinitely remote from mine, in which you lived, concerned with government, with the issuing of orders and with annoyance about their not being obeyed; and finally into a third world where everybody else lived happily and free from orders and from having to obey. I was continually in disgrace, either I obeyed your orders, and that was a disgrace, for they applied, after all, only to me, or I was defiant, and that was a disgrace too, for how could I presume to defy you, or I could not obey because, for instance, I had not your strength, your appetite, your skill, in spite of which you expected it of me as a matter of course; this was the greatest disgrace of all. What moved in this way was not the child's reflections, but his feelings.

VOCABULARY

admonitions

QUESTIONS

A. Discovering Meaning

1. What aspects of his father's behavior made Kafka fear him?
2. How did the writer feel in comparison to his father?
3. How did the writer react to his father's behavior at the table?
4. Why was his father's behavior depressing to Kafka?

B. Examining Method

1. How does Kafka open his letter to his father (see pages 394–398)?

2. How does he organize the discussion after the opening passage (see pages 374–378)?

3. What is the effect of the direct address form "you" in this piece?

4. What do the father's quotations contribute to the effect of the paragraph (see pages 400–403)?

5. Why does he include so many details from his experiences at the dinner table (see pages 400–403)?

6. What kind of person does the writer seem to be? How would you describe the tone of this paragraph? (See pages 421–422.)

C. Shifting Focus

1. Rewrite this experience from the father's point of view.

2. In an effort to account for his fear, Kafka uses exposition (see pages 3–4), narrative (see pages 277–281), and description (see pages 255–258). How does each of these contribute to the clarity and overall message of his approach?

SUGGESTIONS FOR DISCUSSION AND WRITING

A. Using Cause and Effect

1. Think of a person for whom you have a strong emotional reaction—admiration, love, respect, anger, fear—and try to account for it. Remember to give some specific instances and details to illustrate your point, as Kafka does. (Incidentally, it is not necessary to be as serious as Kafka is or serious at all.)

2. Write a letter to someone for whom you have a particularly strong feeling, explaining the reasons for this feeling.

B. Exploring the Options

1. Among other things, this paragraph is also an excellent portrayal of hypocrisy. Describe a scene in which you have also observed such a "don't do as I do, do as I say" attitude.

2. Kafka's biographer, Max Brod, explains that Kafka wanted his mother to deliver this message to his father to "clear up" his relationship with him. Kafka saw autobiographical writing as therapeutic. Write a letter to someone in which you attempt to clarify some aspect of your relationship. (Kafka's mother never delivered the letter.)

Doubting My Major

Tracey Brown (student)

In this essay, an undergraduate student reconsiders her choice of English as a major and offers some reasons why she is now suffering so many doubts. Notice the examples of her "incompetence" and her frequent use of unanswered questions. Much of what Tracey thinks about writing is in this paper, one that clearly grew out of midsemester frustration.

Thinking Ahead Tracey discusses reasons for her doubts about her major. Can you anticipate any? How can she make these reasons interesting to a reader? What are your own thoughts about your major? Can you explain why you feel the way you do?

All through junior high and high school I took honors English classes, and with very little effort I always passed with A's and high B's. I was told I was creative, imaginative, and perceptive. I was told I had a "plethora" (high school vocab.—wouldn't Mrs. Westrate be proud!) of raw talent and "potential" in my writing. And I truly believed these things. I had found my niche. One teacher was sure I'd be the next Agatha Christie. So was I. But I'm not so sure anymore. In fact, I'm positive I won't be. After a long and mostly unproductive absence, I'm back in school and very discouraged. I've chosen English as my major. "Why English?" people ask me, amazed. "Lack of talent in other areas, I guess" is my standard response. And judging from the way things are going, I'm lacking talent in this area too. As the English classes get more specific and in depth, I'm finding an A no longer comes with the territory. I had planned to become an English teacher, but during the past year I've discovered a few reasons why I don't think I have what it takes. 1

For one thing, English teachers know how to interpret literature, and I haven't the vaguest idea how to interpret literature. I only know how to read it. In fact, there's a part of me that doesn't really care how to interpret it. Don't misunderstand me. I've enjoyed all the books I've read for classes, but I don't see the importance of them unless someone tells me the importance. I don't notice symbols as readily as others do. Who says Harper Lee meant for the mockingbird to symbolize innocence? Why 2 should I believe that the girdle Sir Gawain accepted to save his life stood for cowardice? How do these teachers know these things? Is it inherent? If I'm a true English scholar, shouldn't I be able to see these things immediately? I thought *The Chosen* was a great book, but please don't ask me the significance of it for I haven't the faintest! I simply do not see this "stuff," as I call it, until someone points it out to me.

I thought *Beowulf* a disjointed and tiresomely interrupted story 3
(poem, excuse me). According to my lit. teacher, however, these interruptions are necessary and planned. They are intricately woven into the "scheme of things." They are forewarnings, harbingers, "if you will," of things to come. I thought they were annoying. Literature teachers always seem to know exactly what the author means. The part of me who likes trashy novels far better than the classics doesn't care what the author means as long as it's entertaining. That's not a very good attitude for an English teacher. Shouldn't my major reading overlap into my personal reading? Shouldn't I be enthralled by Dickens and all the rest of them? I am not enthralled, and concerned I might never be.

Another problem is writing. I just can't seem to write *right.* Teachers 4
know how to write properly. They understand structure, and thesis sentences, and voice, and purpose. Unless a paper is terribly confusing or disjointed, I do not see these things. As with literature, I focus on enjoying the content. No longer do I get A's on my first try. No longer are there inspiring compliments written on the last page of my essays. It now takes several tries to get a B, ever mind an A, and the last pages of my essays are defiled with ugly red criticisms about purpose and structure and more STUFF!

—"What is the purpose of this paper?" I don't know! I just wrote it!
—"Where's the thesis sentence?" I don't know! What's a thesis?
—"Your structure needs some work." Huh?
—"What voice are you using?" So what's voice?

Help! Besides these major problems with my writing, I have several minor ones. My language is not consistent: too stuffy here, too slangy there, too wordy, not wordy enough. My spelling is a mess, and I need old Noah's advice for nearly every other syllable. How can I correct papers with these problems? How can I teach students to write *right* when I can't?

The romantic vision I had of myself teaching has also changed. I had 5
pictured this rather eccentric professor. You know the type—long peasant skirts, beat-up cowboy boots, baggy old sweaters, bracelets and amulets clinking as she waves her arms emphatically about some big scene in Shakespeare. That picture has disappeared. I now see a timid girl, no amulets (she can't get a decent teaching position, thus can't afford them), clad in a cheap brown polyester suit, wringing her hands in confusion. My students and I aren't sitting in a circle anymore—reading, writing, discussing, learning. I'm now at the blackboard stammering, with nothing

pertinent to say about Chaucer, or *Beowulf,* or thesis sentences. My students are yawning with boredom, looking forward to an easy "A" from this incompetent. My colleagues and I no longer share ideas about teaching and English—they are laughing behind my back. I'm a failure, a loser, in the wrong profession.

Yet, when I try and think of doing anything other than becoming an English teacher, I draw a blank. What else is there I truly love besides English? I could run my Dad's collection agency, I guess. I'd be good at it, but I think I would feel unsatisfied at the end of the day. I'm told if I stay in school and stick with it I'll learn all these things I complain about endlessly. I hope so. Maybe. We'll see. 6

QUESTIONS

A. Discovering Meaning

1. What are the most important reasons this student gives for feeling she is unequal to her major?
2. How did she imagine herself before she came to college and took English courses?
3. What has happened to her fantasy?
4. Most of this piece focuses on causes of her doubts. What are some of the effects of her experience as an English major?

B. Examining Method

1. How does she introduce this piece (see pages 394–398)?
2. What is the relationship between the introduction and the conclusion (see pages 435–439)?
3. Why does she mention the mockingbird and Gawain's girdle in paragraph 2 (see pages 400–403)?
4. What is the tone of the piece (see pages 421–422)?
5. How does the writer's choice of words contribute to the tone or the attitude that emerges as you read (see pages 422–423)?
6. This student frequently uses contrast to make her points. Look particularly at the "romantic vision" of paragraph 5 and the reality she now fears. How does this contrast help us to understand her present situation?
7. Why does she ask so many unanswered questions?

C. Shifting Focus

1. Beyond explaining her problems with her major, what is the writer's purpose in this piece (see pages 368–371)?

2. Paragraph 5 contains many descriptive details (see pages 400–403). Why?

SUGGESTIONS FOR DISCUSSION AND WRITING

A. Using Cause and Effect

1. What is your attitude toward your own major? Evaluate in detail what causes you to feel this way.

2. Why did you choose your present major? Do you have a "romantic vision" of yourself with a degree in this major?

B. Exploring the Options

1. Write a letter to Tracey, referring specifically to comments makes in her essay.

2. Write a "career" paper in which you attempt to draw a picture of your future working self (maybe ten years from now). Describe your location, your daily routine, your wardrobe, your salary, your co-workers (if any). (See pages 253–258.)

3. Write an essay in which you compare this piece with Jane Jerrard's "In Defense of English Majors" on page 227. (See pages 33–35.)

The Strand: My Own Movie

Christopher John Stephens (student)

This piece evaluates the reasons why an old theater remains so important as a memory for the writer. About writing it, Chris says, "This piece began as rough notes in my multi-volume journal, but I kept on coming back to it. It took countless drafts and workshop classes (see pages 364–365) to get control of it."

Thinking Ahead Why does this student have such strong feelings for the old theater? Do you have a particular place from your past that stirs such feelings?

The Ipswich Strand had been shut down and boarded up for almost four years. In the summer 1986, it was leveled, leaving a sad emptiness in the place where I'd done so much growing up. From 1972 to 1983, between the ages of eight and nineteen, I frequented this modest theater, the only palace I've ever known, where I learned the true magic of the movies. These eleven years cannot be destroyed by a wrecking ball, though, and I make no apologies for feeling so attached to the memory of an inanimate building. 1

I liked the physical experience of being there. By most standards, the Strand was shamelessly dirty and poorly-run. It probably had a span of glory years, but they were before my time. In the end, apathy and poor business left the besieged owners waiting for the inevitable. As a child, though, I was never bothered by appearances. Settled into my favorite last row balcony seat, I'd acclimate myself to the clatter of the broken heating system. Eventually, I'd work it into the movie. The sticky floor and stony seats were harder to ignore, as was the rude yet lively audience. I took it all as part of the experience, though, and never gave a thought to how long this time of joy and discovery might last. I was in awe of the wide screen, the endless rows of seats, and a balcony that seemed to have been built in a perfect viewing area, right there in the clouds painted on the ceiling. With noisy friends and a sister by my side, I sat quietly, absorbed by the images, sounds, and colors before me. The impact was immediate. One afternoon there could carry me through anything. 2

I must have seen hundreds of movies there through those eleven years—originals, re-runs, some many times over. I'm standing in a line winding down the sidewalk, and around the bank and post office, waiting to see "Close Encounters of the Third Kind." The excitement is almost unbearable. I'm nine years old again and falling into an uncomfortable sleep through "The Sting," because it's long and hard to understand. I laugh along with the foolish humor of "The Bad News Bears." The terror of "Jaws" is so great I see it a few times, nearly hiding under the seats when Richard Dreyfuss takes that dive and discovers the skeleton in the ship. My brother takes Dave Hurlburt and me to the Strand when we're thirteen to see "Rocky." There, in the downstairs third row, we're swallowed up by the movie. Almost. Directly in front of us are a boy and a girl our own age groping each other, awkwardly kissing in the dark. Something changes in me that night, and I curiously split my attention between the movie and this couple. When Rocky kisses Adrienne he knows exactly how to begin and precisely where to end. The couple doesn't seem so sure. 3

I found a purpose at the Strand. During those long hours at the movies, 4
I got ideas about where my life should go. The flickering images on the

screen convinced me that a small town childhood was only the start of things. I knew I would have to leave. And as a member of the audience, I learned what it felt like to be part of something much larger than where I was, larger than I could imagine by myself. The dialogue was of other places, and I desperately wanted to discover those worlds for myself. I felt too comfortable with my unsuffering childhood and typical teen years. I envied the artists who could create such worlds, and I wanted to try to make some on my own. I wanted to get others to feel something of what I felt. In the Strand, the reality of my daily life could be blanked out with the flick of a switch. The movies never let me down.

After I graduated from high school, I lost track of the Strand. The last 5 movie I saw there was "The Right Stuff," heroic, predictable. Leaving that night, I had no idea that was all there'd be, and I didn't really care. I'd grown, and had no more time for such a shambles. It became important as a place to reject. I was going into Boston and Cambridge, having pretentious discussions with new friends about Bergman and Fellini double features. I was craving anything with sub-titles. I felt better than the common folk who went to this worn-out, small-town theater with its second-run movies, and came out satisfied, as if what they'd seen was high art. They were boring and complacent, but I was having new and better experiences in strange places. My world expanded to the high-brow, and those few years after high school left no time for reminiscence. That came later.

The loss of the Strand didn't really bother me until late summer of last 6 year, when I drove through downtown and felt a sudden ghost-town feeling as I passed the pit where the theater once stood. I didn't want to think of the old days dreaming in the balcony, nor did I want to recall the hopes I had then. I didn't want to admit that the dreams up there in the clouds have mostly faded. But the emptiness made me face the questions. "Have you finished your screenplay?", they ask. "When will your book be in the stores?" Friends get married and start their own families. I'm still alone. Life lets me down the way the movies never did.

I still retreat to the movies, but most theaters now are just holding 7 cells with no individual souls. I no longer have a special refuge. I've come to see the Strand as a part of my own Cecil B. De Mille movie, the part where the music starts and the opening titles flash on the screen. I'm eight years old, with my friends and a sister, and we're upstairs in the balcony for the first Saturday matinee of "Willy Wonka and the Chocolate Factory." The camera pans the crowded seats, then slows for a close-up of my face, all fresh and innocent, and the movie begins. . . .

QUESTIONS

A. Discovering Meaning

1. Why is the Strand so important to the writer?

2. Why did he give up on the Strand before it was destroyed?
3. What did it mean to him as a child?
4. What has it come to mean to him as an adult?

B. Examining Method

1. What is the main purpose of this essay (see pages 368–371)?
2. Why is the couple in paragraph 3 included?
3. What is the purpose of paragraph 5?
4. What is the purpose of paragraph 6?
5. Why does he mention so many movie titles by name (see pages 400–403)?
6. Why does he mention the sticky floor and stony seats in paragraph 2 (see pages 400–403)?
7. Why does he refer to the clouds in paragraph 7 (see pages 400–403)?
8. For what audience was this piece written (see pages 370–371)?

C. Shifting Focus

1. Rewrite paragraph 2 as if the child hated going to the movies.
2. What is the tone, the attitude of the writer toward the subject (see pages 421–422)? The writer told a workshop class that his intention was to avoid sentimentality, or "sappy reminiscence," as he called it. Has he succeeded? Discuss your response with specific references to the paper.
3. How do comparison and contrast contribute to the overall meaning of the piece (see pages 33–35)?

SUGGESTIONS FOR DISCUSSION AND WRITING

A. Using Cause and Effect

1. Think of a place that has had a powerful effect on you—a house, an apartment, a school, a room, a vacation spot—and account for its significance. Have your feelings changed about the place? (You might consider revisiting it.)

2. An all too common experience for Americans is to discover that a once familiar or beloved place has been destroyed—for example, a favorite restaurant, school, or house. If such an experience has happened to you, write about the effects on you.

B. Exploring the Options

1. Write on the American "throw-away" attitude as it relates more broadly to the passion for the new to replace the old. (You may want to read the section on argumentation or persuasion on pages 180 and 214.)
2. Write an essay on a location, an object, or a person of shifting significance for you. Trace these changing feelings, but be sure to think of *why* your feelings have shifted and of what your purpose of writing about them is (see pages 368–371). (One student wrote about a ring that changed its meaning as her relationship with her boyfriend changed. Another wrote of a hill behind his elementary school, which now is a condominium.)
3. Relate the experience described in Stephens' essay to the comments on the American character by Alexis de Tocqueville (pages 322–325).
4. Compare this piece with "Once More to the Lake" by E. B. White (see pages 340–345).

Some Major Effects of Divorce on Children

Linda Alves (student)

This research paper presents information gathered from both older and current research. About writing this, Linda explains, "The research wasn't always easy to find, especially since some of it was coming out at the same time I was writing this. Also, one of the major problems was that it was often overlapping, making the same points over and over. I had to select carefully to avoid being repetitive."

Thinking Ahead From your experience or research, can you identify some of the major effects of divorce? How can Linda keep this paper from becoming simply a list? For any other major change in life, can you identify some of the important effects?

With the divorce rate in the United States higher than any time in its 1
history, it is not at all uncommon for children to be forced to cope with

the break-up of their families. The situations differ within each divorce. Some children are so young, they may remember little of the actual divorce, and grow up with one parent or a new family. Others, the older ones, must watch as the only home they have ever known shatters before their eyes. Some families are supportive and helpful during this extremely difficult adjustment in their children's lives. Others, for whatever reasons, are less aware, less concerned, less able to handle the emotional burden they are placing on the youngest members of their family. But whenever the divorce is experienced, however it is handled, the difficulties do not disappear when the final divorce papers are signed. Research has shown that the effects are many and often long-lasting.

One of the more immediate effects of divorce may be denial. Some 2
children deny because they feel shocked, as if the divorce is occurring without warning. In a series of interviews, Terry Grossman discovered that "Sixty out of the sixty-six children interviewed stated that they had been surprised by the news of the divorce and/or couldn't believe that it was actually taking place" (80). Dr. Richard Gardner suggests that parents who do not fight in front of the children make such denial easier (90), but also suggests that children may deny the divorce simply because of the extreme pain involved (93). Yet one more source of denial is a lingering hope that the parents will get back together. According to Bruce Fisher, these children are not yet able to accept the fact that they will not (34). Parents who disagree openly with one another and who share feelings along the way may help to make denial less likely.

When denial is no longer possible, however, other feelings may take 3
its place. One of these may be guilt. Children may come to believe that their own behavior caused the divorce. Florence Kaslow suggests that children sometimes blame their own misbehavior (176), and Glynnis Walker sees a tendency in children to make things up as a way of explaining the split (129). This guilt is one of the many bad effects of not talking to children about the divorce and of not assuring them that they are guiltless. Explanations may hurt, but the versions the imagination creates may be far more painful for the children who feel that they are at fault.

Related to these feelings is the very common feeling of grief. Glynnis 4
Walker says that children "may feel the loss of their father, usually the absentee parent, acutely, and at the same time may feel that mother's love and attention are also missing from their lives" (126–127). It is a kind of double loss. This grieving is normal and often extreme, but according to Stuart Berger, it may become less painful over time (124), as does the mourning for someone's death. Once they become accustomed to the absence of a parent, once they become adjusted to living in the new situation, they may return to their normal attitudes and routines, particularly if they trust their parents.

Worse than temporary grief, however, is deep sadness or, more seri- 5
ously, depression. Sadness is the less worrisone and ". . . almost always exists initially and should be considered normal unless it continues for months," explains Susan Arnsberg Diamond (23). She goes on to suggest that some children find ways to forget these feelings, by getting involved

in school, for example, but she also points out that some children cannot easily dismiss their misery:

> They may feel down and fail to find satisfaction in any of the activities they used to consider fun; they may withdraw from their friends and drift off into daydreams; they may easily burst into tears; they may have difficulty concentrating (23).

Even this sadness is, however, usually for a short time. Depression, on the other hand, according to a doctor who has studied the serious effects of divorce, often "lingers on and begins to interfere in a very basic way with the child's ability to learn, to work, to play, to make friends—in short, to lead a normal life" (Berger 128). A depressed child also may not eat, may walk around looking glum, and may complain of headaches (Salk 48). Diamond suggests that these children feel as if it can not get any better; they feel helpless and empty (23). The love of both parents is important to help children avoid such serious depression, but if this fails, psychological help should be sought out.

Another common reaction is a feeling of rejection. In a questionnaire 6
study, Glynnis Walker found that many children felt deserted by the parents, particularly by the one leaving home (130). Children fear that the parent who leaves home will not be seen again, and they also fear that the absent parent does not love them anymore. According to Bruce Fisher, many children therefore cling to the parent they stay with, for fear of losing that one also, and he also suggests that such children need to be told that the second parent has no intention of leaving them (35). These children need to know that both parents will continue to love them, that their love for them does not stop with the divorce.

Once the child does accept the divorce and its consequences, anger 7
may become one of the strongest effects. Experts agree that children often become angry at the one seen as the cause of the divorce or at the parent who leaves home (Fisher 52). Often children of divorce do not get along with the absent parent. Some may express this anger by becoming destructive, by becoming involved in fights, or by vandalizing (Salk 47). Some children may also deal with anger by taking drugs and alcohol as a way of getting back at their parents. Parents need to recognize this anger as a symptom of deeper problems and seek out the help their children need if the anger is destructive or out of control.

One cause of the anger, in addition to the fact of the divorce itself, is 8
the embarrassment many children feel when the family breaks up. Tracy Grossman's interviews showed that 37 out of 66 did not tell anyone that their parents were divorced, unless they had no choice (85). Their friends often live with two parents, so they feel different, sometimes making up stories about the missing parent. Susan Grobman, for example, always told her friends, whenever they slept over, that her father was away on business (40). Unfortunately, this embarrassment can last for many years after the divorce and lead to much misery for the children who have not been able to adjust to the facts of their own lives. Children need to learn how to accept the divorce, without shame.

Some effects of divorce on children are clearly short-term, lasting anywhere from a few months to a year. Others are more long-lasting, carrying over into later stages of life, even into adulthood. 9

Judith Wallerstein, a psychologist, has recently studied the long-term effects of divorce and has found many examples of extended difficulties caused by the parents' divorce during their childhoods. She studied 60 families with a total of 131 children from 5 to 10 years after the divorce. In the five year follow-up, interviewing 56 of the 60 families, she found that only 34% of the children were doing fine (20). The other "37% were depressed, could not concentrate in school, had trouble making friends and suffered a wide range of other behavior problems" (29). Children are generally expected to improve, not decline, in their recovery from divorce, but Wallerstein found otherwise. In her ten-year follow-up, 45% were doing fine; they could be described as successful people. But 41% were not, feeling angry and worried as adults, and having difficulty reaching desired goals (20). 10

In this ten-year study, she also found the "sleeper effect," a belated feeling of betrayal experienced mostly by women, particularly when about to make a long-term decision about their futures—marriage or other commitments. The fears and the feelings of betrayal associated with their parents' experiences come to the surface and make them afraid to take actions in their own lives. They may carry fears, anger, and a sense of rejection into adulthood, and thus bring these troubles into their own relationships, whether or not they are appropriate. 11

The possible effects, both short-term and long-term, of divorce on children are many and complex. Not all children experience all of them, nor do all cope with the divorce in the same way. Clearly one of the major factors in the immediate effects experienced by children and in the lingering effects many years down the road is the behavior of the parents at the time of the divorce. At a time when they are often caught up in the difficulties of their own emotions, parents must take the time to recognize the feelings of their children. The ones who talk with their children about the feelings, who share the anger, the frustration, the sadness, the decisions, have a far better chance of protecting them from the worst effects of the breakup of the family. If they themselves are unable to do this, they should provide for the attention of some other adult to support and guide them through this most difficult experience. 12

WORKS CITED

Berger, Stuart M. D. *Divorce Without Victims.* New York: Signet, 1986.

Diamond, Susan Arnsberg. *Helping Children of Divorce: A Handbook for Parents and Teachers.* New York: Schocken Books, 1985.

Fisher, Bruce. *Rebuilding: When Your Relationship Ends.* California: Impact Publishers, 1987.

Gardner, Richard A. *The Parents Book About Divorce.* Garden City: Doubleday, 1977.

Grobman, Susan. "Child of Divorce." *USA Today* July 1987: 40–42.

Grossman, Tracy Barr. *Mothers and Children Facing Divorce.* Michigan: UMI Research Press, 1986.

Kaslow, Florence W., and Lita Linzer Schwartz. *The Dynamics of Divorce: A Life Cycle Perspective.* New York: Brunner/Mazel Publishers, 1987.

Salk, Dr. Lee. *What Every Child Would Like Parents to Know About Divorce.* New York: Harper & Row Publishers, 1978.

Walker, Glynnis. *Solomon's Children: Exploding the Myths of Divorce.* New York: Arbor House, 1986.

Wallerstein, Judith S. "Children After Divorce: Wounds That Don't Heal." *The New York Times Magazine* 22 Jan. 1989.

QUESTIONS

A. Discovering Meaning

1. What are the major effects of divorce on children?
2. What are the two major kinds of effects?
3. What do parents need to do at the time of the divorce?
4. Does this seem an adequate assessment of the major effects of divorce, or can you think of other important effects?

B. Examining Method

1. How does the writer introduce the subject of her research (see pages 394–398)?
2. What transitions does she use as she moves from one paragraph to the next (see pages 415–418)?
3. How does the writer introduce information drawn from research?
4. How is the information drawn from other sources distinguished from Linda's own writing? (An important concern in research is to avoid plagiarism, or the representation of someone else's words or *thoughts* as your own).
5. What is the purpose of paragraph 9?
6. What kind of conclusion does the writer use? How does it relate to her procedure throughout the paper? (See pages 435–439.)

C. Shifting Focus

1. Could narrative be profitably worked into this piece? Where?

2. In research, the writer should never disappear beneath a stack of notecards and borrowed quotations. The writer must be the "guiding light" *through* the information gathered from other sources: introducing the entire piece, creating a thesis, organizing the information in the best possible order, preparing the reader for outside information, commenting upon and evaluating it; making transitions from paragraph to paragraph, from idea to idea, drawing conclusions. It's the writer's job to make sense of the information gathered from outside sources; the writer must not leave this task up to the reader. In short, the writer has to be *everywhere* in a research paper, or the reader will be lost. How does this writer work herself into her paper? Has she fulfilled these requirements for successful research?

SUGGESTIONS FOR DISCUSSION AND WRITING

A. Using Cause and Effect

1. Write a paper in which you analyze the effects of an important change in your life—becoming a mother or a father, experiencing the death of a friend or a parent. If you choose to write on one of the effects of divorce, like moving in with a stepparent or getting adjusted to joint custody, you may want to use a closer focus than in Linda's paper. Remember to consider what kind of paper you are writing: Is it a paper about personal experience, in which case you will probably include examples and possibly narrative, or is it a research paper based on what you have discovered in the library, through interviews, and any other sources.

2. Write a research paper on the major causes of divorce.

3. Write a paper based on personal experience, research, or both, on some possible effects of an incompatible couple staying together "for the sake of the children."

B. Exploring the Options

1. Do you think that married couples turn too easily to divorce rather than work out their difficulties? Is marriage another thing Americans throw away? (See pages 180–183 for a discussion of argument.)

2. Oscar Wilde, an English playwright of the late nineteenth century, once said, "Divorces are made in heaven." Write your response.

The Effects of Steroids

The NCAA Drug Education Committee

This is an excerpt from an information pamphlet provided to both coaches and athletes by the NCAA. It focuses primarily on the effects of using steroids.

Thinking Ahead Are you aware of any of the side effects of using steroids? What do you think should be the primary concerns of this committee as they provide this information? Can you think of any other drug, substance, or activity for which you could identify the side effects?

It should be emphasized that the steroids being discussed here are anabolic steroids,* not the corticosteroids often used by physicians to reduce tissue swelling and inflammation. Anabolic steroids and corticosteroids are completely different types of compounds with different actions in the body. In the 1930s it was reported that testosterone had an "anabolic" action in laboratory animals, causing nitrogen to be retained and body protein, including muscle, to be developed. The term "anabolic" implies that the substance under consideration is being synthesized and stored. The general athletics world began to hear of the "possibilities" of anabolic steroids in the early 1960s. The prevalent story was that the drugs first had become available to weightlifters and body builders in the 1950s and thereafter the use spread widely among participants in the athletic throwing events. 1

In athletics, objective evidence of the efficacy and safety of the "anabol- 2

---

*

Some Commonly available anabolic steroids:

Common Name	*Oxymetholone*
Methandrostenolone	Oxandrolone
Ethylestrenol	Stanozolol
Nadrolone	Brand Name
Adroyd, Anadrol	Dianabol
Anavar	Maxibolin
Winstrol	Durabolin

ics" is sparse an contradictory, and there appears to be a considerable placebo effect. It is not likely that many approved studies involving the use of high doses of the "steroids" in athletics will be undertaken, primarily based on ethical considerations. Some athletes have been reported to ingest five to 15 times the medically approved therapeutic dosage of anabolic steroids. The dangers and side effects inherent in the therapeutic use of the "anabolics" are well documented in the scientific literature.

A brief summary of some of these adverse effects of "steroid" therapy 3
includes:

- enlargement of the prostate gland,
- loss of libido,
- testicular atrophy resulting in sterility and
- weight gain caused by fluid retention and associated elevation in blood pressure.

In prepubertal males, another adverse effect of anabolic steroid use is 4
premature closure of the epiphyseal plates (growth areas) in long bone. This means that a person who takes anabolic steroids while still growing will quite likely not grow to the full height they would have attained if they had not started taking anabolic steroids.

Other less serious effects of the misuse of anabolic steroids are: loss of 5
hair, acne, nose bleed and stomach disorders. Liver disorders are the most serious and most frequent disorders resulting from "steroid" therapy. The most serious liver disorder associated with normal anabolic steroid therapy is cancer. The potential accelerated development of atherosclerosis, which leads to heart disease, strokes and peripheral vascular disease, may be anticipated with chronic use of these drugs because of disturbances in carbohydrate and lipid metabolism. It should be mentioned that many of these adverse side effects of anabolic steroid use result from normal therapeutic doses. It is unknown what will be the long-term effects of the massive doses taken by athletes. Some of the side effects may take 20 to 30 years to become apparent.

Studies on the effect of anabolic steroid therapy upon females is sparse. 6
Based upon the evidence available, however, it is strongly recommended that anabolic steroids not be taken by prepubertal females. Reports in the scientific literature describe several undesirable side effects occurring from anabolic steroid therapy on human females, such as masculinization, excessive hair and disruption of normal growth patterns. Most of these side effects are irreversible.

As mentioned earlier, there is apparently a large "placebo" effect asso- 7
ciated with the use of anabolic steroids by athletes. Those who decide to use steroids *expect* to increase muscle mass and strength and tend to train a littler harder in anticipation of this result. Many researchers feel that most, if not all, of any resulting increase in muscle mass and strength is due to the increased training rather than the anabolic steroids. Yet it

is difficult to convince some athletes and coaches, and even some physicians, of this because they are certain it is the anabolic steroids causing the changes. Their arguments are bolstered by many "personal testimonials" passed along in the weight room, and even by a few studies found in scientific journals. Unfortunately, careful analysis of the studies showing positive effects of anabolic steroids use indicate many of them are not well-designed or well-controlled. Most of the arguments in favor of anabolic steroids boil down to anecdotal evidence or poorly designed studies. This is a poor basis for making decisions about whether or not to use anabolic steroids.

The problem of eliminating the use of anabolic steroids by athletes is 8
difficult because of the popular perception that an athlete has to take steroids in order to "compete with those who do." A coach or any other person who encourages an athlete to use anabolic steroids for this reason is only perpetuating a myth. It is possible to compete successfully without using steroids. An example is Randy Matson, one of the great shot putters and discus throwers in the history of track and field. He tried anabolic-androgenic steroids in 1964 and 1965. He states he abandoned them because he found no real evidence that they improved his performance. Two years later, after hard work, demanding training and persistent practice without drugs, he set a world shot put record of 71 feet, 51/2 inches, a distance very few have surpassed even today.

Seeking to improve athletic performance, various athletes have experi- 9
mented through the years with a variety of drugs. Based on scientific evidence, however, it is difficult to find athletes who in fact improved their performance. Natural production in the human body of the four major and many minor steroid hormones is interdependent and delicately balanced and is crucial to physical and mental health. Supplementation of these natural levels cannot be undertaken without disturbing the balanced production of all these hormones and causing harmful secondary effects.

In summary, in spite of reports that steroids increase muscle mass and 10
definition, the potential adverse effects appear to clearly outweigh any potential benefit that may be derived from use of these drugs. The only objectively proven way to increase muscle fiber mass and strength is through work overload. That means the best (and certainly the safest) method is the basic approach of good nutrition and a good weightlifting program.

VOCABULARY

anabolic (1), placebo (2), therapeutic (2), inherent (2), atrophy (3), prepubertal (4), atherosclerosis (5), peripheral (5), vascular (5), lipid (5), metabolism (5), anecdotal (7)

QUESTIONS

A. Discovering Meaning

1. What are the major effects of the use of anabolic steroids?
2. What kinds of steroids do the writers discuss here?
3. What is the placebo effect?
4. What is the source of many of the arguments in favor of the use of anabolic steroids?

B. Examining Method

1. What kind of introduction does the committee use (see pages 394–398)?
2. What is the purpose of paragraph 2?
3. Why is the list in paragraph 3 included so early in the report (see pages 400–403)?
4. Why do the writers mention and discuss the placebo effect?
5. How does the diction reflect the purpose of the piece (see pages 422–423)?
6. What is the purpose of the piece?
7. What kind of conclusion do the writers use? Is it effective?

C. Shifting Focus

1. Are you convinced by the arguments in this paper? If so, explain what led you to accept the information. If not, explain what you feel could be improved and what might not be accurate. (Thoughts for this question may lead you to a fuller writing project.)
2. This information is organized around effects and is presented straightforwardly. Is the purpose purely expository?

SUGGESTIONS FOR DISCUSSION AND WRITING

A. Using Cause and Effect

1. Write a piece on the effects of some drug, substance, or activity with which you are familiar—good, bad, or mixed. Be sure to consider your

purpose in writing it. Do you want to encourage or discourage your readers, or are you simply being informative?

2. Write a piece on the causes of using such substances or of taking part in such activities. Remember: Decide whether you intend to be critical or not.

B. Exploring the Options

1. Compare this piece to two others on steroids in this collection: a definition (page 165) and a narrative (page 292). What are the major similarities and differences in approach and purpose? This is as much an analysis of writing as it is of steroids. This suggestion is meant to encourage analysis of writing in *different* ways on the *same* subject. (See pages 368–371 for a discussion of purpose, pages 364–366 for a discussion of working with a raw material, pages 310–314 for an essay addressing the issue of *finding* meaning.)

I Want a Wife

Judy Syfers

Born in 1937, Judy Syfers, was married in 1960 and raised two daughters. Following her divorce, she began working full time as a secretary during the day and going to school at night. In this piece, written in 1971, she gives several reasons why she would like to have a wife of her own.

Thinking Ahead Can you think of possible reasons why the writer would like to have a wife? Is there any other type of person you would like to have in your life?

I belong to that classification of people known as wives. I am A Wife. 1
And, not altogether incidentally, I am a mother.

Not too long ago a male friend of mine appeared on the scene fresh 2
from a recent divorce. He had one child, who is, of course, with his ex-wife. He is obviously looking for another wife. As I thought about him while I was ironing one evening, it suddenly occurred to me that I, too, would like to have a wife. Why do I want a wife?

I would like to go back to school so that I can become economically 3
independent, support myself, and, if need be, support those dependent upon me. I want a wife who will work and send me to school. And while I am going to school I want a wife to take care of my children. I want a wife to keep track of the children's doctor and dentist appointments. And

to keep track of mine, too. I want a wife to make sure my children eat properly and are kept clean. I want a wife who will wash the children's clothes and keep them mended. I want a wife who is a good nurturant attendant to my children, who arranges for their schooling, makes sure that they have an adequate social life with their peers, takes them to the park, the zoo, etc. I want a wife who takes care of the children when they are sick, a wife who arranges to be around when the children need special care, because, of course, I cannot miss classes at school. My wife must arrange to lose time at work and not lose the job. It may mean a small cut in my wife's income from time to time, but I guess I can tolerate that. Needless to say, my wife will arrange and pay for the care of the children while my wife is working.

I want a wife who will take care of *my* physical needs. I want a wife 4
who will keep my house clean. A wife who will pick up after me. I want a wife who will keep my clothes clean, ironed, mended, replaced when need be, and who will see to it that my personal things are kept in their proper place so that I can find what I need the minute I need it. I want a wife who cooks the meals, a wife who is a *good* cook. I want a wife who will plan the menus, do the necessary grocery shopping, prepare the meals, serve them pleasantly, and then do the cleaning up while I do my studying. I want a wife who will care for me when I am sick and sympathize with my pain and loss of time from school. I want a wife to go along when our family takes a vacation so that someone can continue to care for me and my children when I need a rest and change of scene.

I want a wife who will not bother me with rambling complaints about 5
a wife's duties. But I want a wife who will listen to me when I feel the need to explain a rather difficult point I have come across in my course of studies. And I want a wife who will type my papers for me when I have written them.

I want a wife who will take care of the details of my social life. When 6
my wife and I are invited out by friends, I want a wife who will take care of the babysitting arrangements. When I meet people at school that I like and want to entertain, I want a wife who will have the house clean, will prepare a special meal, serve it to me and my friends, and not interrupt when I talk about the things that interest me and my friends. I want a wife who will have arranged that the children are fed and ready for bed before my guests arrive so that the children do not bother us. I want a wife who takes care of the needs of my guests so that they feel comfortable, who makes sure that they have an ashtray, that they are passed the hors d'oeuvres, that they are offered a second helping of the food, that their wine glasses are replenished when necessary, that their coffee is served to them as they like it. And I want a wife who knows that sometimes I need a night out by myself.

I want a wife who is sensitive to my sexual needs, a wife who makes 7
love passionately and eagerly when I feel like it, a wife who makes sure that I am satisfied. And, of course, I want a wife who will not demand sexual attention when I am not in the mood for it. I want a wife who

assumes the complete responsibility for birth control, because I do not want more children. I want a wife who will remain sexually faithful to me so that I do not have to clutter up my intellectual life with jealousies. And I want a wife who understands that my sexual needs may entail more than strict adherence to monogamy. I must, after all, be able to relate to people as fully as possible.

If, by chance, I find another person more suitable as a wife than the 8
wife I already have, I want the liberty to replace my present wife with another one. Naturally, I will expect a fresh, new life; my wife will take the children and be solely responsible for them so that I am left free.

When I am through with school and have a job, I want a wife to quit 9
working and remain at home so that my wife can more fully and completely take care of a wife's duties.

My God, who *wouldn't* want a wife? 10

QUESTIONS

A. Discovering Meaning

1. What are the main reasons Syfers would like to have a wife?
2. How would you describe the implied husband in this piece? Do you like him? Does he seem in any way realistic? Why?

B. Examining Method

1. Why does she open the way she does (see pages 394–398)?
2. What is the purpose of paragraph 2?
3. For what audience was this piece written (see pages 370–371)?
4. What is the tone, the attitude of the writer toward the subject (see pages 421–422)?
5. Why does she so repeatedly begin her sentences with "I want"? (Do you hear an echo of any others who so often say "I want"?)

C. Shifting Focus

1. Is this simply a list of reasons for wanting a wife, or does she intend a message beyond her own personal preferences?
2. Is this piece an effective argument for women's liberation? Explain.
3. In the process of explaining why she wants a wife, Syfers defines what a wife is to her. How would you define a "wife?"

SUGGESTIONS FOR DISCUSSION AND WRITING

A. Using Cause and Effect

1. Write an essay in which you give reasons why you want a particular type of person in your life—a secretary, a husband, a physician, a lawyer. Remember to consider purpose. Are you making a straightforward explanation or arguing a larger case as you go along?
2. Based on research, make some judgments about why the husband–wife arrangement has evolved in society.

B. Exploring the Options

1. Write an answer to Syfers as if you were her husband.
2. This article was written in *Ms.* magazine in December 1971. Is it still current, or is it too dated to have any real meaning today?
3. Recent research shows that women still spend far more time than men do on household chores, whether or not they are employed outside the home. The suggestion seems to be that women who "have it all"—career, husband, children, home—may actually have far more than they would like to have and often more than they can manage. Do these conclusions seem accurate? Do they have any effect on choices you might be making as a college student (male or female)?
4. *Alaska Men* is a magazine in which men advertise for mates to move to Alaska and share their lives with them. Write your own advertisement for a perfect mate.
5. If you could create an ideal living situation for yourself, what would it be? If this situation involves a mate, try describing it in letter form to that person.

Defining

"What *is* it?" screams the heroine as the slithery green beast salutes her through the twilight on the misty moor. Is it a primitive creature emerging for a ghoulish feast in the surrounding villages? Is it an optical illusion, really a tree distorted by the mist? Is it a friend on the way to a costume party at the nearby pub? All of these conclusions are possible, and our heroine would certainly like to know who the real beast is. Should she run, get new glasses, or put on her dancing shoes?

Usually the need for definition is not so dramatic. But too often we want to know what things are *and* what they are not. The word *definition* itself comes from the Latin *de* and *finis*, or "concerning limit." Definition helps us to set boundaries around things, to separate one thing from another so that we know what we are confronting—on the moor or elsewhere. It helps us to understand words, ideas, objects, or people with greater accuracy, whether such distinctions are simply interesting or desperately necessary.

Definitions may be brief and straightforward, as in the meanings of words in the dictionary (*teach*—"to impart knowledge or skill to"), or they may be extended into essays ("My Early Years at School," by Philip Lopate) or even books (*The Art of Teaching,* by Gilbert Highet) that attempt, with greater and greater detail and subtlety, to delineate the meaning of something.

Definitions may be abstract, the kind often favored by philosopher: What is truth? What is justice? What is self-respect? They may also be concrete, the kind often sought in examinations: What is a bicameral legislature? What is a drumlin? What is a eukaryotic cell? But however brief or extended, however abstract or concrete, definitions must place the subject in the proper category and identify the particulars.

It is also important to be aware of purpose when you are writing definitions. Is the intent to be as objective as possible, as in a dictionary, or is it to express subjective emotions and possibly to engage those of the reader? It is possible, for example, to define *love* by looking it up in a dictionary ("strong affection or liking for someone or some thing"). It is also possible to define not *love,* but "what love is to me" (working at the church bazaar and staffing the food kitchen for the homeless) or even "what love should be to you" (never having to say you're sorry).

The simple distinction between the words *house* and *home,* for example, suggests such possible variations in emotional content. Both are residences with dictionary definitions (denotations): A *house* is "a structure serving as a dwelling for one or several families"; a *home* is more personal—it is "the place where one resides." But each also has its own special feelings attached to it, its associated meanings (connotations). The word *house* suggests a building;

the word *home,* a place where people who care for one another live (or maybe a euphemistic, smooth-sounding description of a place where people might not want to live at all—a rest home, a home for the terminally ill). The words *cat* and *kitty* do not mean exactly the same thing, nor do *brat* and *toddler,* or *hot shot* and *CEO.* In other words, definitions can also be emotional. Beyond what the dictionary says, they can have purposes other than clarification; they can have effects on the feelings of the reader.

Consider the following examples.

1. What is a dormitory student?

   —One who lives in local housing
   —One who may meet others also living on campus
   —One who may spend more time on campus and may therefore take part in local activities
   —One who has easier access to the library and to other students.

2. What is a dormitory student?

   —One who does not live at home or off campus but, rather, in local housing, near the center of the action
   —One who easily meets many friends because of their proximity and availability
   —One who spends time in the college community and therefore receives the benefits that campus life has to offer
   —One who may have a better chance of receiving good grades because he or she has easier access to the library and the help of other students

(The first definition is expository and explains as objectively as possible what a dormitory student is. The second definition, on the other hand, is persuasive and makes a case for the *value* of living on campus. In the first, the definition simply clarifies; in the second, it encourages agreement.)

Given the many decisions that must be made while writing a definition—the length, the extent of the detail, the degree of abstraction, the emotional content, the overall purpose—it is important for you to decide *how* a definition is to be used within an essay. Short and straightforward definitions might easily be absorbed into the larger essay, as in the following plan for discussing major English literary figures of the eighteenth century.

3. In major writers of the eighteenth century may be traced the development from classicism to romanticism.

   —Introduction with definitions of "classicism" and "romanticism"
   —Discussion of Alexander Pope

—Discussion of Jonathan Swift
—Discussion of Samuel Johnson
—Discussion of William Blake
—Discussion of Samuel Taylor Coleridge
—Discussion of William Wordsworth

(Definitions of the two terms, although important to the meaning of the essay, are used as *background* to the historical discussions.)

It would also be possible to use definitions of "classicism" and "romanticism" as the *major focus* of an essay, selecting writers as illustrations of the meanings.

4. Important characteristics of "classicism" and "romanticism" are clearly reflected in the major writers of the eighteenth century.

    —"Classicism"—literary traditions of Greece and Rome, as in Pope and Johnson
    —"Classicism"—regular forms, as in Pope and Swift
    —"Classicism"—the individual within society, as in Swift and Johnson
    —"Classicism"—faith in reason, as in Pope, Swift, and Johnson
    —"Romanticism"—shift away from ancient traditions, as in Blake
    —"Romanticism"—greater variety of forms, as in Blake, Coleridge, and Wordsworth
    —"Romanticism"—the independent individual, as in Wordsworth
    —"Romanticism"—greater trust in emotion, as in Blake, Coleridge, and Wordsworth

(In this definition essay, the definition dominates the discussion in its constant focus on major characteristics; it is not simply background to a historical analysis.)

Consider the following plan for a definition paper on the "essay" as a literary form.

5. What is an essay?

    —A piece of literary nonfiction prose with roots in classical speech making and letter writing
    —An "essai," an "attempt" to explore a topic, as defined by Montaigne, the "father of the essay"
    —A popular and widely circulated periodical entry of the eighteenth century
    —An expanded literary form of the nineteenth century, including sophisticated works by some of the greatest prose stylists

—After severe competition from the short story and reportorial journalism in the twentieth century, a kind of literature now enjoying a much deserved revival

(In this outline, definition is important throughout, not just as background. The entire plan is organized around some major moments in the historical development to the literary essay. Other "definitions" of the essay could focus instead on various types of essays—formal, informal, travel, historical, biographical, critical, and so forth, or on various analyses by essayists themselves—Montaigne, Addison, Johnson, Chesterton, Woolf, White, and others.)

The writer of definitions then, must make judgments not only about the meaning of the subject but also about the purpose and the shape of the essay that will express it.

WORKING WITH DEFINITION

Consider subjects to which you may give a personal definition: self-respect, insensitivity, the joy of hiking, a particular career or major. Or draw from your fund of knowledge—what is the ultimate French meal, what is bird-watching to me? With research, definitions may include the judgments of others—what is bird-watching to ornithologists and professionals, what is heavy metal, what is an arthropod?

The interest in definition is in making the most enlightening connections and in separating your subject from all others. The challenge for an essay focusing on definition is to avoid the dryness of dictionary denotations. The writer must try to give life to the subject—through details, historical analysis, comparisons, descriptions, storytelling, quotations from others, and so forth.

Example

A definition of a dormitory student:

> A dormitory student is one who lives on campus, not too far from the classrooms, not very far from the next meal, never very far from the action. Whether in the more highly supervised freshman buildings or in the more free senior residences, dorm students can always count on companionship. These students form the core of on-campus life, taking part in activities long after the 2:30 commuters have headed down the highways.

They run the clubs. They act in the plays; they sit in the audiences. Even on weekends, they often turn to the school for friendship and entertainment. Academically, too, they have some advantages: easy access to the library, to the tutors, and to other students with the experience to help them. Without the distractions of home or apartments, they can concentrate on being students.

Warm-Up

Write a paragraph in which you define something personal (a truly bad day), something requiring specialized knowledge (a job as a store manager), or something requiring research (Post-traumatic Stress Disorder). Remember, essay definition must be more interesting than words about words.

What Is Digital Video Imaging?

(paragraph)

Jonathan Hart (student)

In this paragraph, a professional photographer defines a new way to take pictures—one that saves time and improves the satisfaction of the subjects. Notice that this definition is not entirely objective. The writer explains that he wanted to give a "human dimension" to this definition before he got into the technical aspects.

Thinking Ahead What could the writer possibly do to arouse interest in his definition? Are you able to define a "technical" subject about which you are informed?

So you hate to have your picture taken—even in a studio? You practice your best smile, but you come out looking like a phoney? You arrange every strand of hair, yet you come out in disarray? You like only one pose in the set, but unfortunately, that's the one with your eye half closed? As a professional photographer, I can't help agreeing with you. Until the most recent advance in studio photography, Digital Video Imaging, it was hard to avoid the funny smiles, the wild hair, and the nervous twitches. Now, however, it's easier to get a perfect picture before you leave the studio, one you helped to design, one selected from thousands of possible prints. DVI, which combines Super VHS video techniques with Digital computer capabilities, allows the creation of standard color pictures from images originally recorded on video tape. With a normal hand-held Super

VHS camcorder and TV monitors placed where both you and the photographer can see them, possible poses and expressions, hair-do's and clothing can be observed and modified as the tape is being created. You see what the viewfinder sees. You can control the shots. And afterwards, you can select the best ones from the tape. These images are then locked into a computer that replicate the exact pattern of dots from which the original high-resolution tape was made, dots that are entirely invisible to the naked eye. Think of it as a puzzle with half a million pieces that the computer takes apart and puts together again—all in a sixtieth of a second. With DVI, it takes only minutes for you to view the proofs, select the images, and print the negatives that you yourself helped to create. This kind of photography may make your "I hate to have my picture taken" blues a thing of the past.

QUESTIONS

A. Discovering Meaning

1. What is DVI?
2. Why is it preferable to the older methods of studio photography?

B. Examining Method

1. What is the purpose of this paragraph?
2. What is the writer's attitude toward the subject? How do you know?
3. Why does the writer ask the questions at the beginning of the paragraph?
4. How is the paragraph organized (see pages 374–378)?
5. Why is the puzzle image appropriate (see pages 400–403, 431–433)?
6. What is the connection between the opening sentence and the concluding one?

C. Shifting Focus

1. How does process work as part of this definition (see pages 92–95)?
2. This writer uses the second person "you" address. Why? How else could this information be presented? What changes would be necessary?
3. If the writer were not impressed with this new method of photography, how could the same information be used against DVI?
4. Does this paragraph also work as argumentation (see pages 180–183)?

SUGGESTIONS FOR DISCUSSION AND WRITING

A. Using Definition

1. Write a definition of a technical subject about which you are informed. If you need to supplement your knowledge with research or information from interviews, acknowledge your sources. If you can, try to focus on "the latest" in a particular area. Be sure to consider your own attitude toward this development; not all "new" ideas are "bright."

B. Exploring the Options

1. Write a definition that also works as an argument either for or against the subject. Define "Star Wars," for example, or "The Dormitory Residence Rules," while at the same time making your opinion known.

Finding the Missing Penny

(paragraph)

Garbrielle King (student)

This paragraph is part of a longer paper in which an accounting major attempts to define what being an accountant really is. By elaborating on the pleasures she finds in it, she also suggests her attitude toward it. About writing this, Garbrielle says, "My first draft stayed too general (see page 400), so that it was hard to tell what I really knew about the job. The details in later drafts helped."

Thinking Ahead What kinds of details might be used to "define" a job? Think of aspects of a job you hope to have or already do have and brainstorm to think of some details.

> But aside from the chance to play around with cash (even if it's other people's), and to make a better than average salary, accountants love to take on a challenge. They even love the unglamorous job of balancing books. When, for example, my total reads $2,736.03 and the bank statement reads $2,736.02, I take a deep breath and gear up. Never would I try to bury that missing penny. Oh, no! I put my coffee break on hold, I take the phone off the hook and stick it deep inside my desk drawer,

I gather ledger sheets, checks (sometimes 300 of them), deposits, oversized journal sheets, and miscellaneous credit memos, and I start to add. I add and add again. My fingers ache. My electric machine shoots out total after total, sometimes as much as $1,000.00 off, sometimes almost back down to the penny. Things usually get worse before they get better, but no matter what the totals, I love the whooshing sound of that machine. I do finger exercises and return to the sheets. Until I find the penny, I'm never sure I will, but I keep reminding myself that not many pennies get by me undetected. And then, maybe minutes, maybe hours after I began the search, I *find* it—buried in the ledger cards, lurking in the journal entries, or hidden in the missing deposit receipts. But I find it, and, like most accountants, I'm happy. Maybe it's the Sherlock Holmes in us. Admittedly, it takes a certain kind of person to love this job. But I guess I'm one of them.

QUESTIONS

A. Discovering Meaning

1. Based on this paragraph, write a definition of an accountant as "one who. . . ."
2. What does the writer like about accounting?
3. How does she handle an off-balance account?

B. Examining Method

1. How does the writer develop this paragraph as part of a definition (see pages 277–281)?
2. What is the purpose of the first sentence (see pages 277–281)?
3. How does this paragraph help you to understand the nature of the job?
4. Which details contribute best to your understanding of her feelings?
5. Notice that every sentence adds a new piece of information, however small. Choose one of these small details and discuss its effect (see pages 400–403).
6. What is the tone of this piece? (How does the writer see *herself* and her subject?) (See pages 421–422.)
7. What is the meaning of the comparison to Sherlock Holmes near the end?

C. Shifting Focus

1. Is this paragraph part of an objective definition?
2. Does the writer intend to influence the feelings of the reader?

SUGGESTIONS FOR DISCUSSION AND WRITING

A. Using Definition

1. Write a definition of a job or a situation with which you are familiar. Be sure to consider your attitude and your purpose in addressing this to a reader.
2. Write a definition of accounting or some other job as if the writer strongly disliked the subject.

B. Exploring the Options

1. Defend your choice of career against those who may think of it as unwise or unappealing (see pages 180–183).
2. Compare this paragraph to the paper by Tien Truong (pages 12–14). Consider purpose, tone, audience, details, and whatever else seems important to you.

One Man's Briar Patch

(paragraph)

Laurel DeWolf (student)

This paragraph is from a longer paper on family vacations in Nova Scotia. Here the writer defines what her grandparents' raspberry patch was to the children of the family. Laurel explains, "My biggest problem was that I found myself wanting to tell *everything* I loved about my experiences over the years in the raspberry patch. I had to select though, or I wouldn't have a clear definition."

Thinking Ahead How does the writer bring life to her definition of the raspberry patch? Can you find some meaning in a place that had (or still has) special meaning to you? How would you choose to define it?

To my mother, father, uncles, aunts, and grandparents, the raspberry bushes were just a tangle of abandoned, scratchy vines. To us six kids, they were a secret, romantic hideout forbidden to adults. We could spend all day in the tangles, build forts by burroughing through the leaves beneath the bushes and by working the branches around to make the walls. We also made a booby trap, a one-foot deep hole with long grass deceptively spread across it to protect us from invasion. We weren't really trying to trip up the adults, but it was fun to set it for each other, evening up the grass and making the hole as hard as possible to see. Every once in a while, I'd forget and go tumbling into the hole and sprawling onto the trail. After I scrambled up, I was all the more clever at setting the trap for the next victim. We also kept the paths through the bushes trampled down with our running; it was a small highway system, without road signs or stoplights. And on a good autumn day, I could get full just standing in one place eating the juicy berries all around me. Grandparents, parents, aunts, and uncles didn't understand the bushes. They didn't know about our forts, our trap, our trails, our feasts . . . our pleasure being out of their sight for so long.

QUESTIONS

A. Discovering Meaning

1. How would the adults define the raspberry patch?
2. How do the children define it?
3. What are the specific things the children like about it?

B. Examining Method

1. Why does she list the adults in the first sentence?
2. Which details best capture the attitude of the children (see pages 400–403)?
3. What is the purpose of the last sentence (see pages 435–439)?
4. What is the tone of this paragraph (see pages 421–422)?

C. Shifting Focus

1. How does contrast help to define the raspberry patch more sharply (see pages 33–35)?
2. How does description contribute to this definition (see pages 253–258)?

SUGGESTIONS FOR DISCUSSION AND WRITING

A. Using Definition

1. Try to define what a particular place was, or is, to you. Remember to consider tone as well as details.
2. Write a definition paper that reflects possible variations in meaning of a particular subject—abortion, drunk-driving roadblocks, communism, flunking our of college (see pages 364–366)

B. Exploring the Options

1. Describe a place, a situation, or a scene in which a difference between the attitude of adults and the attitude of younger people is clearly felt. (See pages 33–35 for a discussion of comparison and pages 128–129 for Kafka's account of a situation in which he and his father failed to see eye to eye. You might also want to read about description on pages 253–258.)
2. Write your definition of something *through* description. (One student defined *cruelty* by describing a young child's treatment of his elderly grandmother.)

Habit

(paragraph)

William James

Philosopher William James (1842–1910), the elder brother of novelist Henry James, got his medical degree at Harvard University. During years of teaching and doing research there, he wrote often on psychology and philosophy, including *Principles of Psychology* (1890) and *The Varieties of Religious Experience* (1902). This is a brief paragraph of definition in which James typically tries to understand what makes people behave the way they do, in this case, out of habit.

Thinking Ahead What do you think "habit" is? Can you think of situations in which you behaved out of habit? Can habits be changed?

Habit alone keeps us all within the bounds of ordinance, and saves the children of fortune from the envious uprisings of the poor. It alone prevents the hardest and most repulsive walks of life from being deserted by those brought up to tread therein. It keeps the fisherman and the dock-hand at sea through the winter; it holds the miner in his darkness, and nails the countryman to his log cabin and his lonely farm through all the months of snow; it protects us from invasion by the natives of the desert and the frozen zones. It dooms us all to fight out the battle of life upon the lines of our nurture or our early choice, and to make the best of a pursuit that disagrees, because there is no other for which we are fitted, and it is too late to begin again. It keeps different social strata from mixing. Already at the age of twenty-five you see the professional mannerism settling down on the young [salesman], on the young doctor, on the young minister, on the young [lawyer]. You see the little lines of cleavage running through the character, the tricks of thought, the prejudices, the ways of the "shop," in a word, from which the man can by and by no more escape than his coat-sleeve can suddenly fall into a new set of folds. On the whole, it is best he should not escape. It is well for the world that in most of us, by the age of thirty, the character has set like plaster, and will never soften again.

VOCABULARY

mannerism, cleavage

QUESTIONS

A. Discovering Meaning

1. What is the dictionary definition of *habit?*
2. In his definition of the word, what is the writer's main point?

B. Examining Method

1. What are the differences between the dictionary definition of *habit* and James's paragraph?
2. What is the meaning and purpose of sentence 2 (see pages 431–433)?
3. Why does the writer mention the "fisherman," the "dock-hand," and other occupations (see pages 400–403)?
4. What is the effect of the image, "nails the countryman to his log cabin . . ." (see pages 431–433)?

5. What is James's attitude toward habit?
6. Is this definition objective?
7. What is James's purpose in writing it?

C. Shifting Focus

1. James is known for his apt use of imagery. Explain two comparisons used in this paragraph (see pages 431–433).
2. What evidence do you see of James's background in psychology?
3. What was your experience while you were reading and understanding this paragraph? Did your second and third reading differ from your first? Explain. If the reading became easier, what helped to clarify meaning for you?
4. Compare James's comments about the "little cleavage running through the character" with the paragraph by King on page 158.

SUGGESTIONS FOR DISCUSSION AND WRITING

A. Using Definition

1. Write a definition of a frequently used term: *truth, love, happiness, loyalty, procrastination, sportsmanship.* You might, as James does, focus on situations in which this term applies and also consider trying to make some comparisons (see pages 431–433).
2. Write a definition of some other influence that might keep us living with "our nurture" or "our early choice."

B. Exploring the Options

1. Do you sense any evidence of "the professional mannerism" beginning to settle on you, the "little lines of cleavage running through the character, the tricks of thought, the prejudices . . .?" Try to identify and account for them.
2. In his last sentence, James says, "It is well for the world that in most of us, by the age of thirty, the character has set like plaster, and will never soften again." Do you agree with this comment? Are there any parts of you that are already set like plaster?

What Are Steroids?

Philip DePalma

Philip DePalma is a professor of Biology at Salem State College. This paper is a scientific definition. Notice the focus on technical detail and the careful distinctions that are made among scientific terms. About writing this, Professor DePalma says, "I was happy to work on a written definition of steroids, substances I would like more people to understand better."

Thinking Ahead What do you expect from a strictly scientific definition? Are you familiar with a subject that requires specific, careful definition for true understanding?

Steroids are lipids derived from cholesterol. Their classification as lipids, a group of compounds that includes fats, oils, and waxes, is based on their solubility—relatively insoluble in water, but quite soluble in organic solvents such as ether. All steroids share an identical molecular unit of four interlocking carbon rings, but they differ in the position of certain double bonds within the rings and in the type and position of side groups bonded to the ring structure. Often these structural differences are very small, but they may result in molecules of strikingly different functions—testosterone in men, and progesterone in women, for example. Steroids are widely found in nature, occurring in fungi, plants, animals, and they show an equally wide variety of biological activities, functioning as vitamins (vitamin D), as structural components of cell membranes (cholesterol), and as hormones (male and female sex hormones, cortisone, aldosterone, etc.). 1

Some steroid hormones are crucial in the maintenance of homeostasis, 2 i.e., the physiologically optimal conditions for life. The sex hormones, for example, guide the anatomical, physiological, and behavioral changes that mark human sexual development. In the early embryo, they induce formation of the primary sexual characteristics (testes or ovaries), and they initiate the development of secondary sexual characteristics (genitalia, etc.). At puberty, when both primary and secondary sexual characteristics become functional, steroid hormones are again extremely important, regulating sperm production, the menstrual cycle, and pregnancy. Other steroid hormones regulate the metabolism of carbohydrates and proteins and still others regulate salt and water balance in the body.

Like all hormones, steroid hormones are secreted by endocrine glands 3 and are carried to their various targets by the bloodstream. Unlike other kinds of hormones, however, steroids initiate activity in these target cells by activation of genes. They tune a cell to its specific hormone in much the same way that a radio can be tuned to one wavelength. The problem of pseudohermaphroditism, for example, or the apparent "feminization" of chromosomal males, is a result of a defective gene's preventing the testosterone from affecting the target organ. The radio is out of tune.

From conception to death, human development is guided by strictly regulated gene action, the switching of genes on and off at the proper time in the developmental history of the individual. And steroid hormones, like a wide variety of other natural and environmental factors, contribute to this timely regulation. They set off significant chain reactions. After entering the target, for example, the hormone binds to a specific protein receptor molecule, thus activating the receptor which in turn binds to specific regions of DNA known as transcriptional enhancers. The gene then undergoes a process called "transcription," the product of which is messenger RNA, which itself associates with ribosomes and undergoes "translation." Finally, the product of this translation is the protein whose structure and function has been informed by the activated gene. This steroid "informing" and turning on and off of genetic action determines the developmental sequence of life. 4

Because of these many and complex functions, and the influence on so many important life systems, steroids are often used for medical purposes, including treatment of arthritis and other inflammatory diseases, fertility disorders, some metabolic disorders, disorders of menopause, and birth control. Long-term use of some of these preparations can, however, cause side effects worse than the condition being treated: high blood pressure, heart disturbances, excessive hair growth, emotional and mental aberrations, lowered resistance to certain infection, increased susceptibility to peptic ulcers, brittle bones, and deficiencies in the immune system. Steroids must be used with caution. 5

Anabolic steroids, for example, synthetic variants of testosterone, were developed in Germany in the 1930's. Searching for a drug that would reduce the effects of muscle-wasting disorders or the muscle atrophy of patients immobilized for long periods, German scientists turned to the synthetic steroid, the modified form of the natural hormone. They hoped to stimulate increased muscle mass without the masculinizing effects of testosterone. In this they and many others were somewhat successful, but often with significant, undesirable side effects. These synthetics sometimes interfered with the normal production of testosterone and led to such serious problems as shrinkage of the testes, enhancement of breast development, and with long-term use, impotence, kidney and liver damage, cancer, heart disease, failure to achieve full stature in adolescents, plus emotional and behavioral disorders often marked by an increase in aggressive, even violent, behavior. 6

In spite of these problems, however, by 1960, athletes—often on the advice of their coaches—began experimenting with the synthetic compounds in an effort to enhance muscle mass and strength. And in fact, almost thirty years later, use of these steroids among athletes remains common. But even among those in athletic training, there is considerable disagreement about the efficacy and value of such use. These synthetic steroids may indeed increase muscle mass, but what of the risks? 7

The international medical community, on the other hand, shares none 8 of these doubts, being convinced that the risks far outweigh any benefits these drugs may provide to the athlete. Most athletic associations now ban their use and many major athletic events are now requiring testing of the competitors. Ideally, the trend will be away from using synthetic steroids simply to increase muscle mass.

VOCABULARY

solubility (1), anatomical (2), physiological (2). metabolism (2), enhancers (4), aberrations (5)

QUESTIONS

A. Discovering Meaning

1. What is the basic, brief, definition of steroids?
2. In this extended definition of steroids, what are the important facts that further clarify meaning?
3. In addition to definition, what information does the writer provide?

B. Examining Method

1. What is the main purpose of this piece?
2. What is the secondary purpose (see pages 368–371)?
3. How does the diction reflect the intentions of the writer (see pages 422–423
4. What is the tone (see pages 421–422)?
5. For what audience has this piece been written (see pages 370–371)?
6. What is the purpose of the example in paragraph 3?
7. What is the intention of the comparison to the radio, also in paragraph 3?
8. Why are anabolic steroids discussed near the end of the piece?
9. What kind of introduction does the writer use? How does it relate to the conclusion?

C. Shifting Focus

1. How does the scientific information earlier in the piece affect the reading of the comments on anabolic steroids near the end of the piece?

2. If this piece were intended *primarily* as an argument against the use of anabolic steroids, what changes would be necessary (see pages 180–183)?

SUGGESTIONS FOR DISCUSSION AND WRITING

A. Using Definition

1. Write your own definition of something that requires exact knowledge and vocabulary—deconstruction, Reconstruction, the search-and-seizure law, parity. Remember to develop the discussion so that the uninitiated reader will be able to comprehend your meaning.

B. Exploring the Options

1. Read the two other pieces on steroids in this book, found on pages 144–146 and pages 292–294. Analyze in detail the differences in approaches, paying particular attention to purpose, tone, and audience.

2. Based on research on anabolic steroids, write your own report on their effectiveness and dangers.

Portrait of a Credit Card Junkie

Lisa Amore (student)

Here a student defines what it is to be a addicted to the use of credit cards. She defines her addiction mostly through what she does as a result of her addiction. Notice her tone. About writing this paper, Lisa says, "This paper was one of the easiest I've ever written, probably because I'm so involved in the topic, but I think that to write better stuff, I need to *live* more." See the discussion of tone on pages 421–422.

Thinking Ahead What kinds of details might help a writer to define an addiction to credit cards? Do you know of any similar addictions or passions? Could you define one of them according to the behavior it produces?

My mess began in the fall of '86. I got my first credit card: a Weathervane charge. It gave me an unfamiliar sense of power and prestige. It enabled me to purchase an "emergency" pair of jeans on a whim, never even worrying about my empty wallet, and from then on I was hooked. It also opened up a new world to me, the world of credit. Buy now, pay later. Much later. Unfortunately, this "new wealth" can be intoxicating. And despite my now enormous debts (approximately $2,500.00), I still want more cards. I'm addicted to them. 1

The Weathervane charge led me to apply for more store charges. While racking up the bills to the limit in one store, I got cards to do the same thing in two other stores as soon as I had to. Filene's and Cherry, Webb & Touraine were added to my options. With new credit adding up to $1,300.00 in these stores, I once again felt powerful. I could buy clothes I couldn't afford, and I did. My motto was, "If you charge it, it's free." Calvin Klein, Esprit, and Liz Claiborne called out to me, begging to be purchased. And I, spineless and materialistic, bought brand names until my closet and drawers overflowed. Some of these clothes remain in my closet, like the red Esprit shirt with huge purple and green polka dots, my "clown shirt." 2

The cards let me shop whenever I wanted, three days before, three days after pay day, anytime. Money didn't matter. If I was depressed, or mad, or happy, I'd go to the Methuen Mall. I once spent $50.00 at The Gap because I'd had a fight with my typewriter. If the weather was warm, I'd buy a new skirt for school. If it was cold, I'd buy a sweater (Liz's, of course). It didn't really matter what I needed, or what I bought. I just had to come home with something. Even socks and underwear could satisfy me for a while. 3

Soon, however, the three cards weren't enough. I wanted to reach every corner of the mall, of the state. Plus, I had reached my limit on those cards. So I applied for a bank card. Arlington Trust turned down my application because of "insufficient credit experience." Who were they kidding? I could spend on credit better than anyone I knew. So I applied for a Citibank Visa with a student application. And I got it. Seven hundred and fifty dollars to spend anywhere in the country! What a rush! The first thing I bought was a pair of $20.00 sunglasses, expensive to me. I treated them like gold, staying careful not to lose them. Then I went on a spree in Rockport, buying any trinket that caught my eye . . . like a stuffed toy lobster. I also spent plastic money on music tapes. I didn't know that much about the music, but if I liked the name of the group or the cover of the package, I bought it. I have a suitcase full of unheard, un-payed-for tapes. 4

This particular spree lasted only a few months. Considering I shopped at every free moment, I'm surprised I could drag out the $750.00 for so 5 long. At my limit again, I had to budget (a dirty word) my charging so I wouldn't get a humiliating "denied" at the register. The intoxication began to wane as I put boundaries on my spending. But then one day I got a letter from Citibank. They were offering me a Master Card with a limit of $1,600.00 (probably because I was such a good customer). I signed the form immediately and bought myself another "credit high."

The Master Card arrived in May and got "maxed out" before Christmas. 6
I got my summer wardrobe out of it, much of it never worn. The white pumps are still in their box; I hate white shoes. But I had to buy *something* in Boston, didn't I? When I needed to go Christmas shopping, all I could find in my Liz wallet was a pack of useless charge cards. I had no room on any of them. So I got an American Express.

It's been a few months since my last shopping spree, right around the 7
time I spent to the limit on my Amex card. I miss shopping, and I still get hot flashes when I pass The Gap, knowing I can only window shop. the trouble with Amex is that I have to pay in full at the end of every billing period. I had to take a part-time job just to pay off my other "minimum monthly payments" let alone these full payments. Amex is not for the pair of jeans on a whim. I did finally pay off Wheathervane bill, but I need a shopping fix. I'm in as much debt as my friend who bought a car, but I have nothing much to show for it except some unworn clothes and white pumps. Citibank didn't raise my limit when my Visa expired. I was depressed for a week and I couldn't even go to Benetton to cheer up. So I applied for a Shawmut Visa. I'm still waiting.

QUESTIONS

A. Discovering Meaning

1. Based on the writer's experience, how would you define a credit card junkie?

2. How does she spend a major part of her time?

B. Examining Method

1. How does the writer develop the comparison between her own addiction and that of a "junkie" (see pages 431–433)?

2. Is the comparison appropriate and effective for describing her attitude toward credit cards?

3. Which details help you best to understand her problems?

4. What is the writer's attitude toward this addiction (see pages 421–422)?

5. How do you feel about her addiction? Do you share her attitude?

C. Shifting Focus

1. Does the tone of this piece seem consistent with the content (see pages 421–422)?
2. What changes would be necessary if the writer were deeply concerned about her problem? Rewrite a single paragraph with this message in mind.

SUGGESTIONS FOR DISCUSSION AND WRITING

A. Using Definition

1. Write a definition of a particular type of person by describing behavior drawn from personal experience or from observation—for example, an athletic superstar, a professional student, a gambler, a ladies' man, or a sports fan. (You might define your own "ruling passion.")
2. Based on research, define a particular kind of "addictive" behavior—either positive, like a passion for running, or negative, like drug abuse.

B. Exploring the Options

1. Write a letter to Lisa, in which you make suggestions about how she can break her "junkie" habit. Be sure to consider your own tone in this letter.
2. As one cartoonist put it, shopping has become America's new "national pastime." What do you think of the American attitude toward shopping?
3. Read the essay by de Tocqueville on page 322 and discuss what he might say about this essay and the larger issue of happiness in the midst of American plenty.

Watching the Watchers

Ann Taylor

Ann Taylor is a professor of English at Salem State College, where she teaches courses in literature and in writing. She also contributes essays to scholarly journals, newspapers, and magazines. In this piece, written for the Massachusetts Audubon Society, she attempts to define what bird-watching is, partly from what others say about the subject and partly from personal experience. About writing this piece, please see the comments in the "Process" section of this book (pages 368–369).

Thinking Ahead Based on your experience, how would you define bird watching? Are you familiar enough with some hobby or special interest to write a definition of it?

Far from New England, at Italy's Lake Avernus, I'm birdwatching again—or watching for a bird again. Here at this "Birdless Place" of ancient mythology, the poisonous entrance to the Underworld where it was thought no bird could safely fly, I'm looking for a particular little bird—just like the one I photographed twelve years ago. Annually afflicted with watching my slides of Virgilian sites, my classics students have annually declared my bird to be a speck of dust on the film, but I *know* I saw a bird. I remember *wanting* to see a bird at Avernus, and I remember finding one—way beyond my talents as a birdwatcher, but definitely of the small speck species. And I'm here to make another, more convincing slide. 1

As near as I can tell, it was literature that nudged me into watching birds, not only this unidentified speck at Virgil's Avernus, but other literary birds—troubadours' and minnesingers' birds, Dante's and Chaucer's, Keat's and Shelly's; Poe's, Eliot's and Frost's. I recall no particular spark of recognition that flamed into an urge to buy binoculars and a field guide and to set out in hot pursuit, but I can remember my first sure black-capped chickadee. It wasn't exactly an epiphany chickadee, though, as were the special towhees, scarlet tanagers, or green woodpeckers for so many watchers. 2

All I *can* recall is a steadily growing curiosity while reading passages like those in *Walden* where Thoreau follows the devious progress of the loon, "It was a pretty game, played on the smooth surface of the pond, a man against a loon," or where he listens to the owl's "Hoo hoo hoo, hoorer hoo," and exclaims with characteristic directness, "I rejoice that there are owls." Literature and birds are often allied, so often in fact that a graduate student recently asked if a life-list should be required for an M.A. in English (probably not a bad idea). 3

Others come to birdwatching for other reasons, almost as many reasons as there are watchers, and they have just as many reasons for staying with it. To some, it is a sport, a game of recognition, a satisfaction of the hunting and collecting instincts. To others, it is freedom from the artificiality and gadgetry of the man-made, a "ventilation of the psyche," or an opportunity to monitor the environment with an "ecological litmus paper." And to still others, more mystically inclined, it is a pursuit of tranquility, of mystery, of enlightenment, a "quickening of our loftiest compulsions." For many, it is a mixture of all of these. 4

In a much-quoted passage, James Fisher summarizes some possible approaches to birdwatching: 5

> The observation of birds may be a superstition, a tradition, an art, a science, a pleasure, a hobby or a bore; this depends entirely on the nature of the observer.

And more humorously, Joseph Hickey explains:

> By some, it is regarded as a mild paralysis of the central nervous system, which can be cured only by rising at dawn and sitting in a bog. Others regard it as a harmless occupation of children, into which maiden aunts may sometimes relapse.

Now that my motivation is beyond literary annotation, I'm not sure 6
where, among these many types, I would place myself (although I have yet to sit in a bog at dawn for any reason), but I *am* sure I could place many other watchers that I have met in the field. Not surprisingly, I have yet to flush out a cliché birdwatcher (the knobby-kneed simpleton clad in pith helmet, striped shirt, baggy plaid shorts, argyles, and lumpy shoes). My discoveries have been real, not cartoon birdwatchers—some bored, some frustrated, some pretentious, some downright unpleasant, but my favorites worthy of my private birdwatchers' life-list.

I think of the elderly, white-haired gent in a three-piece suit striding 7
from his Illinois Mercedes to Newburyport Harbor to see the visiting Ross' gull. Using his cane like an oar, he propelled himself over a muddy rut and asked breathlessly, "Is he still there?" I think also of the elderly woman, an "old school marm," she said, sitting alone at the rail of the Atlantic-tossed boat, without binoculars but with a firm grip, as the waves poured from the hood of her red cape to the toes of her L. L. Bean boots. She was waiting for a parasitic jaeger. I was inspired that they were so inspired so late in life.

I think too of the watchers at Mt. Wachusett where, every October, 8
thousands of hawks migrate down the Eastern Flyway, riding the thermals with wings stretched flat. The hilltop is prickly with scopes focused long distance in all directions. The mood is relaxed, expectant; that is, until "Kettle of sharpies at two o'clock!" or "Two red-tails trailing left of tower, above the horizon!" sends everyone scurrying. Here I rely on the regulars, who follow the count for days straight and who know their hawks. By the time I decide if a hawk's shin is sharp or not, he'll be sunning in South America, so I quiz the drivers with the "HAWK" or "RAPTOR" license plates and listen for their directions as the birds rise in chaotic spirals above my head—way above my head.

I have met other devotees, the ones who keep not only life-lists, but 9
year, country, state, day, trip, yard, and back-step lists, the ones who wear sweatshirts dedicated to various birdy brethren, and who may well drift off to sleep with visions of 700 lists for a North American year or life-lists with all 8,600-plus worldwide species. On a pelagic trip to Stellwagen Bank, I watched in amazement as some of this type took a humpback

whale in stride, got mildly stirred by a jaeger and a shearwater, but danced with delight as the Sabine's gull emerged from a flock of unremarkables.

"A Sabine's! I can't believe it!" yelled one, as she rummaged through her "Le Bag" for her checklist. 10

"I *thought* it was, but I didn't dare call, because you'd all think I was crazy!" shouted another, dashing to the opposite rail as the boat drifted into a turn. This Sabine's was a life-lister for many of them—old salts of the seabird set (and certainly for me, as were the jaeger and the shearwater). But *I* can still have life-lister thrills in my backyard. 11

They were enthusiasts all, but no birder seemed more enthusiastic than the warbler-watcher of a recent spring on Marblehead Neck. "There are days you'd *kill* for a Wilson's," he said, looking more like an Olympic wrestler than a warbler fan. Almost concealing his binoculars in one huge hand, he focused again on the young birch, "Now take a look at that! Must be 15 in one tree!" Settling on a log at the edge of the clearing, he confessed, "I had to take a day off from work last week 'cause everything that moved began to look like a warbler." Focusing again on the birch he mumbled, "Never saw so many Wilson's," then turning to me, he asked, "By the way, did you see the elusive bay-breasted on the way in here?" Answering that I had seen only a prominent Blackburnian, he looked disappointed, heaved himself off the log and headed back down the trail. "Gotta get that bay-breasted," he sighed, and disappeared into the shadows. 12

Bird artist Lee Jacques once said, "The difference between a warbler and no warblers is very slight," but to the Marblehead watcher, warblers were no slight affair. I hope he got his bay-breasted. 13

These devoted watchers give me courage for the occasional "yellow-bellied sapsucker" joke or for comments like the one from a student who wondered, "Why watch a bird anyway? I can see eating 'em, but just going out watching 'em? No way!" Against such critics, the best watchers make me confident, but when I'm actually in their company, my confidence takes wing. I am inspired by their enthusiasm, but more often awed, even intimidated, by their quick identifications. My comma on the Atlantic horizon is a Manx shearwater to them. My six little birds in a tree are a Wilson's, a parula, three yellows, and a redstart to them. I wouldn't call a bird in their presence if it matched itself up personally with the sketch in my field guide. 14

Probably because of this insecurity, I was delighted to find a passage by E. B. White where he comments on the autumn Chestnut-sided Warbler's lemon-colored shade of green: 15

> Well, it is sufficient for recognition if you happen to be standing, or lying, directly under a Chestnut-sided Warbler in the fall of the year and can remember not to confuse the issue with "adults in spring" or with the Bay-breast at *any* season—specially the *female* Bay-

> breast in spring, which is rather dim and indistinct, the way all birds look to me when they are in a hurry (which they almost always are) or when I am.

Considering how often I share White's frustration, particularly in pursuit of those little avian no-see-ums, I doubt if I would qualify for passage through Peterson's three stages—looker, to lister, to full-fledged watcher. I have no list beyond a spotty life-list; I've never had a Big Day or even a Small One; and I've yet to memorize the chirps, squawks, twitters, thumps, and trills on the Cornell Laboratory's bird-song tapes. I've never studied bird skins or courtship habits. I've never graduated to ecology, breeding bird censuses, banding, conservation, or life histories. Nor have I fallen from a cliff, been attacked by a tawny owl or a lammergeier, or been chased by tribesmen, bandits, bulls, whales, or a flock of frantic flamingos—all documented by Peterson as tell-tale markings of the full-fledged. I haven't even become philosophical about the role of birds in my life or in anyone else's. 16

But I have found myself patting a stuffed dovekie and trailing through the marshy eel grass on Monomoy watching for a Bald Eagle affectionately named E11. I have crawled over craggy boulders for a photo of a feeding puffin, and I have stood in snowy woods while a tape recorder conversed with a Barred Owl. I have held the feathery vitality of an Ovenbird while someone else placed a band on its leg and then felt the peculiar thrill of releasing it to the nearby maple. And I have sat content for an hour while two male mallards competed for a coy female, our guide saying little beyond, "Now *there's* some behavior." I have also made it to my second Peterson *Guide* (autographed at his lecture on penguins). 17

More recently, on re-reading Beston's *Outermost House*, I have been convinced by his comments on birds: 18

> In a world older and more complete than ours they move finished and complete, gifted with extensions of the senses we have lost or never attained, living by voices we shall never hear. They are not our brethren, they are other nations, caught with ourselves in the net of life and time, fellow prisoners of the splendour and travail of the earth.

The longer I watch the birds, the more right he seems to be. Even Wallace Stevens' "Thirteen Ways of Looking at a Blackbird" makes greater sense to me, particularly Stanza V:

> I do not know which to prefer,
> The beauty of inflections
> Or the beauty of innuendoes,
> The blackbird whistling
> Or just after.

Birdwatching helps me read better and, although I'm not full-fledged yet, I may be sprouting some feathers after all.

Here at Lake Avernus, I have just counted 20 kittiwakes soaring over 19
the ancient crater, and I have an indisputable slide for my next twelve years of classics students. I *would* like another try at that small speck though.

VOCABULARY

pelagic (9)

QUESTIONS

A. Discovering Meaning

1. Based on the information provided in this piece, how would you define bird-watching?
2. On what kinds of sources does the writer draw for this definition?

B. Examining Method

1. How does this essay open? How is the introduction related to the conclusion? (See pages 435–439.)
2. What is the writer's attitude toward birds and bird-watchers?
3. What is the writer's attitude toward herself (see pages 421–422)?
4. This piece was written for the members of the Massachusetts Audubon Society. What are the clues? (See pages 370–371.)
5. What is the purpose of the references to professional ornithologists and bird-watchers (see pages 400–403)?
6. How do the literary references and quotations relate to the meaning of the piece?
7. Why is the "private birdwatchers' life-list" included?
8. Why is the bird-watcher of paragraph 10 described and quoted?

C. Shifting Focus

1. This definition includes passages of cause and effect and of exemplification. How do these passages contribute to the overall definition?

2. What would be the effect of removing the personal experience passages from this definition?

SUGGESTIONS FOR DISCUSSION AND WRITING

A. Using Definition

1. Write a paper defining some interest or hobby, based, if possible, on some combination of personal experience, observation, and reading. What is numismatics, dirt-racing, coaching?
2. Write a definition of some interest or hobby of which you are not fond (e.g., driving ORV's across the dunes or hunting with a bow and arrow).

B. Exploring the Options

1. Write a defense of a hobby with which you are familiar (see pages 180–183). Be sure to consider the arguments of your opponents.
2. Naturalist Aldo Leopold defines a hobby as something "in large degree useless, inefficient, laborious, or irrelevant." In relation to some hobby that interests you, discuss this definition.

Influencing Through Argument and Persuasion

In this chapter, the focus is no longer on exposition, but on argumentative writing, which includes both argumentation and persuasion. Unlike exposition, which focuses primarily on setting forth information, both categories of argumentative writing seek to influence the opinion of the reader. Argumentation works primarily through appeals to the reader's intellect, while persuasion works more through appeals to the reader's emotions. Like exposition, argumentative writing may well turn to examples, comparisons, classifications, processes, causes, effects, and definitions to make the point, but the writer's intentions are more directed to achieving the desired response from the reader. The reader's mind and heart are being pursued.

As we have seen, exposition allows the writer simply to add to the reader's treasure trove of things known. The reader may or may not be influenced by the attitude of the writer; the reader may or may not necessarily form an opinion or become emotionally engaged in the discussion. Argumentative writing, however, establishes a different relationship between the writer and the reader. The writer seeks to influence, direct, manage, stir up, enrage, or engage the reader, thus offering an invitation to agree or the pressure to care.

Within argumentation and persuasion, the proportions of facts and feelings may vary greatly, according to the intention and the attitude of the writer. So also may the desired response from the reader vary. The writer may simply seek a reader who agrees, an intellectual ally on the subject, but the writer may also want more than simple agreement. When all is said and argued out, should the reader take up a cause, get out his wallet, feel shocked, or paint up the plackards and join the picket line? It is important for the writer of argument to consider what his or her intentions are with regard to the reader. Just how does the writer want the reader to *feel* about this information? Just what does the writer want the reader to *do* with it?

Arguing by Appealing to Reason

Argumentation involves expressing opinions. It is an effort on the part of the writer to influence the thoughts of the reader. It proceeds mostly by appeals to reason, aiming for agreement based on increased understanding of the subject. Not all subjects are worth an argument, however. It is important to choose subjects about which there is some disagreement in the first place. Making a case for the cuteness of puppies may stir little interest, but one in favor of allowing pets to visit homes for the elderly might be worthwhile:

—Pets provide companionship for withdrawn and lonely patients.
—They provide the opportunity to both give and receive affection.
—They allow for "touching" and "being touched," which sometimes are missing from the experience of the elderly.
—Studies show that they can contribute to both the physical and mental well-being of elderly patients.

(The writer may or may not succeed in convincing reluctant housing administrators to open up their facilities to pets, but the argument is a reasonable attempt to make a positive case.)

As with other kinds of writing, it is possible to argue on large issues requiring some specialized knowledge or focused research, like altering the federal tax structure or impeaching a president, but it is also possible to argue on smaller issues, or those drawn more from personal experience or observation, like the need to change the town leash law, the need for additional parking for students, or the advisability of taking a year off between the last year of high school and the first year of college.

A student who is investigating campus housing may learn from someone who is opposed to off-campus housing for freshmen and argues that it fosters:

—Isolation from the campus before campus life has been experienced firsthand
—Exploitation of naïve students by unscrupulous landlords
—The temptation to party, not to study, because of being away from home and from supervision for the first time
—The possibility of postponement—three more years of off-campus living when the student is more familiar with the campus and with the best options.

(Again, these arguments may or may not succeed, but they do ask for the student to think through the opposing side of the issue.)

Aside from the obvious need for some conflict and for some convincing information in support of an idea, it is also important that the writer choose an appropriate and manageable subject.

"Answer 'yes' or 'no'," commands the television interviewer who is seeking quick responses from "the man in the street." "Should we invade Kuwait?" or "Should parents have the final say about what goes into a high school reading list?" or "Do you think Mrs. M. is guilty of child abuse?" Quick questions like these, and especially the quick answers, may well make responsible argument all the more difficult. Too often our society asks for on-the-spot opinions, with or without necessary information. In fact, thoughtful hesitation may hinder spontaneity, and after all, the show must go on. The poll must get reported.

It's "democratic" to have opinions; we have a "right" to have opinions. Film for the evening news, "talking heads" interviews in campus papers, quick quiz answers for newspapers, push-the-button instant opinion samplings on the television, either—or computer solutions to complex problems all foster a kind of glibness, a reluctance to say, "I don't know," "I need some time to think about this" or "I want some more information." This fast-forward "democracy" encourages fast, thoughtless responses and gives them a credibility and respect they rarely deserve.

When you are choosing a topic to argue, it's important to avoid this pressure for a quick opinion on just about anything. Few complex problems, few real issues can be reduced to simple yes–no, either–or resolutions. Hesitations, moderation, balance, information are not signs of weakness in argument. The "I-don't-care-if-I-understand-it-or-not; I-know-what-I-think" school of thought, is a confession of ignorance, an empty, false confidence that drives thoughtful readers away.

A lifeguard may well be able to make an informed argument about the inadequate safety regulations at the nearby pool. A student with personal experience and some responsible research may be ready to make a case on the use of the SAT's as an admissions tool. Someone who has taken the trouble to learn about the possible harmful effects of passive smoking may be qualified to argue against smoking in public places. Winning arguments are based on what the writer really knows or is willing to learn. Ignorance loses the the intelligent reader and the argument.

One freshman, for example, wrote that the United States was totally correct in the Vietnam War because it was saving a democratic regime in the south. Asked if he had studied the history of the war and its causes, he responded, "Well, I think I know as much as anyone" (after which he admitted that he had done no research). Here is an "F" in the making. This student does not *yet* know "as much as anyone" about the war. What about the scholars who have spent their professional lifetimes on the topic; what about the soldiers who fought in the war; what about the Vietnamese people; what about the policymakers of the time? Obviously, this student does not have to know as much as all of these people put together, but without major research, requiring a lot of time and attention, he will never be ready to argue this case convincingly, whether or not his opinion is valid.

Each subject for argumentation requires a different set of procedures—a journey deep into the heart for personal facts and figures, a excursion into the larger world of experience and information, an exploration in the library, probably for hours or days, possibly for months.

As in all writing, but more particularly in argumentation, the writer must earn the respect of the reader. Agreement is not earned through simple, or simple-minded, assertion.

WORKING WITH ARGUMENTATION

Think of the times you have said "That's ridiculous!" or "No way they should be doing that!" Here may well be a subject about which you have opinions that are serious enough for writing an argument. You need to care what someone else thinks. Convince the college to drop or add a certain requirement, argue why your father should give you an increase in your allowance, or convince an alcoholic friend to talk to the school psychologist. You may also find arguments in your own particular experiences or observations—arguments about keeping fit, about being wary of "cash-back" offers from car dealerships, about the possible "overkill" in requiring so many courses for professional majors. And with the necessary research, you may be able and eager to take on the big subjects like abortion, nuclear power, genetic engineering, deceptive language in television advertisements, environmental pollution, and the rest.

The interest in argument comes from the commitment of the writer to a certain point of view and from the quality of the information selected to make the point best. The challenge is in choosing a subject about which you are able to argue, deciding on the main purpose of your argument, and adapting it to the appropriate reader. Whose judgment are you trying to influence? Why? The writer must have the reader and the purpose in mind.

Example

An argument against off-campus housing may be written by a student who had a bad experience with a landlord:

> When I left my parents' house, I was determined to get away from watch-dogs. I wanted my own place, so I went to a big building near campus with an "Apt.

> for Rent" sign outside and took a studio apartment for what seemed like a steal. Well, it wasn't. And let me warn you, apartments aren't always what they appear to be at first sight. This place *looked* good. The walls were all a new white, and the linoleum looked washed. What I didn't see was the leak that gradually seeped through the white and turned the walls rusty, nor did I see the many entrances for mice who regularly scampered across the kitchen floor. Worse, I didn't see the "no withdrawal" clause in my lease or the landlord's small-print option to raise rents if the town raised property taxes. In short, the quality of the apartment went down as my rent went up—another $25.00 a month to a new total of $325.00. The landlord had told me the place was rent-controlled, but I learned later that he was lying, and that I had to pay. He denied ever mentioning rent control. Granted, this may not happen to you; I'm sure there are good landlords near campus. But it might be wiser to learn more before you sign on the dotted line.

(A comment like this one might be valuable for new students seeking housing near campus, maybe part of an orientation packet. The writer's goal, however, is primarily to inform, and to warn, not to stir a march on the landlord's office. If the goal were more militant, the writer would need to express more outrage and to make an appeal for public, dramatic support.)

Warm-Up

Try writing an argument for or against something about which you have both an opinion and enough information. Be sure to consider the audience and your purpose in making your case. Try to rewrite it after you have studied the following chapter.

The Search Is Off

(paragraph)

Karen Connery (student)

Karen Connery, an adult adoptee with a family of her own, gives some arguments against groups that argue for adoptees' searching out their birth parents as the only "right" thing to do. In earlier paragraphs, she writes of the tendency of these groups to attribute too many problems to the adoptees' not "knowing" and to sentimentalize the "happy" results. She also confesses a lack of need for anyone else in her already large, loving, extended family. In this paragraph, she focuses on her most important argument against the search. Karen explains, "The pressure, almost the expectation, nowadays is that adoptees *should* search. I just wanted to offer an argument on the other side. For some people it may be necessary, but I don't think the issue is as simple as the supporters make it appear."

Thinking Ahead What are some possible arguments both for and against an adoptee's searching out birth parents? Can you think of any subjects about which your opinion is different from the commonly held, current opinion? What about the delights of New Year's Eve or the importance of earning large amounts of money?

> And, in spite of my parents' willingness to have me search, I am concerned about hurting them, or possibly myself. These search groups are not there to deal with the emotional pain that may result. What about the biological child that is rejected by the long-lost parent? What about the biological parent with the unsavory past or present? What about the emotional repercussions for the adoptee within the adoptee's own family—with husband, children, brothers, sisters, and most of all, parents? I don't have the answer to these questions, but I certainly am concerned enough to ask them. I wonder why the supporters of searching don't more often share some of these concerns. I have personally known of "search" missions that turned into "search and destroy," for practically everyone involved. How can people with so little experience over time be so sure that it's the right thing for everyone? My mother and father love me and promise not to be hurt, but I fear that this is an intellectual rather than an emotional promise. The fact is, I don't need another set of parents to help me find myself. Others might; I don't. My own parents have done quite well enough and that's the way I want to leave it. I know who I am and where I came from, and I know where I am today—without my genes to tell me.

QUESTIONS

A. Discovering Meaning

1. What is the main argumentative point in this paragraph?
2. What is the writer's claim to authority in arguing this subject?

B. Examining Method

1. For what readers was this piece written (see pages 370–371)?
2. What is the writer's purpose (see pages 368–371)?
3. How does the writer want the reader to feel?
4. Why does the writer ask so many questions in this paragraph?

5. What is the tone of the paragraph (see pages 421—422)?

6. Why does the writer so often mention the opinions of the supporters of searching?

7. Why does she include references to her parents?

8. Does the paragraph build to a climax (see page 377)?

9. Do you think she succeeded in her goal for this paragraph? As a reader, how did you react? Can you identify any reason for your reaction?

C. Shifting Focus

1. If the writer were convinced that all adoptees should stop searching for their birth parents, what changes would she have to make in her argument?

2. Compare this paragraph to the longer paper by Tina Beecher on page 186. Be sure to focus on audience, purpose, tone, and the nature of the argument.

SUGGESTIONS FOR DISCUSSION AND WRITING

A. Using Argumentation

1. Write a paper in which you argue against a belief that now is commonly held as absolute wisdom (e.g., the importance of exercise or the need to travel in order to "broaden one's horizons.") You might consider simply modifying a current belief, rather than rejecting it entirely, and you might vary the tone to humorous or ironic.

2. If you feel you are well-informed, write an argumentative response to Karen's piece, or do the research necessary to write an informed argument either for or against her point.

B. Exploring the Options

1. Consider the role of the "genes" and the "environment" in creating identity—from personal experience, from interviews, or from research that has often focused on the "nature—nurture" discussion (identical twins adopted into different backgrounds, etc.), or from all of these.

2. Do the research necessary to write an informed argument either for or against the writer's attitude toward the search for adoptees by birth par-

ents. (Or you could research a single aspect of the subject, not necessarily argumentative: agencies providing search services, the history of adoption laws and procedures, case studies, psychological analyses, and so forth.)

What's Wrong with Less Than Perfect?

Tina Beecher (student)

Here a student argues from personal experience with dieting. Notice her larger purposes here, beyond simply sharing her own problems. Tina explains, "I get so tired of reading how 'awful' it is to be fat. It seems that people, even very skinny people, never feel thin enough in this society. And after our class discussion about picking realistic topics to argue, this one came to mind."

Thinking Ahead What are some possible arguments against excessive concern with dieting? Is there any other aspect of physical appearance that seems to receive too much attention?

Rice cakes are disgusting unless they're smothered with peanut butter. 1
They have no taste. I prefer cardboard to dry toast. And what is popcorn without salt and butter? Nothing to me. Diet mayonnaise ruins tuna fish. Diet margarine refuses to melt, on anything. Exercise, aerobic, of course, is necessary at least three times a week. I hate exercising. I got so bored with my health club that I quit after a couple of months. I usually feel guilty about my failures, but then I sometimes wonder about all this huff-and-puff dieting, exercising, and healthy living.

It's hard to keep track of all the good things I should be doing for 2
myself. And the truth is, I don't really want to. By the time I start to do what's good for me, I find out it's bad for me. Jogging is out; walking is in. Red meat is out; chicken-and-fish are in. Fresh fruits and leafy, green vegetables are conducive to perfect health, but then, I read that the vegetables may be sprayed with harmful chemicals, and the fruit could be treated with cyanide. Oat bran *was* the cure-all for cholesterol. They even put the stuff in waffles. I was waiting for the oat bran candy bars. Now it's on the "out" list, so I might as well enjoy my Frosted Flakes. Maybe some day they'll discover that fried chicken and hot fudge sundaes lower cholesterol too. I hope so. Or even better, maybe they'll prove that cholesterol isn't bad for you in the first place.

Six months ago I joined an expensive weight loss program. I figured 3
I'd try to keep up with the girls on television and in magazines. That's

how I'm supposed to look. Right? Every day I ate 6 ounces of protein, 3 servings of fruit, 3 servings of milk, 2 servings of bread, and all the vegetables I could eat. I measured everything I ate on a scale. And guess what? I was allowed 150 optional calories each week. This meant I could use dressing on my salad sometimes. Between meals I snacked on rice cakes, unbuttered popcorn, or raw vegetables. Inhuman. Boring. Torture. Oh, and how could I forget the eight glasses of water a day—2 in the morning, 2 with lunch, 2 at dinner, and 2 before I went to bed. And this is living? I was living at the water faucet.

After six weeks of skinless chicken and broccoli (and then more chicken, broccoli, broccoli, chicken, and broccoli), I lost fifteen pounds. I looked better, but I felt hungry and deprived. I was grouchy. I dreamed of pepperoni pizzas and french fries. Finally, I couldn't stand the monotony. I wanted to eat like a human being, not a bird, but to reach my goal weight I needed to lose ten more pounds. I still need to lose them. 4

What's wrong with pleasingly plump? I think Marilyn Monroe was one of the most beautiful women ever. She wasn't thin. Of course, if she were a star today, she'd be dragged by her platinum blonde hair to a weight loss program. I don't know what Madonna did, but she looked better to me before she lost weight. And what about Oprah Winfrey? I thought I'd have to hear about her 67-pound weight loss for the rest of my life. Now I hear about the 22 pounds she's gained back and about her chances for gaining it *all* back. Always ready with the next problem, the critics are never satisfied. Oprah promises she won't gain it all back. Of course she won't. The tabloids would love to spread the headline across the front page: OPRAH BLOWS UP! 5

The other day I was reading a women's magazine, one with those pictures of starved models and movie stars. It seemed that every other article was on eating right, losing weight, or exercising. One article was titled, "Losing That Extra Blubber." Blubber. I hate that word. It's an insult to heavier people. Do they need to be compared to whales? The article said, "People who are overweight need to learn to eat like thin people." Funny. My friends who look like Barbie Dolls survive on fast food, and they've never exercised in their lives. So much for the "thin people theory." 6

One time my mother's friend came for a visit with her baby girl. I was eating apple pie with whipped cream. I gave the baby a small bite of the cream. The mother screamed, "Oh no! Don't give her that! It's not good for her, and I don't want her to be fat!" Even a baby can't enjoy life these days. 7

I'm not trying to condemn those who choose to lead healthy lives. I want to lead a healthy life too. What I'm complaining about is the crazy pursuit of heath that actually interferes with enjoying life. Is it good to be healthy and miserable at the same time? 8

I now live day by day. One day I "pig out." The next day I eat nothing. It depends on my mood. One time I was down because my boyfriend and I had an argument. I ordered $25.00 worth of Chinese food: chicken 9 fingers, fried shrimp, fried rice, egg rolls, and beef with green peppers (no broccoli!). I ate half for dinner and the rest for breakfast the next morning. I looked four months pregnant, but I sure felt better. The white wine helped too. Maybe some day they'll discover that greasy chicken fingers heal a broken heart (chicken is better with the grease).

I know I'll never look like a fashion model or a movie star. I'll certainly 10
never look like Barbie. I guess I'll have to resign myself to looking like me—less than perfect.

QUESTIONS

A. Discovering Meaning

1. What is the writer arguing in this piece?
2. How does she back up her thesis (see pages 180–183)?
3. What is her purpose in writing this piece?
4. For what audience would this piece be most appropriate?

B. Examining Method

1. What kind of introduction does the writer use? Does it prepare the reader for the argument that follows? How?
2. What is the writer's claim to authority on the subject?
3. Were you convinced by her argument or by parts of her argument?
4. Why does she include so much detail in paragraph 3?
5. What is the tone of the argument (see pages 421–422)?
6. What is the purpose of the conclusion? Is it effective? (See pages 435–439.)
7. What is the purpose of the reference to the women's magazine in paragraph 6?

C. Shifting Focus:

1. How does the writer use examples in support of her point?
2. How might this piece be expanded into a larger research project?
3. Paragraph 7 also makes use of narrative (pages 277–281). Why does she offer this example in story form?

SUGGESTIONS FOR DISCUSSION AND WRITING

A. Using Argumentation

1. Write about some other popular attitude toward physical appearance, making a case for or against current opinion.
2. Write a response to Tina, making your own point of view clear as you communicate with her. Be sure to consider tone and purpose. How do you feel about what she has said here, and what would you like her to do with what you say to her?
3. Write on some other habit, or perhaps a fetish, in our society—for example, the use of Retin A, antismoking movements, or the right to bear arms. Remember not to claim more for your argument than you can. Bigger arguments require more research.

B. Exploring the Options

1. Do some research on attitudes toward physical appearance in other cultures or in other times. How does the current "fat is ugly" idea in America relate to this?
2. Visit a weight loss program and try to learn about the reactions of the clients to Tina's argument and write a report, or possibly an argument, about your discoveries.
3. Write a letter from Tina to either the local weight loss program or to the writer of the article on "blubber."

The Social Set

Edwin Diamond

Edwin Diamond, born in 1925, has been a reporter, a lecturer at MIT, an editor at *Newsweek,* and a science writer. He is now professor of journalism at New York University. His books include *Good News, Bad News* (1978), a study of the news media, and *The Spot: The Rise of Political Advertising on Television* (1988). "The Social Set," too, is about media, specifically television. It is argumentative, an attempt to present his point of view on the social value of television. Notice the extended introduction and conclusion.

Thinking Ahead What are some possible arguments in favor of watching television? Could you write a defense of something that is often attacked?

I suppose there are still some intellectuals who denounce television as the boob tube or idiot box. Perhaps some blinkered critics still believe in "audience flow theory"—that is, viewers sit video-tranquilized in front of the television, tuned to one channel through the evening. 1

The intellectuals and critics, of course, are as behind the times as a black-and-white television set with no remote control or videocassette attachment. Television and the television viewer have changed while the theorists weren't looking. We no longer watch television qua television: we now watch specific programs, and for specific purposes. Television has become a lively part of our social transactions, much like the out-of-town visitor whom we invite our friends to meet, or the late-arriving guest who picks up the party just before it sags. 2

Not all television, obviously, has grown up to be literate and adult; but enough has changed to warrant a systematic look at the social role of television. The contemporary role of television as social instrument recalls the earliest days of the medium: When a family on the block was the first to buy a televison set, the rest of us flocked over to marvel at the new technological wonder. No matter that the wonder brought Uncle Miltie's old burlesque routines or primitive two-camera coverage of sports[1]; television viewing was a social occasion. Later the superhype that preceded each Super Bowl drummed up more social television gatherings. Though the game seldom lived up to the advance billing, the occasion was pleasant in itself—a friendly afternoon for nursing a few drinks and noshing. 3

Special programs have also become occasions for more serious social interaction. Black friends of mine made "Roots" into a family matter, setting their children down in front of the set for each episode. Discussions would follow, and teenage children would check out the Alex Haley book from the library. Jews and their Christian friends watched the "Holocaust" series—usually separately—but met to discuss the programs the next day. 4

As might be expected, television has become a focus of social life for younger men and women, the under-thirty-five-year-olds who have grown up with the medium. A twenty-seven-year-old friend of mine recently threw a big Saturday night party with plenty of food, wine, and disco music. At 11:30 everyone sat down to watch "Saturday Night Live." The party didn't die; it shifted into a different gear, and the hostess didn't complain. 5

---

[1]Uncle Miltie": Milton Berle (b. 1908). American television entertainer.

Some of my older, more sophisticated friends find television much more of a social experience than, say, going to a Broadway play or to the movies. While no talking is allowed in the theater, social television encourages interaction between audience and set, and among the audience. The viewers can guess at the dialogue and plot of dramas, editorialize on the news, predict the Oscar winners, or single out from the semifinalists the next Miss America. It can be much more fun to talk back to the set than to sit silently in a darkened theater (the product on the screen being equal, naturally). 6

I am not claiming that social television has brought back the wit and brilliance of the salon to American homes. Social television can't replace real conversation or tête-á-têtes or a good book or a blazing fireplace or solitary thought. 7

Television has proved, on the whole, to be a good guest in the house, especially when it is not invited to perform too often. Most of our work and much of our play forces us, as individuals, into specialized roles. Even our reading materials have become like private languages—father is down at the *Wall Street Journal* or looking into his *Fortune;* mother can be found, or may be lost, in *The Women's Room;* the college kids are like a *Rolling Stone.* 8

Television can be a national tongue. At its best, television can provide a common basis for experience, maybe a few laughs, some information and insight, perhaps the chance to engage one's intelligence and imagination. In these days of runaway prices, inflated mediocrities, and deflated hopes in our public lives, that's not a bad record. Television has a standing invitation to come to my place. 9

VOCABULARY

tranquilized (1), burlesque (3), noshing (3), salon (7), tête-á-tête (7)

QUESTIONS

A. Discovering Meaning

1. What makes up Diamond's major argument for watching television?
2. Who is his intended audience?
3. What is his possible goal in writing this defense?

B. Examining Method

1. What is the implication of the title?

2. How does the writer introduce his argument? Why? (See pages 394–398.)

3. Why does he mention the "boob tube" and the "idiot box" in paragraph 1?

4. Explain the comparisons in paragraph 2. What do they imply about television? What is the relevance of these comparisons in this essay? What would the relevance be of comparing television to an uninvited guest or to a late-arriving visitor who breaks up the party? (See pages 431–433.)

5. What is the purpose of paragraph 7 (see pages 368–371)?

6. Why does Diamond personify, or give human characteristics to, the television set?

7. What role does personal experience play in this argument?

C. Shifting Focus

1. Were you convinced by this argument? Does he take enough of the arguments against watching television into account? Do you see any way this argument might have been improved?

2. Diamond reacts to a commonly held attitude against watching television. How does this contrast work in his efforts to argue his own point?

SUGGESTIONS FOR DISCUSSION AND WRITING

A. Using Argumentation

1. Write an essay in which you defend something that is frequently attacked—for example, lowering the drinking age, attending spectator sports, or even watching television (if you have additional arguments in its defense). Or, reverse the approach and criticize something that is usually defended—for example, going to college, traveling, being patient, and so on. Be sure to keep the opposition in mind, as Diamond does.

2. Write an argument against watching television, using comments by Diamond as part of your discussion.

B. Exploring the Options

1. Read the essay on television by Marya Mannes on pages 193–196. Write a dialogue between Diamond and Mannes on the subject of watching

television. Try to imitate the tone, as well as the attitude, toward the subject.

2. What is the role of television in your household? Is it a welcome visitor? Convince the reader of your characterization.

3. What is the role of some other nonhuman piece of equipment in your household (or your life)? Has a personal computer moved in?

4. Are critics of watching television as "behind the times" as a "black-and-white television set with no remote control or videocassette attachment"? Daniel Boorstin, in *The Americans: The Democratic Experience*, says, "Before, the desire to share experiences had brought people out of their homes gathering them together (physically as well as spiritually), but television would somehow separate them in the very act of sharing." Discuss.

5. Discuss Diamond's argument. Is his essay convincing? Do you feel he gave the opposition sufficient attention? What would you have added if you were writing a defense of television as "social"?

6. How do you feel about the assertion that "While no talking is allowed in the theater, social television encourages interaction between audience and set, and among the audience"? Do you feel that the experience of watching television is superior to the experience of seeing a movie or a play? You might write a paper comparing seeing movies or plays with watching television.

7. What do you think about the possibility that television helped destroy the "real conversation" to which Diamond refers in paragraph 7? Do you see any evidence of this destruction, or does the claim give too much weight to the bad influence of television? Is television a scapegoat?

The Child Before the Set

Marya Mannes

Marya Mannes was born in 1904 in New York City and died in California in 1990. She was the daughter of two professional musicians who eventually founded the Mannes College of Music. After some time in the theater, she turned to writing and contributed to such periodicals as *Vogue, Theater Arts, Harper's, Glamour,* and *The Reporter.* This piece is taken from a 1958 book, *More in Anger.* About writing, Mannes says that her purpose is to "commun-cate clearly and honestly what I see and what I believe about the world I live in."

Thinking Ahead What are some possible arguments against children's watching television? Think of some other activity or activities among children that you could support as preferable to watching television.

I am sorry for the children who are brought up on television; not so 1
much for the fare they receive, which if often of abysmal quality, as for the hours they lose. For while it is grotesque enough that healthy adults be "entertained"for three hours a day for six days a week (the seventh being mercifully reserved for enlightenment) it is an act of destruction that children should kill time, which is the most precious thing they possess: time to dream, time to imagine, time to make. Until a child can meet reality, he must live in fantasy. But he must create his own fantasy. And it is televison's primary damage that it provides ten million children with the same fantasy, ready-made and on a platter. Nor is this, with very rare exceptions, the fruitful fantasy of poets or artists but the unreal world of television itself, which bears no relation to that of a child but which envelops him, willy-nilly, in a false adult vision which, in turn, is not even truly adult. And on this infinitely sentitive and apparently unerasable recording-tape of the child's mind is printed a shadow world of blurred values, where the only reality is the product Mom must buy.

This need not be so. Television could be the great teacher and the 2.
great revealer to children, and I hope I live till the day when it fulfills its miraculous function as a third eye. But now I can think only of the killing of hours, and remember the hours of one child who grew before television pre-empted them.

In my childhood the days were not regimented. After school and be- 3
fore a homework evening, the time was our own, for us to fill as we chose. In school we were groups, at home we were single; and it never occurred to my parents to arrange my social day with organized activity. They felt that a good school, an affectionate home, and a consistent standard of ethics were enough. The rest was up to us, my brother and me.

I cannot presume that our life was typical, because my parents were 4
making music all day, teaching or playing together or rehearsing for concerts, my mother at the piano, my father with the violin. In time my brother used the piano when it was free, and there were very few hours in my childhood when the air in our home was dead, or empty of meaning. Because of this, the advent of radio, miraculous as we thought it, left us indifferent. What could it give us then that our life could not? What need was there to turn on its scratchy blatancies when musicians like Cortot and Casals and Thibaud[1] came to the apartment and joined my

[1]Alfred Cortot (1877–1962), a famous French pianist; Pablo Casals (1876–1973), reknowned Spanish cellist; Jacques Thibaud (1880–1953), famous French violinist.

parents in the quintets and trios of Brahms, in Schubert quartets? I remember clearly the exaltation this music brought me, a sense of excitement and glory that often impelled me to tears. And I remember sitting in a corner of the living room watching these musicians play and noticing the transfiguration of their faces, which, a moment before had been—to my childish eyes—neither handsome nor extraordinary. I saw what music did to them and I felt great awe.

This was not, I repeat, a typical home; rather it was a rarely fortunate one. Yet there were still those hours in the afternoon when my parents were teaching or on tour, when my brother, whose five-year seniority then kept us worlds apart, was out or away, and when I fended for myself, often alone. And I know that if television had been in the house I would not have done what I did. I read, voraciously and indiscriminately, nearly a book a day, alternating the *Golden Bough* with *Dotty Dimple, Kidnapped* with the *St. Nicholas* magazine. I wrote very bad poems with very deep emotion. I studied Swahili phrases in African adventure stories. I made peculiar figures out of plastecine, I painted messy water-colors of flowers in vases, I practiced the role, patterned on John Barrymore,[2] of Richard III, I tried leaping like Nijinsky[3] in *Spectre de La Rose,* and I spent a considerable amount of time hanging by my knees from a trapeze set in my bedroom door. I liked the feeling. 5

When I was not engaged in any of these pursuits, I was out on Riverside Drive with a friend, usually standing on a bridge where the freight trains came through beneath in a hissing cloud of white steam, or walking along the Hudson smelling the dampness of rotting piers, or climbing granite mountains blazing with mica. The hours were long and the sun was bright and our heads full of crazy thoughts. Even in our teens, nobody told us to join anything, nobody arranged subscription dances so that we could meet the right boys, and, in fact, we never thought of meeting boys. We were in love with Peter Ibbetson.[4] 6

What is more—and what I believe to be most relevant of all to the age before television and mass communication in general—I do not remember in all my childhood any commercial preoccupation. We bought what we needed, but nobody sold anything to us. My parents worried, often, about money, for they made little and lived gracefully. But the talk was of meeting bills, not of buying new things. And we were brought up, if not with frugality, then with a stern sense of the value of money and the sin of waste. To want things without needing them was an impulse to be scorned, and the word "material" in describing a person, an epithet. 7

---

[2]John Barrymore (1882–1942), famous American stage and film actor.
[3]Vaslav Nijinsky (1890–1950), legendary Russian ballet dancer and choreographer.
[4]*Peter Ibbetson,* a novel by George du Maurier, was published in 1892. Peter Ibbetson avoids the harsh reality of his life by escaping into his own dream world.

Listen then to this excerpt from a well-known woman newspaper columnist, Sylvia Porter, writing last year about her eight-year old daughter: 8

> I began to think carefully about her [she wrote] and the millions of children like her, who are extravagant. It is not an extravagance encouraged by us. Rather, it is an extravagance stimulated by the TV shows they see and radio shows they hear—shows which cajole them into buying things and food on a scale which can be believed only by those living the experience. To Cris and all the boys and girls of her age who are allowed to watch TV during the pre-supper hour, the commercials are often more intriguing than the performances themselves.
>
> They feel they must obey when they are told to "go right out and buy" something. They ask and they nag—and finally, most of us give in.
>
> Again, we are not developing the brand name devotion in the youngsters. It is being pounded into them by the ads they see and hear on every side. They don't eat "a" cereal: they eat such-and-such cereal; they don't drink "a" soft drink; they name it by brand name.
>
> In all seriousness, Cris will tell me that a certain food is "good for me"—and she will tell me why in words that obviously come right out of a commercial. I recall my own childhood; I never asked for a food or drink because it would "help me grow."
>
> [Speaking of her own childhood, Miss Porter wrote:] I think I ate some food in the packages which came with the prizes. Not so with Cris and her friends. They grab the package, extract the prize or cut out the gimmick, etc., and that's the end of it. At times, I think that if all the half-consumed boxes of cereal on Americans' pantry shelves right now were collected and shipped overseas, we could solve the hunger problem of a fair-sized nation.
>
> [Then, later] Cris and her friends will actually coo over the color and style of a new car or appliance. In fact I think they're snobbish about it.

After this curdling tale, Miss Porter ends on a happy note. "In short," she concludes, "one decade from today, Cris and her contemporaries will be creating a market in our land, lush and luxurious beyond anything ever seen." 9

While this may delight the country's economists and the makers of goods, it horrifies me. For it is in effect producing a race which believes that a high standard of living is the final aspiration. I would be more inclined to call it the last ditch. 10

I am sorry for the children who grow up on television. they don't know what they've missed, or how rich life can be, in the real and imagined world. 11

VOCABULARY

abysmal (1), blatancies (4), epithet (7)

QUESTIONS

A. Discovering Meaning

1. What is Mannes' main argument against watching television?
2. On what group does she focus?
3. What is her main purpose?
4. Who are her intended readers, and does she have any intentions for them as a result of this argument?

B. Examining Method

1. What kind of introduction does Mannes use?
2. What is the purpose of the reference to the "recording-tape" in paragraph 1?
3. What is the purpose of paragraph 2?
4. Why does the writer include the description of the musicians in paragraph 4?
5. What is the effect of the last sentence in paragraph 5?
6. Why does the writer include the discussion of the "commercial preoccupation" of television?
7. What is the purpose of the extended quotation from Sylvia Porter?
8. How does the piece conclude? What is the connection to the introduction? (See pages 435–439.)

C. Shifting Focus

1. This argument was written in the 1950s. Is it too dated to be convincing, or does it still work for our time?
2. If this piece were intended as a general argument against watching television, what alterations would the writer have to make?

3. This piece discusses several possible effects of television watching for children. How does the writer make these effects a part of her argument?

4. How does this argument differ from the one by Diamond, also on watching television?

SUGGESTIONS FOR DISCUSSION AND WRITING

A. Using Argumentation

1. Mannes describes her happy, creative childhood as a way of arguing against watching television. Write a piece in which you describe some activity of your life as an argument for or against doing something.

2. Write an argument in favor of some activity for children that might be preferable to watching televison.

B. Exploring the Options

1. Mannes complains about the "commercial preoccupation" of children's television. Write a paper on the modern role of commercials in children's television. Research would provide much information on this topic.

2. Both this piece by Mannes and the one by Lillian Ross, "The Halloween Party," on pages 328–330, suggest that something is very wrong in the experience of our children. Do you have the same sense that children are somehow getting the wrong message, that something is wrong in their world and in the upbringing that they are receiving? If so, what evidence or possible explanations do you have for it? Do you have any solutions? Or make a case disagreeing with these grim portrayals. (Given this assignment, one student who was also a part-time day care worker, wrote a strong argument against extended day care for lonely and disturbed children: "One mother, dressed in designer clothes and perfectly groomed, left her four-year-old son at seven every day. He was usually in his pajamas, often dirty, and never fed. This is child abuse," she argued.)

3. Mannes also refers to her freedom from regimentation. Do you see evidence for regimentation among children today? Do you approve of these arrangements for children?

The Meeting with the Old Proletarian in *Nineteen Eighty-Four*

Eileen Drago (student)

Although they often require research to discover what other readers have thought about the subject, critical papers may sometimes be drawn from your own thoughts and feelings about the piece you are reading. Critical papers may simply be one reader's response to a character, a scene, a symbol, or a theme in a text. In fact, even when additional research is required, this personal response is important. It's important to think your own thoughts first, before you invite the professional critics to influence your judgment.

Unlike the review by Joseph Wood Krutch, discussed on page 314, and the one written by Thomas D'Evelyn on page 210, the primary purpose of a critical paper usually is not to recommend either reading or not reading the book but to explain or to clarify certain critical issues in the text. The writer makes an argument for a certain interpretation (or "reading"), hoping to convince other readers of its correctness and thereby to deepen their experience. Ultimately, the goal of this close reading, careful thinking, and argumentative writing is enlightenment for the reader with the help of the informed critic. To be informed and truly convincing, however, this analysis must be more than speculation or random intuition; it must be based firmly on the source. Quote lines and refer to passages that back up your ideas. The reader has the right to ask, "What makes you think so?" In the paper that follows, a student responds to an assignment in answer to the question, "Why is _______ included in *Nineteen Eighty-Four*" (e.g., the paperweight, the character, O'Brien, or a scene, such as the one discussed here)? In this argumentative piece, the answers to the question become the topics of the paragraphs. Eileen says that the first thing was "to read the novel carefully and then to find something that seemed interesting enough to discuss. I almost wrote on the purpose of the paperweight, but then decided the old proletarian interested me more."

Thinking Ahead How does the writer divide up the main parts of her argument? What kind of information does she draw upon to write her analysis? Consider some literary passage, object, symbol, or character and attempt to account for its inclusion in the piece you are reading.

In *Nineteen Eighty-Four,* Orwell's hero, Winston, an alienated member of the Party, often wanders in the proletarian section of town for relief from the surveillance of the Thought Police. In fact, he comes to place his hopes for the future in the eighty-five percent of society that makes 1 up the lowest class: "But if there was hope, it lay in the proles."[1] During one of these excursions, he notices a man, nearly eighty years old, and tries to question him in an effort to discover the truth about life before the Revolution. But the old man answers none of his questions, recalling only random personal facts like the number of years since he has seen a top hat or the day he was pushed off the sidewalk by a drunken gentleman. Winston leaves in despair. Although this early encounter with the old proletarian is minor in comparison to later ones with Julia and O'Brien, Orwell includes it in his novel for a variety of reasons.

First, the meeting is evidence of Winston's desperate eagerness to discover the truth. All along he has been taking chances against the Party and its Thought Police, committing "thought-crime" by questioning the truth of their statements, secretly recording these anti-Party thoughts in an illicit diary, and wandering in a section of town where Party members rarely go. Once he starts the search for the truth, however, these actions are not enough. He cannot stop his quest for information by which he may judge the statements of the party, and so when he realizes that the old prole may remember pre-Revolutionary life, "a lunatic response took hold of him" (39). He knows that for taking actions like this he is "already dead" (13), so that he continues to take even more daring actions. Winston cannot give up. 2

The Party cannot satisfy his desire to learn about the past, in spite of what he knows are the certain odds against him. He will be caught. It is this knowledge that makes the scene with the old man so frightening, another of its purposes in the novel. As in so many scenes before and after this one, the reader expects Winston to be arrested at any moment. Through him, we share the terror of living under the watchful and treacherous Thought Police and through him our fear increases as he slowly drags out useless answers from the tedious old pubber. Every pause in the octogenarian's speech, every drift of his thought adds to the reader's fright: 3

> I was jest thinking, I ain't seen a top 'at in years. Gorn right out, they'ave. The last time I wore one was at my sister-in-law's funeral. And that was—well, I couldn't give you the date, but it must 'a been fifty years ago. Of course it was only 'ired for the occasion, you understand.(41)

It is one of the most frustrating and suspenseful encounters along the way to Winston's final capture.

And, seen in the larger context, it is a foreshadowing of his ultimate 4

[1]George Orwell, *Nineteen Eighty-Four,* in *Orwell's Nineteen Eighty-Four: Text Sources, Criticism,* ed. Irving Howe (New York: Harcourt, Brace Jovanovich, 1963), p. 38. All further page references will be to this text.

defeat. By the end of the novel, the conversation with the old man takes its place among the many pieces of evidence that Winston never could have won. Here, on a minor scale, Winston experiences the crushing of his hope, in this case the hope that he can uncover a fact inconsistent with the Party's presentation of its "fact" and thus prove his mind free from this control. He enters the pub full of hope, he eagerly buys a social drink for the old man, and he patiently quizzes him until he is forced to recognize the futility of his quest. As happens so often in the novel, most powerfully at the end, hope is destroyed, and the Party is the victor. In his intolerable ignorance, the old man deals a blow to Winston's search for a past and for freedom, driving him on to even more desperate and finally fatal chances.

In the old man we see living evidence of the total success of the Thought Police. Members of the Party must think only as Members of the Party. Proletarians must not think at all. Any proletarian who does will be "vaporized" immediately. The fact of the old proletarian's existence at such an advanced age is sufficient evidence for his essential mindlessness, which he proves in every word he utters. He can make no judgments about the past or the present, he has no sense of the relative importance of facts and events, he has no ability to communicate coherently. In short, he cannot think. For all his potential value as a source of information, he might just as well have been "living in the treetops" (40), as the barman says. If he were able to answer Winston's questions satisfactorily about the quality of life before the Revolution, he would not be alive in the first place. His longevity is a sign of his total ignorance, for the Thought Police would not have allowed real thought to thrive for so long. 5

Nor would they have allowed any accurate memory of the historical past to linger even in one man's mind. The most important function of this encounter with the old proletarian is to show the effects of the loss of history. If accurate historical records are destroyed and if historical memory is entrusted to the mindless, history is essentially dead. Winston wants to know about poverty, capitalism, freedom, the relationship between the upper and the lower classes, so that he can compare his time with past time, and thus make an independent judgment, but he is forced to accept the fact that "the old man's memory was nothing but a rubbish heap of details" (41). He is not one of the "last links" (39) to the past, he is a missing link. In the prole's blundering and self-centered recollections, we see the past destroyed—one of Orwell's most sobering warnings in the novel. Once independent thought is gone and once all evidence of anything different from the present is obliterated, Big Brother has won. Later, when Winston finally consents to love Big Brother, he too has joined the old man in his loss of true self, in his mindlessness. He has only to die. 6

Thus, a scene that at first might appear minor, a mere interlude in the long series of exploits for Winston, actually relates to many of the major ideas of the novel and contributes to their development. It helps charac- 7 terize Winston as an eager, if unwise, seeker after truth; it contributes to the fear and suspense of the novel; it warns of Winston's final defeat; it characterizes the perfect proletarian, giving evidence of the efficiency of the Thought Police; and most important, it displays the fatal danger of losing one's sense of the past. The question, "Was life better before the Revolution than it is now?" and all other questions like it are indeed unanswerable. Big Brother has *all* the answers.

QUESTIONS

A. Discovering Meaning

1. What is the main argument, or thesis, of this paper (see pages 364–366)?
2. According to the writer, what are Orwell's major reasons for including the scene in his novel?
3. What kind of information was necessary to develop this argument?

B. Examining Method

1. What is the purpose of the introduction (see pages 394–398)?
2. Around what central idea are the paragraphs organized? In what order are they arranged?
3. For what audience is this piece written? How important is it that the reader be familiar with Orwell's novel? What does she have in mind for the reader?
4. Why does the writer include so many quotations from the novel?
5. What kind of conclusion is it? How does it relate to the introduction?

C. Shifting Focus

1. This argument is based primarily on causes, on reasons for the inclusion of the scene in the novel. What distinguishes this argument from an exposition based on cause and effect?
2. How would you describe the attitude, the tone, of the writer in this piece? How does this attitude affect your response to the writer's judgments in the argument?

SUGGESTIONS FOR DISCUSSION AND WRITING

A. Using Argumentation

1. Write an essay on a literary work in which you answer the question, "Why is ______ included in the work?" Be careful not to get stuck repeating the action of the story; assume your reader is familiar with the text. Try to understand *why* a scene, an object, a character, a theme, or other element is part of the work. Assuming that the writer could have left the page blank by leaving the subject out, why was it put in?

2. Read the poems on pages 59–60 and write an explication of some aspect of either one of them.

B. Exploring the Options

1. Evaluate a critical analysis of a literary work with which you are familiar and write your own critical response. Do you agree with the writer's conclusions? Does the writer help you to appreciate the work? See the *Modern Language Association Bibliography* (the *MLA Bibliography*) for annual lists of articles on a literary work. Books on your particular writer or bibliographies on literary schools or centuries may also offer valuable comments or resources.

2. Consider your own critical response to an aspect of a literary work, read extensively among the critics and commentators, and write a research paper in which you explore the subject and come to an informed conclusion. Be sure to develop your own thesis, not just a patchwork of other writers' thoughts. (See pages 203–208.)

Heroic Eve

Francis Blessington

Francis Blessington was born in 1942 and was educated at Boston Latin School, Boston College, Northeastern University, and Brown University. He now teaches English at Northeastern University, He has published *Paradise Lost and the Classical Epic* (1979); *The Motive for Metaphor* (1983), with Guy Rotella; *Paradise Lost: A Student's Companion to the Poem* (1988); a collection of poems, *Lantskip* (1987); plus essays and poems in a variety of journals. In this essay, he provides a model for a certain type of college research paper: a review of major statements made on a certain topic, followed by evaluation and commentary by the writer. Here, he reviews critical reactions to Milton's Eve in *Paradise Lost* and concludes with his own argument about her role in the poem, that Eve is not a weak figure or an example of Milton's lack of appreciation for women but, in fact, an epic heroine. About writing critical papers, he says, "It's important not to overstate your case or to claim more than the text actually says. It's also important to give other critics fair representation."

Thinking Ahead Part of this argument involves summary of major critical statements about Eve. How are they worked into the writer's argument? Write your own critical review on a character, scene, symbol, or some dilemma that has caused critics to react in a variety of ways, react to these arguments, and draw some conclusions yourself.

While most early commentators on John Milton's *Paradise Lost* make little mention of Eve, Samuel Johnson raised the spectre of Milton's literary misogyny by writing that in his books appears "something like a Turkish contempt for females" (I, 157). Two centuries later, a controversy has arisen, of which the only point of agreement might be Professor Walter Raleigh's contention about Milton that "Of Eve, at least, he never writes indifferently" (145). 1

It was Raleigh who directly answered Johnson: 2

> It would be truer, and weaker, to say that Milton thought woman made for the exercise of private, and man for the exercise of public, virtues. Hence in their mutual relations Eve carries off all the honours, for her duty coincides with her inclination, while in his case the two are at variance. (151)

But inclination aside, feminist readers see in Eve's private virtues the very misogyny Johnson saw, a judgment which by now is axiomatic in feminist criticism. For instance, concerning Satan's temptation of Eve in a dream before the fall, Christine Froula writes: 3

> The cultural economy erected upon Eve's credence exists on condition that Eve can "read" the world in only one way, by making herself the mirror of the patriarchal authority of Adam, Milton's God, Milton himself and Western culture that the voice [in her dream] tells her she is. (329)[1]

In other words, Eve must conform to male authority.

Marcia Landy spells out what that Miltonic mirror of patriarchal authority is: 4

> The woman must also, in learning her place, accept that the man should not allow her to act without his superior judgment. She must know that it is demeaning for a man to obey her; to listen to a woman is to lose one's manhood, to become like a woman, thus abandoning the necessary superior role of guide. (14)

So Eve caused the fall of man by taking over Adam's authority and bidding him to eat the apple.

Joan E. Hartman sees Eve as heroic but only as a self-effacing partner in marriage: 5

> She is actively engaged in serious work, the work of maintaining the relation of marriage. Yet this work is also self-abnegating and self-denying: Eve provides the first great example of female heroism that will be reenacted by her daughters, a heroism of self-effacement rather than self-assertion. (133)

The above statement is true in the sense that Milton accepted the traditional attitudes towards women in his day: that the wife was subservient to her husband. This view had the authority of the Bible: "Neither was the man created for the woman; but the woman for the man" (I Cor. 11:10). But Barbara K. Lewalski demonstrates how Milton's Eve, in spite of this Biblical limitation, shares all the duties, pleasures, and dangers of Eden (7–12). So Hartman's attitude towards Eve, as actively engaged only in the work of marriage, is too narrow. 6

And Milton may be defended on other ground, pointed to by C. S. Lewis, who writes of Eve: 7

> We see her prostrate her self in spirit before Adam—as an Emperor might kneel to a Pope or as a queen curtsies to a King. You must not think but that if you and I could enter Milton's Eden and meet her we should very quickly be taught what it is to speak to the "universal Dame." (120)

While Lewis errs on the side of idolatry, here we can see Eve, not as mere wifely companion, but as a being on a higher plane, indeed a hero in Milton's sense of that term. Thus, Milton's later defenders, such as Diane Kelsey McColley (210), Joseph Wittreich (99), and John Collier (xiii), show that Eve emerges from the fall stronger than Adam and actually enables him to survive the fall. 8

Following this line of defense, we can go further and say that Eve embodies the heroism that Milton upholds as the ideal in *Paradise Lost,* which is also the ideal of Christianity, that of the self-sacrificing hero exemplified in the suffering Christ. Moreover, Adam is shown as inferior to Eve in his behavior at the fall and is later reprimanded for misogyny (11.634–636). Mere self-assertion being Satanic in Milton's world of an 9 omnipotent God, Eve becomes the epic hero, the parallel to the son of God.

She demonstrates this heroism most powerfully after the fall, where 10
we see that the most heroic human action in the poem is Eve's, her action paralleling the Son's promise, earlier in the poem, to sacrifice himself for man on the cross. Overhearing the Father's prophecy of the fall of man, the Son offered to die for man:

Behold mee then, mee for him, life for life
I offer, on mee let thine anger fall;
Account mee man; I for his sake will leave
Thy bosom, and this glory next to thee
Freely put off, and for him lastly die
Well pleas'd, on me let Death wreck all his rage. (3.236–241)

In much the same language, Eve too is moved to pity at the sight of 11
Adam's fall and makes the only other offer of self-sacrifice in the poem. We feel the echo even without the verbal echoing of the first person pronoun in the objective case, *mee:*

On me exercise not
Thy hatred for this misery befall'n
On me already lost, mee than thyself
More miserable; both have sinn'd but thou
Against God only, I against God and thee,
And to the place of judgment will return,
There with my cries importune Heav'n that all
The sentence from thy head remov'd may light
On me, sole cause to thee of all this woe,
Mee mee only just object of his ire.
(10.927–936)

Eve is moved not by familial ties alone, but by the same sympathy that made the Son of God wish to die for fallen man. Eve also feels the guilt of having led Adam into sinning, so her offer of sacrifice derives from a sense of justice as well as a gesture of love. Her imitation of Christ is the true heroism in *Paradise Lost,* as it is the true heroism of Christianity.

That Eve is to be taken as heroic is also obvious from the classical 12
posture of this scene where Eve clasps Adam's knees begging forgiveness. The theme of the suppliant so common in Greek and Roman epic would not be unintentional in a classically-oriented poet like Milton, who throughout the poem raises Eve to heroic stature by constant allusion.[2] The suppliant image is crucial to epic poetry: the suppliants, Chryses and Priam, in the beginning and the end, respectively, of Homer's *Iliad* (1.10–32; 24.476–595); Odysseus in disguise in the *Odyssey,* begging at his own door (17.192–606); Turnus in Virgil's *Aeneid,* stretching out his

arm to Aeneas at the climax of the poem (12.930–952). The epic suppliant is usually rejected and causes the punishment of the rejector, since Zeus protects suppliants. Though a whole morality in the heroic world of battle depended upon the role of mercy in society, even more than pagan heroes, Christian heroes should raise up the suppliant. That a morality of forgiveness should replace a morality of revenge is clearly Milton's point in Eve's supplication.

Luckily for us, Adam relents and tries to match Eve in offering himself. 13
But as the Roman proverb says, "He who gives quickly, gives twice." We may change the pronoun to the feminine gender and claim that Adam is too late. The true heroism is that self-motivated heroism of the Son and of Eve, fulfilling what was prayed for in the ancient epics but seldom achieved. Eve is not the model of Satanic self-assertion, but she is not brow-beaten and self-effacing either. Like all heroes, she stands in the front line to save society.

NOTES

1. Froula is answered by Edward Pechter in "When Pechter Reads Froula Pretending She's Eve Reading Milton; or, New Feminist Is But Old Priest Writ Large." *Critical Inquiry* **11** (1984): 163–170. She responds in the same volume, "Pechter's Specter: Milton's Bogey Writ Small; or, Why Is He Afraid of Virginia Woolf?": 171–178.
2. For example, 4.303; 4.461; 4.714–719; 5.382; 9.387–395; 9.441.

WORKS CITED

Collier, John. *Milton's Paradise Lost: Screenplay for Cinema of the Mind.* New York: Knopf, 1973.

Froula, Christine. "When Eve Reads Milton: Undoing the Canonical Economy." *Critical Inquiry* **10** (1983): 321–347.

Hartman, Joan E. "We Ribs Crooked by Nature: Gender and Teaching *Paradise Lost.*" *Approaches to Teaching Milton's Paradise Lost.* Ed. Galbraith M. Crump. New York: Modern Language Association of America, 1986, pp. 126–134.

Homer, *Iliad.* Trans. Richmond Lattimore. Chicago: University of Chicago Press, 1951

———, *Odyssey.* Trans. Robert Fitzgerald. New York: Anchor, 1963.

Johnson, Samuel. *Lives of the English Poets.* Ed. George Birbeck Hill. Oxford: Clarendon Press, 1905. 3 Vols.

Landy, Marcia. "Kinship and the Role of Women in *Paradise Lost.*" *Milton Studies* **IV** (1972), 1–18.

Lewalski, Barbara K. "Milton on Women—Yet Once More." *Milton Studies* **VI** (1974), 3–20.

Lewis, C. S. *A Preface to Paradise Lost.* New York: Oxford, 1961.

Milton, John. *Complete Poems and Major Prose.* Ed. Merritt Y. Hughes. New York: Odyssey, 1957.

McColley, Diane Kelsey. *Milton's Eve.* Urbana: University of Illinois Press, 1983.

Raleigh, Walter. *Milton.* New York: Putman, 1900.

Virgil. *Aeneid.* Tr. C. Day Lewis. New York: Anchor, 1952.

Wittreich, Joseph. *Feminist Eve.* Ithaca: Cornell University Press, 1987.

VOCABULARY

spectre (1), misogyny (1), axiomatic (3), patriarchal (3), self-abnegating (5), subservient (6)

QUESTIONS

A. Discovering Meaning

1. What is the main point of this argumentative essay?
2. What is the main critical difference between the writer and the critics quoted early in the essay?
3. On what grounds does the writer base his claims for Eve's heroism?
4. How is Milton's Adam viewed by this writer?

B. Examining Method

1. What is the approach of the introduction? What is the connection to the conclusion?
2. Why are so many critics quoted early in the discussion?
3. What is the purpose of the C. S. Lewis quotation in paragraph 7?
4. Upon what kind of information does the writer draw to develop this argument?

5. What is the basis of the writer's disagreement with the critics who see Eve as a sign of Milton's misogyny?

6. What is the writer's aim for the reader of this argument?

C. Shifting Focus

1. This argument proceeds by giving examples of critical statements made about Milton's Eve. How are these examples used in the service of the writer's argument?

2. If the writer had written a personal appreciation of Milton's Eve (see Drago's piece on pages 199–202), in what ways would the essay differ from this one?

SUGGESTIONS FOR DISCUSSION AND WRITING

A. Using Argumentation

1. Write a two-part paper. In the first part, give an objective reporting of what critics say about your chosen subject. In the second part, react to these critical judgments. Finally, draw your own conclusions.

2. Choose one of the poems on pages 59–60 or one of the essays on pages 309–345, think about it carefully, read several critical comments on it, and then write a critical paper of your own. Be sure to review and evaluate what you discover among the critics. (See the advice for suggestion 2 on page 203.)

B. Exploring the Options

1. Compare this paper to the personal analysis by Eileen Drago on page 199 and the review by D'Evelyn on page 210. What are the major differences among them? Consider such matters as assumptions about the reader, overall purpose, tone, thesis, and so forth.

2. About literary criticism, critic and scholar Helen Gardner once wrote in *The Business of Criticism,* "To have seen more promise of value than the work came in time to provide is less destructive to the development of right judgement and true taste than to have been superior to what is of value. Critics are wise to leave alone those works which they feel a cru-

sading itch to attack and writers whose reputations they feel a call to deflate." Evaluate this comment in relation to your own reading of literature and of literary critics.

One Writer's Travels in the World of Words

Thomas D'Evelyn

Thomas D'Evelyn is general editor for the Humanities at Harvard University Press and frequently reviews books for *The Christian Science Monitor,* where this review of Jonathan Raban's *For Love and Money: A Writer's Life* (1989) appeared.

Thinking Ahead On what subjects do you expect a book reviewer to focus? In what ways is a book review argumentative? Have you read a current book about which you have a strong opinion?

This book solves a problem. How to write about the writing life? Use fiction, as novelists Paul Theroux and Peter Handke have done recently? Or the sermon/lecture form, like Annie Dillard? 1

A third way is offered by Jonathan Raban in "For Love and Money." He teaches by example. He includes samples of his output from the last 20 years—fiction, reviews, feature stories. His book, he says, is "partly a collection, partly a case-history." It succeeds on both counts. 2

Despite its complexity, this book does tell a story. Raban experienced two "calls." Because of the first, he left a teaching job and went to London to try his luck as a freelancer. Because of the second, he left London and went to sea. The dirty dishes had piled up with the unpaid bills, but his escape returned him to his vocation. Having decided to be a writer, he needed something to write about. He would become a travel writer and his forte would be travel by boat. 3

In the case-history parts of this collection, Raban analyzes different kinds of writing assignments and what he learned from them. He became a fine book reviewer. Reviewing for the New Statesman, he would see his idol V. S. Pritchett turn in his reviews. "There was no mistaking a manuscript by Pritchett—it was overlaid with small embellishments in longhand, many of them crossed out and recorrected, to the point where the sheet of paper was in places blackened." Raban compares the reviewer to the cartoonist. "The reviewer has to capture a good likeness in as few strokes as possible, with the stamp of his own style in every line, to be vivid, intelligent and impossibly concise." And he correctly notes that "it is in the reviews, more than in the seminar-rooms or in Foundation- 4 funded colloquia, that the main dialogue about modern literature is sustained. . . ."

Raban could go on to greater things, but this collection makes clear, 5
both from the number and relative excellence of the book reviews, that this form of writing, in which the reader finds his thought articulated against the imposing reality of the book, rewards the writer far more than the small pay he receives for it.

Then there's journalism. "With luck, with imaginative commissions, 6
journalism nourishes rather than vitiates the writer's other work. Its technical demands are absorbing." When Raban tried his hand at writing lucrative plays for radio and TV, he found it frustrating: His language (this was early in his career) was stiff. He learned the same lesson from print. "Trying to make real people sound real on the page," he says, was a big challenge. On the plus side, from journalism he learned the place of fiction in reality. "Writing from memory, trying to re-create events on the page as you remember them and building them into the form of a story, is an act of imagination, however closely you try to stick to what seems to have been the facts."

It all comes together in Raban's true calling, travel writing. He comes 7
to its eloquent defense here against chroniclers like Paul Fussell, who proclaimed that travel writing is dead. On the contrary: "Life, as the most ancient of all metaphors insists, is a journey; and the travel book, in its deceptive simulation of the journey's fits and starts, rehearses life's own fragmentation. More even than the novel, it embraces the contingency of things." It also embraces a multitude of forms; "It accommodates the private diary, the essay, the short story, the prose poem, the rough note and polished table talk with indiscriminate hospitality." As a case book of a great travel writer (his "Old Glory: An American Voyage" was a best-seller) and anthology of reviews of travel books, "For Love and Money" constitutes a superb introduction to travel writing. Raban is a true connoisseur.

Things really get serious when Raban writes of the sea. He says it would 8
be "wonderful to salvage just a small fraction of that sense of the philosophical bounty of the sea"; readers of his novel "Foreign Land" (1985) will agree he has done so. In novel and memoir Raban writes eloquently of the cold, complex, mysterious metal thing called a sextant. He describes how it works. He says that with his sextant, the 17th-century navigator was "an exemplary symbol of solitude and independence." Raban confesses to being a "closet-Ptolemaic. This geocentric, egocentric view of the world was infinitely preferable to the icy abstractions and gigantic mileages of the physicists." The navigator "stood outside [the world's] social and political arrangements, conducting himself in strict relation to the tides, the moon, the sun and stars." He tests the contemporary validity of this image of the navigator in his novel. From the course his own life has taken, it's clear that this anachronistic vision has present applications.

"For Love and Money" is an invitation to travel through a world of 9 wonderful books, ideas, places, and people. To use Raban's words about another writer, it's "full of wonder, surprisingly humble." It tells us about the writing life in the best possible way: by praising others who live by writing and showing how hard it is to live up to the standard implicit in the best of them.

VOCABULARY

articulated (5), vitiates (6), geocentric (8), anachronistic (8)

QUESTIONS

A. Discovering Meaning

1. What does D'Evelyn think about Raban's book?
2. What are the major types of writing done by Raban?
3. Of what is Raban a "true connoisseur?"

B. Examining Method

1. How does D'Evelyn open his review? Why?
2. How does he organize his discussion of Raban's book (see pages 374–378)?
3. How does he conclude?
4. What is the purpose of paragraph 4?
5. What is the purpose of the first sentence in paragraph 6 (see pages 415–418)?
6. For what audience has the piece been written (see pages 370–371)?
7. What is the tone of this review (see pages 421–422)?
8. Would you be interested in reading this book, based on D'Evelyn's review? Why?

C. Shifting Focus

1. If D'Evelyn had not liked the book, what kind of changes would be necessary in this review?
2. What would be the effect of dropping the direct quotations from Raban's book?

SUGGESTIONS FOR DISCUSSION AND WRITING

A. Using Argumentation

1. Write a review of a current book, one for which you have an informed response. Be sure to support your judgment by making references to the text. Consider your readers and where a review of such a book might appear. (You may also want to look at the comments of Joseph Wood Krutch on page 314.)

B. Exploring the Options

1. Read "What Is a Good Review?" by Joseph Wood Krutch on page 314 and evaluate D'Evelyn's review in the light of Krutch's comments.
2. Read several reviews about a current book with which you are familiar, write a summary, and evaluate it in the light of your own experience.

Persuading by Appealing to the Emotions

Like argument, persuasion attempts to influence the opinion of the reader. The difference is in the *approach* to the point being made and to the reader. As we have seen, argument appeals primarily to the thoughts of the reader, whereas persuasion seeks also to stir the emotions. With well-chosen, often emotionally laden words, images, comparisons, incidents, and quotations (i.e., anything that works), the persuader leads the reader to *feel* inclined to agree.

The writer may also have strong enough feelings about the subject to seek not only agreement but also consent, or even action. In fact, so eager in its purposes does persuasion sometimes become that it may even seek to turn off the critical faculty of the reader so that consent will be all the more enthusiastic. Advertisers are professional persuaders. So are politicians. See the discussion of propaganda on pages 80–85.

Also, as in argument, the persuader must understand the reader, must be aware of the emotional appeals most likely to strike a responsive chord or to create such unbearable disharmony that the reader refuses to listen. Mocking religious sermons in a fundamentalist magazine would not be wise or convincing. Singing the praises of an upscale shopping mall to be built over the local swamp may not be appealing to members of the society for the protection of wetlands. The wrong message to the wrong readers, the wrong attitude toward them, the wrong tone, or the wrong vocabulary will destroy any effort at persuasion, no matter how strong the feelings of the writer or how forcefully they are expressed. In fact, the emotion may rebound on the writer, causing the reader to disagree all the more firmly. No one likes to feel demeaned or bullied. The reader must trust the persuader, must feel a certain alliance, not hostility, to the one attempting to convince.

Consider the following outlines for persuasive papers.

1. A student tries to persuade the Speech Department to eliminate the public speaking requirement:

    —The classes are interesting, but they serve so many students that opportunity for speaking is limited and thus not as instructive as they might be. The department should be larger, or the requirement should be dropped.

    —The requirement, as valuable as it may be for some majors, especially those in education and business, has little value for those whose careers will never require speaking in public.

—It is one of the many "important" courses that simply do not fit into today's tightly structured major programs that take up almost four years with requirements and allow little room for exploration.

(Notice the student does not simply attack the course, calling it an overcrowded, anachronistic waste of time, but instead acknowledges its value while at the same time asks for reconsideration as a requirement. To make the points even more persuasive, the student would need to develop them by adding some "convincers"—maybe a verbal sketch of a student lost in a huge classroom reciting a few lines per semester, some quotations from students who chose majors specifically because they do not *want* to speak in public, or a comparison with other courses that have also been dropped from the general curriculum, for example, handwriting. The reader should feel the dead weight of tedium.)

2. The speech teachers would, of course, have their own "convincers".
   —Students who pass a proficiency examination are not required to take the course. The department is hiring three new instructors. The portrait of the "ignored" student is inaccurate, exaggerated.
   —College is about learning what we *don't* know, breaking down old fears, acquiring new strengths. It is impossible to predict the needs of a lifetime, but it is likely that most college graduates, at one time or another, will be called upon to speak in public. This experience is invaluable. Reluctance to do so may hinder professional advancement.
   —Speaking in our age of instant media communication is more, not less, important than it ever was. The course is not at all out of date. (And maybe students should be learning to write legibly, too).

(Here the faculty responds to the student's complaints but would also need to develop emotional content, possibly by showing students getting more than enough attention, by portraying a stumbling, unschooled candidate in the process of losing a job, or by listing contemporary occasions when students might be called upon to speak with confidence. The reader should feel that the course is indispensable.)

3. On the matter of student housing, parents may be so against off-campus housing that the argument may become an effort to persuade, especially if the freshman wants an apartment in town:

   —Remember the last semester of your senior year, when you were so involved with end-of-school parties that you forgot to study and almost didn't graduate? We worry that something like this might happen before you ever get a chance to become involved in college.

—We don't want to make you feel guilty, but we are concerned about the financial investment we're making for just this one year of college. The initial cost of off-campus housing would be very difficult, if not impossible, for us (without dad's taking on extra work, that is).

—You know we trust you, but we'd be so much happier if you could live on campus just for a while, maybe just for the freshman year.

(Again, the argument is not forced, and possible emotional appeals are suggested: concern for the student's well-being, even academic survival; the possibility of an already overworked parent's being forced to take on yet more work; the parents' ultimate trust in the student; and the promise of reconsideration later. These appeals would need development.)

More consistently and seriously than any other kind of writing, persuasion involves thinking of the readers and what may be effectively said to them.

WORKING WITH PERSUASION

It is important to choose topics about which you feel strongly, subjects that stir your feelings of anger, frustration, delight, concern, and so forth. Think of times when you said, "I can't believe this!" or "I just have to protest!" or "Who do they think they're kidding?" Consider subjects for which lively examples, stories, quotations, descriptions, character studies, and a ready vocabulary come to mind—the all-college requirements, the street parking ban near the college, your reaction to a certain film or television program (Have you ever called a station to protest a certain broadcast?), restrictions on the sale of handguns. As emotional as you may be, however, you must also know what you're talking about if you want others to share your feelings. Research may be necessary.

The interest is in the curiosity readers are likely to have about a subject that stirs such feelings in the writer. The challenge is in turning the feelings into readable, convincing prose and in getting the reader to care. Emotion, although possibly entertaining to read, is not enough to influence an uncaring, untrusting, or even hostile reader. Screaming may shut down the receivers.

Example

To the son who wants an off-campus apartment, a mother might write the following letter.

> **Dear Tom,**
>
> We don't want to make you feel guilty, but we are quite concerned about the financial investment we're making for just this one year of college. It's going to cost us about $12,000.00 this year by the time we get finished with tuition, books, board, and the rest. This apartment in town would add another $2,000.00 to the bill. Even with our savings, $12,000.00 is already more than we expected, and I just don't see how we can add to it. I know you'll be able to understand our predicament. Dad could, I suppose, take another job, but he's already getting worn out with the two jobs he has now and, just between you and me, he's already worried about the bills as they are. On the financial basis alone, then, I'd really appreciate your holding off on the apartment idea. Maybe at some later date we can reconsider.
>
> **Love,**
> **Mom**

(Notice that the mother appeals to the conscience, the good nature, and the affection of her son as she writes this letter of refusal. The specific amounts of money are mentioned so that he will understand clearly how much his year in school will cost. She makes her point, while at the same time giving him some hope for the future. If she were expressing anger that her son had the nerve to ask for the money in the first place, this letter would be entirely different, possibly charging selfishness and lack of sympathy. If she took this negative, unpersuasive approach, she might indeed gain obedience but also many bad feelings and no true assent.)

Warm-Up

Write a paragraph of persuasion in which you try to convnce someone to agree or to act as you would like them to act. Consider writing a return letter from the son to the mother. Identify the audience and the purpose of your writing.

After you have studied the examples in this chapter, try to rewrite the paragraph.

The Caterer Told You So!

(paragraph)

Nancy Gilman (student)

In this paragraph, a student, who also runs a catering service, tries to persuade prospective brides to avoid major mistakes at their weddings. In an essay called, "Because You Don't Get Married Every Day," she attempts to persuade indirectly, as if she were talking to a bride who didn't listen. The reader "overhears" the lessons without feeling preached at and, ideally, becomes convinced before the wedding. Nancy says, "I tried to establish a friendly, close-to-my-reader tone by writing in the first person and by bringing in humor and hypothetical anecdotes."

Thinking Ahead What is the goal of this persuasive paragraph? What persuasive techniques does the writer use? Are you well informed in a particular area, so that you feel qualified enough to persuade others of potential problems?

The caterer really shouldn't be an "I told you so," especially after your wedding, but who else will say why Uncle George gobbled every tid-bit in sight, while Aunt Martha ate as if her ninety-eight pound skeleton had been seized by a tapeworm? And what about the dieting bridesmaids, who ate like the proverbial horses? I told you so. You *can't* have a cocktail buffet on Saturday night at 6:30. As the wedding day wears on, people get hungry and want to be fed. No, they *expect* to be fed. They feel that a hundred dollar lamp or even a twenty-five dollar gift certificate entitles them to a substantial dinner, even if it's only chicken supreme. These guests have already gawked for hours at you and your wedding gown, wept at the ceremony, stood patiently in the receiving line, endured the photo session, and pretended to care for relatives and acquaintances they've not seen in ages. Now they want to eat. And these people are not moderately hungry; they're ravenous. I know hors d'oeuvres might be elegant and stylish, but they serve only to pique appetites, not satisfy. No, tiny horseradish cream canapés, dainty snow peas with lovely St. André cheese, and minikin cheddar wafers do absolutely nothing for the hulking twenty-three-year-old usher who's just downed a couple of beers to whet his appetite. By dinner time, elegance and romance are lost causes. Your party is over; now it's their turn. Uncle George and Aunt Martha came to your wedding with visions of veal oscar, lobster thermidore, and filet mignon dancing in their heads. You gave them a cheddar wafer. I've seen it all before. I told you so.

QUESTIONS

A. Discovering Meaning

1. What is the major persuasive point of this paragraph?
2. Why is a 6:30 P.M. wedding buffet a problem?

B. Examining Method

1. What persuasive techniques does the writer use to make her point?
2. What is the effect of addressing the bride who has already made the mistakes?
3. Why does the paragraph begin and end with specific references to one wedding, while the middle part contains general advice given to the bride by the caterer?
4. What is the writer's tone, her attitude, in this paragraph (see pages 421–422)?
5. How does her role as caterer affect the persuasiveness of this paragraph?
6. For what audience was this piece written?
7. What does the writer have in mind for her readers?
8. If you were planning a wedding, how would this paragraph affect you?

C. Shifting Focus

1. If you were going to rewrite this paragraph primarily as argument rather than persuasion, what changes would be necessary?
2. This paragraph contains specific advice about the timing of a wedding celebration. It also contains some lessons about the nature of weddings themselves and about wedding guests. What are these lessons, and why are they included here?

SUGGESTIONS FOR DISCUSSION AND WRITING

A. Using Persuasion

1. Write a persuasive paper in which you attempt to warn someone about something, based on your own special expertise. (One student gave ad-

vice to a freshman about studying; another warned about taking a job as a stock boy in a supermarket, on pages 220–221). Remember to consider your audience and purpose.

2. Write a persuasive letter from Uncle George and Aunt Martha in which they attempt to express their true feelings about the wedding, politely.

B. Exploring the Options

1. Write a response to the caterer from the bride, not necessarily persuasive.

2. How do you react to the sentence, "They feel that a hundred dollar lamp or even a twenty-five dollar gift certificate entitles them to a substantial dinner, even if it's only chicken supreme"?

The Not So Super Market

(paragraph)

Michael Brangiforte (student)

In the longer version of this paper, the student tries humorously to convince anyone contemplating a low-level supermarket job *not* to take it. He complains about the terrible wages, with raises "in 20¢ increments," the "slavery" of bagging, carriage retrieving, and stocking Jiffy Pop until 2 A.M., and worst of all, the customers. Michael says that it was a relief to write this paper. "Funny, I didn't feel quite as angry when I was done."

Thinking Ahead What might be some persuasive complaints against customers as experienced by a store clerk? Could you write a persuasive paragraph in which you attempt to make your case by humorous complaint?

If my stories about the minimum wage and the Jiffy Pop don't bring you to your senses before you sign the contract, consider the customers—visitors from Hell, I think. No matter how hard you try to hide, they sniff you out. No matter how polite you try to be, they finally bring you to a desire to kill. It's as if your name tag says, "Hello! I'm a sub-human. Please treat me accordingly!" They love to deliver lines like, "Hey! where're ya' hidin' the tomatoes?" "How come you're chargin' 89¢ for this mustard when it's only 79¢ down the street?" (as if I had anything to do with pricing mustard). "Get me some plastic bags, now!" And their favorite, "Where's the boss?" I have a particular affection for customers with kids, especially the ones who play in the salad dressing aisle. They try to jump on the green tiles only (or they'll "blow up"). While their parents punch numbers into their calculators or argue with me about the price of lettuce, their little brats leap over the white tiles and skid into a special Wishbone display. As we slop up the oozy oils, we learn from mom and dad that it's our fault anyway for stacking bottles in such a stupid place. I hear it's no better when these customers finally get to the registers.

QUESTIONS

A. Discovering Meaning

1. What is wrong with the customers?
2. Does their behavior convince you that a supermarket job is not worth taking?

B. Examining Method

1. What is the writer's major persuasive purpose in writing this paragraph, for himself and for his readers? How serious is he?
2. For what readers is this paragraph intended?
3. The writer often uses hyperbole, deliberate exaggeration, to make his point. How does it contribute to the writer's persuasive purposes?
4. Why does he include quotations?
5. Explain the irony of the writer's "particular affection."
6. Why does he mention the Wishbone display?
7. What particular vocabulary words contribute to your understanding of the writer's feelings (see pages 422–423)?

C. Shifting Focus

1. This paragraph gives many examples of things the writer does not like about his customers. How do these examples contribute to his persuasive purpose?
2. Rewrite this paragraph without using the persuasive elements and analyze the effect.
3. What might be the implied message to a general audience, not just to those considering a supermarket job?
4. Compare this paragraph to the paper by Tien Truong on page 12. Consider especially purpose, audience, and tone.

SUGGESTIONS FOR DISCUSSION AND WRITING

A. Using Persuasion

1. Write a persuasive paragraph or a longer piece based on complaint. Consider using humor and exaggeration to make your point.
2. Become one of the writer's customers and write a persuasive letter to the management about him or write directly to him.
3. Rewrite this paragraph, changing the purpose and tone, as if the writer were persuading his reader to take the job.

B. Exploring the Options

1. Write your own account of what it's like to deal with the public. Remember to consider for whom you are writing and why.
2. Write a one-paragraph job description as if you were a manager attempting to hire the writer's replacement.

Why Wilderness?

(paragraph)

Edward Abbey

Edward Abbey (1927–1989) attended the University of Michigan and then worked as a park ranger and as a forest fire lookout before becoming a full-time writer. His works, primarily personal essays and journals about the American West and the preservation of the environment, include such titles as *Desert Solitaire* (1968), *The Journey Home* (1977), *Abbey's Road* (1979), and *One Life at a Time, Please* (1988). About the essays in his collection, *The Journey Home,* from which this paragraph has been taken, Abbey writes, "If certain ideas and emotions are expressed in these pages with what seems an extreme intransigence, it is not merely because I love an argument and wish to provoke (though I do), but because I am—really am—an extremist, one who lives and loves by choice far out on the very verge of things, on the edge of the abyss, where this world falls off into the depths of another. That's the way I like it."

Thinking Ahead How is Abbey's persuasive paragraph organized? Do you have any strong feelings about the maintenance of the wilderness?

We need wilderness because we are wild animals. Every man needs a place where he can go to go crazy in peace. Every Boy Scout troop deserves a forest to get lost, miserable, and starving in. Even the maddest murderer of the sweetest wife should get a chance for a run to the sanctuary of the hills. If only for the sport of it. For the terror, freedom, and delirium. Because we need brutality and raw adventure, because men and women first learned to love in, under, and all around trees, because we need for every pair of feet and legs about ten leagues of naked nature, crags to leap from, mountains to measure by, deserts to finally die in when the heart fails.

QUESTIONS

A. Discovering Meaning

1. What is Abbey's main point in this persuasive paragraph?
2. How does he organize the supporting arguments for his strong feelings?

B. Examining Method

1. What is the purpose of the first sentence?
2. Notice the frequent repetitions in this paragraph: "Every. . . . Every," "for a run . . . for the sport . . .for the terror . . .," "Because . . . because . . . because. . . ." What are the purpose and the effect of these repetitions?
3. What feelings of the writer become apparent as you read? What are the clues?
4. What is the overall purpose of the paragraph?
5. To what audience is it directed?
6. How is the final sentence organized? Why?

C. Shifting Focus

1. Much of the emotional force of this paragraph comes from the structure of the sentences and their relationship to one another. Analyze the paragraph sentence by sentence.
2. Rewrite this paragraph, using a reasoned approach to argument, rather than an emotional approach to persuasion.

SUGGESTIONS FOR DISCUSSION AND WRITING

A. Using Persuasion

1. Write a paragraph or a longer paper in defense of one of your most strongly held beliefs about "What we need" or about some other topic. Convince your readers of its importance.

2. Write a close imitation of Abbey's paragraph, beginning with "We need ________." Try to echo his tone and his sentence structure. Make it sound as if Abbey wrote it.

3. Write a persuasive piece of your own about the preservation of wilderness, whether or not you agree with Abbey.

B. Exploring the Options

1. Read the quotation by Abbey in the introduction to this piece and discuss it in relation to this paragraph. Do you see any evidence for the tone he describes there?

2. In the eighteenth century, essayist Charles Lamb rejected invitations from poet William Wordsworth to come and visit him in the wild Lake District of England. Please read the quotation from a letter on page 263. Clearly, he preferred London to the wilds of Windermere. Discuss this attitude in an essay of your own.

The Down Side of Rock and Roll

Robert Salerno (student)

In this piece, a student who is the group leader and manager for a rock group writes a persuasive account of what can be "down" about playing rock and roll. About writing this piece, Robert says, "The examples were easy; the selection was hard."

Thinking Ahead Anticipate some possible disadvantages of being a rock musician. How could these be presented persuasively? Think about a topic with a down side that is not always apparent.

A rock show is an explosion of energy. Tension builds as two hundred 1
fans sit in a packed club to greet their heroes. The band strides confidently on stage and with a stirring drum roll ignites the already charged room. Every chord, every beat, sounds right, better than the hundreds of times in practice. The crowd responds between songs, echoing the decibel level, the excitement of the music. That stage is the best possible place to be. Fame and fortune seem inevitable.

I'm the group leader for a band called "A Boy's Will," and I can say 2
we've had some nights like this, scaled-down versions of big pop concerts. It's a good thing, because given our usual nights, I doubt we'd still be looking for stages to play on. Success is for the few, and the task of becoming a popular band, even just on the local level, is disheartening.

For one thing, we aren't the only band out there looking. Literally hun- 3
dreds of us are calling, visiting, prodding, to get our bands on stage. And the club owners could care less. They're interested in money, not music. Most of them refuse to meet bands in person, and even find the telephone too much to handle sometimes. I'm also the manager of the group, so I get to do the calling:

"Hello, I'm Bob from "A Boy's Will . . ." 4

"Ah . . . listen . . . I'm busy right now. Why don't you call back next 5
Tuesday?"

On Tuesday, I discover he just left for a two-week vacation to a place 6
without phones. Sometimes, this goes on for months. One hundred and ninety-nine other managers got to him before me.

If we do finally get a booking, it usually comes with tickets attached. 7
Owners require members to solicit people for the gig, usually on the awful Monday–Wednesday nights when the club would be almost empty anyway. They get the business. The band gets next to nothing. I remember one grim Wednesday night in Rowley when our audience consisted of my two roommates, my drummer's girlfriend, a bartender, and a soundman. We sat in the empty room enjoying the beer more than the prospect of getting on stage. We sulked or tried to laugh. Then we turned on each other, fighting over little things.

"What about playing 'Round Up'?" 8

"No. That's too fast. I'm not in the mood for a fun song. How about 9
an extended version of 'Layers upon Layers'? *That's* nice and slow and depressing."

"Just because you're slow and depressing, the music doesn't have to 10
be!"

It's hard enough to get friends to come out on school nights to drink 11
pitchers of beer, but it's next to impossible to get exposure to a new audience, especially when we get crammed into a thirty-minute segment with four other bands. The only chance of moving to better nights is directly tied to the number of tickets peddled and to the amount of beer consumed by the audience.

At gigs like this, the music flickers and fades, barely able to ignite any- 12
thing, let alone an audience. The downbeat becomes a dull thud. So much

for the fame. And the fortune? The money is minimal, anywhere from nothing to $50.00. One "big" night, we got a whopping $75.00—divided by four, minus twenty bucks to our then manager for getting us the gig, plus a $60.00 bar tab. You figure it out.

And not all of the problems are with the clubs and managers. As anyone 13
knows who has been a member of a group, it's almost impossible to find players with attitudes you can work with. Clashing personalities and demanding egos sometimes create more problems than the club managers. The drummer and the bassist want to jam some funk, the lead singer wants to do his Sting imitation, and the guitarist wants everyone to hear only his screaming solos. The members of the band can wear on each others' nerves, especially when they begin to take sides. The drummer allies himself with the sulky lead singer and refuses to go on unless he has more to say.

What do you do when you feel your own enthusiasm slipping, when 14
going to a movie begins to look better than practicing another song that might never get a fair hearing? Maybe it's the hope of one of those magical, exciting explosions—without the down side that keeps us playing.

QUESTIONS

A. Discovering Meaning

1. What is the thesis?
2. What does the writer identify as the "down side" of rock and roll?

B. Examining Method

1. What is the persuasive purpose of this piece?
2. What kind of introduction is it, and how does it relate to the body of the essay (see pages 394–398)?
3. For what audience has this piece been written (see pages 370–371)?
4. What is the purpose of paragraph 2 (see pages 415–418)?
5. Why include the dialogue between the writer and the club manager?
6. What is the tone, the attitude of the writer, in this piece?
7. What particular vocabulary words best reveal the writer's attitude?
8. What particular aspect of the paper best captures the "down side" for you. What contributes to the feeling, as well as the understanding, that rock and roll can be a "downer?"

C. Shifting Focus

1. How does contrast contribute to the writer's overall persuasive purpose?
2. How is the persuasion affected by the role of the writer as the leader of the group?

SUGGESTIONS FOR DISCUSSION AND WRITING

A. Using Persuasion

1. Write a persuasive paper about the down side of something that often appears "up." Be sure to consider your overall purpose and the intended audience.
2. Write a letter as if you were the leader of a rock group. Convince the manager of the Club Musica to give you a performance date at his club.

B. Exploring the Options

1. Write a description of a rock concert—good or bad—from the point of view of a member of the audience. (Remember that concerts usually have sounds as well as sights. See pages 253–258 for a discussion of description.) Also consider the *point* of your description.
2. What do you think of this system of hiring young talent? Consider possibly similar situations. Give examples and reasons for your judgment. In other words, use details. (See pages 400–403.)

In Defense of English Majors

Jane Jerrard

Here a student who has recently graduated from college gives several defenses of her major to those who do not understand the reasons for her choice. Notice the tone and any devices she uses to persuade her readers. Her motivation for writing the piece is clear.

Thinking Ahead What are some possible persuasive techniques she could use to demonstrate that English is a wise choice as a major? Do you have any defenses for your own major?

When my father told a friend what I was studying in college, the friend replied. "Having a daughter who tells you she wants to major in English ranks right up there with having your son tell you he wishes he'd been born a girl." 1

This remark nicely sums up the attitude I've constantly run into during the two and one-half years I've been an English major. Any conversation with any acquaintance, relative, or stranger always manages to swing around to the subject of school. And once it's been discovered that I'm a college student, the next question or comment is never, "So how much do you drink?" or even, "I hear your football team really stinks," but inevitably, "What's your major?" Then comes my one-word answer, followed by stunned silence. Then, tentatively, "Are you going to teach?" 2

No, no, no! I don't want to teach; I don't want to "go into something a little more practical"; I don't even want to pick up a few secretarial courses! I'm tired of giving quiet, polite explanations that border on apology, tired of having to justify a liberal arts degree in the modern world. So let me take this opportunity to clear up a few misconceptions (now *there's* a good sentence—and notice the use of the colon coming up): studying English means more than correcting people's grammar at cocktail parties or reading *The Divine Comedy* just for the hell of it. The fact is, we can WRITE, damn it, and we think at least as clearly as we write. We have creativity, organizational skills, self-discipline, "culture," and research skills. An English major can rip through a page of data, analyzing, summarizing, and sorting with a finely tuned mind comparable only to the finest in small-business computers. 3

OK, maybe I'm exaggerating a bit, but the point I'm trying to make is that we don't spend four years getting an education just so we can chuckle dryly over literary jokes like that incredibly bad Dante pun in the last paragraph. 4

There are lots of possible fields open to English majors. How about editing, advertising, public relations, journalism, technical writing, BUSINESS (don't forget those communication skills); we can go on to graduate school to become lawyers and hot-shot executives—all these possibilities besides teaching and writing novels or poetry, or being housewives or manual laborers. 5

The problem is that many employers don't see the marvelous flexibility of an English major, replete with real abilities and potential skills that should make the hardiest of personnel directors envious. Really, though, when English majors are given a chance in the Real World that we hear so much about in college, they prove that they are not idealistic poets, but real folk, with useful skills and good clear minds. 6

No matter how I get to use these skills, I will be doing something I like. Even if I must look forward to being underpaid and overqualified, I 7 do not regret my choice. Literature is what I love and what I've always loved. I'm not going to switch to something more "secure" because I feel safest where I am now, hanging out with Hemingway and Emily Brontë. If I have no interest in courses in computer science and business in school, how can I seriously consider a career in those fields?

I will admit I don't see how Chaucer applies to my life or how knowing 8
the phonetic alphabet will make me a better person. But I'll also admit that I've learned more than I can say from the literature I've studied—all the facts and techniques and ideas from fiction and poetry, as well as the practical skills that helped me to extract and expand on that knowledge. My field has taught me to think and to work no less than if I were a student of accounting or business administration.

So let this be a lesson to you: a college education is not simply a step- 9
ping stone to a career. If it were, universities would be replaced by vocational schools, and then where would we English majors be? A college degree is part of your life, not part of your resumé, Whatever you study will benefit you because any education is a good education, regardless of the condition of the job market.

College is a time for making decisions and beginning to act on them. 10
Many students have to decide between what they've wanted and what they feel they should have; what they're best in and what their parents say is best for them; what gives them pleasure and what will get them more money. The general attitude toward an "impractical" liberal arts degree is enough to push any student into the field that comes closest to guaranteeing a safe future.

I don't mean to encourage everyone in college to leap into liberal arts 11
with both feet (although it would be interesting to see a shortage of business graduates and a glut of philosophy majors). All I want is a serious consideration of the good old humanities—by students, employers, and the man in the street who keeps asking me what my major is.

And the next time someone asks me what in God's name I'm going to 12
do with an English major, I'll say, "Flaunt it."

QUESTIONS

A. Discovering Meaning

1. What are the writer's major points in defense of being an English major?
2. What are some of the attitudes she persuasively rejects during the course of her argument?

B. Examining Method

1. What is the persuasive purpose of her essay (see pages 368–371)?

2. For what audience has this piece been written? What is her attitude toward her audience (see pages 370–371)?

3. How does she acknowledge the possible attitudes of her readers?

4. What is the connection between the introduction and the conclusion (see pages 435–439)?

5. What persuasive techniques does the writer use to express her strong feelings?

6. Why does she include so many quotations in paragraph 2?

7. What particular vocabulary words seem best to express her mood (see pages 422–423)?

C. Shifting Focus

1. Does the writer's approach to her subject and to her readers work for you? Are you persuaded that English is a worthy major? Explain your response?

2. Compare this piece to one of the other persuasive pieces in this chapter, paying particular attention to point, purpose, and voice, the assumed attitude of the writer as the case is being made.

SUGGESTIONS FOR DISCUSSION AND WRITING

A. Using Persuasion

1. Write a defense (or possibly an attack on) your own choice of a major. Try to persuade an uninformed or unconvinced reader. You might also consider an ironic defense, one in which you argue just the opposite of what you really believe. Be sure to evaluate how you really *feel* about this subject and just how firmly committed you are to a particular point of view. Also, anticipate what your readers might think.

2. Write a persuasive essay in which you argue for or against a certain program of study, or some aspect of that program, even if it is not your own choice. Do you think, for example, that a program devoted almost entirely to career training is a good idea? Do you have any strong feelings about a certain course? Remember that strong feelings are not usually enough to convince a reader. Your subject may well demand some inter-

views with faculty and students or some research in the working world or in the library. In any case, be informed enough to reach a reader.

B. Exploring the Options

1. Consider why you have chosen a certain major or possibly why you have come to college in the first place (see pages 120–123).
2. Compare this piece to Tracey Brown's on page 131. Compare subject matter, examples, conclusions, purpose, tone, and effectiveness in making your point.

Running on Empty

John Speziale

Among many other things, including managing and playing in a rock band and landscaping, John Speziale is a teacher of college English. Here he writes a piece in which he strongly disapproves of long-distance running. About writing this piece, John says,

> I write in a frenzy, excited about what I have to say. It's fun, but the resulting first draft can be somewhat overzealous, requiring editing to avoid disaster. Supercharged, near-obnoxious passages must be softened so as not to alienate the reader.
>
> For example, the passage in this essay which reads
>
> > Long distance running is . . . about us entertaining as watching someone deliberately stick himself in the eye with a finger.
>
> was originally written in the following way, though I hesitate to admit it:
>
> > Long distance running is . . . about as entertaining as watching someone stick himself in the eye with a stiletto.
>
> I decided the line had limited appeal. It's easier to convince a reader if you can avoid making him cringe.
>
> On the way to my final version of the sentence I tried a slightly different wording:
>
> > Long distance running is . . . about as entertaining as watching someone deliberately poke a finger into his eye.

But this was *too* soft. "Poke" is something that children do because they don't know any better. The word "stick" is stronger, connoting more deliberation and thus conveying more of the sense of masochism I needed. Also, the syntax of this sentence is not properly effective. The reader knows too soon that it's only a finger doing the poking. Making "finger" the last word in the sentence allows the line to retain a bit of shock value until its very end, which suited my purpose more aptly.

Thinking Ahead Can you think of any persuasive reasons why long-distance running should be considered the "world's worst" sport? Do you have your own candidate for world's worst?

I haven't got time for the pain.

Carly Simon

Catching the Boston Marathon highlights on the news, I was reminded of the campaign metaphor employed by Massachusetts Governor Michael Dukakis during his ill-fated run for the presidency. Many had already rejected "The Duke" because his campaign lacked focus; others because they could foresee the Commonwealth's impending budget crisis. But it was the metaphor that shook my faith in the man. 1

For Dukakis cast himself as "The Marathon Man," the guy who could go the distance. How unfortunate, I thought, comparing himself to a participant in the world's worst sport, long distance running. 2

True, running is sometimes necessary and often valuable. Running to catch a bus or a train, for example, can guarantee punctuality and even result in some awe-inspiring barroom anecdotes. And jogging about the neighborhood is a convenient, inexpensive way to stay in shape. 3

But long distance running is lowest on the totem of bad competitive sports (far below frog jumping contests and bear baiting). The sports media may glorify it as a competition both entertaining an admirable, but it fails to be either because it is too masochistic, requires little skill and almost no strategy. 4

Long distance running is blatantly self-punishing and, as such, about as entertaining as watching someone deliberately stick himself in the eye with a finger. And while the sadistic among us might pay good money to watch someone put out his eye, you won't catch that event on Wide World of Sports. Yet the one-eyed "athlete" probably has done himself less physical harm than a marathoner who has run himself so hard he can't climb stairs for a month. 5

Bottom line: How entertaining was it to watch Boston Marathoner Joan Benoit Samuelson limp across the finish line "like a broken puppet," as television reporter Hank Phillipi so aptly put it? The puppet image conveys more irony than Ms. Phillipi intended. Real puppet shows are enter- 6 taining, but watching Ms Samuelson cripple herself was like watching a puppeteer who has cast herself as Punch's Judy, whacking herself with a big, bad stick—odd, and a little disgusting.

And it's difficult to admire such behavior, though sportscasters insist 7
on labeling it "guts." Keep in mind that "guts" and "absurd risk of personal injury" have been confused throughout history. One man's hero is another man's fruitcake. (The jury is still out on Generals Custer and Patton and Captain Ahab, for example.) And, certainly, it was not admiration that prompted us to laugh the first time we heard the old joke about the guy who kept hitting himself in the head because it felt so good when he stopped.

At least that guy had the sense to stop *in time* to feel good. According 8
to one reporter, the last stop for many Boston Marathoners was a first aid post so full of casualties it came to resemble "a M.A.S.H. unit."

Some will inevitably argue that, masochistic aspects aside, marathons 9
offer the traditional "Thrill of the Race." But the thrill of watching a *real* race is at least partially derived from each participant's ability to maneuver a vehicle or an animal strategically over a given course. The dominant skills applied in running are basic motor skills which should have been developed since early childhood. And the strategies involved are pretty simple, too. It all comes down to playground activities: running right or left or straight ahead, watching not to trip, dodging the other children. You hear the sportscasters talk about runners playing "mind games." But all that ever amounts to is sticking close to the heels of one's strongest opponent in order to rattle him a bit. Not exactly as intimidating as some hell-bent Indy driver buzzing your tail at 200-plus miles per hour in a Formula One machine. And darn less fun to watch.

Yes, real racing is dangerous and can be much more violent than run- 10
ning. But one of the goals of such racing—and of most other real sports—is to apply incredible skill toward the *avoidance* of tragedy. Physical pain in such sports comes, more often than not, from the failure to circumvent dangerous obstacles. In running, however, pain *is* the obstacle, the only obstacle. And it's self-inflicted.

I realize that long distance running is a time-honored activity which 11
recalls an ancient, noble era when messengers, unless they were lucky enough to have stolen a horse, ran on foot and thus became the most respected, the most valuable men in their warring tribes. That was running for a purpose, all right. But today that purpose can be achieved by the telephone, the fax machine and jet-age couriers who can get your message anywhere, guaranteed overnight.

I wish The Duke had gotten the message. His unfortunate metaphor 12
had to have cost him votes.

I voted for him anyway, of course, despite his poor taste in sports. 13
What choice did I have? His opponent portrayed himself as an avid fisherman and hunter, killing animals for no practical reason whatsoever (such "sports" are not even included on the totem).

By now it's likely that Governor Dukakis has realized his mistake. He wasn't on the Boston Marathon finish line to hand out the laurels; he sent Lt. Governor Murphy in his place. 14

QUESTIONS

A. Discovering Meaning

1. What does the writer dislike about long-distance running?
2. What are his feelings as he watches it?

B. Exploring Method

1. What is the writer's persuasive purpose (see pages 368–371)?
2. For what audience is the piece intended?
3. What is the meaning and the purpose of the quotation preceding the body of the paper?
4. How is the paper introduced (see pages 394–398)?
5. What is the tone of this piece?. In what ways does the writer reveal tone? (See pages 421–422.)
6. What is suggested by the reference to Governor Dukakis?
7. What is the purpose of the references to frog jumping and bear baiting?
8. Why does the writer include the description of Joan Benoit Samuelson limping across the finish line?
9. What is the purpose of the reference to an "Indy driver"?
10. Why does the writer refer to the "time-honored" activity of long-distance running?

C. Shifting Focus

1. If the piece were intended more as argument than as persuasion, what changes would be necessary?
2. Were you persuaded by the writer's argument against this sport?
3. How does humor contribute to the writer's point? What effect does it have on his overall purpose?

SUGGESTIONS FOR DISCUSSION AND WRITING

A. Using Persuasion

1. Write a persuasive paper on your choice for the world's worst sport or the world's worst ________. Be sure to work on convincing your reader of your judgment, not just on stating an opinion. (Students have written on the world's worst job, kind of friend, school, government program, or character trait. Some required personal experience; some, wide observation; and some, research.)
2. Write a defense of long-distance running. Address it directly to the writer, if that approach seems to work.

B. Exploring the Options

1. Do you agree that " 'guts' and 'absurd risk of personal injury' have been confused throughout history"? Are they confused in modern sports?
2. What do you think about the level of violence in modern sports? Be sure to determine the *purpose* implied in your answer; are you *primarily* giving examples, analyzing causes, arguing a case, persuading, or making suggestions? What do you have in mind for your reader?

I Have a Dream

*Martin Luther King, Jr.**

Martin Luther King, Jr. (1929–1968), president of the Southern Christian Leadership Conference, winner of the Nobel Peace Prize, and author of *Stride Toward Freedom* and *Why We Can't Wait,* was one of the most active and influential of the civil rights leaders until his assassination. He actively opposed all forms of racial discrimination while also preaching the virtues of nonviolence and brotherhood. In his famous speech, "I Have a Dream," delivered at

*Transcribed from recording, "The Great March on Washington," November 1983 by the King Library and Archives. Protected by Copyright. Not to be reproduced without written permission.

the March on Washington on August 28, 1963, he calls for a new commitment to the cause of freedom. Notice the persuasiveness of the appeal—the repetitions, the short phrases, the figurative language, the crescendo of the message. Developed from themes used in previous speeches, this speech was composed throughout the entire evening before its delivery. Limited to eight minutes at the end of the ceremonies, King was eager to express the emotions of the crowd of 200,000 that had gathered at the Lincoln Memorial. Near the end, he abandoned his preprepared text and spoke directly to the audience, calling on him to "Dream some more."

Thinking Ahead In a persuasive speech calling for racial harmony, what points could King most effectively make to an audience that had marched to Washington in support of his cause? Do you, too, have a "dream" that reaches beyond your own personal aspirations?

I am happy to join with you today in what will go down in history as 1
the the greatest demonstration for freedom in the history of our nation.

Five score years ago, a great American, in whose symbolic shadow we 2
stand today, signed the Emancipation Proclamation. This momentous decree came as a great beacon light of hope to millions of Negro slaves who had been seared in the flames of withering injustice. It came as a joyous daybreak to end the long night of their captivity.

But one hundred years later, the Negro still is not free; one hundred 3
years later, the life of the Negro is still sadly crippled by the manacles of segregation and the chains of discrimination; one hundred years later, the Negro lives on a lonely island of poverty in the midst of a vast ocean of material prosperity; one hundred years later, the Negro is still languished in the corners of American society and finds himself in exile in his own land.

So we've come here today to dramatize a shameful condition. In a sense 4
we've come to our nation's capital to cash a check. When the architects of our republic wrote the magnificent words of the Constitution and the Declaration of Independence, they were signing a promissory note to which every American was to fall heir. This note was the promise that all men, yes, black men as well as white men, would be guaranteed the unalienable rights of life, liberty, and the pursuit of happiness.

It is obvious today that America has defaulted on this promissory note 5
in so far as her citizens of color are concerned. Instead of honoring this sacred obligation, America has given the Negro people a bad check; a check which has come back marked "insufficient funds." But we refuse to believe that the bank of justice is bankrupt. We refuse to believe that there are insufficient funds in the great vaults of opportunity of this nation. And so we've come to cash this check, a check that will give us upon demand the riches of freedom and the security of justice.

We have also come to this hallowed spot to remind America of the 6
fierce urgency of now. This is no time to engage in the luxury of cooling off or to take the tranquilizing drug of gradualism. Now is the time to

make real the promises of democracy; now is the time to rise from the dark and desolate valley of segregation to the sunlit path of racial justice; now is the time to lift our nation from the quicksands of racial injustice to the solid rock of brotherhood; now is the time to make justice a reality for all of God's children. It would be fatal for the nation to overlook the urgency of the moment. This sweltering summer of the Negro's legitimate discontent will not pass until there is an invigorating autumn of freedom and equality.

Nineteen sixty-three is not an end, but a beginning. And those who 7
hope that the Negro needed to blow off steam and will now be content, will have a rude awakening if the nation returns to business as usual. There will be neither rest nor tranquility in America until the Negro is granted his citizenship rights. The whirlwinds of revolt will continue to shake the foundations of our nation until the bright day of justice emerges.

But there is something that I must say to my people, who stand on the 8
worn threshold which leads into the palace of justice. In the process of gaining our rightful place, we must not be guilty of wrongful deeds. Let us not seek to satisfy our thirst for freedom by drinking from the cup of bitterness and hatred. We must forever conduct our struggle on the high plain of dignity and discipline. We must not allow our creative protests to degenerate into physical violence. Again and again we must rise to the majestic heights of meeting physical force with soul force. The marvelous new militancy, which has engulfed the Negro community, must not lead us to a distrust of all white people. For many of our white brothers, as evidenced by their presence here today, have come to realize that their destiny is tied up with our destiny. And they have come to realize that their freedom is inextricably bound to our freedom. We cannot walk alone. And as we walk, we must make the pledge that we shall always march ahead. We cannot turn back.

There are those who are asking the devotees of Civil Rights, "When 9
will you be satisfied?" We can never be satisfied as long as the Negro is the victim of the unspeakable horrors of police brutality; we can never be satisfied as long as our bodies, heavy with the fatigue of travel, cannot gain lodging in the motels of the highways and the hotels of the cities; we cannot be satisfied as long as the Negro's basic mobility is from a smaller ghetto to a larger one; we can never be satisfied as long as our children are stripped of their selfhood and robbed of their dignity by signs stating "For White Only"; we cannot be satisfied as long as the Negro in Mississippi cannot vote and a Negro in New York believes he has nothing for which to vote. No! No, we are not satisfied, and we will not be satisfied until "justice rolls down like waters and righteousness like a mighty stream."

I an not unmindful that some of you have come here out of great trials 10
and tribulations. Some of you have come fresh from narrow jail cells. Some of you have come from areas where your quest for freedom left you battered by the storms of persecution and staggered by the winds of

police brutality. You have been the veterans of creative suffering. Continue to work with the faith that unearned suffering is redemptive. Go back to Mississippi. Go back to Alabama. Go back to South Carolina. Go back to Georgia. Go back to Louisiana. Go back to the slums and ghettos of our Northern cities, knowing that somehow this situation can and will be changed. Let us not wallow in the valley of despair.

I say to you today, my friends, so even though we face the difficulties 11
of today and tomorrow, I still have a dream. It is a dream deeply rooted in the American dream. I have a dream that one day this nation will rise up and live out the true meaning of its creed, "We hold these truths to be self-evident, that all men are created equal." I have a dream that one day on the red hills of Georgia, sons of former slaves and the sons of former slave owners will be able to sit down together at the table of brotherhood. I have a dream that one day even the state of Mississippi, a state sweltering with the heat of injustice, sweltering with the heat of oppression, will be transformed into an oasis of freedom and justice. I have a dream that my four little children will one day live in a nation where they will not be judged by the color of their skin, but by the content of their character.

I HAVE A DREAM TODAY! 12

I have a dream that one day down in Alabama—with its vicious racists, 13
with its Governor having his lips dripping with the words of interposition and nullification—one day right there in Alabama, little black boys and black girls will be able to join hands with little white boys and white girls as sisters and brothers.

I HAVE A DREAM TODAY! 14

I have a dream that one day every valley shall be exalted, every hill 15
and mountain shall be made low. The rough places will be plain and the crooked places will be made straight, "and the glory of the Lord shall be revealed, and all flesh shall see it together."

This is our hope. This is the faith that I go back to the South with. With 16
this faith we will be able to hew out of the mountain of despair, a stone of hope. With this faith we will be able to transform the jangling discords of our nation into a beautiful symphony of brotherhood. With this faith we will be able to work together, to pray together, to struggle together, to go to jail together, to stand up for freedom together, knowing that we will be free one day. And this will be the day. This will be the day when all of God's children will be able to sing with new meaning, "My country, 'tis of thee, sweet land of liberty, of thee I sing. Land where my father died, land of the pilgrim's pride, from every mountain side, let freedom ring." And if America is to be a great nation, this must become true.

So let freedom ring from the prodigious hilltops of New Hampshire; 17
let freedom ring from the mighty mountains of New York; let freedom ring from the heightening Alleghenies of Pennsylvania; let freedom ring from the snow-capped Rockies of Colorado; let freedom ring from the curvaceous slopes of California. But not only that. Let freedom ring from

Stone Mountain of Georgia; let freedom ring from Lookout Mountain of Tennessee; let freedom ring from every hill and mole hill of Mississippi. "From every mountainside, let freedom ring."

And when this happens, and when we allow freedom to ring, when we 18
let it ring from every village and every hamlet, from every state and every city, we will be able to speed up that day when all of God's children, black men and white men, Jews and Gentiles, Protestants and Catholics, will be able to join hands and sing in the words of the old Negro spiritual, "Free at last. Free at last. Thank God Almighty, we are free at last."

QUESTIONS

A. Discovery Meaning

1. What is the main subject of King's speech?
2. What are his major complaints?
3. What are his most strongly held hopes?

B. Examining method

1. What is the main purpose of this speech (see pages 368–371)?
2. Who is King's intended audience, and what is his relationship to them (see pages 370–371)?
3. What is the echo in the first line of paragraph 2? For what purpose?
4. Why does King repeat the phrase, "One hundred years later" in paragraph 3? Is it a weakness in his style or an effective repetition? Why?
5. What is the purpose of the extended comparison to banking in paragraphs 4 and 5 (see pages 431–433)?
6. Find another comparison that contributes both directly and indirectly to King's meaning and explain it.
7. What is the implied reference in paragraph 6: "This sweltering summer of the Negro's legitimate discontent. . . ."?
8. Why does King say "dignity and discipline" in paragraph 8 rather than "dignity and training that develops self-control, efficiency, and so on" (a dictionary definition of discipline) (see pages 406–411)?
9. What is the purpose of paragraph 9? How does it contribute to the persuasiveness of King's speech?

10. From paragraphs 11–15, King repeatedly uses the word "dream." What is the effect of this repetition? (See pages 422–423.)
11. Why does he so often say, "Let freedom ring"?

C. Shifting Focus

1. King is certainly attempting to persuade his audience of his point of view. What other purposes does he have in mind?
2. What emotions does he express in this very emotional speech?
3. Notice the sophisticated diction and sentences, the many biblical echoes. What does this sophistication suggest about King's background, his audience, and his intended purpose?

SUGGESTIONS FOR DISCUSSION AND WRITING

A. Using Persuasion

1. Write a persuasive essay on a dream you might have that reaches beyond your own personal aspirations, one that might contribute to a larger good.
2. What is your most compelling personal "dream" at this time in your life? Write a personal essay in which you attempt to lead others to share your feelings about it.

B. Exploring the Options

1. In persuasive speaking, according to Charles S. Mudd and Malcolm O. Sillars, *Speech: Context and Communication* (San Francisco: Chandler Publishing Co., 1969), p. 319, "The rational and non-rational elements of proof combine to influence audience response. Indeed, they are closely intermingled in any persuasive speech that only the critic who is consciously looking for them can isolate one aspect of the proof from another." In the light of this comment on persuasive speaking, discuss King's speech.
2. Write an essay in which you analyze the qualities of a speech you have heard. Identify and illustrate what contributed to the speaker's effectiveness or lack of it. This assignment may require your attending a speech for this specific purpose and taking notes as you listen. Notice all aspects

of persuasion—clothing, haircut, gestures, posture, tone of voice, facial expressions, as well as the persuasive aspects of what is actually said. If you were "put off," what put you off; if you were involved and convinced, why?

3. About this speech by Martin Luther King, writer James Baldwin said, "That day, for a moment, it almost seemed that we stood on a height, and could see our inheritance; perhaps we would make the kingdom real perhaps the beloved community would not forever remain that dream one dreamed in agony." Comment on Baldwin's reaction and evaluate your own.

Three Reviews of *Batman*

Orli Low, John Simon, Pauline Kael

These three reviews give individual reactions to the film that earned a record-breaking $100 million in the first ten days of distribution, plus profits from Batman paraphernalia that flew out across the land in the summer of 1989. But, in spite of the media hype and film marketing, it is the reviewer's job to evaluate a film on its merits and to write persuasively of these reactions. Notice the differences in approach and purpose as these three reviewers evaluate the same film. Orli Low writes for *On Line at the Movies,* a full-color pamphlet distributed at movie theaters. John Simon reviews films regularly for *National Review,* and Pauline Kael is one of the most widely read of all modern film reviewers, periodically publishing her articles in *The New Yorker* and then in book form.

Thinking Ahead: What are some possible persuasive purposes in writing a film review? If you were to review *Batman* or a film similar to it for a school newspaper, what might your persuasive purpose be?

Orli Low

Wham! Pow! Holy Silver Screen! The keeper of Gotham City is back! 1
It's Batman, making his feature-length debut on the big screen. Leaping into movie theatres June 23rd, the legendary DC Comics hero is celebrating 50 years of seeking to right the underworld's wrongs. Michael Keaton stars as the masked wonder, with Jack Nicholson as his arch enemy, The Joker. Kim Basinger plays the beautiful and talented photo-journalist Vicki Vale in this kaleidoscopic action-packed film.

"Batman" is set in the rich textures of Gotham City where we find the 2

Caped Crusader's alter-ego Bruce Wayne, back after some years away perfecting his physical and scientific skills. As a young boy, Wayne had witnessed the brutal murder of his well-to-do parents, and though devastated, pledged his life to law and order. Upon his return, he discovers his hometown to be highly corrupt, and Wayne, who appears to be merely a wealthy philanthropist, assumes his second identity, the powerful and terrifying crimefighter known only as Batman. He then spends his life battling evil and its malevolent personification, The Joker.

The movie boasts a series of breathtaking encounters where the two 3
antagonists use a myriad of unique skills, trickery, and weapons to fight the battle over justice. The new Batmobile looks like a cross between an early-model Corvette and Darth Vader's mask, and a new gadget in the war on crime is the ultra-sleek and sophisticated Batwing airplane.

The film has a much more gritty and realistic tone than the wildly 4
successful tongue-in-cheek television series of the late 1960s, which is still in world-wide syndication—and *the* hot show on British morning telly. In the movie, Gotham City is a web of ominous skyscrapers, built like upside-down pyramids and joined by massive bridges, which allow little sunshine to creep through, make the streets dark and desolate—and evoke an eerie vision of a futuristic New York.

The Batcave, too, has been recreated with a *noir* twist, as the under- 5
ground headquarters in the deep recesses of Wayne Manor no longer has the shiny high-tech look of the television series. It is now populated with building pylons and rudimentary carpentry fixtures. Only The Joker is excused from the film's somber-hued tones. His costume of bright orange and green, topped off by white face, bright red lips and yellow hair are true to their shock value.

Batman was originally created in 1939 for Detective Comics by Bob 6
Kane (who serves as the film's technical consultant), and has gone through numerous incarnations: a half-century of continuous comic-book publication, now more popular than ever and published in 20 languages in over 45 countries; a series of paperback "graphic novels," featuring a 50-year-old Batman donning his cowl and cape one more time; newspaper comic strips; animated Saturday morning television series; and a line of licensed Bat-merchandise so vast that even Alfred the faithful butler would have trouble keeping track of it all.

From costumes to sets to characters, the movie's look and feel bring 7
back Batman's original "dark" image and allow a whole new generation of fans to follow the Caped Crusader as he continues his quest for justice in a tough world. Judging by his resurgent popularity and the rage for Bat-related memorabilia in recent years, it looks like Batmania is back . . . with a Bang.

John Simon

You must have noticed that more and more American movies are based 1
on comic strips (the *Superman* series, *Batman,* the upcoming *Dick*

Tracy), or on what might as well be comic strips (the Indiana Jones series, the so far only two *Ghostbusters, Who Framed Roger Rabbit?,* and scads more). You will also have noticed how many movies are sequels (the list is endless). What does this mean? It is the sinister confluence of two unwholesome manifestations: rabid nostalgia and a frenzy for playing it safe.

The comic-strip is the epitome of nostalgia, sequels, and playing it close 2
to the vest. The nostalgia is for when one was young and devouring comic strips, sequentiality is built into the daily or weekly comic strip, and what could be financially safer than translation to the big screen—with stars—of a story that delighted fans for decades on end? In the case of *Batman,* there is also a TV version haunting the collective memory. So the public's attitude to this one is roughly what the ancient Greeks' would have been to a movie adaptation of the *Odyssey.* I have seen people in the *Batman* line picnicking on the sidewalk while awaiting their spiritual sustenance.

Well, *Batman* does provide spectacular production design. Gotham 3
City, as dreamed up by Anton Furst, is an amazing amalgam of present-day New York, Fritz Lang's *Metropolis,* Victor Hugo's Notre Dame and environs, the Temple of Karnak, Art Deco as Edgar Allan Poe might have conceived it, and perhaps also post-modernism after acid rain has had its well-deserved way with it. It is a parody city, but with a certain sinister beauty about it as well as genuine horror. Furst is the relatively rare case of an art director who is not only a director of art but also a connoisseur. With sets like these, one could have made an adult movie, perhaps a satirical dystopia that might have commented sardonically, wittily, seriously on the way of our world. What a pity to waste such visual talent—not to mention such money—on a comic strip.

Of course, the film will recoup its investment many times over, and is 4
very likely to become one of the top grossers in cinema annals. But isn't there something truly gross about such unmitigated waste, such downright concupiscent greed? If the history of trash is ever written—and, unbeknown to me, it probably has been already—wouldn't it have to distinguish between trash with some redeeming inventiveness and excitement, and trash of the callously exploitative and predictable sort, such as this *Batman?* (Not having ever caught Bob Kane's cartoon or the campy TV show it generated, I cannot speak about other *Batmen* or *Batmans.*) Will audiences never get tired of invincible Good disguising itself in mask and cape and, with or without a faithful companion (Tonto, Robin, Lois Lane), foiling vincible Evil in the nick of time? And what is so fascinating—except to nerds, who can identify themselves, realistically, with the Clark Kent persona while dreaming themselves into the Other—about the cut-and-dried dual personality of the superman-hero?

And speaking of Robin, he is conspicuous by his absence from the new 5
Batman. The thinking was that, in this less innocent age, he would give rise to speculations about a possible homosexual relationship between himself and Batman, or Batman's other persona, the immensely wealthy playboy Bruce Wayne. That at least would have given the movie some

crude interest of the do-they-or-don't-they kind. Instead, we get the glamorous photographer Vicki Vale, who is prompt to tumble into bed with Bruce but excruciatingly slow about deducing his other identity.

The entire story, after that dalliance, is a protracted coitus semi-interruptus until, at film's end, Vicki is reunited with Bruce. Well, not quite with Bruce, but with his Jeevesian valet/chauffeur, Alfred, and Bruce's Rolls-Royce, comfier than the Batmobile, a product of miscegenation between a Maserati and a finned Cadillac. Alfred makes her get in and assures her that his master will join them presently. Yet the concluding shot offers Bruce still in full Batman regalia, surveying, from the pinnacle of the tallest building, his beloved Gotham City, temporarily purified by him. I am not sure what this mild ambiguity portends; most likely, heaven help us, a sequel. 6

There are only two scenes in the two-hour movie that have any resonance, and neither of them has anything to do with Michael Keaton, who spends much of his screen time in Batman costume, which exposes (other than those radar eyes) only the tip of his nose, the rosebud mouth (suggestive of Betty Boop or, just possibly, a fruit bat), and the chin, with which he is pretty much forced to lead. The scenes do, however, involve Jack Nicholson, as the petty thief Jack Napier, who, in his other persona, becomes the Joker, the hideously laughing supervillain with the disfigured mouth, supposedly caused by Batman's having tossed him into a vat of boiling, viridescent chemicals, but more plausibly derived from Victor Hugo's *L'Homme qui rit* (or its silent-movie version). Nicholson gives an inspiredly comic-epic performance as the cackling sadist whose rictus would spell the last laugh for the world, were it not for Batman. 7

In Nicholson's material there is even a smidgen of comic invention by the scenarists, Sam Hamm and Warren Skaaren. (Are these real names? Real people? I'd like to think that they are merely a team of screenwriting jingles. Surely "Warren" and "Skaaren" must be pronounced so as to rhyme, as "Sam" and "Hamm," and "love" and "dove," do.) There is a bit of cleverness in having the Joker poison various cosmetics so that, used in certain combinations, they will induce the same clownish grin as his, followed by swift death. Although such a conceit lacks the minimal illusion of credibility that lends piquancy to the incredible, it is still good for a disgruntled guffaw or two. But if Nicholson's performance steadily transcends the Joker's material, nothing much follows suit. 8

To return, however, to the two scenes that almost do. The first is the one where the Joker and his goons invade the local art museum and, while he sings and cavorts outrageously, deface the masterpieces from all periods hanging there—except for a Francis Bacon, whose work pleases the Joker. There is, thanks largely to Nicholson, a ghastly vandalistic humor to this, but the filmmakers missed a chance to do something positive by not showing Pollocks, Rauschenbergs, Warhols, and the like being defaced. 9

The other scene of some interest is the dark-garbed Joker's crazed skyscraper-top waltz with the white-clad, fainting Vicki (Kim Basinger), 10 whom he intends to ravish and destroy as he already did a previous girlfriend, played, alas, by Jerry Hall (Mick Jagger's mistress), whose face before disfigurement is not much better than after it. As Nicholson whirls about laughing fiendishly with the limp and all but lifeless Vicki in his malefic arms, it conjures up images of Death and the Maiden, Dr. Miracle and Antonia, Svengali and Trilby, and other mythic or near-mythic archetypes.

The direction by Tim Burton is appropriately slick and mindless. Bur- 11
ton allows the scenarists to come up with several shaggy-dog plot elements (an imminent bicentennial celebration for which the city has no funds, a crusading D.A. who does absolutely nothing, a police commissioner who arbitrarily fades in and out of the action), and he cannot give shape to the material. But that is the occupational hazard in making movies out of comic strips, a non-art form that is all middle and no end. Kim Basinger has been lovelier and more effective in other movies; her main distinction here is that she sheds or loses her shoes in three separate scenes, either because she thinks she is playing Shoeless Joe or because she is taller than her leading man. Jack Palance, Pat Hingle, and especially the good Michael Gough are stuck with no-account roles; as Gotham City's mayor, Lee Wallace is a perfect Ed Koch lookalike, but nothing is made of that, either.

Pauline Kael

In "Batman," the movement of the camera gives us the sensation of 1
swerving (by radar) through the sinister nighttime canyons of Gotham City. We move swiftly among the forbidding, thickly clustered skyscrapers and dart around the girders and pillars of their cavelike underpinnings. This is the brutal city where crime festers—a city of alleys, not avenues. In one of these alleys, Bruce Wayne as a child watched, helpless, as his parents were mugged and senselessly shot down. Now a grown man and fabulously wealthy, Bruce (Michael Keaton) patrols the city from the rooftops. He has developed his physical strength to the utmost, and, disguised in body armor, a cowl, and a wide-winged cape, and with the aid of a high-tech arsenal, he scales buildings and swoops down on thugs and mobsters—Batman.

There's a primitive visual fascination in the idea of a princeling ob- 2
sessed with vengeance who turns himself into a creature of the night, and the director, Tim Burton, has given the movie a look, a tone, an eerie intensity. Burton, who's thirty, has a macabre sensibility, with a cheerfulness that's infectious; his three films ("Pee-wee's Big Adventure" and "Beetlejuice" are the other two) get you laughing at your own fear of death.

Seen straight on, the armored Batman is as stiff and strong-jawed as a 3
Wagnerian hero. His cowl-mask has straight-up sides that end in erect ears; he gives the impression of standing at attention all the time. (He's on guard duty.) But something else is going on, too. The eye slits reveal

only the lower part of his eyes—you perceive strange, hooded flickers of anger. When Batman is in motion, what you see can recall the movies, such as "The Mark of Zorro" and the 1930 mystery comedy "The Bat Whispers," that the eighteen-year-old cartoonist Bob Kane had in mind when he concocted the comic-book hero, in 1939. Though the Tim Burton film is based on Kane's characters, it gets some of its funky, nihilistic charge from more recent "graphic novels" about Batman, like Frank Miller's 1986 "The Dark Knight Returns" and Alan Moore's 1988 "The Killing Joke." This powerfully glamorous new "Batman," with sets angled and lighted like film noir, goes beyond pulp; it gallops into the cocky unknown.

In the movie's absurdist vision, Batman's antagonist is the sniggering 4
mobster Jack Napier (Jack Nicholson), who turns into the leering madman the Joker. Clearly, Batman and the Joker are intended to represent good and evil counterparts, or, at least, twin freaks, locked together in combat; it was Jack Napier who made an orphan of Bruce Wayne, and it was Batman who dropped Jack into the vat of toxic chemicals that disfigured him. That's the basic plan. But last year's writers' strike started just as the movie was set to go into production, and the promising script, by Sam Hamm (it reads beautifully), never got its final shaping; the touching up that Warren Skaaren (and uncredited others) gave it didn't develop the characters or provide the turning points that were needed. With the young hipster Keaton and the aging hipster Nicholson cast opposite each other, we expect an unholy taunting camaraderie—or certainly some recognition on Batman's part that he and the Joker have a similarity. And we do get a tease now and then: when the two meet, their actions have the formality of Kabuki theatre. But the underwritten movie slides right over the central conflict: good and evil hardly know each other.

At times, it's as if pages of the script had drifted away. The mob kingpin 5
(Jack Palance, in a hearty, ripe performance) is toppled by Jack Napier, who moves to take control of the city, but we're not tipped to what new corruption he has in mind. We wait for the moment when the photojournalist Vicki Vale (Kim Basinger), who's in love with Bruce Wayne and is drawn to Batman, will learn they're the same person. She's just about to when the scene (it's in her apartment) is interrupted by the Joker, who barges in with his henchmen—we expect him to carry her away. The revelation of Batman's identity is suspended (we never get to see it), and the Joker trots off without his prize. After this double non-whammy, a little air seems to leak out of the movie. And it's full of these missed moments; the director just lets them go. Vicki and Bruce, dining together, are seated at opposite ends of an immense banquet table in a baronial hall in Wayne Manor; two thousand years of show business have prepared us for a zinging payoff—we feel almost deprived when we don't get it. Yet these underplayed scenes have a pleasing suggestiveness. The dinner scene, for example, shows us that Bruce is flexible, despite his attraction to amor. (He collects it.) And Vicki quickly realizes that the Bruce Wayne–Batman identity is less important than the question Is he mar-

ried only to his Batman compulsion or is he willing to share his life with her?

The movie has a dynamics of feeling; it has its own ache. Michael 6
Keaton's poor-little-rich-boy hero is slightly dissociated, somewhat depressed, a fellow who can take his dream vehicle, the Batmobile, for granted. How do you play a guy who likes to go around in a bat costume? Keaton has thought out this fellow's hesitations, his peculiarity, his quietness. In some situations, the unarmed Bruce is once again a passive, helpless kid. (In a triste scene at night, he hangs by his ankles on gym equipment, rocking softly—trying to lull himself to sleep.) Keaton's Bruce–Batman is really the only human being in the movie; he gives it gravity and emotional coloring. This is a man whose mission has taken over his life. The plangent symphonic score, by Danny Elfman, might be the musical form of his thoughts; it's wonderfully morose superhereo music.

When Nicholson's Joker appears for the first time, the movie lights up 7
like a pinball machine: the devil has arrived. (Nicholson is playing the role Keaton played in "Beetlejuice.") The Joker is marvellously dandified—a fashion plate. The great bohemian chapeaus and the playing-card zoot suits, in purple, green, orange, and aqua, that Bob Ringwood has designed for him have a harlequin chic. They're very like the outfits the illustrator Brian Boland gave the character in "The Killing Joke," and Nicholson struts in them like a homicidal minstrel, dancing to hurdy-gurdy songs by Prince—the Joker's theme music. But the grin carved into the Joker's face doesn't have the horror of the one on Conrad Veidt's face in the 1927 "The Man Who Laughs" (where Bob Kane acknowledges he took it from). Veidt played a man who never forgot his mutilation. Nicholson's Jack Napier is too garish to suffer from having been turned into a clown; the mutilation doesn't cripple him, it fulfills him. And so his wanting to get back at Batman is just crazy spite.

This may work for the kids in the audience, and the Joker's face stirs 8
up a child's confused fear of—and delight in—clowns. (They're like kids made hideous and laughed at.) But possibly the Joker's comic-book dazzle diminishes the film's streak of morbid grandeur—the streak that links this "Batman" to the reverbs that "The Phantom of the Opera" and "The Hunchback of Notre Dame" set off in us. When the adversaries have their final, moonlight encounter, among the gargoyles on the bell tower of Gotham's crumbling, abandoned cathedral, they could be like the Phantom of the Opera split in two, but there's pain in Keaton, there's no pain in Nicholson. The Joker may look a little like Olivier as the John Osborne vaudevillian, but he isn't human: he's all entertainer, a glinting-eyed cartoon—he's still springing gags after he's dead. This interpretation is too mechanical to be fully satisfying. And is Nicholson entertainer enough? He doesn't show the physical elegance and inventiveness we may hope for.

The master flake Tim Burton understands what there is about Batman 9
that captures the moviegoer's imagination. The picture doesn't give us any help on the question of why Bruce Wayne, in creating an alternate

identity, picked a pointy-eared, satanic-looking varmint. (Was it simply to gain a sense of menace and to intimidate his prey?) But Burton uses the fluttering Batman enigmatically, playfully. He provides potent, elusive images that draw us in (and our minds do the rest). There may be no more romantic flight of imagination in modern movies than the drive that Vicki and Batman take, by Batmobile, rocketing through a magical forest. Yet though we're watching a gothic variation of the lonely-superhero theme, we're never allowed to forget our hero's human limitations. He's a touchingly comic fellow. When he's all dressed up in his bat drag, he still thinks it necessary to identify himself by saying, in a confidential tone, "I'm Batman."

The movie's darkness is essential to its hold on us. The whole concep- 10
tion of Batman and Gotham City is a nighttime vision—a childlike fantasy of the big city that the muggers took over. The caped crusader who can find his way around in the misasmal dark is the only one who can root out the hoods. The good boy Batman has his shiny-toy weapons (the spiked gauntlets, the utility belt equipped with projectile launcher, even the magnificent Batwing fighter plane), but he's alone. The bad boys travel in packs: the Joker and his troupe of sociopaths break into the Flugelheim Museum, merrily slashing and defiling the paintings—the Joker sees himself as an artist of destruction.

Batman and the Joker are fighting for the soul of the city that spawned 11
them. We see what shape things are in right from the opening scenes. Gotham City, with its jumble of buildings shooting miles and miles up into the dirty skies, is the product of uncontrolled greed. Without sunshine or greenery, the buildings look like derelicts. This is New York City deliberately taken just one step beyond the present; it's the city as you imagine it when you're really down on it. It's Manhattan gone psycho. But even when you're down on it you can get into your punk fantasies about how swollen it is, how blighted and yet horribly alive.

The designer, Anton Furst, seems to have got into that kind of jangled 12
delight, putting together domes and spires, elongated tenements, a drab city hall with statues bowed down in despair, and streets and factories with the coal-mine glow of the castles and battlements in "Chimes at Midnight." Gotham City has something of the sculptural fascination of the retrofuture cities in "Blade Runner" and "Brazil"—it's like Fritz Lang's "Metropolis" corroded and cankered. If H. G. Wells' Time Machine took you there, you'd want to escape back to the present. Still, you revel in this scary Fascistic playground: the camera crawls voluptuously over the concrete and the sewers, and the city excites you—it has belly-laugh wit.

When Gotham City celebrates its two-hundredth birthday, the big pa- 13
rade balloons are filled with poison gas—an inspiration of the Joker's. (He rides on a float, jiggling to the music; his painted red grin has wing tips.) Paranoia and comic-book cheesiness don't defeat Tim Burton; he feels the kick in them—he likes their style. The cinematographer, Roger Pratt, brings theatrical artifice to just about every shot—a high gorgeousness, with purples and blacks that are like our dream of a terrific rock

concert. The movie even has giant spotlights (and the Bat-signal from the original comic books). This spectacle about an avenging angel trying to protect a city that's already an apocalyptic mess in an American variant of "Wings of Desire." It has a poetic quality, but it moves pop fast. The masked man in the swirling, windblown cape has become the hero of a comic opera that's mean and anarchic and blissful. It has so many unpredictable spins that what's missing doesn't seem to matter much. The images sing.

VOCABULARY

Orli Low: kaleidoscopic (1), rudimentary (5), cowl (6), resurgent (7). *John Simon:* confluence (1), sequentiality (2), sustenance (2), amalgam (3), dystopia (3), sardonically (3), concupiscent (4), dalliance (6), miscegenation (6), viridescent (7), rictus (7), smidgen (8), piquancy (8), malefic (10) *Pauline Kael:* macabre (2), camaraderie (4), dissociated (6), plangent (6), enigmatically (9), miasmal (10).

QUESTIONS

Orli Low

A. Discovering Meaning

1. What does Low think about the film *Batman?*
2. Is there anything she doesn't like?

B. Examining Method

1. What is the persuasive purpose of her review?
2. What is the effect of her introductory sentence (see pages 394–398)?
3. What is the tone (see pages 421–422)?
4. What is the intention of the phrase, "kaleidoscopic action-packed film"?
5. What is the purpose of the second paragraph?
6. For what audience was this piece written? What assumptions does the writer make about this audience—age, experience, interest in movies, for example?

7. Select some individual vocabulary words that best give clues to what the writer's main purpose is.

8. Are you convinced by this piece? Is the writer?

C. Shifting Focus

1. What is the intended effect of the "punchy" vocabulary ("Wham," "Pow"), the breezy, and the frequent clichés ("wildly-successful," "hot show,")?

2. What do these stylistic traits suggest about her readers—their likely point of view, the time available to them for reading, their desire for analysis?

John Simon

A. Discovering Meaning

1. What is Simon's thesis?

2. What does he like about the film?

3. What does he dislike?

4. Why do audiences seek out film versions of comic strips, according to Simon?

5. What does Simon think of the Jack Nicholson role in the movie?

B. Examining Method

1. What is Simon's attitude toward his subject and his readers?

2. Why does he mention Pollock, Rauschenberg, and Warhol in paragraph 8?

3. What assumptions does he make about *his* audience?

4. What is the purpose of the final paragraph?

C. Shifting Focus

1. Compare the commentary by Low with the one by Simon. Be sure to consider point, purpose, style, and attitude of the writer, and the relationship with the readers.

2. As you read this review, it is also possible for you to get a sense of what the *writer* is like. Why does he reveal so many of his own personal traits as well as those he sees in the film?

3. Is this review appropriate for the readers of the *National Review?* (If you are not familiar with the source, study it in the library.)

Pauline Kael

A. Discovering Meaning

1. What is Kael's thesis?
2. What does she like about the film?
3. What does she dislike about the film? On what does she blame some of the film's weaknesses?
4. Which character seems the most human to Kael?
5. What does she think about the setting?

B. Examining Method

1. What is her purpose in writing this piece?
2. What assumptions does she make about her readers? What is her intention for them as a result of reading her review?
3. What kind of introduction does she use? How does it compare to Low's and Simon's? (See pages 394–398.)
4. Why does she refer to the books in paragraph 3?
5. What does she mean when she says that the film "goes beyond pulp; it gallops into the cocky unknown"?
6. What is the "double non-whammy" in the film? What is the effect of this diction? (See pages 422–423.)
7. Compare the concluding paragraphs of all three reviewers. What do they reveal about the approach and the judgment of each? (See pages 435–439.)

C. Shifting Focus

1. Why does Kael refer so often to films other than *Batman?*
2. What does the reference in paragraph 4 to the writer's strike suggest about Kael as a reviewer?
3. Is this review appropriate for *The New Yorker?* (Check the source in the library, if necessary.)

SUGGESTIONS FOR DISCUSSION AND WRITING

A. Using Persuasion

1. Write your own review of a film you have seen recently. Be sure to look up the necessary information on actors and other facts so that your discussion will be concrete. (It might be wise to attend a film for the purpose of reviewing and to take notes while you are watching it.) Identify your readership and your place of publication, and keep both in mind as you write. Think of what you would like your readers to take away from your review.

2. Find two or three reviews of a film about which you have strong feelings and a clear recollection, summarize their judgments, and then evaluate them. (*The Reader's Guide to Periodical Literature* lists film reviews at the back of each volume. Don't forget newspaper indexes.) The first part of your essay will most likely be expository (see pages 3–4), and the second part will be persuasive. (For a critical paper following a similar pattern, see "Heroic Eve" on pages 203–208.)

B. Exploring the Options

1. Compare these three reviews of *Batman.* Which one do you find the most informative and convincing. Which one would most influence your decision on whether or not to see the film? Why? Which one would have the least effect on your decision?

2. Evaluate a review of a recent film that you have not yet seen. Do you have faith in the reviewer? If you go to see the film, you might write a comparative paper on your expectations based on the review and your actual experience of the film.

Creating Images Through Description

Description is bringing something to life, most often through the senses. It is the writer's portrayal of the world as it looks, feels, smells, sounds, and maybe even tastes. But, delightful and engaging as it may be, it rarely stands on its own; it is usually a *part* of what the writer is trying to say. It may, for example, be straightforward, as in scientific reports or medical diagnoses, in which exactness of detail is essential, but it may also be suggestive, evoking meanings and feelings associated with the subject.

Description may be a vivid support for an argumentative thesis, as is Jonathan Kozol's description in *The New Yorker* (January 25, 1988), in which he argues for better treatment of homeless families in New York:

> . . . many of the children have on coats and sweaters. After they eat, some of them come back to the table, timidly. They ask if there are seconds. There are no seconds. Several families at the back of the line have to be turned away. In my pocket I have one enormous apple, which I bought in Herald Square for fifty cents. I give it to a tall Italian man who comes back to the table to request an extra meal. He doesn't eat the apple. He polishes it against his shirt. He turns it in his hand, rubs it some more. I watch him take it back to where he's sitting, with his children—one boy, two little girls.

(Notice the details that contribute to this picture of desperation—the timid children returning to the table, the turning away of late families, the Italian man cherishing the apple for his children.)

Description may be indirectly persuasive, as in Henry Beston's *The Outermost House.* After living on outer Cape Cod for a year, Beston concludes by describing his feelings, feelings he hints we might share:

> . . . I had seen the ritual of the sun; I had shared the elemental world. Wraiths of memories began to take shape. I saw the sleet of the great storm slanting down again into the grass under the thin seepage of the moon, the blue-white spill of an immense billow on the outer bar, the swans in the high October sky, the sunset madness and splendour of the year's terns over the dunes, the clouds of beach birds arriving, the eagle solitary in the blue. And because I had known this outer and secret world, and been able to live as I had lived, reverence and gratitude greater and deeper than ever possessed me, sweeping every emotion else aside, and space and silence an instant closed together over life. Then time gathered again like a cloud, and presently the stars began to pale over an ocean still dark with remembered night.

(In this passage, Beston traces visual images of the past year to his inspiring moment of "reverence and gratitude," a moment he shares through his writing and lures us to appreciate.)

Description may contribute to the theme of a larger work, as in H. T. Lowe-Porter's translation of Thomas Mann's famous account of plague-ridden Venice, where the artist-hero gradually succumbs to the lethal atmosphere:

> There was a hateful sultriness in the narrow streets. The air was so heavy that all the manifold smells wafted out of houses, shops, and cook-shops—smells of oils, perfumery, and so forth—hung low, like exhalations, not dissipating. Cigarette smoke seemed to stand in the air, it drifted so slowly away.

(The Venetian authorities may be keeping the plague a secret, but Mann's ominous, even sickening, description warns of what is to come.)

Description may also contribute to characterization, as in M. F. K. Fisher's travel piece, "I Was Really Very Hungry," in which she suggests something of the French reverence for food through the behavior of a relentless waitress:

> . . . The cork was very tight, and I thought for a minute that she would break it. So did she; her face grew tight, and did not loosen until she had slowly worked out the cork and wiped the lip. Then she poured an inch of wine in a glass, turned her back to me like a priest taking Communion, and drank it down. Finally some was poured for me, and she stood with the bottle in her hand and her full lips drooping until I nodded a satisfied yes. Then she pushed another of the plates toward me, and almost rushed from the room.

(Fisher's description moves slowly through the sequence and helps us to *see* the waitress's attitude.)

Description may characterize the writer, as in Aldous Huxley's detailed description of one of the world's most-admired sites, the Taj Mahal in Agra, India:

> . . . Nature did its best for the Taj. The west was duly red, and orange, and yellow, and, finally, emerald green, grading into pale and flawless blue towards the zenith. Two evening stars, Venus and Mercury, pursued the sunken sun. The sacred Jumna was like a sheet of silver between its banks. Beyond it the plains stretched greyly away into the vapours of distance. The gardens were rich with turf, with cypresses, palms, and peepul trees, with long shadows and rosy lights, with the noise of grasshoppers, the calling of enormous owls, the indefatigable hammering of a coppersmith bird. Nature, I repeat, did its best. But though it adorned, it could not improve the works of man. The Taj, even at sunset, even reverberated upside down from tank and river, even in conjunction with melancholy cypresses—the Taj was a disappointment.

(Huxley's description of the Taj at sunset moves from the distant to the closer details, all leading to his surprising and unconventional conclusion. He describes in lush detail what it was that failed to move him.)

Description may also help the reader to understand an abstract concept or a difficult idea, particularly through comparison, as in Leonard Bernstein's account of what it's like to conduct an orchestra:

> So the conductor is a kind of sculptor whose element is time instead of marble; and in sculpting it, he must have a superior sense of proportion and relationship. He must judge the largest rhythms, the whole phraseology of a work. He must conquer the form of a piece not only in the sense of form as a mold, but form in its deepest sense, knowing and controlling where the music relaxes, where it begins to accumulate tension, where the greatest tension is reached, where it must ease up to gather strength for the next lap, where it unloads that strength.

(In this passage, the background image of a sculptor at work helps the reader to visualize and understand what the conductor's job is like. The more concrete art form lends solidity to the art of conducting.)

Evocative description, simply for its own sake, particularly of the clichéd, rosy sunsets, glistening snows, and broad horizons sort, is usually boring, because it is all too familiar and it makes no point beyond itself. As in the preceding examples, description needs to make a dominant impression, and there must be a reason for including it. It needs to make a point.

For the student who is wondering where to live, a description of an off-campus apartment in a housing office notice will probably have occupancy as a goal:

> Large apartment a stone's throw from campus! Spacious, sunny, furnished! Sitting room, modern kitchen, plus a private bedroom with hardwood floors and fireplace. Available immediately for mature female.

An even more detailed, persuasive description of the apartment may appear in the student's letter to her parents, in which the student requests more money for rent, or a very different description may be part of a letter of complaint to the landlord, in which the tenant explains why two months' rent has yet to be paid:

> The rotting wood on the front steps is a safety hazard, as is the clanging heating system that rarely works on days when the temperature goes below freezing. Yes, the place is furnished as you promised, but I now discover that the best pieces—the blue couch, the Shaker desk, the brass floor lamp—belonged to the former tenant who just last week lugged them to his U-Haul. The stainless steel stove in the "modern" kitchen looks good, but it's more likely to produce a fire than a good dinner. Throughout the apartment, from the entrance hall to the far corner of the bedroom, the wiring is frayed and dangerous, probably from many, many years of neglect.

(Written by a tenant who is not planning to pay the rent, this description focuses on the negative details and explains why the landlord should not be expecting the rent.)

Description contributes to the larger point the writer is trying to make.

WORKING WITH DESCRIPTION

Consider places or people you know well—sights, sounds, colors—that appear vividly in your imagination. Description is not only visual. Think of the rooms, houses, camps, clubs, schools, yards, and vacation sites you have visited. Describe a salty view from a rocky point overlooking the Atlantic; the sights, sounds, and smells of a local fair; or the atmosphere of a class conducted by an excellent teacher. You might also try describing something abstract by means of something concrete—your idea of boredom compared to the grinding movement of a glacier, busy-ness compared to the activities of leaf-cutter ants.

The interest in description is in sharing the writer's true sense of a place or an experience, or the writer's evocation of the world as it looks, smells, feels, sounds, and tastes. The challenge is to avoid clichéd descriptions, the ones too often portrayed on souvenir posters and placemats, and to avoid descriptions without meaning. Description needs a dominant impression and a point. Is the room, so lovingly described, a haven from the chaos surrounding it, or is it a painful memory of a lost childhood? Is the dance club a "meat market," an insult of all of your senses, or is it a model of what clubs for the enlightened should be?

Descriptions must also take organization into account, the order of the details of the description. Is the reader supposed to look around a room from the door to the window, to the closet, and back to the door again? Is the reader supposed to move from a general impression to a particular detail, or from top to bottom, or from the larger setting to the furnishings? There is no rule about order, except that the best arrangement is the one that helps the reader *best* to experience what is described.

In a classroom exercise, for example, students listed random details about their classroom: humming fluorescent lights, cold drafts near the windows, streaky blackboards, colorful spring-break posters, desks with outdated graffiti, dull yellow walls, the clock that always tells the wrong time, the new linoleum, and so forth. After examining these details, they chose to suggest that the dominant impression of the room is *unpleasant* and selected the particulars that backed up the point. The final plan for the paragraph moved from things that contribute to a general impression (walls, blackboards) to closer details, which take more time to detect (cold, desks, clock, lights).

Example

In this letter, a student describes what he enjoys about his new dormitory room.

Hi Mom,

I'm glad you convinced me to hold off on the apartment idea. Someone named Jack Allen (a friend of Elizabeth's) took it, and isn't too happy with the leaky pipes or the mice. I really lucked out on this room, though. It's private! I just happened to be in the right place at the right time. After I got your letter, I went to the housing office just when the sophomore who used to live here decided to join the Army. Most of the space was already assigned, so they let me have it. I was dreading a room like the one Tom had last year, with a roommate who piled dirty laundry in the corner, stayed up all night listening to tapes, and stole his class notes. This room is *my* space, only about 8' by 10', but still mine. The swaybacked bookshelves run from ceiling to floor on two of the walls and even reach out over the bed. I have to watch my head when I get up. The closet space isn't much, but neither is my wardrobe. The sixth floor window looks out on a New England autumn scene, sort of like the one on the cover of the catalog. Trouble is my desk is right at this window, so I spend too much time appreciating the view. Guess I'd better ask for a shade. It's real quiet here, because all the rooms on this level are private, mostly honors students, I guess. The floor is stained, rough cement, but when I buy myself a cheap rug, and bring in my TV and my hockey stuff, it'll seem almost like home. I hope that guy likes the Army. Gotta go.

Ryan

(Notice that the dominant impression of this description is positive. The student *likes* this room. Also notice that this description begins generally, with dimensions, then moves to the bookshelves lining the walls, and to the closet space. The view outside the window adds to a generally positive impression, and even the stained floor is worked into the overall good feeling about the place.)

Warm-Up

Write a paragraph in which you describe something particular in great detail. Remember that description is usually spatial, moving from top to bottom, near to far, right to left. Consider your feelings about what you are describing. (You might try describing a bad experience that Ryan might have in a dorm room, thus making it part of another appeal for an apartment.)

The New Year's Flower Market in Canton

(paragraph)

Weijon Chu (student)

This paragraph is a detailed description of just one of the many colorful and flowery aspects of the Chinese New Year's celebration. Although Weijon hasn't seen this market for many years, the descriptive details came crowding in: "As I worked on new drafts, I had to keep dropping details so I could put in better ones."

Thinking Ahead What are some descriptive details that Weijon is almost compelled to include? Could you describe a particular aspect of a periodic celebration, one of those transient, yet vivid moments during the course of a year?

The February New Year's celebrations in China are many and colorful, but the one I remember most vividly from my childhood is the Flower Market in Canton's Dong Chuan Road. For a period of three days, a half mile stretch of this wide road is devoted entirely to flowers. I remember the tall, blooming peach trees at the huge temporary gateway and the horizontal scrolls with characters saying, "Welcome to the Flower Market." Surrounding this gateway were small colorful triangular flags, and near the entranceway every half hour was a lively lion dance. I remember the shining multi-colored lights, and down the center of the road, a double row of high flower stands, offering an array of red roses, white narcissi, yellow and purple chrysanthemums, and symbolic golden tangerines to the New Year's crowd. Some flowers were erect, some slender and graceful, some bending gently. I felt they were beautiful and loved them all. At any one time during the peak hours of 7 P.M. to 1 A.M., as many as 40,000 people may make their way down one side of the stand then back the half mile to the exit. Tall red flags flap in the breeze, bright lights trim the stands, the mixed scent of flowers floats in the air, folk music sings out over the noisy throng—the violin, the drum, the plucked instrument, or "pipa," and the bamboo flute, or "xiao." I remember it as a noisy, colorful scene, so crowded sometimes, that I envied the goldfish swimming freely in their tanks at some of the stands. But I also remember loving this market and wishing I had another pair of eyes to take it all in. After some time just looking, the adults push their way into the stands to bargain for the New Year's flowers and then carry them high above their heads to protect them from the crush. I can still see my parents and I making our way carefully to the exit, usually two and a half hours after we entered. My legs always told me it was time to go home.

QUESTIONS

A. Discovering Meaning

1. Which senses does the writer call upon to describe the market?
2. What is the dominant impression in his description?
3. What is the emotional effect of this description on the reader? How does it make you feel?

B. Examining Method

1. Which details help you best to understand what the market was like to a young child?

2. What is the tone of the paragraph?
3. How does the writer suggest his emotional reaction to the experience of going to the market?
4. What is the writer's purpose for his readers?
5. How are the experiences of the paragraph organized?

C. Shifting Focus

1. Rewrite this paragraph as if the writer hated being dragged annually to the market.
2. How does the writer combine his description of a past scene with his present feelings about it?
3. Can you imagine how the writer's parents might have described the same market (or maybe how the goldfish might have)? What kinds of changes would be necessary?

SUGGESTIONS FOR DISCUSSION AND WRITING

A. Using Description

1. Write a description of a public festival or ceremony. Remember to choose the most characteristic details and to think of the dominant impression you want to make. What is your point?
2. Describe in detail an event that you would see as characteristic of a particular culture. What aspect does it characterize?

B. Exploring the Options

1. What are the feasts and celebrations that seem most important to Americans? Do we have our own peculiarly "American" way of celebrating, say, New Years?
2. About travel writing, author and editor Caskie Stinnett once suggested that it needed a "sting," something to keep it from the simple-minded false adoration of marketers or chambers of commerce. Describe a place that is well known, a place for which certain reactions are almost predictable. After your own description, discuss how your reaction compares to what might be expected.

3. In an article entitled, "Why We've Failed to Ruin Thanksgiving" (*Time,* November 27, 1989), Walter Shapiro argues that Thanksgiving is "the one holiday that cannot be bought," primarily because "more than any other date on the calender, Thanksgiving has remained private and personal, devoid of the tinsel trappings that mar the rest of contemporary life." Do you agree that Thanksgiving has not yet been ruined? Do you think that other holidays ***have*** been "bought"? (See pages 180–183 for a discussion of argument or pages 214–218 for a discussion of persuasion.)

Camping I Hate!

(paragraph)

Sally Atwater (student)

This paragraph is part of a longer paper on this student's honeymoon, which was a camping trip. Here she describes the many things she doesn't like about camping, especially on her honeymoon. In her first draft, Sally wrote about several aspects of the newlywed couple's trip: routes they took, sights they enjoyed, and places they visited, and she just mentioned that camping was not much fun. On rewriting it, after a workshop class asked her to specify her central point, she "decided to focus more on the contrast between my dreams of a honeymoon and what I actually got. We came home a week early."

Thinking Ahead What could the writer describe if she wanted the reader to share her displeasure with camping? Do you have any particular reaction to the great outdoors?

One of the worst aspects of my honeymoon trip was the camping. I hated the much-praised woodsy smell, the dampness, the crowding into a stuffy tent. I hated sleeping in a sleeping bag. I *didn't* sleep in a sleeping bag. I wanted a hotel room with a view and After Eights on my down pillow. What I got was a sleeping bag and bugs. I hated the mosquitoes, fleas, flies, and pinchers that love camping, and campers. And the sticky repellant wasn't much better than the bugs. I also hated the showers that I needed to get the sticky stuff off. I haven't been camping much, but every time I've gone, I've had to take a cold shower, usually in an old roofless bathhouse, somewhere far off in the woods. This time was no exception. The mosquitoes didn't give up in the bathhouse, either. In fact, they liked it there, taking perverse pleasure in biting while I tried to lather my hair with one hand and pull the shower rope with the other. Before I left, I had to spray on my first sticky layer of new repellant. All the time I was camping I was missing not only my hotel room with the view, but also my own new apartment—with screened-in windows, hot water, faucets, lightbulbs, and a kingsized waterbed. I never want to leave home again without them.

QUESTIONS

A. Discovering Meaning

1. What does the writer dislike about camping?
2. Which senses does she use to describe the experience?

B. Examining Method

1. Which details contribute most to your understanding of the writer's dislike of camping (see pages 400–403)?
2. Why does she use lists at the beginning of her paragraph (see pages 394–398)?
3. What is the tone of the piece? Does the writer take this experience seriously? (See pages 421–422.)
4. What is the reference in the last line? How does it contribute to tone?

C. Shifting Focus

1. How does contrast work within this description? Could the passage be written without the contrast?
2. What is the main purpose of this paragraph? What does the writer have in mind for her reader?

SUGGESTIONS FOR DISCUSSION AND WRITING

A. Using Description

1. Write an account of a type of vacation or a vacation spot primarily through description of the details of the experience. Remember to consider thesis and tone.
2. In a letter to William Wordsworth, on January 30, 1801, Charles Lamb refuses an invitation to join his friend in the country, announcing that, "... I don't much care if I never see a mountain in my life."

> I have passed all my days in London, until I have formed as many and intense local attachments, as any of you mountaineers can have done with dead nature. The lighted shops of the Strand and Fleet Street, the innumerable trades, tradesmen and customers, coaches, waggons, playhouses, all the bustle and wickedness round about Covent Garden, the very women of the Town, the Watchmen, drunken scenes, rattles—life awake, if you awake, at all hours of the night, the impossibility of being dull in Fleet Street, the crowds, the very dirt and mud, the Sun shining upon houses and pavements, the print shops, the old book stalls, parsons cheap'ning books, coffee houses, streams of soups from kitchens, the pantomimes, London itself a pantomime and a masquerade—all these things work themselves into my mind and feed me, without a power of satiating me. The wonder of these sights impells me into night-walks about her crowded streets, and I often shed tears in the motley Strand from fulness of joy at so much Life.

(Write an imitation of this paragraph, using as subject matter a particular place that you enjoy.)

B. Exploring the Options

1. Write a letter to Sally from the Crow's Nest Campground Management. (Be sure to consider tone and purpose. Why are they writing to her?)
2. Write a personal response to her, either agreeing or disagreeing with her assessment of camping.
3. Why do so many people crave "roughing it" in the wilderness? (You might want to see the passage by Abbey on page 222 and the one by Beston on page 254.)

Body Shop

(paragraph)

Paul Grasso (student)

This is one paragraph from a paper describing the many "mutilations" this student's 21-year-old body has undergone—on the football field, in a fight, off the back of a pick-up truck—none of which are flattering and all of which occurred as a result of making a bad decision. This paragraph describes an intentional "mutilation," getting a tattoo. Paul says that "in early drafts, I left out many of the best details—the photogaphs lining the walls, Davey's wife, the message on Davey's lower lip. The paragraph got better as I added them in."

Thinking Ahead Which senses do you expect the writer to use in this description? Do you have an unusual experience or maybe a "coming-of-age" ritual that you could describe in detail?

> As I approached Davey's Tattoo Studio on my sixteenth birthday, I was planning to research the subject of tattoos thoroughly before going through with it. I checked out all the photos of tattooed women lining the walls in the waiting room, and I glanced at Davey's wife, also tattooed. A while later, in the back room, I reclined uneasily in one of Davey's cold metal chairs and looked at Davey, weighing in at around 300 pounds. I believe he was white, but I'm just guessing because every square inch of exposed skin was covered with tattoos, including eyelids and the top of his bald head. On the inside of his lower lip was a cheerful two-word phrase that won't be found in greeting cards. As we discussed details, I started to have my doubts, so I asked this sympathetic presence whether or not it would hurt. He pushed me further back into the chair, stuck a very large needle in my left thigh, and said, "Nope". It hurt. About an hour and a half later, I re-emerged into the bright June sunshine. I felt relieved, but also very cool and rock-star-like with my new tiger tattoo running down my thigh. I was sure that "Wanna see my tattoo?" would be foolproof with the ladies. Once again, I was wrong.

QUESTIONS

A. Discovering Meaning

1. What does the writer actually describe in this paragraph? Do you see any need for further description?
2. In the longer paper, the writer describes the damage to his body as helping him to learn to think more carefully about what he is doing. His "scars" are his constant reminders. How does this description of getting a tattoo fit the larger point of his paper?
3. When does the writer "come of age" or recognize the lesson in his experience?

B. Examining Method

1. Why does the writer mention his sixteenth birthday in the first sentence?
2. Which details help you best to share the writer's experience (see pages 400–403)?

3. Why does he mention the photographs of the tattooed women?

4. How do you feel about the subject and the writer as you read this account? (Do you have different reactions to the writer as he was then, at 16, and as he is now, a college junior?)

5. What is the writer's own attitude toward this experience (see pages 421–422)?

6. What is the writer's purpose for the reader?

C. Shifting Focus

1. In this description, the writer tells a small "story" of his visit to the studio. What is the connection between the description and the narration?

2. If the writer were very serious about his experience and deeply concerned about the errors of his past, what changes would be necessary in this paragraph?

SUGGESTIONS FOR DISCUSSION AND WRITING

A. Using Description

1. Write an essay in which you use description as the central focus of a set of experiences. This writer, for example, organized each paragraph around a physical sign of his bad decisions—a cleat mark, a short scar, a long scar ("like a railroad track"). Another student described the customers in several stores where she has worked: how their clothing, appearance, and manners told something about the values of the community from which they came.

2. Describe a "coming-of-age" of your own, one in which you at least thought you were taking a step toward adulthood. Be sure to consider any possible differences between the person you were then and the one you are now.

B. Exploring the Options

1. Write a paragraph in which Davey advertises for his Tatoo Studio.

2. Why would anyone, including a 16-year-old boy, want a tattoo? (Interviews and research may add further interest to your speculations here.)

3. Consider some American "coming-of-age" ritual—for example, getting a driver's license, going out on a first date, or possibly the irony of getting

drunk as a way of proving one's "manhood." What do such rites of passage suggest about American society and about growing up in America? Describing the ritual would certainly be important, but remember to consider what point you are trying to make *through* your description. (One student described a drunken party in his apartment, in which "everyone passed out." When asked *why* he was describing this scene to his readers, he said that had no idea. He had forgotten the difference between living and writing. The writer *must* have an idea. Was he bragging, was he horrified, was he disgusted, was he going on the wagon, was he looking for new friends? Except for a secondhand hangover, what does he want the reader to get from his experience?)

4. Follow the same instructions for the previous suggestion and write about a coming-of-age ritual in some other culture.

Getting Through to Students

(paragraph)

Gilbert Highet

Gilbert Highet (1906–1978) was born in Glasgow, Scotland and graduated from Glasgow University and Oxford. Married to novelist Helen Clark MacInnes, Highet was a professor of Greek and Latin at Columbia University, New York for most of his teaching career. He became an American citizen in 1951. His many publications, include ***The Classical Tradition: Greek and Roman Influence on Western Literature*** (1949), ***The Art of Teaching*** (1950), ***Talents and Geniuses*** (1957), ***The Anatomy of Satire*** (1962), and ***The Immortal Profession*** (1976), from which this passage is taken. Here Highet describes the difficulties of trying to get through to students, given the many distractions surrounding them. The paragraph is an extended comparison between teaching in the classroom and making a long-distance telephone call during a noisy party. Notice the many descriptive details. About writing essays, Highet says, "The first essential is to choose a subject which is clear and precise in your mind and which interests you personally—so that you really enjoy thinking and talking and writing about it."

Thinking Ahead Which sense do you think Highet will use most often in his description? Can you think of any apt comparison for describing the difficulty of getting through to someone?

Have you ever attempted to take a long-distance call in the middle of a party at someone else's house? The host says: "This is for you, Cleveland calling," and hands you the receiver. Distant and uneven, a little voice speaks in your ear, explaining something you have forgotten and asking questions you cannot answer. From time to time it is interrupted by surges and crackles of electricity; occasionally the voice of a total stranger, like a disembodied ghost, floats along the wire uttering fragments of an unintelligible conversation. But your caller in Cleveland goes on earnestly explaining and eagerly enquiring. Meanwhile your host has gone back to the other guests, and is engaged in a loud argument about the Middle East that comes into your free ear with much more force and stridency than the Cleveland talker. Two late-comers are taking off their coats and chatting just beside you in the hall. Music is coming from the middle distance, where Jeff and Valerie have been persuaded to do their own special version of "Baby, it's cold outside"; and there are shouts of laughter at the end of each verse. And you are hemmed in by a stream of miscellaneous noise, random interjections and isolated phrases and hum and clink and clatter, topped off by the furious blares of taxis threading their way past the double-parked cars outside the door. At last Cleveland says: "O.K., you've got all that. Nine o'clock on Tuesday without fail, and bring *both* zizms, they're sending Presjunks as well. 'Bye now." And you go back to the party, wondering what on earth that was all about, and trying with a sense of overhanging despair to make a connected story out of the message. Sometimes you ring back next morning for confirmation. Sometimes you put the bits together into the wrong shape, and blame the telephone company. Sometimes you get it right, and it is at least partly luck.

QUESTIONS

A. Discovering Meaning

1. According to Highet, what is it like trying to communicate with students?
2. What are the distractions that interfere with communication?
3. Based on this paragraph, how might a teacher cope with these problems in communication?
4. Upon what sense is most of this description based? Why?

B. Examining Method

1. Why does Highet include this paragraph in a book on teaching?
2. Who is his likely audience? What is his purpose for this audience? (See pages 370–371.)

3. What is the tone? Can you get any sense of what Highet might have been like as a teacher (see pages 421–422)?
4. How does the extended comparison to a telephone call work (see pages 431–433)?
5. Why is so much of the paragraph devoted to dialogue, some of which is nonsense?

C. Shifting Focus

1. Is Highet's purpose simply to describe the difficulty of teaching?
2. Could Highet have described this difficulty without using the extended comparison? Try it. What is the effect?

SUGGESTIONS FOR DISCUSSION AND WRITING

A. Using Description

1. Write a descriptive paragraph using extended comparison, for example, doing X is like Y: sailing a boat is like trying to talk to my mother; going to a club is like taking a test; and so forth.
2. Write a description of a classroom experience from a student's point of view. If possible, try to use extended comparison.

B. Exploring the Options

1. What are some of the ways students themselves might cope with the "long-distance telephone call" experience in the classroom?
2. What are some of the ways professors might cope with this difficulty of getting through to students?

My Room, My Prison

Vladimir Glezer (student)

Recently settled in America, this adult student describes a room in Moscow in which he passed a significant part of his life. Vladimir says that it was "sometimes difficult to write this piece, because it brought back some bad memories and at the same time made me lonely for my old homeland."

Thinking Ahead Given the title, what kinds of details do you expect the writer to include in his description? Do you have a particular place that over the years has remained significant for you?

In Moscow, when I was young, I was fond of Byron. Some of his poems I had a hard time understanding, but the one I liked best was "The Prisoner of Chillon." Perhaps because of the place I was living, I liked his description of his cell, but it wasn't until much later that I could comprehend the meaning of his conclusion: 1

My very chains and I grew friends,
So much a long communion tends
To make us what we are:—even I
Regain'd my freedom with a sigh.

I lived right in the center of Moscow, in a room I'll never forget: an ugly, one-room apartment in a six-story private house. It's the place where I spent my childhood and my youth. And ugly as it was, with its strange angles and crowded corners, it's a permanent part of my life. When I was a two-week-old baby, my father left this room for the front, and he never came back, killed at the age of 34. It is this room where my wife and I spent our honeymoon. It's the same room where my mother lived her last years. This room is a witness of both good and bad times, and I remember it as it was. 2

My first recollection belongs to a time when I was about three. It was the third year of the war as well, and there was no food, no clothes, little furniture. The winter was terrible, and I see clearly—a little iron stove in the middle of the bare room. We called this stove "bourgois." I don't know why; maybe it was because it ate too much and didn't work. I remember piles of firewood in the corner, but they weren't enough, and all our wooden furniture was used to feed the stove too. It was so cold that the wall between the two great windows was covered with ice. My mother put a huge cupboard there to protect us, but it was useless. That winter, I had a terrible case of pneumonia. I remember two beds on both sides of the door: iron ones for me and my older sister. I don't remember my mother's bed. Possibly she had no bed at all. 3

As I got older, there were times I actually enjoyed this ugly little room, maybe because there were six other rooms in the house and we had lots of neighbors with children. A long corridor connected our rooms and flowed into a long kitchen with seven tables and two gas stoves. Our family's table stood in the corner, close to the only window, which in winter served as a refrigerator (we didn't know refrigerators in those times). Our table had a good position in the room because it didn't verge on any other table, and this aroused envy in our neighbors. The other object of envy was the position of our room, close to a bathroom. Though there were two bathrooms in our common living area, I remember a long line of neighbors in the morning, all waiting and quarrelling. These quarrels were common, but we children took little notice of them. We 4 liked running along the corridor and the kitchen, causing the ire of adults carrying hot kettles and pans. We had no toys so we made them ourselves of whatever we could find. Imagination made them beautiful. I had a box of such toys near our door, a collection worth more than jewels to me.

When I got still older and went into the army, I finally got a chance to live away, but even then, I had some affection for the place. My mother still lived there and maybe I associated it with security. During the war, I actually found myself missing it, but when I returned everything seemed different. 5

The room still looked the same. It was still its same old ugly shape. It was still near the bathroom. It still came with its well-situated table in the kitchen. But I began to feel trapped, more and more like a prisoner. My toy box was just a fond memory. I tried to make the place seem like home again by bringing in a big collection of books. I put them everywhere—on shelves, in the wardrobe, upon and under the desk, on the refrigerator (we finally got one), on the TV. I enjoyed these books, but as the Russian proverb says, "You can't make a black dog white simply by washing it." Whenever I read Byron, I tried to imagine his cell, and it always seemed as if he were describing this room, maybe because I too *couldn't* leave. I was at the university, and I couldn't afford to live elsewhere. As Byron said, 6

> And it was liberty to stride
> Along my cell from side to side,
> And up and down, and then athwart,
> And tread it over every part.

Even after I married, my new wife and I lived with my mother for several years in this same room. We re-decorated—new brown carpet, soft, stuffed furniture, new curtains to match, but no matter what we did, the room felt more and more prison-like. All of my old neighbors were gone, and the new ones were not fun at all. The quarrels over tables and bathrooms went on as usual, but I couldn't escape with the children this time. And, worst of all, some neighbors were anti-Semites; we were Jewish. 7

My wife and I finally bought another apartment—a two-room luxury apartment near the center of the city. It was clean and new and even had a private bath. I liked this place, but strangely, I sometimes found myself wanting the old room again. From a distance and bad as it was, it still seemed more like home than the new place did. It would take me only one hour actually *in* the old room, however, in the ugly, cramped surroundings, and I'd want to escape again. My feelings about this room have never been simple. 8

Eventually, my mother died and the room passed to other people, but when I received permission to emigrate after an eight-year wait, I was allowed to visit once more. I wanted to say farewell to the place that sheltered me for such a large part of my life. There was no one there at 9 the time, so I had a chance to go over the many years I spent there. I studied the walls, the windows, the ceiling, the floor. I noticed the ugly, uneven shape once again, and a strange, sweet feeling began to take me over. I realized then that I would feel the loss of this room wherever I lived and that I would recall it in memory before my death, as Bryon's prisoner remembered his cell when he acquired freedom. I finally understood the conclusion to his poem. "... even I/Regain'd my freedom with a sigh."

QUESTIONS

A. Discovering Meaning

1. How would you describe the attitude of the writer toward this room? Does he have one or many?
2. What does the writer describe about this room?
3. What is the writer's thesis, his main point about the room?

B. Examining Method

1. Is there a dominant impression in this description?
2. What is the writer's purpose in describing this room to his readers? What does he want them to understand through his description?
3. How does the writer organize his discussion of the room?
4. Why does he trace the appearance of this room through several changes in time?
5. What does Byron's poem have to do with the meaning of this piece?
6. What is the purpose of paragraph 5?
7. Which descriptive details recreate the room most clearly for a reader who has never seen it (see pages 400–403)?

C. Shifting Focus

1. What does the description actually contribute to the meaning of this piece? Could the writer make his point without any descriptive detail? What would happen to his essay?
2. If the writer had intended this description to work also as a criticism of the Soviet system of government, what kinds of changes would be necessary?

SUGGESTIONS FOR DISCUSSION AND WRITING

A. Using Description

1. Write a description of a place that over the years has remained significant for you. Choose either a single point in time or possibly trace its transformation and yours, as the writer of "My Room, My Prison" does. What point are you trying to make about the place?
2. Describe a place with which you have a love–hate relationship. Can you think of any reasons why?

B. Exploring the Options

1. Discuss the point made by Byron and this writer about the possible relationship between ourselves and our "chains":

   My very chains and I grew friends,
   So much a long communion tends
   . . .

   Can you think of any situations in which this kind of "friendship" might develop?
2. This book contains several essays on homes. Read them and write a comparison of their approach to subject matter, their overall point, their purpose, and their audience.

The Subway to the Synagogue

(introduction)

Alfred Kazin

Born in 1915, Alfred Kazin has written literary criticism and essays about personal experiences, as well as anthologies of both literature and criticism. He has taught at Harvard, University of California, Smith, Black Mountain College, University of Minnesota, City University of New York, and other universities here and abroad. His books include *Starting out in the Thirties, New York Jew, On Native Grounds,* and *A Walker in the City,* from which this description has been taken. Kazin has written, "I looked to literature for strong social argument, intellectual power, human liberation . . . salvation would come by the word, the long-awaited and fatefully exact word that only the true writer would speak."

Thinking Ahead This description moves spatially down a city street. What kind of details might Kazin observe there? Think of a walk or a journey that you have taken so frequently that the details have become very familiar.

In every cry of every man,
In every infant's cry of fear,
In every voice, in every ban,
The mind-forg'd manacles I bear.

William Blake: London

Every time I go back to Brownsville it is as if I had never been away. From the moment I step off the train at Rockaway Avenue and smell the leak out of the men's room, then the pickles from the stand just below the subway steps, an instant rage comes over me, mixed with dread and some unexpected tenderness. It is over ten years since I left to live in "the city"—everything just out of Brownsville was always "the city." Actually I did not go very far; it was enough that I could leave Brownsville. Yet as I walk those familiarly choked streets at dusk and see the old women sitting in front of the tenements, past and present become each other's faces; I am back where I began. 1

It is always the old women in their shapeless flowered housedresses and ritual wigs I see first; they give Brownsville back to me. In their soft dumpy bodies and the unbudging way they occupy the tenement stoops, their hands blankly folded in each other as if they had been sitting on these stoops from beginning of time, I sense again the old foreboding that all my life would be like this. *Urime Yidn. Alfred, what do you want of us poor Jews?* 2

The early hopelessness burns at my face like fog the minute I get off the subway. I can smell it in the air as soon as I walk down Rockaway Avenue. It hangs over the Negro tenements in the shadows of the El-darkened street, the torn and flapping canvas sign still listing the boys who went to war, the stagnant wells of candy stores and pool parlors, the torches flaring at dusk over the vegetable stands and pushcarts, the neon-blazing fronts of liquor stores, the piles of *Halvah* and chocolate kisses in the windows of the candy stores next to the *News* and *Mirror,* the dusty old drugstores when urns of rose and pink and blue colored water still swing from chains, and where next door Mr. A.'s sign still tells anyone walking down Rockaway Avenue that he has pants to fit any color suit. It is in the faces of the kids, who before they are ten have learned that Brownsville is a nursery of tough guys, and walk with a springy caution, like boxers approaching the center of the ring. Even the Negroes who 3 have moved into the earliest slums deserted by the Jews along Rockaway Avenue have been infected with the damp sadness of the place, and slouch along the railings of their wormy wooden houses like animals in a cage. The Jewish district drains out here, but eddies back again on the next street; *they* have no connection with it. A Gypsy who lives in one of the empty stores is being reproached by a tipsy Negro in a sweater and new pearl-gray fedora who has paid her to tell his fortune. *You promis' me, didnja? Didnja promis', you lousy f...?* His voice fills the street with the empty rattle of a wooden wheel turning over and over.

The smell of damp out of the rotten hallways accompanies me all the way to Blake Avenue. Everything seems so small here now, old, mashed-in, more rundown even than I remember it, but with a heartbreaking familiarity at each door that makes me wonder if I can take in anything new, so strongly do I feel in Brownsville that I am walking in my sleep. I keep bumping awake at harsh intervals, then fall back into my trance again. In the last crazy afternoon light the neons over the delicatessens bathe all their wares in a cosmetic smile, but strip the street of every personal shadow and concealment. The torches over the pushcarts hold in a single breath of yellow flame the acid smell of half-sour pickles and herrings floating in their briny barrels. There is a dry rattle of loose newspaper sheets around the cracked stretched skins of the "chiney" oranges. Through the kitchen windows along every ground floor I can already see the containers of milk, the fresh round poppy-seed evening rolls. Time for supper, time to go home. The sudden uprooting I always feel at dusk cries out in a crash of heavy wooden boxes; a dozen crates of old seltzer bottles come rattling up from the cellar on an iron roller. Seltzer is still the poor Jew's dinner wine, a mild luxury infinitely prized above the water out of the faucets; there can be few families in Brownsville that still do not take a case of it every week. It sparkles, it can be mixed with sweet jellies and syrups; besides, the water in Europe was often unclean. 4

In a laundry window off Dumont Avenue a printed poster with a Star of David at the head proclaims solidarity with *"our magnificent brothers in Palestine."* A fiery breath of victory has come to Brownsville at last! Another poster calls for a demonstration against evictions. It is signed by one of those many subsidiaries of the Communist Party that I could detect if it were wrapped in twenty layers of disguise. "WORKERS AND PEOPLE OF BROWNSVILLE . . .!" Looking at that long-endured word *Landlord,* I feel myself quickening to the old battle cries. 5

And now I go over the whole route. Brownsville is that road which every other road in my life has had to cross. 6

VOCABULARY

fedora (3), briny (4), chiney (4)

QUESTIONS

A. Discovering Meaning

1. What does the writer like about this road? What does he dislike? How does he suggest these reactions through his description?
2. What is his thesis?
3. Why does he return to this road?

B. Examining Method

1. What senses does Kazin call upon throughout his description?
2. What type of introduction does he use (see pages 394–398)? What is the purpose of the details he includes there?
3. What is the tone of the introduction? Is this mood consistent with the rest of the piece?
4. What role does memory play in this description?
5. What is his purpose in writing this description?

C. Shifting Focus

1. These paragraphs also serve as an introduction to a longer chapter in a book. As introductory paragraphs, are they successful in leading you to read the rest of the chapter? Why?
2. In this selection, Rockaway Avenue takes on a symbolic meaning beyond its literal existence as a road through Brownsville. What does it mean to Kazin? What descriptive details contribute to this larger meaning?

SUGGESTIONS FOR DISCUSSION AND WRITING

A. Using Description

1. Write a description of a road with which you are quite familiar. Think about how you feel about this road. What point do you want to make about it?
2. If the road has changed, write a descriptive piece comparing the way it once looked with the way it looks now. Use more than the visual sense

and consider what point you are trying to make. How does the change make you feel? What would you like your reader to feel? (You might want to read pages 33–35 for a discussion of comparison.)

B. Exploring the Options

1. Return to a place you often frequented when you were young or to a place ten years in your past and compare your feelings then to those you have now.

Telling What Happened Through Narration

"And then what happened?" is the question answered in narration (coming from the Latin *narrare,* "to tell a story"). It is the telling of events through time: First this happened, then this, then this. It is *also* the relating of these events to one another and giving them significance beyond the usual daily sequence of activities. Narrative is selective, or should be. Unlike the child's simple listing of events at a birthday party—"We came. We played catch. We tossed water balloons. We ate cake. We gave presents. We went home"—narrative requires comparison, weighing, a sense of what is important and what isn't, a sense of purpose, and a decision as to what the whole thing means.

It is important to ask, "Why is this tale being told? What's the point?" Think of how you sometimes feel when you hear, "Let me begin at the beginning," especially from a storyteller who does not usually select well or get to the point quickly. You can feel yourself wishing the beginning were somewhere nearer the middle, or even better, at the end. The person who gives you a "double-feature" account of the weekend may leave you preferring short subjects—the highlights, not the whole 48-plus hours. A reader may not share your endurance for reliving every stop on your European itinerary, menus included, or your fascination with all five fun-filled days at Disney World. The writer must offer some meaning; the reader must care about what the writer is telling.

And often the events that we experience are much less compelling than the European menu or the parade at Disney World. They may not even bear contemplating, let alone narrating to someone else. For example, consider your usual activities from the time your alarm clock goes off at 7 A.M. to your first class at 8:30 A.M.: "The clock radio came on, I got up, I put on my clothes, I ate breakfast," and so on. It is possible to "save" such flat information, but it would require *making* something of this early morning routine: "Morning is the best part of the day for me" or "My mornings are a constant struggle between my desire to sleep and the world's desire to wake me up" or even "Getting up in the early morning is just one more of the indignities imposed on the common man by the capitalistic system." If you do not "make something" of this early morning routine, the material will remain flat and unengaging.

Writing narrative essays requires the skills of the storyteller—the ability to describe scenes, to bring characters to life, and to make them talk to one another. As in all writing, details are important, but in narration they are essential to meaning. As short story writer Anton Chekhov said:

> Everything that has no direct relation to the story must be ruthlessly thrown out. If you write in the first chapter that a rifle hangs on the wall it must without fail fire in the second or third chapter. And if it isn't going to fire, it mustn't hang, either.

Narration also requires attention to tone, to the writer's attitude toward the events in the story. A "What I Did Last Summer" essay, the school assignment that most often is accused of being instantly tedious, can be made into good narrative with the selection of the right details and the right attitude for reporting them.

One student, for example, recently wrote a successful and humorous essay on his summer that was devoted entirely to boring himself to death. Here is his outline:

—When summer began, I wanted to relax, so I ended up hanging around watching game shows in the morning and soaps in the afternoon. (In the paper, this paragraph was developed with sample quiz questions, descriptions of fake, tense struggles to come up with the right answers, and intricate plot summaries for the soaps.)

—I thought things would pick up when I went to the cottage, the same cottage my family has been going to for the past 12 years. The lake was polluted this year, but I didn't want to go swimming anyway. Most of the kids were younger than I was, so I ended up babysitting for my nieces and nephews and grilling hot dogs for two weeks. (The paragraph is developed with wake-up calls from 3-year-olds and shopping trips with them to purchase hot dogs).

—My end-of-the-summer job at the video shop from 7 to 12 every night made grilling hot dogs seem lively. After my all-day nap, I spent the night reshelving misplaced empty tape boxes. (The paragraph is developed with long lists of video titles and categories, echoing the tedium).

(Generally a contented person, this writer was mildly amused by his awful summer, so his tone was light and self-mocking. He could, however, have been genuinely depressed over his failure to make more out of his free time; he could even broaden his frustration and turn the paragraph into a serious criticism of the plight of American teenagers, tortured by boredom and unaware of the remedies.)

The college student who is looking for housing could tell a story of her search, focusing on the various agents who took her to the vacant dumps near campus, the places where the agents admired the six layers of muddy royal blue paint around the bathroom mirror, or making it a "coming of age" story, in which her disillusionment with the wonders of college life grows.

For the narrative essayist, the facts of life are the materials; what to make of them is the art.

WORKING WITH NARRATION

We are constantly telling tales to one another. Some of them are worth telling; some are not. Try to think of some true stories that would hold someone's interest, stories you would *care* to tell. Think also of the meaning of each one. Is the point of each story a lesson learned, a character revealed, a hidden meaning discovered, or a humorous side perceived? Narrative essays do not have to be personal. It is possible to tell a story about someone else, based on insider's information, or to base a narrative on research, as with an event drawn from a historical biography.

The interest in narration is in the reader's curiosity about what happened next and in the involvement with events as they are reported. How many of you have intentionally eavesdropped on an argument or on a conversation at a nearby table in a restaurant? Most of us are somewhat nosy. The challenge, though, is in using this natural nosyness to keep the story interesting by selecting details that have some relevance to the point (assuming, of course,

that there *is* a point) and, in nonfiction narration, by telling the truth without distorting or without lying for effect. Short-story writing allows you to express your impulses to make up a story. The reader of nonfiction narration expects the truth and deserves to get it.

Example

Here is a paragraph written by a student who is telling her friends what it's like to live at home:

> So you think you'd rather commute than live in the dorms? Well, think again. Take just one typical day in my life. Last Thursday, I woke up at 7 to get to my 8:30 class, but by the time I got the $19.00 worth of gas into my antique auto, through the one-ways in the center, and into the crowded parking lot, I was late anyway. At 2:30, as usual, I rushed out of my Comp. class and headed for Zayre's where I worked registers, wrote up returns and exchanges, and stocked cosmetics until 6:30. (Don't forget, I have to keep the car on the road and buy gas.) By 7:30, I got home for what was left of the cold meatloaf. My mother wanted a ride to a Tupperware party and my brother needed to be picked up from hockey practice. I needed to study for a test at 8:30 on Friday. My mother's response

was her usual, "Now Janice, you get free room and board here. It wouldn't hurt to give just a little, would it?" By 9:00, I was studying, but by 10:00, I was asleep, that is, until my sister decided she needed a heart-to-heart about her new boyfriend. I'll trade my commuter's life for a dorm room any day.

Warm-Up

Write a brief narrative account of some event that seemed important to you at the time—for example, an incident at a party, a conversation in the cafeteria, or an event during a recent school break. You could also rewrite Janice's paragraph, turning her narrative into one that is in favor of commuting. Be sure to think of the reasons *why* you are selecting certain details. What is your main point?

Reefing in a Brisk Wind

Erick Scheiderman (student)

Written by the same student who wrote the process paragraph on reefing (page 95), this paragraph is one of a series of stories about knowing what you're doing when you're on a boat. This is a "reefing story," a narrative account of a frightening occasion when reefing a sail became necessary. Please reread the process paragraph after you have read this one. About the difference in writing the two, Erick says that writing the narrative was "easier than telling how to reef. I didn't have to be as technical. I just had to remember what actually happened."

Thinking Ahead This is an "adventure" narrative. What kind of details should Erick include? Do you have a brief story of a situation in which you were forced to act quickly to prevent disaster?

With Mike and Paul as crew, I set sail in my Santana 20 across San Diego Bay. The sun shone brightly and the full mainsail pulled taut in a brisk 10 knot (13 m.p.h.) wind—good signs for this three hour, ten mile race. We were optimistic. But almost immediately, a dark front of black cloud wedged its way from the ocean and over the strand into the bay. Within minutes, the darkness bore down upon us, the wind picked up, and the rain sliced across the deck and into our faces. The wind almost tripled, with gusts up to 40 m.p.h. and three to five foot waves crashed against the side of the boat. Our progress slowed to about 8 m.p.h., and the little twenty-footer heeled over, its rudder out of the water. At the wheel, I had almost no control of the steering. With its keel almost parallel to the surface, the boat began to drift sideways. I wasn't at all scared, but my less-experienced crew went silent, waiting for some words from me, namely, instructions on how to get control of the situation. I guess experience really does count. "Reef the mainsail!" I ordered, as clearly as I could. Step by step, I guided them. "O.K., Paul, tie the lines there!" "Mike, lower the main halyard!" The sail luffed and cracked in the wind; the boat rocked unevenly. "Paul, tie the loose sail to the boom, and Mike, bring in the outhaul!" I then told both of them to raise the remaining sail as high as they could, get it tight, and tie the halyard to the cleat. With all of this done within about two minutes, the shorter sail filled taunt and the boat righted in the still-brutal breeze. After Paul replaced the 150 jib sail with a 110, we made it back on course to the finish. (We came in sixth.) As we crossed the line at the yacht club, the clouds dispersed, the wind died, and the sun came out. I love adventures like these. Mike and Paul wanted some hot chocolate at the club.

QUESTIONS

A. Discovering Meaning

1. What happened to the writer and his crew?
2. How does the writer react to his experience?
3. How does the crew react?

B. Examining Method

1. Why is the story told in the first person?
2. What is the purpose of the first sentence? Of the last sentence? (See pages 394 and 435.)
3. Which details help you best to imagine the predicament?
4. How does the writer's attitude toward this experience support the main point that it is important to know how to handle emergencies?
5. What was your attitude as you read this paragraph?

C. Shifting Focus

1. If the writer's purpose were to frighten his readers rather than to warn them, what changes would be necessary in his paragraph?
2. What would be the effect of telling this story in the present tense?
3. Compare this paragraph to the process paragraph by the same writer on page 95. Consider point, purpose, tone, and audience.

SUGGESTIONS FOR DISCUSSION AND WRITING

A. Using Narration

1. Write an account of a situation in which you were required to act quickly to prevent disaster or some other undesirable result.
2. Write a narrative telling of a situation in which your expertise was called upon. Remember to consider your purpose and your reader.

B. Exploring the Options

1. Rewrite this same story from the point of view of Mike or Paul.

I'll Take the Low Road

(paragraph)

John Baron (student)

This paragraph is part of a longer paper in which the writer confesses his childhood terrors at the amusement park—for example, the roller coaster, the merry-go-round with its "equestrian gargoyles," and the ride operators with their engineer boots and contempt for their passengers. Here he gives a narrative account of a terrifying ride with his more daring sister. John says that he is still slightly embarrassed by his fears, but that "this is the way it happened. Maybe I'll help someone else feel a little better."

Thinking Ahead How does the writer help the reader to share his fears in this narrative? What do you expect the writer's attitude to be so many years after the event? Can you recall a childhood terror that has since become more amusing than frightening?

Because of my sister's boldness when it came to choosing hazardous rides, I usually turned to my mother for company on the more sedate ones. Once, only once, did I get the urge to be bold myself and only once did Mary consent to go on a ride with me. It was a six-armed contraption with a Flash-Gordon-vintage rocket at the end of each arm. Terrified before I got on, I began to feel dizzy when the ride operator threw a lever, and each arm moved slowly in concert about the base of the machine. I didn't know that each rocket had a control stick that could raise the rocket up to a twenty-five foot orbit. But after only a few feet, Mary yanked back the stick and my heart lumped into my throat. Our rocket lifted off while the ones in front of us scissored up and down as their manic little pilots maneuvered them through the atmosphere. Watching them, I felt a more sickening vertigo. Peering below, I could see the indifferent operator, chomping his wet cigar and leaning casually on the lever. I begged Mary to bring us back down. She yelled to me that it was a baby ride and I belonged on it. I was desperate and though I was six and she ten, fear brought strength. I grabbed the stick and held it down for the remainder of our flight, my knuckles turning white and my pale and knobby knees trembling. As an astronaut, I was a failure. Our ship was the first to re-enter and the only one to hold a steady three-foot orbit for the entire ride. These were probably the longest two minutes of my sister's life. I know they were mine.

QUESTIONS

A. Discovering Meaning

1. What didn't the writer like about this ride?
2. How did the writer as a child react to his fear?

B. Examining Method

1. What is the point of this story?
2. What is the writer's purpose in telling it?
3. How does he want his readers to feel while reading it?
4. What is the connection betwen the first sentence and the last (see pages 435–439)?
5. How is the narrative organized (see pages 374–378)?
6. Does the paragraph rise to a climax? Should it? (See page 377.)
7. What is the tone?
8. How does the present writer compare to the little boy in the rocket? What are the signs of the difference?

C. Shifting Focus

1. Rewrite this paragraph from Mary's point of view. What point could she make through *her* experience of this ride?
2. How else could this same story be told? What other meanings could be derived from it?

SUGGESTIONS FOR DISCUSSION AND WRITING

A. Using Narration

1. Write an account of an experience you once had that at one time seemed very different from the way it does now—for example, flying, speaking in public, dancing, or going to the dentist. This requires a dual perspective, a simultaneous awareness of both feelings. (Your present feelings about it may not be superior to your past feelings about it.) Remember to consider *why* you are telling the story. What is your point? How do you want your readers to react?

2. Write a narrative account of a frightening experience. Remember to think of your readers.

B. Exploring the Options

1. Why do some of us, like Mary, feel compelled to take part in "daredevil" amusements?

2. Do you ever see anything sinister in situations that are intended to be simply fun or that others see as fun?

The Purse Test

(paragraph)

Anne McKay (student)

This paragraph is taken from a longer paper in which the writer tells of her various experiences with clothing styles at several different schools she attended as she was growing up. Here she focuses on a particular scene at one school where she was taught a lesson by an older student, "Miss S." About writing it, Anne says she found it interesting to trace her school experiences by focusing on something that revealed a great deal about the values of each place—clothing. "This particular experience is probably the one I remember with least pleasure, however."

Thinking Ahead In this paragraph, the writer tells about an experience that was intended to teach her a lesson. Did she learn it? Have you experienced a "learning session" that you did not bring upon yourself?

One thing I noticed the moment I arrived at the local junior high was that all the girls carried purses. So a purse was one of the first things I looked for on my first shopping trip, even though I had no desire or need to carry one. I got a very small one, thinking it would be perfect, and then I tried to fill it up. Miss S's purse literally overflowed with makeup. With great curiosity, I had watched her dig down through heaps of clutter to get to a pencil at the bottom. I didn't wear makeup yet, so I bought a little Kleenex purse pack like the one my mother always carried. I didn't have a cold, but it seemed like a good filler. Next, I packed in an extra small comb that couldn't possibly get through my hair, but anything larger wouldn't fit. A small plastic change purse for lunch money and extra pencils stuffed it to the brim. I was running out of ideas, but that night I remember rather liking my new purse. Not for long. Next day, at the clay sculpting table in art class, Miss S. spotted it. She zoomed in and snatched it away before I could hide it under the table. "Oh, it's such a *little* one," she sneered, "and such a *cute* style!" I tried to grab it from her, but she was too fast. Next, she dumped the contents into the middle of the big oil-cloth-draped table. Holding and dangling each object for display, she announced to her attentive audience, "Now, isn't this a practical little packet of Kleenex . . . and, oh, *I* wish *I* could have a teeny-weeny comb just like this one!" They laughed; she laughed. I had all I could do to keep from crying. I had gotten "A's" in many a math and science test, but that didn't matter at this school. I failed the purse test.

QUESTIONS

A. Discovering Meaning

1. What was the test that the writer had to pass?
2. What kind of person was the writer at the time of the experience?
3. What kind of person was Miss S.?

B. Examining Method

1. Why does the writer give so much background to the actual narration?
2. How does the writer feel now about this experience? What are the indications?
3. Which detail of the narrative helps you best to imagine the writer's experience?
4. Does the paragraph rise to a climax (see pages 374–378)?
5. What is the real "lesson" in this paragraph? Is there more than one?

C. Shifting Focus

1. Suppose that the writer were still deeply upset by this experience. What changes would be necessary in her paragraph?
2. Rewrite this narrative from the point of view of Miss S. What point might she try to make through her story?

SUGGESTIONS FOR DISCUSSION AND WRITING

A. Using Narration

1. Write a narrative account of a situation in which you were intentionally or unintentionally embarrassed. Remember to consider your attitude toward the experience now.
2. Write about a situation in which you were required to learn a lesson that possibly was not sought by you.
3. Write a short narrative that includes a portrayal of character.

B. Exploring the Options

1. Compare the experience of this narrator with that of Langston Hughes in "Salvation" (pages 305–307) or with that of Updike in "Three Boys" (pages 27–30).
2. Write an essay on the pressure to conform in American society. The approach could be argumentative (see pages 180–183) or possibly on how to cope with pressure (see pages 92–95).

Beating for the Hunt

Scott Russell Sanders

Scott Russell Sanders was born in 1945 in Memphis, Tennessee. He received his M.A. from Brown University and his Ph.D. from Cambridge University, and he now teaches literature at the University of Indiana. He is the author of several books, including *Hear the Wind Blow: American Folk Songs Retold*, *Wilderness Plots*, *Stone Country*, *Bad Man Ballad*, and *The Paradise of Bombs*, from which this selection has been taken.

This paragraph, from a longer essay, "At Play in the Paradise of Bombs," is an account of Sanders' early years living among the armaments of the Ohio Arsenal. It was a time of exploration, war games, and hunting. Here he tells of herding deer for a hunting party of Pentagon "military brass." About writing an essay, Sanders says, "It must not be idle movement, however, if the essay is to hold up; it must yield a pattern, draw a map of experience, be driven by deep concerns."

Thinking Ahead This paragraph tells of a coming-of-age experience that led the writer to make a permanent decision in his life. Do you see the "map of experience," the "deep concerns" mentioned by Sanders in his comment? Think of an experience that led you to make an important decision in your life.

> A freezing rain the night before had turned the world to glass. As we fanned out over the brittle snow, our bootsteps sounded like the shattering of windows. We soon found our deer, lurking where they had to be, in the frozen field where hay had been dumped. Casting about them our net of bodies, we left open only the path that led to the ravine where the officers waited. With a clap of hands we set them scurrying, the white tails like an avalanche, black hoofs punching the snow, lank hams kicking skyward. Not long after, we heard the crackle of shotguns. When the shooting was safely over, I hurried up to inspect the kills. The deer lay with legs crumpled beneath their bellies or jutting stiffly out, heads askew, tongues dangling like handles of leather. The wounded ones had stumbled away, trailing behind them ropes of blood; my father and the other seasoned hunters had run after to finish them off. The generals were tramping about in the red snow, noisily claiming their trophies, pinning tags on the ear of each downed beast. The local men gutted the deer. They heaped the steaming entrails on the snow and tied ropes through the tendons of each hind leg and dragged them to the waiting jeeps. I watched it all to the end that once, rubbed my face in it, and never again asked to work as a beater, or to watch the grown men shoot, or to hunt.

QUESTIONS

A. Discovering Meaning

1. What particular experience is told in this paragraph?
2. What was the writer's attitude at the time of the experience? How do you know?

B. Examining Method

1. What is the main point of his narrative?

2. How does the writer want his readers to react to his experience?

3. Sanders' narrative contains vivid and detailed description. Why is it so important to this piece?

4. Why does he present so many descriptive details in the sentence that tells of the deers' scurrying away after the hunters' clapping?

5. Why does he use the monosyllables, "white tails," "black hoofs," and "lank hams"?

6. Why does he present the scene after the shooting in such vivid and unpleasant detail?

C. Shifting Focus

1. What changes would be necessary if the narrator had enjoyed the experience and had even gone on to be a hunter?

2. Remove the details that describe the deer. What is the effect on the quality and the message of the paragraph?

SUGGESTIONS FOR DISCUSSION AND WRITING

A. Using Narration

1. Write an account of an experience that led you to make an important decision in your life.

2. Tell a story of an event that appeared very different to you in comparison to the view of others who were observing or partaking in the same event.

B. Exploring the Options

1. In this story, the deer are "lurking where they had to be, in the frozen field where hay had been dumped" and then driven into the guns of the "generals." Do the "generals" have a right to claim "their trophies"? Some people have charged that bullfighting, too, is a contrived and unfair "battle" to the animal's death. Is there any true sport in such activity?

What the Dog Did

Ian Frazier

This is a very short narrative piece on a dog named Tiffany. On writing this piece, Frazier comments fully in his own author's note.

Thinking Ahead What does Frazier do to ensure his reader's interest in his story? Can you write on an equally stirring event that also would be worthy of being told in *The New Yorker?*

I came home the other day and my Saint Bernard, Tiffany, had a really guilty expression on her face, with her ears all hanging down. I got a hunch. I went into the living room, and there were all cushions on the floor, and dog hairs all over the davenport. She knows she's not supposed to be up there. I said, "Come here, you!" and I whacked her with a rolled-up newspaper. She knew she had it coming. She went out in the mud room and lay down with her head right on the floor while I cleaned up the mess she'd made. Finally, I figured she'd had enough, so I said, "Come on, girl, you're a good dog now." I went to give her a Liv-a-Snap, and the next thing I knew she wagged her tail so hard she knocked a full ashtray right off the kitchen table!

A NOTE ON THE AUTHOR: *Ian Frazier is a writer who soaks up experience like a sponge. He experiences life as vividly and adjectivally as he writes about it. His appetite for life is as large as the man himself, or even somewhat larger, since Ian Frazier is of average size and his appetite for life is way above average. He has been embracing all of experience since he was eleven years old, when he began riding his bike to school and so escaped the crushing, stultifying influence of his parents. He spent his pre-teen years travelling, hunting, and fishing as a protégé of novelist Ernest Hemingway, whom he later broke with when he noticed that the older writer continually addressed him as "Daughter." Now in his mid-thirties, a mature writer who has triumphantly found his own voice, he remains (paradoxically) very much a child in many ways. He has that type of courage which one finds so rarely in an adult in our society, and that is the courage to play. It's been said that the eminent student of the human mind Carl Jung abandoned his career and his responsibilities in his sixties and spent a year building sand castles on the beach; that would be as nothing to Ian Frazier. He is just constantly playing. Sometimes he'll give oranges to people on the subway. Sometimes he'll pull a chair out from under a friend when that friend is about to sit down. Sometimes he'll send people unnecessary packages Air Express, making sure that the package will arrive at an inconvenient time. He is blessed with a fractured vision, and a conviction that the world is mad. In spite of that (or perhaps because of that), he doesn't judge another fellow until he has walked around for a while in that fellow's shoes. And not just guys' shoes—sometimes he walks around in ladies' shoes, too: ankle-straps, Mary Janes, high heels, flats,* *and sling-backs. And all the people coming around his apartment trying to get their shoes back, and the confusion, the arguments—unpleasant, perhaps, but all part of a writer's life. Any experience that happens, it doesn't just have to be a good experience, and—*BAM*—Ian Frazier will convert it to writing of some kind. Say he's flying from New York to Miami and his plane has a layover at a Southern airport like Atlanta. Within a matter of minutes, he'll be writing a postcard, the scent of heliotrope and verbena and honeysuckle pervading his prose, and he will be infused with a tremendous sense of place. Or, to give another example, say he's sitting around at a party and someone puts an old song on the record-player and the song reminds him of eighth grade. Suddenly it will be as if he actually is in eighth grade for a while in his mind. Then maybe he'll notice a Fedders air-conditioner in the window next to where he's sitting and he'll be reminded of a Fedders air-conditioner he owned in 1975 that broke down once in the hottest part of the summer. Then something else will bring another memory to mind and off he'll go again. He'll be in the same room with you and yet not there, all at the same time. His writing shows evidence of the strong influence of Sardou, Mazo de la Roche, and Juanita Bartlett. Some critics have called him the white Paul Laurence Dunbar. He lives in Paris, France, with eight mistresses, one of whom is a former Miss Universe runner-up. Everyone he has ever met is completely crazy about him.*

QUESTIONS

A. Discovering Meaning

1. What did the dog do?
2. What did the writer do?

B. Examining Method

1. What is Frazier's overall purpose in telling this story?
2. *The New Yorker* usually places the author's name at the end of the piece and does not include authors' notes at all. Why did the magazine make an exception in Frazier's case?
3. Where is the climax of the narrative?
4. Did you find the story about Tiffany interesting? Would you like to read more of Frazier's stories?
5. If you could characterize the author based on his own notes about himself, what would you mention?

C. Shifting Focus

1. Do you think that the author of the notes is the same as the *real* Ian Frazier, born in 1951, and author of several books, including *Nobody Better, Better Than Nobody,* and *Great Plains* (1989)?

2. What is the tone of the piece? Are there signs that Frazier's purposes might be humorous, even satiric?

SUGGESTIONS FOR DISCUSSION AND WRITING

A. Using Narration

1. Write an equally interesting short narrative on a subject that interests you (or maybe doesn't interest you).

B. Exploring the Options

1. Write an extensive and detailed author's note on yourself. Be sure to consider what you want your readers to think about you. Are you writing this "straight," or are you trying something different?

Bigger and Better?

Paul Grasso (student)

In this essay, a student tells the story of a friend who has turned to steroids to improve his athletic ability. Paul says, "This friend has been on my mind a lot recently, and so was his story when I was asked to write a narrative essay."

Thinking Ahead What could be a possible purpose of telling a story about a user of steroids? This entire piece focuses on someone else's behavior. Do you have a "character" that you could bring to life through telling a story about him or her?

A year ago, my friend Rob, a football player at a major college, weighed 195 pounds. In the weightroom, he could bench press about 215 pounds. Today, he weighs around 250 and can press well over 400 pounds. He has also lost most of his hair, suffers from severe mood swings, and has become unpredictably aggressive and violent. He has been taking anabolic steroids for the last year. 1

I know a lot about steroids now. I wish I had known more about them then. Maybe I could have done something. Steroids are a drug. Their main use is to increase muscle size, mostly through water retention, to enhance an athlete's performance. They come in two basic forms, liquid and pill. Someone told Rob that not too many people took pills, known to cause more serious liver damage. So Rob chose to inject himself up to six times a week. 2

We were in a local gym, our workout finished. It was in April, about a week before spring football practice began. "I've gotten the crap kicked out of me for two years," Rob said. "All the guys are a lot bigger than me. I've gotta do something. I've gotta get on the juice." 3

"Steroids?" I said. "No way, Rob. I played ball for six years without 'em and I did OK." 4

He just shook his head and went over to a guy in the corner of the gym. This guy was a definite user. His skin was all tight and shiny. He looked bloated, like someone had pumped him up with air. I was tempted to stick a pin in him, half expecting him to fly around the room, deflating. He weighed at least 280 pounds. It seemed as if 90% of it was from the waist up. 5

The next day Rob came to my house. As he ripped open a small brown package, he looked like a kid on Christmas morning. 6

"Got it!" he said. "hGH, human growth hormone. Seven hundred fifty bucks for three weeks worth, but worth it. This other one's rhesus monkey hormones. The guy said it was the best he could do." 7

Rob drew out a syringe and probed around his arm. Finally, he found a vein and slid the needle soundlessly in, grimacing. "I'm on my way, baby." 8

A few weeks later, a bunch of us were sitting around Rob's dorm room. A knock sounded at the door. Starting to show some real muscle definition, Rob answered. A small delivery guy from the Chinese restaurant down the street came in. He and Rob spoke for a moment. Rob picked the man up easily. He started tossing him around the room, screaming, "NO WAY this should cost ten bucks!" Then he began to slam the man up against the wall, in time with his words. "That's!" Slam. "TOO!" Slam. "MUCH!" Slam. We finally grabbed him and forced his arm behind his back. The delivery man wasted no time scurrying out the door. 9

I didn't see Rob for quite a while after that, but about five months after he started using steroids, he came into a bar where I work. At first I didn't recognize him. His bushy black hair had receded, and a neat round bald spot had appeared on the back of his head. He couldn't stop moving around; he was shoving chairs and tables aside, bothering everybody. The Rob I knew a few months earlier had been painfully shy. I was sure I didn't like the new pumped-up version. His arms bulged out against his form-fitting shirt, and his back was enormous. He looked and acted like a completely different person. I just watched. 10

He went over to a girl by the jukebox and began to rub her back. (He used to be shy with girls too.) Then he slipped his hand down a little 11 lower. I was only about ten feet away when she turned sharply and slapped him in the face. Without budging an inch, Rob grabbed her arm and punched her on jaw. She hit the floor hard. As she lay there, Rob picked up a chair and raised it. I have no doubt that his intention was to smash her head with it. Several of us grabbed the chair, and forced him to sit down. Looking into his wildly unfocused eyes, I tried to calm him. I called to him. Nothing. I shook him by the shoulders. Nothing. I had no idea what to do or say.

I tried again, yelling, "What the hell are you doing to yourself?" 12

Finally, he answered, with almost no force to his voice, "I'm just playin' 13 ball," and pulled away from me.

A few months after this incident, Rob checked into a drug rehab. hospi- 14 tal. I went to see him. He told me that the feeling of power and invincibility he got from steroids was unlike anything he had ever experienced before. He motioned me closer and looked around the room to see if anyone could overhear. Softly, he whispered, "As soon as I'm out of here I'm back on the juice. The coaches love me. I've got a chance to start this year." It was hard to believe what I was hearing.

He's out of the hospital now. But I haven't seen him yet. 15

QUESTIONS

A. Discovering Meaning

1. What happens to Rob as this story progresses?
2. What happens to the writer?

B. Examining Method

1. What is the writer's purpose in telling this story (see pages 368–371)?
2. Which details contribute best to the overall point (see pages 400–403)?
3. Is the paper effective in bringing Rob's experience to life?
4. Why does the writer so often use quotations in this piece?
5. Why does he so often use short sentences (see pages 426–428)?
6. What is the attitude of the writer in relation to Rob and to steroids?
7. How do you feel as you read this athlete's experience?

C. Shifting Focus

1. How does description contribute to the effect of this story?

2. Given the same information, what other points could possibly be made? If, for example, it were turned into a "friendship" story, rather than one with drug use at its center, what adaptations would the writer have to make?

3. Rewrite this paragraph from Rob's point of view. What point would Rob possibly be able to make from the same set of incidents? What changes in the story would be necessary?

SUGGESTIONS FOR DISCUSSION AND WRITING

A. Using Narration

1. Write a character sketch in which you use narrative as a major part of your portrayal. Remember to decide what you are trying to *say* as you tell about this person.

2. Tell a story that dramatically illustrates the effects of a certain choice (good or bad)—for example, driving while drunk, getting engaged, leaving college, going into therapy, cheating, or joining a sorority or a fraternity.

B. Exploring the Options

1. How did you react to Rob's story in the larger context of competitive sports? Is it true that it is necessary to take steroids or other "enhancers" in order to compete? Are competitive sports, in college and elsewhere, given too much importance? (Answer one of these questions or make up and answer your own question. Then develop an argumentative or persuasive paper with a clear thesis. See pages 180–183 for a discussion of argumentation or pages 214–218 for a discussion of persuasion.)

2. Compare this piece to the two others on steroids (page 144 and page 165) in this book. Consider purpose, tone, audience, and style.

3. Do you see any way in which the *kinds* of information presented in each of the three pieces mentioned in question 2 could be selected and combined into one essay on steroids? Try it. (You might also consider enhancing the information with some research of your own or by drawing on some of your own experiences.) Again, be sure to consider *your* main point.

Epiphany

Don Paskowski (student)

In this essay, a student tells the story of one of many operations for his cerebral palsy. Please see the writer's extended analysis of writing this piece on pages 107–109 of this book.

Thinking Ahead This essay is a narrative account of a particularly sad experience from which Don struggles to find meaning. Have you ever had an experience that could be described as an "epiphany" (a significant discovery or a sudden perception of the meaning of something, as in the Magis' first recognizing Jesus as the Christ of the Gentiles)?

This is how I remember it: 1

Out in the hall, dressed in a cotton loin cloth and johnnie too, I lie on 2
a gurney, look up at the square lights and the dimpled ceiling tiles, look at the white wall that chills my arm when I brush against it, look through the restraining bar that makes sure I won't fall off. I see surgeons in blue gowns with sweat-stained fronts, masks dangling, see their heads and feet wrapped in sterile caps and paper booties. I see the anesthetist, dressed like the surgeons, glide by me into Pre-Op carrying an I.V. kit. The breeze he creates adds to my goose flesh. My mouth is dry; my stomach burns.

"Relax," Mom says, patting my hand, the hand that I forgot has been 3
clutching the restraining bar with force enough to whiten the fingers and slick the palm.

The bar rings as I let go. I look at her and half smile while running the 4
hand down my shirt front. Now my hands drum my chest in time to my fidgeting heart.

"Why am I so *nervous,*" I almost squeak. "It's not like I've never been 5
through this before."

I had been through it before. Ten times Cerebral Palsy had sent me 6
into Boston Children's to have various foot, leg, hip and ankle bones broken and rearranged so I could get from here to there without looking bad doing it. I also had my heel cords, abductors and hamstrings lengthened to increase flexibility. All between 1966 and 1985, averaging one operation about every two years.

So why was I nervous about this Pre-Op? 7

I tried to figure it out as I lay there waiting for somebody to roll me 8
into Pre-Op, pierce a vein on the back of my hand and start a sugar and water feeding.

Mom taps my hand again, brushes a strand of hair off my forehead. "It's 9
the first time you've come down here without being prepped a few hours ahead of time," she says.

True. Because of an insurance policy quirk, I'd come in the day before 10 for the blood test, urinalysis, weigh-in, temperature, but I couldn't stay overnight; I arrived an hour before the operation and I wasn't yet sedated. Never had I been so alert.

I knew that was part of it. 11

A nurse approaches us, introduces herself. I don't catch her name. "Are 12
you Donald?" she says. Her voice sounds like Gilda Radner doing Emily Latella.

"Yup." I twist my wrist, showing her the ID braclet as proof. Like she 13
wouldn't believe me.

She knows I'm on edge. "Little nervous?" she says. 14

I lie. "Not very." 15

Mom hiccups a laugh. "Not very?" 16

We all laugh. 17

"I'll see if we can't get you calmed down," Emily says. She pivots into 18
Pre-Op, cotton pant bottoms whipping, white hospital jacket billowing out behind her, straight black hair sweeping side to side.

Why are you nervous, I think. *Is it the thought of the I.V. needle sliding* 19
into that vein? Is it the way you think you can hear it—the sound of a toothpick puncturing cellophane? No, it's not that. Even though the last time it took two guys seven tries just to find the vein. That's always over soon enough. Tape always hides that mosquito prong, anyway.

So what is . . . 20

Emily is back with nembutal. Must they carry one pill in those tiny 21
paper cups? "Here you go."

I down it. "Hope this works fast." 22

The anesthetist is now behind her. He's hairier than Jamie Farr. The 23
bifocals give him a look of prominence. "I'll be along to give you the snake bite in a bit."

"Give me what?" I say. 24

He smiles. "The I.V. Didn't mean to scare you. Little humor." 25

"Oh." I sigh. 26

Jamie forces a laugh. Flashing a tight-lipped smile, he turns down the 27
hall.

It seems like forever before Emily finally rolls me into Pre-Op. Jamie 28
finds the vein on the first try. Even so, I'm still uptight. The nembutal isn't dousing the fireflies that torch my stomach.

And you're supposed to be the "Old Pro." The babies on the other 29
gurneys are all more calm than you.

To take my mind off it, I scan the walls, seeing cardboard cut-outs of 30
Charlie, Lucy and the rest of the Peanuts in various poses of inanimate happiness. I scan the TV fastened to the wall, catching clips of the space shuttle Columbia launch. I scan once more the babies around me. Nothing holds my attention.

Emily swoops to my bed, covering me with a heated blanket. "The 31
anesthetist is going to give you something else to calm you a bit more."

"Great." 32

Moments later. He empties a fat syringe into the I.V. tube. My hand is 33
ice. "What is it?" I ask.

"Instant six pack." 34

He isn't kidding. Within ten seconds I'm a flaming mess, laughing and 35
ready to tell everybody where to go. "Ma! . . . Ma!" I gasp the words. "Let's skip it. I like this better." I can't stop laughing. My eyes close. I sing in a whisper: "She loves you, yeah . . . yeah . . . yeah . . ."

Emily swoops in again. "How are you, Donald?" 36

"Effing great!" Another guffaw. 37

I got this nerve stuff beat now. This ain't nothing . . . I was nervous? 38

Then I'm rolled through the operating room doors. I have nothing 39
beat.

I see baby blue tiles, notice a thermometer that reads 40 degrees, no- 40
tice the stainless steel tables. A woman to the left sorts instruments. I see her holding the scalpel. To the right, a man is busy checking the EEG or EKG—I'm not sure which. I look up. There it hovers, the shell that houses the lights.

As they wire me up to the machines, the fireflies return, and I wonder 41
again why I'm nervous. It's not the room. I'll be unconscious within ten minutes.

My mind drifts to yesterday's talk with a woman who asked me if I'd 42
want a local or a general anesthetic . . .

"I want general," I say. 43

"Okay," she says. "Would you sign this release, please." She extends 44
her clip board and pen to me; I take it. It's what she says now that nerves me.

"When you first go under anesthetic, we have a maximum of four mi- 45
nutes to breathe for you, or you could die. Also, be sure not to eat anything after midnight because the anesthesia could cause you to vomit, and the vomit would fill the lungs, causing them to collapse."

"Okay," I mumble and sign . . . 46

I knew these things, except for the part about the vomitting, but it was 47
the first time the anesthetist had ever talked to *me,* told me the details. All other times, I'd simply been told not to eat after midnight. Then there would be a huddle in the hall with my parents, and my father would sign the release.

Here, on the operating table, I shut off that memory, but it's no good. 48
My mind rolls. . . . the climactic scene of *Coma* . . . Genevieve Bujould white-faced on the table. The operation is over. The anesthetist, expecting a breath, arches her neck, forcing her head back. But she doesn't breathe . . .

Maybe that's it? No. I know I'll come out all right. 49

So *what is it?* Why *is this operation day working me up so? Is it Pre-* 50
Op? Is *it the conversation with the anesthetist . . .?*

A woman's voice jolts me out of this reverie: "Your hand will feel cold 51
for a second. Count backwards from a-hundred."

"A-hundred, ninety-nine, ni . . ." 52

I come to in my fourth floor room. Mired by a film of anesthetic 53
goo, my eyes flutter open. The light hurts them. For a moment I'm disoriented, but then, as if through seashells, I hear sit-com laugh tracks bubble from a TV. Some of my bed-ridden mates laugh too. I realize where I am.

On my back, I raise my head too fast, looking for Mom and— 54

Mom is sitting beside me, reading. I don't disturb her. 55

Nausea sends bile inching past my sternum. Soon it recedes. I lower 56
my head, but not before I catch a blurry glimpse of one roommate's parents: his mother—

His *father,* sitting beside his bed, resting a forearm on the mattress, 57
watching TV while his son sleeps.

A pang of depression squeezes my chest, deflates my lungs. 58

Finally I discover the truth behind today's nervousness. 59

Saddened but not crying (for my mother's sake), I stare at the ceiling 60
through gluey eyes.

And I remember. 61

I remember how my father always had a way of easing my tension. 62
Many times he'd send me into the operating room laughing at his "funny face." His favorite was a cross between Mr. Ed and Mr. Magoo's oriental butler Charlie. He'd bloat his cheeks and let his false teeth hang half out of his mouth while pinching his eyes shut and curling up his top lip.

And he was always there with mom when I woke up . . . 63

Not this time. 64

No, not this time. 65

My mother gone, my eyes clear, and my nausea overcome, my mind 66
replays the last time I'd talked to my father at home. The cancer had spread to his lungs; a hospital room lay in waiting.

I stand in our livingroom, angry. In he comes, coat draped over his 67
arm. The lone lamp fans light over his own drawn, tired face. We stand nose to nose.

"How do you feel," I ask, voice cracking, weak. 68

He puts a hand on my shoulder. "Remember how I felt last week?" 69

"I drop my eyes, "Like shit?" then raise them again to meet his. 70

"Yup. Like shit." 71

We hug tight. 72

"I love you," I say, words muffled by his neck. 73

"I love you," he says, cupping my head and neck with a hand whose skin is rough . . . 74

The memory trails off. I see my reflection in the blackened windows of the hospital room. 75

How much I need another of his hugs. 76

QUESTIONS

A. Discovering Meaning

1. During this particular operation, what was the experience of the writer?
2. What does he finally discover as the cause of his uneasiness? In other words, what is the "epiphany" of this piece?

B. Examining Method

1. Why does the writer tell this story?
2. Why does he include the comments he made to himself, unheard by others?
3. Which details best help the reader to understand the writer's nervousness?
4. What is the tone of the piece? Does the tone shift as the story develops (see pages 421–422)?
5. Why does the writer move away from the normal, "first-to-last-time" sequence in this story?
6. What is the climax of the story (see pages 374–378)?
7. How does the introduction relate to the conclusion (see pages 435–439)?
8. What do you think of the diction of paragraphs 70 and 71? Discuss.

C. Shifting Focus

1. How does comparison and contrast contribute to the effect of this narrative essay?
2. Read the writer's account of composing this piece on pages 107–109 of this book. What does his own discussion of process contribute to your reading of this piece?

SUGGESTIONS FOR DISCUSSION AND WRITING

A. Using Narration

1. Write a narrative account of an experience that was particularly unpleasant for you. What, if anything, did you learn from it?

2. Write an account of an experience in which you, too, experiencd an "epiphany," a discovery about yourself or your situation as the writer describes his here. Or write possibly on a discovery about someone else. (Sherwood Anderson's short story, "I Want to Know Why," is an excellent account of a discovery about someone else.)

B. Exploring the Options

1. Write a piece in which you compare an experience with another, similar experience. What is the point of your comparison? Did you learn something from the contrast? (One student wrote an essay on shifting family relationships by comparing what it is like to visit an uncle's cottage now with what it was like when she and her cousins were children. Another student compared living with his mother, who suffered from alcoholism, to his new concern about his *own* drinking and its effect on his small son.)

2. Write an analysis of the process of composing any one of the previous essays. As you work, keep notes on what you are going through. What were you saying to yourself, what did others say, what did you decide to leave, and what did you have to change?

Traveling South: Circa 1950

Gwendolyn L. Rosemond (student)

In this narrative, a college administrator reflects back upon an experience of her childhood—traveling as a black child through the South of the 1950s. About writing, Gwendolyn advises, "One ought to just start writing; never mind beginning, middle, or end. Like a jigsaw puzzle, one can piece it together later."

Thinking Ahead This is a narrative of a past event as remembered by an adult. How does the writer manage the dual time perspective? Could you write a story in which you reveal how you learned a "survival lesson"?

An entire generation, nearly two, does not know the South I know. A friend from Alabama said to me, "Our students don't believe that the George Wallace sitting in his wheelchair is the same one in their history books." I mulled the irony, remembering the man who stood in the schoolhouse door, barring it to the parents of my friend's students. That events of my childhood and youth have found their way into the history books gives pause, but most of all I think of that particular South through which I traveled year after year, losing innocence and gaining identity. 1

We change trains in Cincinnati, Mama and I, and board the Carolina Special. All the way there, and for weeks before we begin the trip, she admonishes me. 2

"At Cincinnati we head South, into Jim Crow country. You say 'ma'm' and 'sir' if anybody white says anything to you." 3

Something is unspoken. What will happen if I don't? 4

From Columbus to Cincinnati white people share our coach. From Cincinnati, where we cross the Ohio, the only white person to pass through is the conductor. Although he and the porter both wear uniforms (though not identical), I can tell the conductor from the porter. The conductor is white and takes our tickets. He never speaks. The porter is black, carries our baggage, smiles, and flirts with Mama. When Mama wants to know anything, she asks the porter. 5

Mama says, "They always put the colored coach up front, nearest the engine. That way we get the smoke and cinders and the white folks don't." 6

The day before we leave, Mama fries chicken, bakes plain cake, makes bread and butter sandwiches, and packs our meals for the trip. The dining car is for white folks only, but whatever they have there is not as sweet and peppery and fresh as Mama's day-old fried chicken, washed down with icy water from the fountain in a tiny paper cone. 7

In Spartanburg, Auntie meets the train. A bustling, fair-skinned, no-nonsense woman, she hustles us into an ancient waiting cab. Year after year, the driver is always black, even though shinier and newer cabs with white drivers stand nearby. Auntie averts her eyes from them, not in a humble way; they just aren't there in her vision. No, I cannot stop for a drink or go to the restroom; we'll be at Auntie's momentarily. I wait. I know that the water in the verboten white fountain is sweet and cold and pure and clear. That in the colored fountain is not. Only in the most dire and potentially embarrassing emergency will Mama relinquish her fragile power over custom and permit use of the colored facilities. 8

We make Auntie's our base from which we travel by bus or by car to family not accessible by train. On the bus we sit in the rear, or stand, or 9 crouch upon our luggage. Air conditioning is not yet a standard feature; open windows bring exhaust fumes and dust, humidity and dirt. At rest-stops we grab a Coke from an outside window. Mama breaks out the ubiquitous fried chicken. Traveling by car for any long distance requires two drivers to relieve one another. The vacancy sign in the motel or hotel means "white only." We drive day and night, virtually non-stop. During the day, we stop briefly at dingy, filthy restrooms marked just for us. Mama carries kleenex; we develop strong bladders. At night, the men drive, the children sleep, the women keep watch, praying silently.

From Auntie's we journey "down home," into the country. Usually my uncle drives, having arrived from Cleveland in his Chrysler New Yorker. His Ohio license plate brands him as a Northerner, the car as an "uppity negro." If his son drives, my uncle nags him all the way. 10

"Don't call attention to yourself. You want to land in a cracker jail, or worse?" 11

Or worse. The phrase hangs over every thought, every word, every gesture. In this year, Brown vs. the Board of Education is inconceivable; "civil rights" is not yet a phrase; Emmett Till is not yet dead. Late one night, in the rain and fog, another uncle is stopped for speeding. We follow the county sheriff's car to somewhere, in heavy and absolute silence. The joyous return from a full day at church vanishes, vanquished by palpable fear. Even Auntie is subdued. The uncle returns to the car, humiliated, poorer, but he escapes the "or worse." 12

One year, Mama and I begin our trip under unusually worrisome circumstances. 13

"They say in the news that colored and white can ride on the same coach on the train. But I doubt if it's really true." 14

At Cincinnati I rehearse my ma'ms and sirs and we board the old Carolina Special. The conductor directs us to our coach. White people get on our coach; they sit down. They look at us; we look out the window. Mama tenses. Finally, the porter comes through. 15

"Are we in the right car?" Mama whispers. 16

He nods. I don't think he believes it either. 17

On our next trip we eat in the dining car; we do not order fried chicken. 18

Nearly forty years have passed. I stay at the best hotels between here and South Carolina. Black bus drivers speed along the Interstates. Martin Luther King has come, and gone. I am driving a new Chrysler New Yorker with Massachusetts plates on a state highway near the Georgia-South Carolina line. Outside the car the temperature sears at 107 degrees. The red clay, glimmering in the August heat, dusts the brush. I fly by isolated one-pump service stations advertising Redman tobacco, and tin roofed outbuildings scattered among brick ranches and resplendent neo-antebellum dwellings. A dusty pick-up truck passes me. I love this countryside, its mystery, its secrets, its tragedies, its honesty. If I roll down the 19 window, the oppressive heat reminds me of broom swept yards, cool well water, and bare feet, a happy childhood reverie.

My daughter interrupts. 20

"Why are you slowing down, Mom?" 21

I am not aware that I have, that my foot has eased off the accelerator, 22 the involuntarily resurrection of something deeply buried.

I pause before I answer her; she will not understand and I will have to 23 go into a long explanation.

" 'Cause I can't deal with the county sheriff," I tell her. And then I tell 24 her about late one night, in the rain and fog, and how it used to be.

QUESTIONS

A. Discovering Meaning

1. What kinds of experiences stand out in the writer's mind as she recalls her trips to the South?
2. How did the child react to those experiences?
3. How does the adult see them?

B. Examining Method

1. Why does the writer tell this story of her past?
2. What does she have in mind for her reader (see pages 368–371)?
3. How do you feel as you read this story?
4. What is the tone (see pages 421–422)?
5. Why does she include so many quotations?
6. How would you describe the relationship between the introduction and the conclusion? Why mention the Chrysler New Yorker?
7. Where did you become most involved in the narrative? Why?

C. Shifting Focus

1. What does comparison and contrast contribute to this narrative?
2. Suppose that the writer had chosen to express profound anger about the experiences described in this essay. What changes would be necessary? Try rewriting one paragraph, in which you alter the emotional content, possibly to anger or to some other feeling.

SUGGESTIONS FOR DISCUSSION AND WRITING

A. Using Narration

1. Tell a story about a time when you learned an important lesson for your own well-being or possibly your survival. Think about why you are sharing this lesson with a reader. Are you primarily saying something about yourself or about the situation?

2. Write a narrative account of the experience of prejudice, either personal or observed. Be sure to evaluate your own attitudes toward the events in your story and to have a point to make.

B. Exploring the Options

1. Read Reverend Martin Luther King's persuasive "I Have a Dream" speech and compare it to this narrative account of living with prejudice. Consider subject, point, purpose, tone, audience, and details.

Salvation

Langston Hughes

Langston Hughes (1902–1967), black American poet, short-story writer, playwright, lyricist, lecturer, professor of creative writing, was known as "the poet laureate of Harlem." Having studied at Columbia University and graduated from Lincoln University, he traveled widely and devoted much of his life to bringing black achievements to the attention of a public who often ignored them. His works include *The Book of Negro Humor* (1966); *The Best Short Stories by Negro Writers* (1967); autobiographical works, *The Big Sea* (1940) and *I Wonder as I Wander* (1956); a history of the NAACP, *Fight for Freedom* (1962); and many poems strongly influenced by jazz and blues.

Thinking Ahead This is a narrative recollection of a childhood experience, at a time when the author did not, and could not, conform to the expectations of adults. Could you tell a similar story?

I was saved from sin when I was going on thirteen. But not really saved. 1
It happened like this. There was a big revival at my Auntie Reed's church. Every night for weeks there had been much preaching, singing, praying,

and shouting, and some very hardened sinners had been brought to Christ, and the membership of the church had grown by leaps and bounds. Then just before the revival ended, they held a special meeting for children, "to bring the young lambs to the fold." My aunt spoke of it for days ahead. That night I was escorted to the front row and placed on the mourners' bench with all the other young sinners, who had not yet been brought to Jesus.

My aunt told me that when you were saved you saw a light, and some- 2
thing happened to you inside! And Jesus came into your life! And God was with you from then on! She said you could see and hear and feel Jesus in your soul. I believed her. I had heard a great many old people say the same thing and it seemed to me they ought to know. So I sat there calmly in the hot, crowded church, waiting for Jesus to come to me.

The preacher preached a wonderful rhythmical sermon, all moans and 3
shouts and lonely cries and dire pictures of hell, and then he sang a song about the ninety and nine safe in the fold, but one little lamb was left out in the cold. Then he said: "Won't you come? Won't you come to Jesus? Young lambs, won't you come?" And he held out his arms to all us young sinners there on the mourners' bench. And the little girls cried. And some of them jumped up and went to Jesus right away. But most of us just sat there.

A great many old people came and knelt around us and prayed, old 4
women with jet-black faces and braided hair, old men with work-gnarled hands. And the church sang a song about the lower lights are burning, some poor sinners to be saved. And the whole building rocked with prayer song.

Still I kept waiting to *see* Jesus. 5

Finally all the young people had gone to the altar and were saved, but 6
one boy and me. He was a rounder's son named Westley. Westley and I were surrounded by sisters and deacons praying. It was very hot in the church, and getting late now. Finally Westley said to me in a whisper. "God damn! I'm tired o'sitting here. Let's get up and be saved." So he got up and was saved.

Then I was left all alone on the mourners' bench. My aunt came and 7
knelt at my knees and cried, while prayers and songs swirled all around me in the little church. The whole congregation prayed for me alone, in a mighty wail of moans and voices. And I kept waiting serenely for Jesus, waiting, waiting—but he didn't come. I wanted to see him, but nothing happened to me. Nothing! I wanted something to happen to me, but nothing happened.

I heard the songs and the minister saying; "Why don't you come? My 8
dear child, why don't you come to Jesus? Jesus is waiting for you. He wants you. Why don't you come? Sister Reed, what is this child's name?"

"Langston," my aunt sobbed. 9

"Langston, why don't you come? Why don't you come and be saved? 10
Oh, Lamb of God! Why don't you come?"

Now it was really getting late. I began to be ashamed of myself, holding everything up so long. I began to wonder what God thought about Westley, who certainly hadn't seen Jesus either, but who was now sitting proudly on the platform, swinging his knickerbockered legs and grinning down at me, surrounded by deacons and old women on their knees praying. God had not struck Westley dead for taking his name in vain or for lying in the temple. So I decided that maybe to save further trouble, I'd better lie, too, and say that Jesus had come, and get up and be saved. 11

So I got up. 12

Suddenly the whole room broke into a sea of shouting, as they saw me rise. Waves of rejoicing swept the place. Women leaped in the air. My aunt threw her arms around me. The minister took me by the hand and led me to the platform. 13

When things quieted down, in a hushed silence, punctuated by a few ecstatic "Amens," all the new young lambs were blessed in the name of God. Then joyous singing filled the room. 14

That night, for the last time in my life but one—for I was a big boy twelve years old—I cried. I cried, in bed alone, and couldn't stop. I buried my head under the quilts, but my aunt heard me. She woke up and told my uncle I was crying because the Holy Ghost had come into my life, and because I had seen Jesus. But I was really crying because I couldn't bear to tell her that I had lied, that I had deceived everybody in the church, and I hadn't seen Jesus, and that now I didn't believe there was a Jesus any more, since he didn't come to help me. 15

QUESTIONS

A. Discovering Meaning

1. What happened at the time the writer was supposed to be saved?
2. What did the writer *want* to happen at that time?

B. Examining Method

1. What point is Hughes trying to make through this narrative?
2. How does the writer portray the child's attitude toward the adults?
3. How does the writer portray his present attitude, as he writes this piece?
4. How does the reader get the sense of being present at the ceremony?
5. What is the connection between the introduction and the conclusion (see pages 435–439)?

6. What is the climax of the story (see pages 374–378)?
7. Why does he mention the boy, Westley?

C. Shifting Focus

1. How does description contribute to the overall meaning of this essay?
2. What would be the effect of telling this story in the present tense?
3. Suppose that the writer had gone on to become a preacher in the style of the preacher who is in the story. How might he tell this story to his congregation?
4. Suppose the writer were more angry than sad over his forced salvation. How would he alter his account?

SUGGESTIONS FOR DISCUSSION AND WRITING

A. Using Narration

1. Write a narrative account of an occasion when you were required to fake the way you really felt, when you had to act a part rather than show your real feelings. Are there occasions like this now?
2. Write an account of an experience in which you learned something about adult values that you had not yet recognized.
3. Describe a group experience of which you were a part. What were your reactions to the behavior of this group? Did you join in? Did you watch? Did you run away? Do you see any meaning now in your behavior? (One student wrote about the need to separate from his intolerant, hard-drinking, and sometimes cruel high-school friends if he wanted to go on to college. He had become to feel more and more alien among them.)

B. Exploring the Options

1. How would you define hypocrisy? (See pages 152–156 for a discussion of definition.)
2. Try writing an account of a story in which the result was, ironically, just the opposite of what others had intended for you.

Reading for Further Insight

Like the selections in the earlier chapters of this book, the essays in this chapter are good examples of certain modes—exposition, argumentation, description, narration. And they may in some ways be good models for your own writing, for all of these writers are skilled at making a point and making it well.

But they are also examples of writing that goes beyond strict boundaries or simple definitions. Many of these writers do work within certain predictable guidelines, but they also readily turn to whatever variations may be necessary for their meaning. Where narrative helps the argument, they tell a story; where description enlivens the narration, they describe.

And just as they take literary form and make it their own, so do they make the experiences of life their own. Rarely do they take life at face value or exactly as others might see it. As Frank Conroy points out, they are always searching for the significance of their experiences; they are always moving toward the more universal applications of their thoughts.

As you read them and think about them, notice how they adapt the writing to their own purposes and how they explore their subjects through language.

Think About It

Frank Conroy

Frank Conroy is director of the Iowa Writers' Workshop and author of *Stop-Time* and *Midair.* His stories and essays have appeared in *The New Yorker, Esquire, GQ,* and *Harper's Magazine,* from which this essay has been taken. He has worked as a jazz pianist and has often written about American music.

When I was sixteen I worked selling hot dogs at a stand in the Fourteenth Street subway station in New York City, one level above the trains and one below the street, where the crowds continually flowed back and forth. I worked with three Puerto Rican men who could not speak English. I had no Spanish, and although we understood each other well with regard to the tasks at hand, sensing and adjusting to each other's body movements in the extremely confined space in which we operated, I felt isolated with no one to talk to. On my break I came out from behind the counter and passed the time with two old black men who ran a shoeshine stand in a dark corner of the corridor. It was a poor location, half hidden by columns, and they didn't have much business. I would sit with my back against the wall while they stood or moved around their ancient elevated stand, talking to each other or to me, but always staring into the distance as they did so. 1

As the weeks went by I realized that they never looked at anything in their immediate vicinity—not at me or their stand or anybody who might come within ten or fifteen feet. They did not look at approaching customers once they were inside the perimeter. Save for the instant it took to discern the color of the shoes, they did not even look at what they were doing while they worked, but rubbed in polish, brushed, and buffed by feel while looking over their shoulders, into the distance, as if awaiting the arrival of an important person. Of course there wasn't all that much distance in the underground station, but their behavior was so focused and consistent they seemed somehow to transcend the physical. A powerful mood was created, and I came almost to believe that these men could see through walls, through girders, and around corners to whatever hyperspace it was where whoever it was they were waiting and watching for would finally emerge. Their scattered talk was hip, elliptical, and hinted at mysteries beyond my white boy's ken, but it was the staring off, the long, steady staring off, that had me hypnotized. I left for a better job, with handshakes from both of them, without understanding what I had seen. 2

Perhaps ten years later, after playing jazz with black musicians in various Harlem clubs, hanging out uptown with a few young artists and intellectuals, I began to learn from them something of the extraordinarily varied and complex riffs and rituals embraced by different people to help themselves get through life in the ghetto. Fantasy of all kinds—from play- 3 ful to dangerous—was in the very air of Harlem. It was the spice of uptown life.

Only then did I understand the two shoeshine men. They were trapped in a demeaning situation in a dark corner in an underground corridor in a filthy subway system. Their continuous staring off was a kind of statement, a kind of dance. Our bodies are here, went the statement, but our souls are receiving nourishment from distant sources only we can see. They were powerful magic dancers, sorcerers almost, and thirty-five years later I can still feel the pressure of their spell. 4

The light bulb may appear over your head, is what I'm saying, but it may be a while before it actually goes on. Early in my attempts to learn jazz piano, I used to listen to recordings of a fine player named Red Garland, whose music I admired. I couldn't quite figure out what he was doing, with his left hand, however; the chords eluded me. I went uptown to an obscure club where he was playing with his trio, caught him on his break, and simply asked him. "Sixths," he said cheerfully. And then he went away. 5

I didn't know what to make of it. The basic jazz chord is the seventh, which comes in various configurations, but it is what it is. I was a self-taught pianist, pretty shaky on theory and harmony, and when he said sixths I kept trying to fit the information into what I already knew, and it didn't fit. But it stuck in my mind—a tantalizing mystery. 6

A couple of years later, when I began playing with a bass player, I discovered more or less by accident that if the bass played the root and I played a sixth based on the fifth note of the scale, a very interesting chord involving both instruments emerged. Ordinarily, I suppose I would have skipped over the matter and not paid much attention, but I remembered Garland's remark and so I stopped and spent a week or two working out the voicings, and greatly strengthened my foundations as a player. I had remembered what I hadn't understood, you might say, until my life caught up with the information and the light bulb went on. 7

I remember another, more complicated example from my sophomore year at the small liberal-arts college outside Philadelphia. I seemed never to be able to get up in time for breakfast in the dining hall. I would get coffee and a doughnut in the Coop instead—a basement area with about a dozen small tables where students could get something to eat at odd hours. Several mornings in a row I noticed a strange man sitting by himself with a cup of coffee. He was in his sixties, perhaps, and sat straight in his chair with very little extraneous movement. I guessed he was some sort of distinguished visitor to the college who had decided to put in some time at a student hangout. But no one ever sat with him. One morning I approached his table and asked if I could join him. 8

"Certainly," he said. "Please do." He had perhaps the clearest eyes I had ever seen, like blue ice, and to be held in their steady gaze was not, at first, an entirely comfortable experience. His eyes gave nothing away about himself while at the same time creating in me the eerie impression that he was looking directly into my soul. He asked a few quick questions, 9 as if to put me at my ease, and we fell into conversation. He was William O. Douglas from the Supreme Court, and when he saw how startled I was he said, "Call me Bill. Now tell me what you're studying and why you get up so late in the morning." Thus began a series of talks that stretched over many weeks. The fact that I was an ignorant sophomore with literary pretensions who knew nothing about the law didn't seem to bother him. We talked about everything from Shakespeare to the possibility of life on other planets. One day I mentioned that I was going to have dinner with Judge Learned Hand. I explained that Hand was my girlfriend's grandfather. Douglas nodded, but I could tell he was surprised at the coincidence of my knowing the chief judge of the most important court in the country save the Supreme Court itself. After fifty years on the bench Judge Hand had become a famous man, both in and out of legal circles—a living legend, to his own dismay. "Tell him hello and give him my best regards," Douglas said.

Learned Hand, in his eighties, was a short, barrel-chested man with a large, square head, huge, thick, bristling eyebrows, and soft brown eyes. He radiated energy and would sometimes bark out remarks or questions in the living room as if he were in court. His humor was sharp, but often leavened with a touch of self-mockery. When something caught his funny bone he would burst out with explosive laughter—the laughter of a man who enjoyed laughing. He had a large repertoire of dramatic expressions involving the use of his eyebrows—very useful, he told me conspiratorially, when looking down on things from behind the bench. (The court stenographer could not record the movement of his eyebrows.) When I told him I'd been talking to William O. Douglas, they first shot up in exaggerated surprise, and then lowered and moved forward in a glower. 10

"*Justice* William O. Douglas, young man," he admonished. "Justice Douglas, if you please." About the Supreme Court in general, Hand insisted on a tone of profound respect. Little did I know that in private correspondence he had referred to the Court as "The Blessed Saints, Cherubim and Seraphim," "The Jolly Boys," "The Nine Tin Jesuses," "The Nine Blameless Ethiopians," and my particular favorite, "The Nine Blessed Chalices of the Sacred Effluvium." 11

Hand was badly stooped and had a lot of pain in his lower back. Martinis helped, but his strict Yankee wife approved of only one before dinner. It was my job to make the second and somehow slip it to him. If the pain was particularly acute he would get out of his chair and lie flat on the rug, still talking, and finish his point without missing a beat. He flattered me by asking for my impression of Justice Douglas, instructed me to convey his warmest regards, and then began talking about the Dennis case, which he described as a particularly tricky and difficult case involving the prosecution of eleven leaders of the Communist party. He had just started in on the First Amendment and free speech when we were called in to dinner. 12

William O. Douglas loved the outdoors with a passion, and we fell into the habit of having coffee in the Coop and then strolling under the trees 13 down toward the duck pond. About the Dennis case, he said something to this effect: "Eleven Communists arrested by the government. Up to no good, said the government; dangerous people, violent overthrow, etc. First Amendment, said the defense, freedom of speech, etc." Douglas stopped walking. "Clear and present danger."

"What?" I asked. He often talked in a telegraphic manner, and one was expected to keep up with him. It was sometimes like listening to a man thinking out loud. 14

"Clear and present danger," he said. "That was the issue. Did they constitute a clear and present danger? I don't think so. I think everybody took the language pretty far in Dennis." He began walking, striding along quickly. Again, one was expected to keep up with him. "The FBI was all over them. Phones tapped, constant surveillance. How could it be clear and present danger with the FBI watching every move they made? That's a ginkgo," he said suddenly, pointing at a tree. "A beauty. You don't see those every day. Ask Hand about clear and present danger." 15

I was in fact reluctant to do so. Douglas's argument seemed to me to be crushing—the last word, really—and I didn't want to embarrass Judge Hand. But back in the living room, on the second martini, the old man asked about Douglas. I sort of scratched my nose and recapitulated the conversation by the ginkgo tree. 16

"What?" Hand shouted. "Speak up, sir, for heaven's sake." 17

"He said the FBI was watching them all the time so there couldn't be a clear and present danger," I blurted out, blushing as I said it. 18

A terrible silence filled the room. Hand's eyebrows writhed on his face like two huge caterpillars. He leaned forward in the wing chair, his face settling, finally, into a grim expression. "I am astonished," he said softly, his eyes holding mine, "at Justice Douglas's newfound faith in the Federal Bureau of Investigation." His big, granite head moved even closer to mine, until I could smell the martini. "I had understood him to consider it a politically corrupt, incompetent organization, directed by a power-crazed lunatic." I realized I had been holding my breath throughout all of this, and as I relaxed, I saw the faintest trace of a smile cross Hand's face. Things are sometimes more complicated than they first appear, his smile seemed to say. The old man leaned back. "The proximity of the danger is something to think about. Ask him about that. See what he says." 19

I chewed the matter over as I returned to campus. Hand had pointed out some of Douglas's language about the FBI from other sources that seemed to bear out his point. I thought about the words "clear and present danger," and the fact that if you looked at them closely they might not be as simple as they had first appeared. What degree of danger? Did the word "present" allude to the proximity of the danger, or just the fact that the danger was there at all—that it wasn't an anticipated danger? Were there other hidden factors these great men were weighing of which I was unaware? 20

But Douglas was gone, back to Washington. (The writer in me is tempted to create a scene here—to invent one for dramatic purposes— 21 but of course I can't do that.) My brief time as a messenger boy was over, and I felt a certain frustration, as if, with a few more exchanges, the matter of *Dennis v. United States* might have been resolved to my satisfaction. They'd left me high and dry. But, of course, it is precisely because the matter did not resolve that has caused me to think about it, off and on, all these years. "The Constitution," Hand used to say to me flatly, "is a piece of paper. The Bill of Rights is a piece of paper." It was many years before I understood what he meant. Documents alone do not keep democracy alive, nor maintain the state of law. There is no particular safety in them. Living men and women, generation after generation, must continually remake democracy and the law, and that involves an ongoing state of tension between the past and the present which will never completely resolve.

Education doesn't end until life ends, because you never know when 22
you're going to understand something you hadn't understood before. For me, the magic dance of the shoeshine men was the kind of experience in which understanding came with a kind of click, a resolving kind of click. The same with the experience at the piano. What happened with Justice Douglas and Judge Hand was different, and makes the point that understanding does not always mean resolution. Indeed, in our intellectual lives, our creative lives, it is perhaps those problems that will never resolve that rightly claim the lion's share of our energies. The physical body exists in a constant state of tension as it maintains homeostasis, and so too does the active mind embrace the tension of never being certain, never being absolutely sure, never being done, as it engages the world. That is our special fate, our inexpressibly valuable condition.

What Is a Good Review?

Joseph Wood Krutch

Joseph Wood Krutch (1893–1970), literary critic, naturalist, philosopher, and college professor, wrote nonfiction throughout his professional career on a great variety of topics. Some of his books include *The Modern Temper: A Study and a Confession* (1929), *Samuel Johnson* (1948), *Henry David Thoreau* (1948), *The Desert Year* (1952), *More Lives Than One* (1962), *If You Don't Mind My Saying So* (1964), and *And Even If You Do* (1967). This selection is from *If You Don't Mind My Saying So.*

Of all literary forms the book review is the one most widely cultivated 1
and least often esteemed. To many the very phrase "literary form" may smack of pretense when applied to a kind of writing which is usually so

casual; and formlessness may, indeed, be the only form of many commentaries on books. Book reviewing can, nevertheless, become an art in itself and would be such more often if the ambitious reviewer would only devote himself to the cultivation of its particular excellences instead of attempting, as he so often does, to demonstrate his capacities by producing something "more than a mere review." The best review is not the one which is trying to be something else. It is not an independent essay on the subject of the book in hand and not an aesthetic discourse upon one of the literary genres. The best book review is the best review of the book in question, and the better it is the closer it sticks to its ostensible subject.

To say this is not to say that a good review is easy to write; in certain 2
technical respects it is, indeed, the most difficult of all forms of literary criticism for the simple reason that in no other is the writer called upon to do so many things in so short a space. The critical essay, no matter how extended it may be, is not compelled to aim at any particular degree of completeness. It may—in fact it usually does—assume that the reader is sufficiently familiar with the work under discussion to make description unnecessary and it may also confine itself to whatever aspects of the subject the critic may choose.

But the book review as a literary form implies completeness; it has not 3
really performed its function unless, to begin with, it puts the reader in possession of the facts upon which the criticism is based, and unless—no matter upon how small a scale—its consideration is complete. However penetrating a piece of writing may be, it is not a good review if it leaves the reader wondering what the book itself is like as a whole or if it is concerned with only some aspects of the book's quality.

I shall not pretend to say how large a proportion of the so-called re- 4
views published in *The Nation* or anywhere else actually achieve the distinguishing characteristics of the book-review form, but a certain number of them do, and the sense of satisfactoriness which they give can always be traced to the fact that, whatever other qualities they may have, they accomplish the three minimum tasks of the book reviewer. They describe the book, they communicate something of its quality, and they pass a judgment upon it.

Each of these things is quite different from the others, but only the last 5
is usually considered as carefully as it ought to be by either reader or writer. Adequate description implies a simple account of the scope and contents of the book; its presence guarantees that the reader will not be left wondering what, in the simplest terms, the book is about. "Communication of quality" implies, on the other hand, a miniature specimen of what is commonly called "impressionistic criticism"; it means that the reviewer must somehow manage to re-create in the mind of the reader some approximation of the reaction produced in his own mind by the book itself. And in however low esteem this form of criticism may be held as a be-all and end-all (Mr. Eliot calls it the result of a weak creative instinct rather than of a critical impulse), it is indispensable in a book

review if that review is to perform the function it is supposed to perform, and if it is to become what it is supposed to be—namely, not merely an account of a book on the one hand or an independent piece of criticism on the other, but a brief critical essay which includes within itself all that is necessary to make the criticism comprehensible and significant.

Your "reviewer" often envies the more lofty "critic" because the critic 6
is supposed to be read for his own sake while the reviewer must assume that the reader is attracted more by his interest in the book discussed than by the reviewer himself. For that very reason he is likely either to treat reviewing as a causal affair or to seek for an opportunity to write something else under the guise of a review. He might be happier himself and make his readers happier also if he would, instead, take the trouble to ask what a review ought to be and if he would examine his own work in the light of his conclusions. It is not easy to do within the space of a thousand words or less the three things enumerated. It is less easy still to combine the description, the impression, and the judgment into a whole which seems to be, not three things at least, but one.

How many reviewers of novels, for instance, seem to know how much 7
of a particular story has to be told in order to provide a solid basis for the impression they intend to convey? And if it is decided that some part of the story must be told, how many know, as a story-teller must, whether the incidents are striking enough to come first or must be introduced with some comment which creates interest? Yet a first-rate review, despite its miniature scale, raises precisely the same problems as long narratives or expositions raise, and each must be solved as artfully if the review is to have such beauty of form as it is capable of. Doubtless the finest reviewer can hardly hope to have his art fully appreciated by the public. But there is every reason why he should respect it himself.

Can Society Banish Cruelty?

J. H. Plumb

Born in 1911, educated at Cambridge University and associated with that university for most of his professional career, J. H. Plumb is the author of several major historical works. Some of his titles include *England in the Eighteenth Century, The Horizon Book of the Italian Renaissance, Royal Heritage: The Reign of Elizabeth II,* and *In the Light of History* from which this essay has been taken.

No one can doubt that cruelty is a major obscenity of modern life. A 1
woman of eighty is thrown over a railing in Central Park and raped; a small girl is murdered for sexual pleasure: an old man is bayoneted to

death for the sake of five dollars. "Snuff films," which progress from mass sex to the deliberate murder and dismemberment of the "actress," are rumored to be displayed in New York City for $200 a seat. Leaving aside the organized violence of war, are we as individuals more cruel than our ancestors? Are we more wanton in our infliction of pain?

In January, 1757, Robert François Damiens made a feeble attempt to 2
assassinate Louis XV of France. Though his small knife barely penetrated the king's thick winter clothes, causing little more than a four-inch scratch, Damiens was caught and tortured to make him name his accomplices. He had none. Then he became the centerpiece of a theatre of cruelty. The philosopher La Condamine, for one, was so fascinated by the prospect of such an extravagant spectacle that he got himself a place on the scaffold to watch the victim. He was part of a huge audience that paid exorbitant prices to see Damiens's flesh pulled off with red-hot pincers and his battered body pulled apart by horses. After that the Parisians—aristocrats, bourgeoisie, and workingmen alike—went back to their dinners.

True, this execution was rather more elaborately staged than most in 3
the eighteenth century, but it was highly traditional. Damiens's executioners had carefully copied, with scrupulous attention to detail, the way François Ravaillac, the assassin of Henry IV, had been put to death in 1610. The French, however, must not be regarded as peculiarly ferocious. The treatment of traitors in England, a method of execution that had first been used against Catholic priests in Queen Elizabeth's reign, was particularly horrifying. Before a vast crowd in a carnival-like atmosphere, the traitor was hanged, but taken down while still alive; then his genitals were cut off and stuffed in his mouth, he was disemboweled, and finally his head was cut off and his trunk quartered. The head, stuck on a pike, would festoon Temple Bar for years; sometimes the quarters were sent to decorate provincial cities.

These were but upsurges in an ocean of cruelty. Several times a year 4
huge crowds swarmed to Tyburn (near Marble Arch in London) to watch and enjoy the executions by hanging of men and women, youths and girls, turned off the ladder into eternity for minor robberies and petty pilfering, as well as murder and mayhem. Such sadism was not merely an occasional visual thrill, for cruelty had been deeply embedded in western European society for centuries and was still to be for a century or so more. It was a constant theme of everyday life, a continuing event of family experience.

Cruelty to animals was widespread—one might say total. Cocks fought 5
each other to the death, bulls and bears were baited by specially trained dogs: cats were sewn up in effigies of the pope to create realistic howls when they were burned. Oxen and horses were driven and flogged until they died. And yet animals were not treated much worse than infants or small children.

The callous behavior of parents and adults to infants in seventeenth- 6
century England or eighteenth-century France is scarcely credible. The

women of the poor suckled for a trade, getting as many babies to a meager breast as they could. Naturally their own child was fed first; often the other sucklings were half starved, and frequently hand fed on an appalling diet of pap—a little flour and water. The broken-down hovels to which babies were consigned for wet-nursing were as dirty as they were pitiable. Often there was a dung heap at the door to give warmth, and the floor was strewn with filth of every kind.

Swaddling was universal. Newborn babies were stretched out on a board, a piece of diaper stuck between their thighs, and then were strapped down so tight that they could not move. Swaddled infants were frequently hung up on pegs on the wall and left there, and, of course, they lived in their own feces and urine until they were reswaddled. It is not surprising, therefore, that the death of an infant was an even of small consequence and of exceptional frequency—50 per cent of all infants died before they were a year old. 7

Childhood was little better. Children were remorselessly flogged. A middle-class child in England was required to stand whenever he was in the presence of his parents and would be savagely punished if he did not. The children of the poor were expected to work as soon as they could walk and were often driven from home to work when little more than seven or eight. Born and bred in a world of callous brutality, the men and women of those days took torture and dismemberment in their stride, were indifferent to the horrors of slavery and the slave trade, and thought nothing of tormenting an idiot or an animal or throwing a witch onto a bonfire. 8

And then, about 1700, attitudes among the prosperous commercial classes in England began to change, for reasons that are difficult to comprehend. John Locke protested against swaddling and child beating and argued powerfully that mothers should suckle their own children. Hogarth's satirical prints show that by 1750 hatred of cruelty had a market. Take a long look at his bitter satire *The Four Stages of Cruelty,* in which animals are being flogged to death or tortured, or children casually killed. One print in this series, *Cruelty in Perfection,* depicts a savage and murderous rape. The very fact that Hogarth satirized cruelty shows that there were some flickers of sensitivity to horror. 9

Men and women formed societies to prevent the worst exploitation of child labor—the young chimney sweeps; they banded together against the slave trade; they helped suppress the most savage type of blood sports. In children's books after 1740, the horrors of cruelty to birds and animals, to fellow human beings, are stressed over and over again. Children were taught to regard cruelty as evil, as sinful. The result was the great wave of humanitarianism that swept Europe and America in the nineteenth century. Wherever we look we find a positive gain over cruelty: public executions largely vanished, torture was stopped. Of course, and this must be stressed, a great tide of cruelty remained, but it was steadily diminishing. 10

The fight against cruelty was long and arduous: it was largely the cam- 11 paign of a social and cultural elite whose greatest success may have been in conditioning their own children in the horrors of cruelty. This attitude never permeated the whole of society or restrained the behavior of governments. Its influence was always fragile, and in this century cruelty has been widespread and growing toward individuals and toward classes of men and women. True, in previous centuries there would not have been the twentieth-century storms of protest against the more outrageous forms of government cruelty; neither are the worst excesses of personal cruelty allowed to flourish unchecked. But we have no cause to congratulate ourselves, for the position is insecure, and permitting the pornography of violence, which stirs deep and dangerous emotions, is a risk that society can ill afford.

12 And yet, maybe we should worry more about children's books, which seem singularly devoid of overt morality. Perhaps we are too concerned with the happiness of the child, rather than with the community's happiness with him. Most children are instinctively cruel to animals, and sensitivity toward pain and suffering must be taught. At the same time, the adult world should take a far sterner view of cruelty than it currently does. We need to think clearly about it; we ought to think more carefully about what ought to be forbidden and what not. Surely, there would be no greater folly than to suppress all pornography simply because some of it extols violence. But certainly a good place to start would be the prohibition of *wanton* infliction of pain on another human being.

The Ambivalence of Abortion

Linda Bird Franke

A journalist and biographer, Linda Bird Franke, born in 1939, is the author of *Growing up Divorced: Children of the Eighties* (1983) and has collaborated with Rosalynn Carter on *First Lady from Plains* (1984) and with Geraldine Ferraro on *Ferraro* (1986). Since 1972, she has been a general Editor of *Newsweek*.

1 We were sitting in a bar on Lexington Avenue when I told my husband I was pregnant. It is not a memory I like to dwell on. Instead of the champagne and hope which had heralded the impending births of the first, second and third child, the news of this one was greeted with shocked silence and Scotch. "Jesus," my husband kept saying to himself, stirring the ice cubes around and around, "Oh, Jesus."

2 Oh, how we tried to rationalize it that night as the starting time for the

movie came and went. My husband talked about his plans for a career change in the next year, to stem the staleness that fourteen years with the same investment banking firm had brought him. A new baby would preclude that option.

The timing wasn't right for me either. Having juggled pregnancies and child care with what freelance jobs I could fit in between feedings, I had just taken on a full-time job. A new baby would put me right back in the nursery just when our youngest child was finally school age. It was time for *us,* we tried to rationalize. There just wasn't room in our lives now for another baby. We both agreed. And agreed. And agreed. 3

How very considerate they are at the Women's services, known formally as the Center for Reproductive and Sexual Health. Yes, indeed, I could have an abortion that very Saturday morning and be out in time to drive to the country that afternoon. Bring a first morning urine specimen, a sanitary belt and napkins, a money order or $125 cash—and a friend. 4

My friend turned out to be my husband, standing awkwardly and ill at ease as men always do in places that are exclusively for women, as I checked in at nine A.M. Other men hovered around just as anxiously, knowing they had to be there, wishing they weren't. No one spoke to each other. When I would be cycled out of there four hours later, the same men would be slumped in their same seats, locked downcast in their cells of embarrassment. 5

The Saturday morning women's group was more dispirited than the men in the waiting room. There were around fifteen of us, a mixture of races, ages and backgrounds. Three didn't speak English at all and a fourth, a pregnant Puerto Rican girl around eighteen, translated for them. 6

There were six black women and a hodgepodge of whites, among them a T-shirted teenager who kept leaving the room to throw up and a puzzled middle-aged woman from Queens with three grown children. 7

"What form of birth control were you using?" the volunteer asked each one of us. The answer was inevitably "none." She then went on to describe the various forms of birth control available at the clinic, and offered them to each of us. 8

The youngest Puerto Rican girl was asked through the interpreter which she'd like to use: the loop, diaphragm, or pill. She shook her head "no" three times. "You don't want to come back here again, do you?" the volunteer pressed. The girl's head was so low her chin rested on her breastbone. "*Si,*" she whispered. 9

We had been there two hours by that time, filling out endless forms, giving blood and urine, receiving lectures. But unlike any other group of women I've been in, we didn't talk. Our common denominator, the one which usually floods across language and economic barriers into familiarity, today was one of shame. We were losing life that day, not giving it. 10

The group kept getting cut back to smaller, more workable units, and finally I was put in a small waiting room with just two other women. We changed into paper bathrobes and paper slippers, and we rustled when- 11 ever we moved. One of the women in my room was shivering and an aide brought her a blanket.

"What's the matter?" the aide asked her. "I'm scared," the woman said. "How much will it hurt?" The aide smiled. "Oh, nothing worse than a couple of bad cramps," she said. "This afternoon you'll be dancing a jig." 12

I began to panic. Suddenly the rhetoric, the abortion marches I'd walked in, the telegrams sent to Albany to counteract the Friends of the Fetus, the Zero Population Growth buttons I'd worn, peeled away, and I was all alone with my microscopic baby. There were just the two of us there, and soon, because it was more convenient for me and my husband, there would be one again. 13

How could it be that I, who am so neurotic about life that I step over bugs rather than on them, who spend hours planting flowers and vegetables in the spring even though we rent out the house and never see them, who make sure the children are vaccinated and inoculated and filled with vitamin C, could so arbitrarily decide that this life shouldn't be? 14

"It's not a life," my husband had argued, more to convince himself than me. "It's a bunch of cells smaller than my fingernail." 15

But any woman who has had children knows that certain feeling in her taut, swollen breasts, and the slight but constant ache in her uterus that signals the arrival of a life. Though I would march myself into blisters for a woman's right to exercise the option of motherhood, I discovered there in the waiting room that I was not the modern woman I thought I was. 16

When my name was called, my body felt so heavy the nurse had to help me into the examining room. I waited for my husband to burst through the door and yell "stop," but of course he didn't. I concentrated on three black spots in the acoustic ceiling until they grew in size to the shape of saucers, while the doctor swabbed my insides with antiseptic. 17

"You're going to feel a burning sensation now," he said, injecting Novocain into the neck of the womb. The pain was swift and severe, and I twisted to get away from him. He was hurting my baby, I reasoned, and the black saucers quivered in the air. "Stop," I cried. "Please stop." He shook his head, busy with his equipment. "It's too late to stop now," he said. "It'll just take a few more seconds." 18

What good sports we women are. And how obedient. Physically the pain passed even before the hum of the machine signaled that the vacuuming of my uterus was completed, my baby sucked up like ashes after a cocktail party. Ten minutes start to finish. And I was back on the arm of the nurse. 19

There were twelve beds in the recovery room. Each one had a gaily flowered draw sheet and a soft green or blue thermal blanket. It was all very feminine. Laying on these beds for an hour or more were the shocked victims of their sex, their full wombs now stripped clean, their futures less encumbered. 20

It was very quiet in that room. The only voice was that of the nurse, locating the new women who had just come in so she could monitor 21 their blood pressure, and checking out the recovered women who were free to leave.

Juice was being passed about, and I found myself sipping a Dixie cup of Hawaiian Punch. An older woman with tightly curled bleached hair was just getting up from the next bed. "That was no goddamn snap," she said, resting before putting on her miniskirt and high white boots. Other women came and went, some walking out as dazed as they had entered, others with a bounce that signaled they were going back to Bloomingdale's. 22

Finally then, it was time for me to leave. I checked out, making an appointment to return in two weeks for an IUD insertion. My husband was slumped in the waiting room, clutching a single yellow rose wrapped in a wet paper towel and stuffed into a Baggie. 23

We didn't talk the whole way home, but just held hands very tightly. At home there were more yellow roses and a tray in bed for me and the children's curiosity to divert. 24

It had certainly been a successful operation. I didn't bleed at all for two days just as they had predicted, and then I bled only moderately for another four days. Within a week my breast had subsided and the tenderness vanished, and my body felt mine again instead of the eggshell it becomes when it's protecting someone else. 25

My husband and I are back to planning our summer vacation and his career switch. 26

And it certainly does make more sense not to be having a baby right now—we say that to each other all the time. But I have this ghost now. A very little ghost that only appears when I'm seeing something beautiful, like the full moon on the ocean last weekend. And the baby waves at me. And I wave at the baby. "Of course, we have room," I cry to the ghost. "Of course, we do." 27

Why the Americans Are So Restless in the Midst of Their Prosperity

Alexis de Tocqueville

Alexis de Tocqueville (1805–1859) was a French historian and author of *Democracy in America* (1835–1839), an early study of America, its institutions, and its democratic way of life. He was a keen and sometimes prophetic observer, and he is still often quoted. The following is from the Henry Reeve translation.

In certain remote corners of the Old World you may still sometimes stumble upon a small district that seems to have been forgotten amid the general tumult, and to have remained stationary while everything around it was in motion. The inhabitants, for the most part, are extremely ignorant and poor, they take no part in the business of the country and are frequently oppressed by the government, yet their countenances are generally placid and their spirits light. 1

In America I saw the freest and most enlightened men placed in the happiest circumstances that the world affords; it seemed to me as if a cloud habitually hung upon their brow, and I thought them serious and almost sad, even in their pleasures. 2

The chief reason for this contrast is that the former do not think of the ills they endure, while the latter are forever brooding over advantages they do not possess. It is strange to see with what feverish ardor the Americans pursue their own welfare, and to watch the vague dread that constantly torments them lest they should not have chosen the shortest path which may lead to it. 3

A native of the United States clings to this world's goods as if he were certain never to die; and he is so hasty in grasping at all within his reach that one would suppose he was constantly afraid of not living long enough to enjoy them. He clutches everything, he holds nothing fast, but soon loosens his grasp to pursue fresh gratifications. 4

In the United States a man builds a house in which to spend his old age, and he sells it before the roof is on; he plants a garden and lets it just as the trees are coming into bearing; he brings a field into tillage and leaves other men to gather the crops; he embraces a profession and gives it up; he settles in a place, which he soon afterwards leaves to carry his changeable longings elsewhere. If his private affairs leave him any leisure, he instantly plunges into the vortex of politics; and if at the end of a year of unremitting labor he finds he has a few days' vacation, his eager curiosity whirls him over the vast extent of the United States, and he will travel fifteen hundred miles in a few days to shake off his happiness. Death at length overtakes him, but it is before he is weary of his bootless chase of that complete felicity which forever escapes him. 5

At first sight there is something surprising in this strange unrest of so many happy men, restless in the midst of abundance. The spectacle itself, however, is as old as the world; the novelty is to see a whole people furnish an exemplification of it. 6

Their taste for physical gratifications must be regarded as the original source of that secret disquietude which the actions of the Americans betray and of that inconstancy of which they daily afford fresh examples. He who has set his heart exclusively upon the pursuit of worldly welfare is always in a hurry, for he has but a limited time at his disposal to reach, to grasp, and to enjoy it. The recollection of the shortness of life is a constant spur to him. Besides the good things that he possesses, he every instant fancies a thousand others that death will prevent him from trying 7 if he does not try them soon. This thought fills him with anxiety, fear, and regret and keeps his mind in ceaseless trepidation, which leads him perpetually to change his plans and his abode.

If in addition to the taste for physical well-being a social condition be added in which neither laws nor customs retain any person in his place, there is a great additional stimulant to this restlessness of temper. Men will then be seen continually to change their track for fear of missing the shortest cut to happiness. 8

It may readily be conceived that if men passionately bent upon physical gratifications desire eagerly, they are also easily discouraged; as their ultimate object is to enjoy, the means to reach that object must be prompt and easy or the trouble of acquiring the gratification would be greater than the gratification itself. Their prevailing frame of mind, then, is at once ardent and relaxed, violent and enervated. Death is often less dreaded by them than perseverance in continuous efforts to one end. 9

The equality of conditions leads by a still straighter road to several of the effects that I have here described. When all the privileges of birth and fortune are abolished, when all professions are accessible to all, and a man's own energies may place him at the top of any one of them, an easy and unbounded career seems open to his ambition and he will readily persuade himself that he is born to no common destinies. But this is an erroneous notion, which is corrected by daily experience. The same equality that allows every citizen to conceive these lofty hopes renders all the citizens less able to realize them; it circumscribes their powers on every side, while it gives freer scope to their desires. Not only are they themselves powerless, but they are met at every step by immense obstacles, which they did not at first perceive. They have swept away the privileges of some of their fellow creatures which stood in their way, but they have opened the door to universal competition; the barrier has changed its shape rather than its position. When men are nearly alike and all follow the same track, it is very difficult for any one individual to walk quickly and cleave a way through the dense throng that surrounds and presses on him. This constant strife between the inclination springing from the equality of condition and the means it supplies to satisfy them harasses and wearies the mind. 10

It is possible to conceive of men arrived at a degree of freedom that should completely content them; they would then enjoy their independence without anxiety and without impatience. But men will never establish any equality with which they can be contented. Whatever efforts a people may make, they will never succeed in reducing all the conditions of society to a perfect level; and even if they unhappily attained that absolute and complete equality of position, the inequality of minds would still remain, which, coming directly from the hand of God, will forever escape the laws of man. However democratic, then, the social state and the political constitution of a people may be, it is certain that every member of the community will always find out several points about him which overlook his own position; and we may foresee that his looks will be 11 doggedly fixed in that direction. When inequality of conditions is the common law of society, the most marked inequalities do not strike the eye; when everything is nearly on the same level, the slightest are marked enough to hurt it. Hence the desire of equality always becomes more insatiable in proportion as equality is more complete.

Among democratic nations, men easily attain a certain equality of condition, but they can never attain as much as they desire. It perpetually retires from before them, yet without hiding itself from their sight, and in retiring draws them on. At every moment they think they are about to grasp it; it escapes at every moment from their hold. They are near enough to see its charms, but too far off to enjoy them; and before they have fully tasted its delights, they die. 12

To these causes must be attributed that strange melancholy which often haunts the inhabitants of democratic countries in the midst of their abundance, and that disgust at life which sometimes seizes upon them in the midst of calm and easy circumstances. Complaints are made in France that the number of suicides increases; in America suicide is rare, but instantly is said to be more common there than anywhere else. These are all different symptoms of the same disease. The Americans do not put an end to their lives, however disquieted they may be, because their religion forbids it; and among them materialism may be said hardly to exist, notwithstanding the general passion for physical gratification. The will resists, but reason frequently gives way. 13

In democratic times enjoyments are more intense than in the ages of aristocracy, and the number of those who partake in them is vastly larger: but, on the other hand, it must be admitted that man's hopes and desires are oftener blasted, the soul is more stricken and perturbed, and care itself more keen. 14

What's Wrong with 'Me, Me, Me'?

Margaret Halsey

Margaret Halsey, born in 1910, graduated from Skidmore and Teachers College of Columbia University. In 1938, she wrote a comic best seller on the English, *With Malice Towards Some.* In New York, During World War II, she worked at one of the only two canteens in the country open to black as well as white servicemen. Her 1946 book about racial integration was called *Color Blind.* In 1977, she published *No Laughing Matter: The Autobiography of a WASP.* This article was first published April 17, 1978 in *Newsweek.*

Tom Wolfe has christened today's young adults the "me" generation, and the 1970s—obsessed with things like consciousness expansion and self-awareness—have been described as the decade of the new narcissism. The cult of "I," in fact, has taken hold with the strength and impetus of a new religion. But the joker in the pack is that it is all based on a false idea. 1

The false idea is that inside every human being, however unprepossessing, there is a glorious, talented and overwhelmingly attractive personality. This personality—so runs the erroneous belief—will be revealed in all its splendor if the individual just forgets about courtesy, cooperativeness and consideration for others and proceeds to do exactly what he or she feels like doing. 2

Nonsense. 3

Inside each of us is a mess of unruly primitive impulses, and these can sometimes, under the strenuous self-discipline and dedication of art, result in notable creativity. But there is no such thing as a pure, crystalline and well-organized "native" personality, though a host of trendy human-potential groups trade on the mistaken assumption that there is. And backing up the human-potential industry is the advertising profession, which also encourages the idea of an Inner Wonderfulness that will be unveiled to a suddenly respectful world upon the purchase of this or that commodity. 4

However, an individual does not exist in a vacuum. A human being is not an isolated, independent thing-in-itself, but inevitably reflects the existence of others. The young adults of the "me" generation would never have lived to grow up if a great many parents, doctors, nurses, farmers, factory workers, teachers, policemen, firemen and legions of others had not ignored their human potential and made themselves do jobs they did not perhaps feel like doing in order to support the health and growth of children. 5

And yet, despite the indulgence of uninhibited expression, the "self" in self-awareness seems to cause many new narcissists and members of the "me" generation a lot of trouble. This trouble emerges in talk about "identity." We hear about the search for identity and a kind of distress called an identity crisis. 6

"I don't know who I am." How many bartenders and psychiatrists have stifled yawns on hearing that popular threnody for the thousandth time! 7

But this sentence has no meaning unless spoken by an amnesia victim, because many of the people who say they do not know who they are, actually *do* know. What such people really mean is that they are not satisfied with who they are. They feel themselves to be timid and colorless or to be in some way or other fault-ridden, but they have soaked up enough advertising and enough catch-penny ideas of self-improvement to believe in universal Inner Wonderfulness. So they turn their backs on their honest knowledge of themselves—which with patience and courage could start them on the road to genuine development—and embark on a quest for a will-o'-the wisp called "identity." 8

But a *search* for identity is predestined to fail. Identity is not found, the way Pharaoh's daughter found Moses in the bulrushes. Identity is built. It is built every day and every minute throughout the day. The myriad choices, small and large, that human beings make all the time determine identity. The fatal weakness of the currently fashionable approach to personality is that the "self" of the self-awareness addicts, the self of Inner Wonderfulness, is static. Being perfect, it does not need to change. But genuine identity changes as one matures. If it does not, if the 40-year-old has an identity that was set in concrete at the age of 18, he or she is in trouble. 9

The idea of a universal Inner Wonderfulness that will be apparent to all beholders after a six-week course in self-expression is fantasy. 10

But how did this fantasy gain wide popular acceptance as a realizable fact? 11

Every society tries to produce a prevalent psychological type that will best serve its ends, and that type is always prone to certain emotional malfunctions. In early capitalism, which was a producing society, the ideal type was acquisitive, fanatically devoted to hard work and fiercely repressive of sex. The emotional malfunctions to which this type was liable were hysteria and obsession. Later capitalism, today's capitalism, is a consuming society, and the psychological type it strives to create, in order to build up the largest possible markets, is shallow, easily swayed and characterized much more by self-infatuation than self-respect. The emotional malfunction of this type is narcissism. 12

It will be argued that the cult of "I" has done some individuals a lot of good. But at whose expense? What about the people to whom these "healthy" egotists are rude or even abusive? What about the people over whom they ride roughshod? What about the people they manipulate and exploit? And—the most important question of all—how good a preparation for inevitable old age and death is a deliberately cultivated self-love? The psychologists say that the full-blown classic narcissists lose all dignity and go mad with fright as they approach their final dissolution. Ten or fifteen years from now—when the young adults of the "me" generation hit middle age—will be the time to ask whether "self-awareness" really does people any good. 13

A long time ago, in a book called "Civilization and Its Discontents," Freud pointed out that there is an unresolvable conflict between the human being's selfish, primitive, infantile impulses and the restraint he or she must impose on those impulses if a stable society is to be maintained. The "self" is not a handsome god or goddess waiting coyly to be revealed. On the contrary, its complexity, confusion and mystery have proved so difficult that throughout the ages men and women have talked gratefully about *losing* themselves. They *lose* the self in contemplating a great work of art, or in nature, or in scientific research, or in writing poetry, or in fashioning things with their hands or in projects that will benefit others rather than themselves. 14

The current glorification of self-love will turn out in the end to be a 15 no-win proposition, because in questions of personality or "identity," what counts is not who you are, but what you do. "By their fruits, ye shall know them." And by their fruits, they shall known themselves.

Halloween Party

Lillian Ross

Lillian Ross has been a regular contributor to *The New Yorker* since 1948. She has written many things, including numbers of "Talk of the Town" pieces, of which this essay is one. Her nonfiction books include *Picture* (1952), *Portrait of Hemingway* (1961), *Adlai Stevenson* (1966), and a collection of "Talk" pieces, *Takes* (1983).

A letter has arrived from a woman we know: 1

My thirteen-year-old son gave a Halloween costume party for a bunch 2 of boys and girls. I became his financier as he talked endlessly about his Count Dracula costume. Count Dracula seems to have been the most popular Halloween costume for the past ten years—a black satin Count Dracula cape ($18.95), Count Dracula fangs ($1.25), clown whiteface makeup ($2), and Zauders stage blood ($2). The menu for the party included fried chicken, spaghetti, Cokes, salad, and cupcakes with orange or chocolate icing (cost per guest: $7). The candy, for visiting trick-or-treaters as well as for the guests, was orange and black jelly beans, sugar pumpkins, Candy Corn, Tootsie Rolls, Raisinets, Almond Joys, Nestlé Crunch, Baby Ruths, Milky Ways, Heide Jujyfruits, Peanut Chews, and Cracker Jacks (total: $38.65). My son also had eight cookies, six inches in diameter and decorated with black cats ($1.25 each); eight little plastic pumpkins full of hard candies, each with a trembly plastic spider on top ($2.50 each); eight orange-colored balloons that blew up to resemble cats (eighty-five cents each); eight orange-colored lollipops with jack-o'-lantern faces (seventy cents each); a larger paper tablecloth showing a black witch standing over a black caldron with spiders popping out of the caldron ($2.25); matching napkins ($1.10); matching paper cups ($2); matching paper plates ($1.75); a "HAPPY HALLOWEEN" sign ($1.25); a dancing skeleton ($3.99); something called a Happy Spider ($4); a classic jack-o'-lantern, made of a real pumpkin ($4, plus labor). Total investment in props: $181.59. Total investment of labor in jack-o'-latern, kitchen cleanup, and laundry: $35. Total investment in emotion and puzzlement: indeterminable.

I watch the guests arrive. The first one, A, comes as Darth Vader, of "Star Wars." B comes as Luke Skywalker, of "Star Wars." C comes as The Incredible Hulk. D comes as a tramp. E comes as a ghost. F comes as a ballerina. G comes, in one of her mother's old evening gowns, as Bette Midler. All are in an advanced stage of hysteria. A pulls at C's costume. G immediately starts throwing sugar pumpkins at E. They've given themselves an hour before they move the party out to ring doorbells and see what they get. They tear into the fried chicken, most of them eating three bites and wasting the rest. They sprinkle jelly beans on the chicken and on the spaghetti. They pick at the spaghetti, which is on the menu because my son said everybody likes spaghetti. They eat it one strand at a time, dropping a strand on the floor for each strand they consume. They gulp down the Cokes, another "must"—their appetite for the caffeine insatiable. And what are they talking about, these eighth graders who are eying each other fishily? They are talking about their *careers.* They are talking about getting into Exeter. They are talking about Yale and Yale Law School. They are talking about how to get in here and how to get in there. They are talking about who makes more money, the president of Chase Manhattan or the president of General Motors. Nobody is talking kid talk. Nobody is talking about the present time and what to do with it. Nobody is talking about learning. Nobody sounds *young.* A, a pudgy boy who tries to find out the marks of every other child in his class, wants to be "a successful corporation lawyer." He doesn't say just "corporation lawyer." It's success that he's bent on. He informs my son that he intends to have more money than his uncle, who is a corporation lawyer in Philadelphia. Next, A tells my son that he wants to go to Exeter. Why? "Because Exeter is a stepping-stone to Harvard," he says. Not Exeter for the wonders of Exeter but Exeter because it will be useful *after* he leaves it. 3

B, with his mouth full of Almond Joy, is asking the others a question: "Do you want to be a little fish in a big pond or a big fish in a little pond?" 4

What has that got to do with getting an education? How about the excitement of learning algebra? How about that wonderful grammar teacher who showed you how to recognize the participle absolute? Why aren't you talking about your French teacher's getting you to speak French with an accent that would wow them in Paris? I want to butt in with my questions, but I keep my mouth shut. 5

Now A is talking. His mother, he is saying, has taken him rock climbing, because rock climbing is an impressive activity to put down as his "interest" on the application to Exeter. 6

But you *hate* rock climbing!" says D, who is a mischief-maker with the face of an angel under his tramp makeup. "You hate to move your *ass,*" D adds. 7

All right, who else is here? C, who is wearing a mask of The Incredible Hulk. C is the jock of the group. He has been in training since the age of 8 two in the craft of giving nothing away. He's wary and tight and already immunized to the teeth against charity for its own sake. He, too, wants to be a corporation lawyer; so do B and D. The girls, though—the ballerina and Bette Midler—both want to be big-corporation presidents. They are both relaxed, being well aware of what women's lib has done for them. E, the ghost, is the only one with a simple costume, made of a sheet. A, talking to B, points out what E doesn't have to bother about a costume, because he's rich, very rich. His grandfather lives in Texas and owns real oil wells—not new ones but very old and very productive oil wells. E wants to be a movie director and has promised to give my son, who at the moment wants to be an actor, a starring part in his first movie. They are pals. Both of them are regarded with suspicion by the ones who want to be corporation lawyers.

What else are they saying? They're still talking about Exeter. Appar- 9
ently, A is obsessed by Exeter—it is he who keeps bringing the conversation back to it.

"They ask you to write a "personal letter' to them," this little busybody 10
says. "They say, 'This letter should represent you as accurately as possible.' But then they tell you in the catalogue what they want, so all you have to do is tell it back to them."

C finally talks. "The way *you* always figure out what the teacher wants 11
and give it right back to *him*," he says.

D squirts a little Coke at A, and the future lawyers get up and make for 12
the door. They cram their loot bags with the orange and black jelly beans, the Candy Corn, the cookies, the trembly spiders, the balloons, the jack-o'-lantern lollipops, and the rest. They make a big point of thanking me loudly. The girls amble out, smiling knowledgeably at each other. E and my son run to catch up to them. They, too, thank me extravagantly. And they all go off, in their disguises, to do their tricks and get their treats. I am left wondering what it's all about.

Japanese and American Workers

William Ouchi

Born in 1943, William Ouchi was one of the first to study what it was that gave Japanese industry the competitive edge during the 1960s and 1970s. A professor of management at University of California at Los Angeles, he published his conclusions in *Theory Z: How American Business Can Meet the Japanese Challenge* (1981), from which this selection has been taken.

Perhaps the most difficult aspect of the Japanese for Westerners to comprehend is the strong orientation to collective values, particularly a collective sense of responsibility. Let me illustrate with an anecdote about a visit to a new factory in Japan owned and operated by an American electronics company. The American company, a particularly creative firm, frequently attracts attention within the business community for its novel approaches to planning, organizational design, and management systems. As a consequence of this corporate style, the parent company determined to make a thorough study of Japanese workers and to design a plant that would combine the best of East and West. In their study they discovered that Japanese firms almost never make use of individual work incentives, such as piecework or even individual performance appraisal tied to salary increases. They concluded that rewarding individual achievement and individual ability is always a good thing. 1

In the final assembly area of their new plant, long lines of young Japanese women wired together electronic products on a piece-rate system: the more you wired, the more you got paid. About two months after opening, the head foreladies approached the plant manager. "Honorable plant manager," they said humbly as they bowed, "we are embarrassed to be so forward, but we must speak to you because all of the girls have threatened to quit work this Friday." (To have this happen, of course, would be a great disaster for all concerned.) "Why," they wanted to know, "can't our plant have the same compensation system as other Japanese companies? When you hire a new girl, her starting wage should be fixed by her age. An eighteen-year-old should be paid more than a sixteen-year-old. Every year on her birthday, she should receive an automatic increase in pay. The idea that any of us can be more productive than another must be wrong, because none of us in final assembly could make a thing unless all of the other people in the plant had done their jobs right first. To single one person out as being more productive is wrong and is also personally humiliating to us." The company changed its compensation system to the Japanese model. 2

Another American company in Japan had installed a suggestion system much as we have in the United States. Individual workers were encouraged to place suggestions to improve productivity into special boxes. For an accepted idea the individual received a bonus amounting to some fraction of the productivity savings realized from his or her suggestion. After a period of six months, not a single suggestion had been submitted. The American managers were puzzled. They had heard many stories of the inventiveness, the commitment, and the loyalty of Japanese workers, yet not one suggestion to improve productivity had appeared. 3

The managers approached some of the workers and asked why the suggestion system had not been used. The answer: "No one can come up with a work improvement idea alone. We work together, and any ideas that one of us may have are actually developed by watching others and talking to others. If one of us was singled out for being responsible for 4 such an idea, it would embarrass all of us." The company changed to a group suggestion system, in which workers collectively submitted suggestions. Bonuses were paid to groups which would save bonus money until the end of the year for a party at a restaurant or, if there was enough money, for family vacations together. The suggestions and productivity improvements rained down on the plant.

One can interpret these examples in two quite different ways. Perhaps the Japanese commitment to collective values is an anachronism that does not fit with modern industrialism but brings economic success despite that collectivism. Collectivism seems to be inimical to the kind of maverick creativity exemplified in Benjamin Franklin, Thomas Edison, and John D. Rockefeller. Collectivism does not seem to provide the individual incentive to excel which has made a great success of American enterprise. Entirely apart from its economic effects, collectivism implies a loss of individuality, a loss of the freedom to be different, to hold fundamentally different values from others. 5

The second interpretation of the examples is that the Japanese collectivism is economically efficient. It causes people to work well together and to encourage one another to better efforts. Industrial life requires interdependence of one person on another. But a less obvious but far-reaching implication of the Japanese collectivism for economic performance has to do with accountability. 6

In the Japanese mind, collectivism is neither a corporate or individual goal to strive for nor a slogan to pursue. Rather, the nature of things operates so that nothing of consequence occurs as a result of individual effort. Everything important in life happens as a result of teamwork or collective effort. Therefore, to attempt to assign individual credit or blame to results is unfounded. A Japanese professor of accounting, a brilliant scholar trained at Carnegie-Mellon University who teaches now in Tokyo, remarked that the status of accounting systems in Japanese industry is primitive compared to those in the United States. Profit centers, transfer prices, and computerized information systems are barely known even in the largest Japanese companies, whereas they are a commonplace in even small United States organizations. Though not at all surprised at the difference in accounting systems, I was not at all sure that the Japanese were primitive. In fact, I thought their system a good deal more efficient than ours. 7

Most American companies have basically two accounting systems. One system summarizes the overall financial state to inform stockholders, bankers, and other outsiders. That system is not of interest here. The other system, called the managerial or cost accounting system, exists for an entirely different reason. It measures in detail all of the particulars of transactions between departments, divisions, and key individuals in the organization, for the purpose of untangling the interdependencies between people. When, for example, two departments share one truck for deliveries, the cost accounting system charges each department for part 8 of the cost of maintaining the truck and driver, so that at the end of the year, the performance of each department can be individually assessed, and the better department's manager can receive a larger raise. Of course, all of this information processing costs money, and furthermore may lead to arguments between the departments over whether the costs charged to each are fair.

In a Japanese company a short-run assessment of individual performance is not wanted, so the company can save the considerable expense of collecting and processing all of that information. Companies still keep track of which department uses a truck how often and for what purposes, but like-minded people can interpret some simple numbers for themselves and adjust their behavior accordingly. Those insisting upon clear and precise measurement for the purpose of advancing individual interests must have an elaborate information system. Industrial life, however, is essentially integrated and interdependent. No one builds an automobile alone, no one carries through a banking transaction alone. In a sense the Japanese value of collectivism fits naturally into an industrial setting, whereas the Western individualism provides constant conflicts. The image that comes to mind is of Chaplin's silent film "Modern Times" in which the apparently insignificant hero played by Chaplin successfully fights against the unfeeling machinery of industry. Modern industrial life can be aggravating, even hostile, or natural: all depends on the fit between our culture and our technology. 9

. . .

The *shinkansen* or "bullet train" speeds across the rural areas of Japan giving a quick view of cluster after cluster of farmhouses surrounded by rice paddies. This particular pattern did not develop purely by chance, but as a consequence of the technology peculiar to the growing of rice, the staple of the Japanese diet. The growing of rice requires the construction and maintenance of an irrigation system, something that takes many hands to build. More importantly, the planting and the harvesting of rice can only be done efficiently with the cooperation of twenty or more people. The "bottom line" is that a single family working alone cannot produce enough rice to survive, but a dozen families working together can produce a surplus. Thus the Japanese have had to develop the capacity to work together in harmony, no matter what the forces of disagreement or social disintegration, in order to survive. 10

Japan is a nation built entirely on the tips of giant, suboceanic volcanoes. Little of the land is flat and suitable for agriculture. Terraced hillsides make use of every available square foot of arable land. Small homes built very close together further conserve the land. Japan also suffers from natural disasters such as earthquakes and hurricanes. Traditionally homes are made of light construction materials, so a house falling down during a disaster will not crush its occupants and also can be quickly and inexpensively rebuilt. During the feudal period until the Meiji restoration of 1868, each feudal lord sought to restrain his subjects from moving 11 from one village to the next for fear that a neighboring lord might amass enough peasants with which to produce a large agricultural surplus, hire an army and pose a threat. Apparently bridges were not commonly built across rivers and streams until the late nineteenth century, since bridges increased mobility between villages.

Taken all together, this characteristic style of living paints the picture 12 of a nation of people who are homogeneous with respect to race, history, language, religion, and culture. For centuries and generations these people have lived in the same village next door to the same neighbors. Living in close proximity and in dwellings which gave very little privacy, the Japanese survived through their capacity to work together in harmony. In this situation, it was inevitable that the one most central social value which emerged, the one value without which the society could not continue, was that an individual does not matter.

To the Western soul this is a chilling picture of society. Subordinating 13 individual tastes to the harmony of the group and knowing that individual needs can never take precedence over the interests of all is repellent to the Western citizen. But a frequent theme of Western philosophers and sociologists is that individual freedom exists only when people willingly subordinate their self-interests to the social interest. A society composed entirely of self-interested individuals is a society in which each person is at war with the other, a society which has no freedom. This issue, constantly at the heart of understanding society, comes up in every century, and in every society, whether the writer be Plato, Hobbes, or B. F. Skinner.

In order to complete the comparison of Japanese and American living 14 situations, consider flight over the United States. Looking out of the window high over the state of Kansas, we see a pattern of a single farmhouse surrounded by fields, followed by another single homestead surrounded by fields. In the early 1800s in the state of Kansas there were no automobiles. Your nearest neighbor was perhaps two miles distant; the winters were long, and the snow was deep. Inevitably, the central social values were self-reliance and independence. Those were the realities of that place and age that children had to learn to value.

The key to the industrial revolution was discovering that non-human 15 forms of energy substituted for human forms could increase the wealth of a nation beyond anyone's wildest dreams. But there was a catch. To realize this great wealth, non-human energy needed huge complexes called factories with hundreds, even thousands of workers collected into one factory. Moreover, several factories in one central place made the generation of energy more efficient. Almost overnight, the Western world was transformed from a rural and agricultural country to an urban and industrial state. Our technological advance seems to no longer fit our social structure: in a sense, the Japanese can better cope with modern industrialism. While Americans still busily protect our rather extreme form of individualism, the Japanese hold their individualism in check and emphasize cooperation.

The Family/Career Priority Problem

Ellen Goodman

Ellen Goodman writes a column for the *Boston Globe* that is syndicated by the Washington Post Writers Group and appears in more than 400 newspapers across the country. She won the Pulitzer Prize in 1980. Among her collections of essays are *Close to Home, Turning Points, At Large,* Keeping in Touch and most recently, *Making Sense.*

One day last week Ed Koch left his Greenwich Village apartment to take the M-6 bus downtown. About the same time he was being sworn in as mayor of New York City, my friend Carol was turning down a job as a top executive of a New York corporation. 1

On the surface, these two events seem to be totally unrelated, except for the fact that they took place in the same city. But I don't think they are. You see, Ed Koch is a bachelor, and my friend Carol is married and a parent, and there's a difference. 2

No, this isn't a story that ends with a one-line complaint from Carol: "If it hadn't been for you, I would have been a star." (Or a mayor, for that matter.) Nor is it a story of discrimination. Her husband didn't put his foot down. Her parents didn't form a circle around her shouting, "*Bad* mother, *bad!*" until she capitulated. 3

Carol chose. She wanted the promotion so much she could taste it. But the job came with weekends and evenings and traveling attached, and she didn't want to miss that time with her husband and sons. She couldn't do both. Knowing that didn't make it any easier. 4

Carol isn't the only one I know making these decisions. Another friend refused to move up a rung on the professional ladder because it would have meant uprooting his family and transferring his wife out of a career of her own. A third couple consciously put their careers on the back burner in order to spend time with the family they'd merged out of two previous marriages. 5

These were not bitter choices, but tough ones. As Carol said, it isn't possible to give overtime at work and decent time at home. 6

Once it was normal for a man to devote his energy entirely to his work, while his family was taken care of by his wife. Once men led the public lives and women the private lives. Now that gap is closing, and another one is growing between family people and single people. Everywhere it seems that men and women who care the most about their private lives are living them that way, while the single people have become the new upwardly mobile. 7

In Washington you can see the difference. There, a twenty-eight-year-old bachelor such as White House aide David Rubinstein works more 8 than sixteen hours a day and eats vending-machine meals, while a guy like Representative Lloyd Meeds (D-Washington) decides not to take his family through another congressional election fight and drops out. There, despite the attempts of the Carters to encourage family time, the government still runs on excess. As one observer puts it, the only way to get the work done is to be single or to have a lousy marriage.

In New York the successful politicians (aside from Koch) now include Carol Bellamy, the single head of the city council, and Andrew Stein, the divorced borough president. The governor is a widower, the lieutenant governor is legally separated. 9

All around us the prototypical workaholics are single, with Ralph Nader leading the Eastern division, and Jerry Brown bringing up the West. And in the U.S. Senate last year there were enough divorces to justify legal insurance. 10

I don't think that this is something "movements" or legislation can solve. I am reminded of the moment in the movie *The Turning Point* when Anne Bancroft and Shirley MacLaine realize that they both wanted it all. These two women hadn't chosen in their lives between work and family in the classic sense, but between workaholism and family: between the sort of success that demands single-minded devotion to a goal and the sort of "balanced" life that includes family and work, but precludes overachieving. In the end the star was a bachelor. 11

The decisions they faced are the rock-bottom ones, the toughies. How do you divide the pie of your life—your own time and energy? 12

Today, the cast of characters is changing. It isn't only men in high-powered work lives and women at home. But the choices have remained the same. There seems to be an inherent contradiction between the commitment to become number one, the best, the first, and the commitment to a rich family life. A contradiction between family-first people and work-first people. 13

Aria

Richard Rodriguez

Born (1944) to Mexican-American parents in San Francisco, California, Richard Rodriguez did not learn to speak English until he was in grammar school. He eventually attended Stanford University and the University of California at Berkeley, where he received his Ph.D. in English literature. He is now associate editor at the Pacific News Service in San Francisco and publishes articles in such publications as *Saturday Review, College English,* and *Harper's.* His prize-winning memoir, *Hunger of Memory* (1982), from which this selection

has been taken, tells of his experiences growing up in the Mexican "private" culture and the English "public" culture.

Supporters of bilingual education today imply that students like me 1
miss a great deal by not being taught in their family's language. What they seem not to recognize is that, as a socially disadvantaged child, I considered Spanish to be a private language. What I needed to learn in school was that I had the right—and the obligation—to speak the public language of *los gringos.* The odd truth is that my first-grade classmates could have become bilingual, in the conventional sense of that word, more easily than I. Had they been taught (as upper-middle-class children are often taught early) a second language like Spanish or French, they could have regarded it simply as that: another public language. In my case such bilingualism could not have been so quickly achieved. What I did not believe was that I could speak a single public language.

Without question, it would have pleased me to hear my teachers ad- 2
dress me in Spanish when I entered the classroom. I would have felt much less afraid. I would have trusted them and responded with ease. But I would have delayed—for how long postponed?—having to learn the language of public society. I would have evaded—and for how long could I have afforded to delay?—learning the great lesson of school, that I had a public identity.

Fortunately, my teachers were unsentimental about their responsibil- 3
ity. What they understood was that I needed to speak a public language. So their voices would search me out, asking me questions. Each time I'd hear them, I'd look up in surprise to see a nun's face frowning at me. I'd mumble, not really meaning to answer. The nun would persist, 'Richard, stand up. Don't look at the floor. Speak up. Speak to the entire class, not just to me!' But I couldn't believe that the English language was mine to use. (In part, I did not want to believe it.) I continued to mumble. I resisted the teacher's demands. (Did I somehow suspect that once I learned public language my pleasing family life would be changed?) Silent, waiting for the bell to ring, I remained dazed, diffident, afraid.

Because I wrongly imagined that English was intrinsically a public lan- 4
guage and Spanish an intrinsically private one, I easily noted the difference between classroom language and the language of home. At school, words were directed to a general audience of listeners. ('Boys and girls.') Words were meaningfully ordered. And the point was not self-expression alone but to make oneself understood by many others. The teacher quizzed: 'Boys and girls, why do we use that word in this sentence? Could we think of a better word to use there? Would the sentence change its meaning if the words were differently arranged? And wasn't there a better way of saying much the same thing?' (I couldn't say. I wouldn't try to say.)

Three months. Five. Half a year passed. Unsmiling, ever watchful, my 5
teachers noted my silence. They began to connect my behavior with the

difficult progress my older sister and brother were making. Until one Saturday morning three nuns arrived at the house to talk to our parents. Stiffly, they sat on the blue living room sofa. From the doorway of another room, spying the visitors, I noted the incongruity—the clash of two worlds, the faces and voices of school intruding upon the familiar setting of home. I overheard one voice gently wondering, 'Do your children speak only Spanish at home, Mrs. Rodriguez?' While another voice added, 'That Richard especially seems so timid and shy.'

That Rich-heard! 6

With great tact the visitors continued, 'Is it possible for you and your husband to encourage your children to practice their English when they are home?' Of course, my parents complied. What would they not do for their children's well-being? And how could they have questioned the Church's authority which those women represented? In an instant, they agreed to give up the language (the sounds) that had revealed and accentuated our family's closeness. The moment after the visitors left, the change was observed. '*Ahora,* speak to us *en inglés*' my father and mother united to tell us. 7

At first it seemed a kind of game. After dinner each night, the family gathered to practice 'our' English. (It was still then *inglés,* a language foreign to us, so we felt drawn as strangers to it.) Laughing, we would try to define words we could not pronounce. We played with strange English sounds, often over anglicizing our pronunciations. And we filled the smiling gaps of our sentences with familiar Spanish sounds. But that was cheating, somebody shouted. Everyone laughed. In school, meanwhile, like my brother and sister, I was required to attend a daily tutoring session. I needed a full year of special attention. I also needed my teachers to keep my attention from straying in class by calling out, *Rich-heard*—their English voices slowly prying loose my ties to my other name, its three notes *Ri-car-do.* Most of all I needed to hear my mother and father speak to me in a moment of seriousness in broken—suddenly heartbreaking—English. The scene was inevitable: One Saturday morning I entered the kitchen where my parents were talking in Spanish. I did not realize that they were talking in Spanish however until, at the moment they saw me, I heard their voices change to speak English. Those *gringo* sounds they uttered startled me. Pushed me away. In that moment of trivial misunderstanding and profound insight, I felt my throat twisted by unsounded grief. I turned quickly and left the room. But I had no place to escape to with Spanish. (The spell was broken.) My brother and sisters were speaking English in another part of the house. 8

Again and again in the days following, increasingly angry, I was obliged to hear my mother and father: 'Speak to us *en inglés.*' (*Speak.*) Only then did I determine to learn classroom English. Weeks after, it happened: One day in school I raised my hand to volunteer an answer. I spoke out in a loud voice. And I did not think it remarkable when the entire class understood. That day, I moved very far from the disadvantaged child I had been 9 only days earlier. The belief, the calming assurance that I belonged in public, had at last taken hold.

Shortly after, I stopped hearing the high and loud sounds of *los gringos.* A more and more confident speaker of English, I didn't trouble to listen to *how* strangers sounded, speaking to me. And there simply were too many English-speaking people in my day for me to hear American accents anymore. Conversations quickened. Listening to persons who sounded eccentrically pitched voices, I usually noted their sounds for an initial few seconds before I concentrated on *what* they were saying. Conversations became content-full. Transparent. Hearing someone's *tone* of voice—angry or questioning or sarcastic or happy or sad—i didn't distinguish it from the words it expressed. Sound and word were thus tightly wedded. At the end of a day, I was often bemused, always relieved, to realize how 'silent,' though crowded with words, my day in public had been. (This public silence measured and quickened the change in my life.) 10

At last, seven years old, I came to believe what had been technically true since my birth: I was an American citizen. 11

But the special feeling of closeness at home was at home; rare was the experience of feeling myself individualized by family intimates. We remained a loving family, but one greatly changed. No longer so close; no longer bound tight by the pleasing and troubling knowledge of our public separateness. Neither my older brother nor sister rushed home after school anymore. Nor did I. When I arrived home there would often be neighborhood kids in the house. Or the house would be empty of sounds. 12

Following the dramatic Americanization of their children, even my parents grew more publicly confident. Especially my mother. She learned the names of all the people on our block. And she decided we needed to have a telephone installed in the house. My father continued to use the word *gringo.* But it was no longer charged with the old bitterness or distrust. (Stripped of any emotional content, the word simply became a name for those Americans not of Hispanic descent.) Hearing him, sometimes, I wasn't sure if he was pronouncing the Spanish word *gringo* or saying gringo in English. 13

Matching the silence I started hearing in public was a new quiet at home. The family's quiet was partly due to the fact that, as we children learned more and more English, we shared fewer and fewer words with our parents. Sentences needed to be spoken slowly when a child addressed his mother or father. (Often the parent wouldn't understand.) The child would need to repeat himself. (Still the parent misunderstood.) The young voice, frustrated, would end up saying, 'Never mind'—the subject was closed. Dinners would be noisy with the clinking of knives and forks against dishes. My mother would smile softly between her remarks; my father at the other end of the table would chew and chew at his food, while he stared over the heads of his children. 14

Once More to the Lake

E. B. White

E. B. White (1899–1985), born in Mount Vernon, N.Y., was thought by many to be the finest essayist in the United States. In 1926, after graduating from Cornell University, White joined the staff of the *New Yorker* and also wrote a column, "One Man's Meal" for *Harper's.* His great variety of books includes *The SubTreasury of American Humor* (1941) written with his wife, Katharine S. White, children's books *Stuart Little* (1945), *Charlotte's Web* (1952), and *The Trumpet of the Swan* (1970), the well-known revision of William Strunk's *Elements of Style* (1959), *The Points of My Compass* (1962), *The Letters of E. B. White* (1976), and *Essays of E. B. White* (1977).

One summer, along about 1904, my father rented a camp on a lake in Maine and took us all there for the month of August. We all got ringworm from some kittens and had to rub Pond's Extract on our arms and legs night and morning, and my father rolled over in a canoe with all his clothes on; but outside of that the vacation was a success and from then on none of us ever thought there was any place in the world like that lake in Maine. We returned summer after summer—always on August 1 for one month. I have since become a salt-water man, but sometimes in summer there are days when the restlessness of the tides and the fearful cold of the sea water and the incessant wind that blows across the afternoon and into the evening make me wish for the placidity of a lake in the woods. A few weeks ago this feeling got so strong I bought myself a couple of bass hooks and a spinner and returned to the lake where we used to go, for a week's fishing and to revisit old haunts. 1

I took along my son, who had never had any fresh water up his nose and who had seen lily pads only from train windows. On the journey over to the lake I began to wonder what it would be like. I wondered how time would have marred this unique, this holy spot—the coves and streams, the hills that the sun set behind, the camps and the paths behind the camps. I was sure that the tarred road would have found it out, and I wondered in what other ways it would be desolated. It is strange how much you can remember about places like that once you allow your mind to return into the grooves that lead back. You remember one thing, and that suddenly reminds you of another thing. I guess I remembered clearest of all the early mornings, when the lake was cool and motionless, remembered how the bedroom smelled of the lumber it was made of and of the wet woods whose scent entered through the screen. The partitions in the camp were thin and did not extend clear to the top of the rooms, and as I was always the first up I would dress softly so as not to wake the others, and sneak out into the sweet outdoors and start out in the canoe, 2 keeping close along the shore in the long shadows of the pines. I remembered being very careful never to rub my paddle against the gunwale for fear of disturbing the stillness of the cathedral.

The lake had never been what you would call a wild lake. There were 3
cottages sprinkled around the shores, and it was in farming country although the shores of the lake were quite heavily wooded. Some of the cottages were owned by nearby farmers, and you would live at the shore and eat your meals at the farmhouse. That's what our family did. But although it wasn't wild, it was a fairly large and undisturbed lake and there were places in it that, to a child at least, seemed infinitely remote and primeval.

I was right about the tar: it led to within half a mile of the shore. But 4
when I got back there, with my boy, and we settled into a camp near a farmhouse and into the kind of summertime I had known, I could tell that it was going to be pretty much the same as it had been before—I knew it, lying in bed the first morning smelling the bedroom and hearing the boy sneak quietly out and go off along the shore in a boat. I began to sustain the illusion that he was I, and therefore, by simple transposition, that I was my father. This sensation persisted, kept cropping up all the time we were there. It was not an entirely new feeling, but in this setting, it grew much stronger. I seemed to be living a dual existence. I would be in the middle of some simple act, I would be picking up a bait box or laying down a table fork, or I would be saying something, and suddenly it would be not I but my father who was saying the words or making the gesture. It gave me a creepy sensation.

We went fishing the first morning. I felt the same damp moss covering 5
the worms in the bait can, and saw the dragonfly alight on the tip of my rod as it hovered a few inches from the surface of the water. It was the arrival of this fly that convinced me beyond any doubt that everything was as it always had been, that the years were a mirage and that there had been no years. The small waves were the same, chucking the rowboat under the chin as we fished at anchor, and the boat was the same boat, the same color green and the ribs broken in the same places, and under the floorboards the same fresh-water leavings and debris—the dead hellgrammite, the wisps of moss, the rusty discarded fishhook, the dried blood from yesterday's catch. We stared silently at the tips of our rods, at the dragonflies that came and went. I lowered the tip of mine into the water, tentatively, pensively dislodging the fly, which darted two feet away, poised, darted two feet back, and came to rest again a little farther up the rod. There had been no years between the ducking of this dragonfly and the other one—the one that was part of memory. I looked at the boy, who was silently watching his fly, and it was my hands that held his rod, my eyes watching. I felt dizzy and didn't know which rod I was at the end of.

We caught two bass, hauling them in briskly as though they were mack- 6
erel, pulling them over the side of the boat in a businesslike manner

without any landing net, and stunning them with a blow on the back of the head. When we got back for a swim before lunch, the lake was exactly where we had left it, the same number of inches from the dock, and there was only the merest suggestion of a breeze. This seemed an utterly enchanted sea, this lake you could leave to its own devices for a few hours and come back to, and find that it had not stirred, this constant and trustworthy body of water. In the shallows, the dark, water-soaked sticks and twigs, smooth and old, were undulating in clusters on the bottom against the clean ribbed sand, and the track of the mussel was plain. A school of minnows swam by, each minnow with its small individual shadow, doubling the attendance, so clear and sharp in the sunlight. Some of the other campers were in swimming, along the shore, one of them with a cake of soap, this cultist, and here he was. There had been no years.

Up to the farmhouse to dinner through the teeming, dusty field, the road under our sneakers was only a two-track road. The middle track was missing, the one with the marks of the hooves and the splotches of dried, flaky manure. There had always been three tracks to choose from in choosing which track to walk in; now the choice was narrowed down to two. For a moment I missed terribly the middle alternative. But the way led past the tennis court, and something about the way it lay there in the sun reassured me; the tape had loosened along the backline, the alleys were green with plantains and other weeds, and the net (installed in June and removed in September) sagged in the dry noon, and the whole place steamed with midday heat and hunger and emptiness. There was a choice of pie for dessert, and one was blueberry and one was apple, and the waitresses were the same country girls, there having been no passage of time, only the illusion of it as in a dropped curtain—the waitresses were still fifteen; their hair had been washed, that was the only difference—they had been to the movies and seen the pretty girls with the clean hair. 7

Summertime, oh, summertime, pattern of life indelible, the fade-proof lake, the woods unshatterable, the pasture with the sweetfern and the juniper forever and ever, summer without end; this was the background, and the life along the shore was the design, the cottages with their innocent and tranquil design, their tiny docks with the flagpole and the American flag floating against the white clouds in the blue sky, the little paths over the roots of the trees leading from camp to camp and the paths leading back to the outhouses and the can of lime for sprinkling, and at the souvenir counters at the store the miniature birch-bark canoes and the postcards that showed things looking a little better than they looked. This was the American family at play, escaping the city heat, wondering whether the newcomers in the camp at the head of the cove were "common" or "nice," wondering whether it was true that the people who drove up for Sunday dinner at the farmhouse were turned away because there wasn't enough chicken. 8

It seemed to me, as I kept remembering all this, that those times and those summers had been infinitely precious and worth saving. There had been jollity and peace and goodness. The arriving (at the beginning of August) had been so big a business in itself, at the railway station the farm wagon drawn up, the first smell of the pine-laden air, the first glimpse of the smiling farmer, and the great importance of the trunks and your father's enormous authority in such matters, and the feel of the wagon under you for the long ten-mile haul, and at the top of the last long hill catching the first view of the lake after eleven months of not seeing this cherished body of water. The shouts and cries of the other campers when they saw you, and the trunks to be unpacked, to give up their rich burden. (Arriving was less exciting nowadays, when you sneaked up in your car and parked it under a tree near the camp and took out the bags and in five minutes it was all over, no fuss, no loud wonderful fuss about trunks.) 9

Peace and goodness and jollity. The only thing that was wrong now, really, was the sound of the place, an unfamiliar nervous sound of the outboard motors. This was the note that jarred, the one thing that would sometimes break the illusion and set the years moving. In those other summertimes all motors were inboard; and when they were at a little distance, the noise they made was a sedative, an ingredient of summer sleep. They were one-cylinder and two-cylinder engines, and some were make-and-break and some were jump-spark, but they all made a sleepy sound across the lake. The one-lungers throbbed and fluttered, and the twin-cylinder ones purred and purred, and that was a quiet sound, too. But now the campers all had outboards. In the daytime, in the hot mornings, these motors made a petulant, irritable sound; at night, in the still evening when the afterglow lit the water, they whined about one's ears like mosquitoes. My boy loved our rented outboard, and his great desire was to achieve single-handed mastery over it, and authority, and he soon learned the trick of choking it a little (but not too much), and the adjustment of the needle valve. Watching him I would remember the things you could do with the old one-cylinder engine with the heavy flywheel, how you could have it eating out of your hand if you got really close to it spiritually. Motorboats in those days didn't have clutches, and you would make a landing by shutting off the motor at the proper time and coasting in with a dead rudder. But there was a way of reversing them, if you learned the trick, by cutting the switch and putting it on again exactly on the final dying revolution of the flywheel, so that it would kick back against compression and begin reversing. Approaching a dock in a strong following breeze, it was difficult to slow up sufficiently by the ordinary coasting method, and if a boy felt he had complete mastery over his motor, he was tempted to keep it running beyond its time and then reverse it a few feet from the dock. It took a cool nerve, because if you threw the switch a twentieth of a second too soon you would catch the flywheel when it still had speed enough to go up past center, and the boat would leap ahead, charging bull-fashion at the dock. 10

We had a good week at the camp. The bass were biting well and the sun shone endlessly, day after day. We would be tired at night and lie down in the accumulated heat of the little bedrooms after the long hot day and the breeze would stir almost imperceptibly outside and the smell of the swamp drift in through the rusty screens. Sleep would come easily and in the morning the red squirrel would be on the roof, tapping out his gay routine. I kept remembering everything, lying in bed in the mornings—the small steamboat that had a long rounded stern like the lip of a Ubangi, and how quietly she ran on the moonlight sails, when the older boys played their mandolins and the girls sang and we ate doughnuts dipped in sugar, and how sweet the music was on the water in the shining night, and what it had felt like to think about girls then. After breakfast we would go up to the store and the things were in the same place—the minnows in a bottle, the plugs and spinners disarranged and pawed over by the youngsters from the boys' camp, the Fig Newtons and the Beeman's gum. Outside, the road was tarred and cars stood in front of the store. Inside, all was just as it had always been, except there was more Coca-Cola and not so much Moxie and root beer and birch beer and sarsaparilla. We would walk out with the bottle of pop apiece and sometimes the pop would backfire up our noses and hurt. We explored the streams, quietly, where the turtles slid off logs and dug their way into the soft bottom; and we lay on the town wharf and fed worms to the tame bass. Everywhere we went I had trouble making out which was I, the one walking at my side, the one walking in my pants. 11

One afternoon while we were there at the lake a thunderstorm came up. It was like the revival of an old melodrama that I had seen long ago with childish awe. The second-act climax of the drama of the electrical disturbance over a lake in America has not changed in any important respect. This was the big scene, still the big scene. The whole thing was so familiar, the first feeling of oppression and heat and a general air around camp of not wanting to go very far away. In the midafternoon (it was all the same) a curious darkening of the sky, and a lull in everything that had made life tick; and then the way the boats suddenly swung the other way at their moorings with the coming of a breeze out of the new quarter, and the premonitory rumble. Then the kettle drum, then the snare, then the bass drum and cymbals, then crackling light against the dark, and the gods grinning and licking their chops in the hills. Afterward the calm, the rain steadily rustling in the calm lake, the return of light and hope and spirits, and the campers running out in joy and relief to go swimming in the rain, their bright cries perpetuating the deathless joke about how they were getting simply drenched, and the children screaming with delight at the new sensation of bathing in the rain, and the joke about getting drenched linking the generations in a strong indestructible chain. And the comedian who waded in carrying an umbrella. 12

When the others went swimming, my son said he was going in, too. He pulled his dripping trunks from the line where they had hung all 13 through the shower and wrung them out. Languidly, and with no thought of going in, I watched him, his hard little body, skinny and bare, saw him wince slightly as he pulled up around his vitals the small, soggy, icy garment. As he buckled the swollen belt, suddenly my groin felt the chill of death.

JUST
WHAT THE HELL
AM I TRYING
TO PROVE ?

PART 2

The Process of Shaping: Prewriting to the Final Draft

Complications to the right of me, complications to the left of me, complex on the page before me, perplex in the pen beside me, duplex in the meandering eyes of me, stuplex in the face that reads me.

James Joyce

PART II OF THIS BOOK traces the sometimes sequential, sometimes chaotic, almost always fascinating process of composing essays, which we will do often by focusing on the students' pieces included in Part I. For the sake of clarity, the process is presented as a *series* of steps, although as any writer knows, most writing does not follow orders, does not move forward to a neat marching beat. Most often, it is steps followed by stumbling and backtracking, retracing steps that shouldn't have been taken in the first place—a devious route to a sometimes undetermined goal. The only thing we can be sure of is that all of the steps do get taken—somehow, sometime, sometimes consciously, sometimes not.

Ideally, all of these steps would be learned at once, so intricate are the relationships. This being impossible, however, it seems best to consider them in isolation and in some approximation of a logical order, disorderly as the actual process of both learning and doing may be.

Each section includes a discussion of a particular step in the process and offers concrete examples of how some writers took that step. The purpose here is entirely practical: to show that writers—all writers—must *work* at what they write and to show *how* some writers worked their writing out. The "Practice" section after each discussion encourages you to apply what you have learned in principle, while the "For Your Own Paper" section leads you to apply these same principles to the paper you are writing at the time.

The ultimate goal is to encourage you, by example and by practice, to take on your own writer's task with greater confidence.

Prewriting

For the sake of clarity, I have divided the process of producing a final manuscript into five major steps, beginning with Prewriting—everything you might do *before* you get the first draft down on paper. It is the idea stage, the time when you think, search, gather, reject, accept, plan, and test. Sometimes, this stage requires the playfulness of a kitten with a ball of yarn, a kind of undirected tossing about, chasing an idea across a room or under a chair. At other times, this stage may call for the calculations of a trial lawyer, carefully balancing the facts in the depositions and the texts, weighing the possibilities of victory.

The delight in these sometimes playful, sometimes strict explorations vary from writer to writer, from situation to situation. Doodling, free-writing, tinkering, poring through journals, being awakened from sleep by a significant thought, or jotting bright ideas as the rising sun shines golden over your pages may be inspiring, but if you are searching at midnight to complete the assignment due at 8:30 the next morning, you may well be immune to the delight or downright cranky. Writing with noisy distractions or writing with an immediate deadline may well eliminate the moments when you might actually enjoy writing. Try not to let this happen. As the Irish poet Seamus Heaney comments, "The important thing is to write from your own joy in it."

It is also important, and possibly consoling, to remember that *most* people, including writers, are busy (Wallace Stevens was an insurance executive, composing poems on his walk to work and during his lunch breaks). Most people are distracted by noise and responsibilities (Jane Austen wrote her novels in the crowded sitting room of her large household). Most writers write with deadlines. (Although he was present, *New York Times* columnist Russell Baker did not actually *see* the first Kennedy–Nixon debate because he was too busy writing his on-the-spot copy for the next edition. He thought Nixon had won.)

One of the challenges of learning about writing, then, is learning how to make room for it in your already overcrowded life. It may require planning ahead, thinking about when things are due *before* you crawl exhausted and drained across a deadline. It requires working regularly, building something out of well-chosen materials, not slapping any old scraps together, all at once. Like John McEnroe's passing shot into the far corner, or Leontyne Price's *Aida*, good writing is neither learned all at once nor *written* all at once.

Good writing may require staying at your desk (when everyone else has gone to the movies), staying up late (without watching David Letterman), or getting up early (for those golden sunrises). To be done well and to be enjoyed, writing requires time—time that may in the past have been spent doing something else (but not necessarily more fun). To feel what Heaney describes as "your own joy in it," you must allow yourself the *time* to feel.

Of the amount of time expended for completing a single piece of writing, prewriting can take up a good portion. But if handled with honesty, if approached with an explorer's curiosity, prewriting may also save time and possibly a grade. Don't allow anything to be wasted. Keep a pad of paper on the passenger seat of your car. Save the bright ideas that go bump in the night. Keep a writer's journal, a daily record of thoughts, experiences, insights, characters, and situations that interest you. As E. M. Forster advised, "Be the kind of person on whom nothing is lost."

Considering the Options

—"Write a three-page paper by next Friday."
—"Write a five-page narrative essay on a childhood experience that changed your life."
—"In a ten-page paper, evaluate five major influences of deconsructionism on modern literary criticism."

Each of these assignments asks for writing; each offers a degree of freedom and restriction. The first one allows prose on any subject in the world, so long as it extends to three pages and is completed by Friday. The second, more restricted one asks for a *kind* of writing—personal storytelling—on an important event of your life (one of many that might be told). The third, a typical study assignment, allows no room for deviation and requires outside information.

Very early in the process of writing, writers must consider *what* they are being asked to do and what they are asking themselves to do. Is the requirement a report, a review of something already known, or is it an "original," creative exploration of something not yet figured out? Will it require digging up information from the past or thinking up bright new ideas? A paper on Caesar Augustus is not the same as one on a favorite dog.

Some subjects require immediate trips to the library (the role of Manifest Destiny in the development of America). Some allow for completion without a step being taken away from the desk (each object on my desk has particular meaning for me). Some subjects benefit from what I like to call "automatic points," an "interest quota" already given in the subject itself (a daring tale of a hike into the crater of Mount St. Helen's or a tragic account of a family's struggle to cope with AIDS). Some require particular ingenuity for salvation (how to change a flat tire; my skiing trip; the drinking age).

It is important to consider what *you* are letting yourself in for, because you are ultimately responsible for the success or failure of what you write. Excuses like, "We had company last weekend," "I ran out of time," "I couldn't get to the library," or "The dog ate my manuscript" do nothing to make a careless or uninformed paper better. The paper either works, or it doesn't. Each writing project given you, each project taken upon yourself, carries its own set of expectations, its own requirements for fulfillment. If you're too busy to get to the library and you have a choice, write an informed paper about the dog rather than a silly one about Caesar. If you *have* to write about Caesar, schedule a trip to the library into your life. Think about your options early.

In this book, many student pieces are presented as examples of a particular

"'How I Spent My Summer Vacation,' a treatment by Todd Mozelle, Grade Three."

rhetorical approach—exposition, argument, description, or narration—and many are developed in certain identifiable ways—comparison, cause–effect, for example. John Baron wrote on the process of collecting autographs (page 101) because a "process paper" was one of the options in the course: "Describe how to do something that you know well," and because he was a collector himself who had specialized knowledge. Sally Atwater's paragraph on camping (page 261) was originally part of a narrative piece about her honeymoon: "Write an account of a recent experience that you would like to do over again." But it eventually became part of a paper describing the many things she did *not* enjoy on her trip to Florida. Chris Stephens began a persuasive paper on the modern failures in movies and ended up with a personal appreciation of an old theater (page 134). All of these students started these papers with *something* in mind, namely a suggested assignment, but they developed or changed them as the writing demanded.

If options are available to you and a particular subject or approach is just not working out, change it. Why would a bride continue to write on the glories of a camping honeymoon when, in fact, it was an inglorious disappointment that sent the couple home early? Change your subject, change your thesis, or change your approach if you discover new meanings or uncover new levels of honesty as you write. Try not to die with a dying paper. Even if you have already expended considerable time, try not to force what you already know is failing. Many readers will appreciate your concern for their well-being.

If, however, your options do not include major changes, do as well as you can. Writing, after all, is not *always* a delight. Think of the undelightful letters of application, apologies to friends you may have hurt, sympathy notes, descriptions of accidents for insurance companies (especially if you were at fault). There may be certain satisfactions in such prose, but sometimes writing must be done simply because it *must* be done. You may try several things to provide a breath of inspiration: Read something new on your topic (as Stutz Plaisted did for his paper on muscle cars on page 125), look at what someone else did with the same assignment (how did Tina Beecher argue against the diet craze? On page 186), or search for a fresh approach (as Don Paskowski did by using interior monologue in his account of his operation for cerebral palsy on page 296).

If all attempts at inspiration fail, simply work through the assignment, paying particular attention to grammar and spelling, to the *way* it is written. Make it a masterpiece of technique.

PRACTICE

1. Evaluate the following options carefully and in detail, considering such questions as how you would go about doing the assignment, how much time it would take to fulfill it, if it can be done independently, or, if research is required, what kind of research may be necessary, how much freedom is allowed within the assignment, how much restriction is there, and any other relevant concerns *before* you make a choice or start to work. Ask if the assignment, whether it is given to you or taken upon yourself, is reasonable or if it will require effort beyond the number of days in the semester. Ask if you are interested enough to stay engaged for the duration. What steps would you take immediately?

   a. By the end of the semester, turn in 25 pages of revised, polished prose, including at least one personal experience piece, one piece written from specialized observation, and one research project.
   b. Read Joseph Wood Krutch's "What Is a Good Review?" (pages 314–316 and discuss Thomas D'Evelyn's review of Jonathan Raban's *For Love and Money: A Writing Life* (pages 210–212) in relation to what he says there.

c. Write a 12–15-page paper on Dante's *Inferno,* in which you identify what changes Dante makes in the classical aspects of his poem. You may, if you prefer, identify and discuss the so-called Italian aspects of this section of his *Divine Comedy.*
d. By your next class, write a narrative essay on an experience from which you learned a valuable lesson.
e. In a sophomore "Introduction to Literary Genre" course you are asked to read Alastair Fowler's *The Kinds of Literature* and to discuss in detail the genre of a particular work read during the semester. Do not simply discuss the work in general but consider it in the light of Fowler's commentary. Write ten pages.
f. As part of an in-class diagnostic, write a short essay on what you would do if the college closed tomorrow. Be specific and be sure to think of how you might feel. Take one hour to write this essay.
g. Write an analysis of Andrew Jackson's handling of the Nullification Controversy and of James Buchanan's handling of the Secession Crisis. Read relevant texts assigned in the course and add some specific research of your own. (Write from eight to ten pages. The assignment is due by the midterm examination.)
h. Write a process essay in which you explain how to do something. It is due in two weeks.
i. Write a nonsense essay in which you compare a "kyroplot" to a "sennogram." Write the essay within 20 minutes.
j. Name three membranous organelles of eukaryotic cells and give the functions of each. You have one hour to do this.
k. In ten pages, discuss the Norman Conquest of England in 1066. The assignment is due at the end of the semester.
l. Write a paper analyzing major ethical problems faced by businesses today and focus on one particular company or issue for a closer analysis. Write 20 pages, due in 4 weeks.
m. For 50 points on a take-home portion of a final examination, write an analysis of the role of recent feminist psychology on current psychoanalytical practice. Be sure to include some of the readings assigned in this course.

FOR YOUR OWN PAPER

Make up a similar analysis of your current writing task—one assigned to you or one you are considering taking upon yourself. Determine the kind of work you will have to do, how much time will be required, how much freedom you are allowed, and your own potential for maintaining interest in the assignment.

Discovering a Subject

As you have seen in the discussion of options, you will have varying amounts of freedom and varying demands upon your creativity according to the demands of the task before you. The process at this stage of discovery, or *invention,* therefore, will vary from essay to essay.

But, even if your subject and outline are already given to you (e.g., "In a ten-page paper, evaluate five major influences of deconstruction on modern literary criticism") or if you have total freedom in the selection of subject and shape (e.g., "Write a three-page paper by next Friday"), some procedures at this stage of writing will be equally valuable to you.

First of all, try to allow yourself a totally free block of uninterrupted time (at least 15 minutes) and some peace for concentration. No matter what the assignment, try to get *something* down on that formidable blank page, which is so familar to those with "writer's block." Consider the comment from Pulitzer-Prize winning columnist, Russell Baker:

> . . . and I think when people sit around complaining about writer's block, what they're doing is saying, "Boy, this is not half as good as Shakespeare could have done it." They're trying to be so terrific that they're not willing to go ahead and be commonplace. And most writing is commonplace, isn't it?

Many writers find it easier to discover an approach by writing ideas on a subject that already has been given; many discover the subject and the approach *within* their own notes and scribblings. If nothing is written down, however, the writer may discover nothing at all and become lost in the labyrinth of unrecorded musings—chaotic, fearful, undirected, and unremembered. It is important to get something written down on paper in order to avoid the dilemma so well described by a student: "I think myself in and out of paper after paper, and I still don't have a word to show for it." As essayist E. B. White once said, "I always write a thing first and think about it afterward, which is not a bad procedure, because the easiest way to have consequential thought is to get something down on paper."

Good writing is a swinging back and forth between play and work. This is the time to play. Although it may be difficult, especially if you have lived through years of red-penciled "awks," "sps," "frags," and "whats?" try not to worry about grammar, spelling, sense, or nonsense. Don't stop to correct anything. This is that delightful stage of writing when nobody, not even your English teacher, cares. Your teacher will not be grading this work at all but, rather, a transformation, worked out as the paper takes real shape. Don't red-pencil yourself into silence.

Again, E. B. White offers an insight on this experience. His wife, Katharine White, was a professional editor, one who made a living polishing other people's manuscripts for publication. When it came to her own writing, however, she couldn't turn off this scrupulous editor in herself, even at the very early stages of composition:

> Katharine's act of composition often achieved the turbulence of a shoot-out. The editor in her fought the writer every inch of the way; the struggle was felt all through the house. She would write eight or ten words, then draw her gun and shoot them down. This made for slow and torturous going. It was simple warfare—the editor ready to nip the writer before she committed all the sins and errors the editor clearly foresaw. Occasionally, I ribbed her about the pain she inflicted on herself. "Just go ahead and write," I said. "Edit it afterwards—there's plenty of time." My advice never had any effect on her; she fought herself with vigor and conviction from the first sentence to the last, drawing blood the whole way.

Try to put your own guns down and simply "go ahead and write," as White suggested to his wife. At this point, no one is there to shoot, except yourself. Draw as little of your own blood as possible. If you have a subject in mind, write anything, absolutely anything, that occurs to you on it. Think of things you have read on it, things said in class on it, things you may have thought about it as you were sitting taking notes, things you wonder about it, things others may have said about it, things you don't like about the subject at all. Think of how you feel about the subject, how informed you already are, and how you might make yourself better informed. Make lists, doodle, write in the margins, leave blanks where facts are missing, and follow your random thoughts wherever they take you. You'll have plenty of time to make sense of these scribblings. Now is the time to get them down.

If the subject is totally open, the process will be similar, except that your writing will, for a while, have no direction whatsoever. The more you try this kind of writing, the less formidable it will seem.

Given an assignment asking for *examples* of a "feeling or a set of feelings at an important time in life," Lyn Capodanno (see page 7) jotted down the following notes for her feelings on the first day of college:

letters
loneliness
Scared
angry
Confused
Worried

Peabody
Parties in Summer
old friends
Car packed
Crying

boyfriend
roommates
Go home!

Here, several feelings emerge, as well as some details that she might want to use later and some that might be irrelevant. Notice that the list is random, jumbled, but already her negative reactions are emerging.

At this stage of writing, nothing is solid. Ideas merge together. Thoughts scramble over one another. But something does get written.

Here is another example: One day in class, while my own students were trying a 15-minute exercise in "free writing," I decided to join them:

Sep 6

Class busy. Me too. Wonder how J.
is doing. Don't really feel back to
school yet. Traveling. So serious
at the end. Students seem bored;
wonder if I should stop. After Italy
Driving Driving Driving Lake
Dachau – Keeps on coming back –
Striped clothes, sunken eyes, blown-up
photos of experiments. Gas Chambers
Horrible – Kept on wanting to walk
away, felt I should look – Frightening
Even in summer – tourists in shorts –
snapping pictures. Spigots.
why turn away
why not
feels like invading privacy
museum needs broad focus on human
potential for violence
we can all be cruel – How cruel?
Time to stop class – 7:47.

(In these quick notes, written on my first day of another school year, I can see even now what was on my mind and what I might be able to work into writing: my concern with my son on his first day in kindergarten (the problems faced by working mothers); my worry about the class (whether they were bored, whether they were learning anything by free writing) that the weeks in semesters have personalities and that the first one feels like a 747 to me, lumbering off the ground, trying to become airborne; my recollections of the recent summer in Europe, especially the concentration camp at Dachau (I'm *still* trying to understand my reactions to the place: nightmares, fear, horror, shock, even though I had seen films and read books; the desire to look away, the need to look); a tendency to be "down" in these notes (to worry about home and school, to worry even about my summer.)

If you let them speak, subjects will gather randomly, group, and lead away to possibilities. Put down the gun.

This rambling, free association is often fun and often reveals a leaning toward a subject before a 15- or 20-minute session is up. When the clock finally stops ticking, reread the ramblings and doodles to see if you were saying anything to yourself. (Much of learning to write is learning to listen to what you have to say.)

Your subject may be staring back at you, as in the following notes by E. B. White—notes that eventually found their way into a rather grim *Letter from the East* (*The New Yorker,* February 24, 1975). In this *Letter,* written from his farm in North Brooklin, Maine, White suggests that "... everything else here in the East is in a mess, just as it is in other parts of the nation, and in all parts of the world" and then provides several examples of this local "mess": the excavation of Goose Cove by a mining company, the governmental threat to the new wing on the hospital, the raising of salmon in an abandoned mine pit, the cultivation of oysters in wire and wood trays, the transformation of a four-story henhouse into a recording studio, a rash of thievery in the area, the excessive speed of the SST, and the topic of these notes, "energy . . . the toughest nut to crack."

White begins to think about energy with pencil scratch notes on small white sheets of paper—his own musings on the subject (shown on page 359). (Note the dashed-out quality to these free, unconnected notions.)

Further contributing to his thoughts on energy was his attendance at a local meeting with a power company executive to discuss the problem. Here he takes notes on a folded yellow sheet of paper (shown on page 360.) (Note here that he not only writes names and quotations, but also that the speaker wore a brown turtleneck. The tone here, too, seems to be negative. He seems to have some second thoughts about nuclear power, even at a "Safe Power for Maine" meeting.)

Your ramblings and notes, too, may wander from a problem at home to what you did last summer, from thermostats to nuclear power. You may move from

(Energy)

We save in little
ways — the lowered
thermostat, the cancelled
motor trips. But the
plain truth is, we are
geared up (in our households)
not for saving but for
spending. The water pump,
the fuel pump, the washer,
the dryer, the dish washer,
the TV the electric heater
the electric toaster, ~~the~~ etc

Emil Garrett — Safe Power for Maine
Basketball court. Central Me Power. Brown
turtleneck - Pick people up and move them
out of the area of radiation. Monitor the milk,
40,000 square miles. High level radioactive
waste. Storage question has not been settled.
Nobody knows what to do with it. My
dentist: Rocket it to the sun.

Mr. John Rundowsi. C Maine Power
Maine Yankee 1972. Yarmouth 1978-
We must be self-reliant.
Cape Rosier - We have no plans for Cape
Rosier at this time.

Fossil fuels.
Supply of uranium - over a thousand years -
Goatherd. Iodine released. Contamination
of milk -
Light water reactor. Breeder reactor.
Very quiet, thoughtful suspicion of the
whole business.
Insurance companies leary of it.
Eisenhower 1952 - peaceful use of
atomic energy. Government picked up the
tab.

the sound of the pen on your paper to sounds at a weekend concert, from the depths of the universe to the depths of the sea, from personal grievances to the grand grievances of the founding fathers. Write what is on your mind, and you will often discover a nugget of a subject. Listen to yourself. Read what you are saying.

If, however, this totally free approach yields little but total freedom, you may want to give yourself some "nudges," some directions for your thoughts: What subjects do I know well enough to handle? Could I tell someone how to do something? What makes me curious? What topic do I really *want* to think about and to learn about, either in the library or elsewhere? (Seeing many of his friends worrying about selling their property, Joe Hession wanted to share what he now knows about owning houses and condos (pages 38–39); Tracey Brown, feeling nervous about her major, asked herself why she had chosen it (pages 131–133).

Ask yourself the following questions. Within the past several days, what subjects got me most involved or upset (see Salerno on rock bands, pages 224–226)? What made me say, "This is ridiculous!" (see Speziale on jogging, pages 231–234) or "I wish" (see White on returning to a childhood lake, pages 340–345)? What are the biggest problems I'm facing right now (see Pennimpede on commuting, pages 40–41)? What advice would I offer to someone who is clearly making a mistake (see Grasso on steroids, pages 292–294)? How do two things compare to each other (see Ross on football versus baseball, pages 46–55)? What are the main causes or effects of a particular event (see Alves on divorce, pages 138–141)? What particular place or person stirs strong feelings in me (see Carbone on her family, pages 15–17)? What makes me angry (see Capodanno, pages 7–8)? What makes me happy (see DeWolf on a briar patch, pages 160–161)?

You may also turn elsewhere: to your instructor's assignments; to reading you have recently done, especially to something that caused you to react strongly; to reading, as in this book, that may inspire you to write something similar; to suggestions for writing in other textbooks; to more general approaches to writing itself (exposition, argumentation, description, narration); to other writing you may have already done in diaries (day-to-day records of activities), journals (daily gleanings from anything that may have interested you—books, events, quotations, newspapers, people), letters, for example. Columnist Ellen Goodman says that she goes through life like a vacuum cleaner, taking in topics to write about. Become a vacuum cleaner.

Some writers get ideas by staring out the window; some, by analyzing other people; some, on subways or in traffic jams on the highway. Others wake up in the middle of the night with a subject demanding to be written. Some always have a subject in mind, which stews on the back burner until the time comes for serving it. Others struggle to find the stove.

In a *New York Times* article (January 12, 1989), Diane Ackerman gives some professional examples. Dame Edith Sitwell used to lie in an open coffin when she needed inspiration. Amy Lowell smoked cigars while writing, Balzac drank more than 50 cups of coffee a day, and Ben Franklin wrote in the bathtub. Others turned to reading—the French civil code, the Bible—to music, or to special colors of paper or ink. Some writers compose standing up.

In short, there isn't any *one* way to come up with subjects or to write about them. The best way is to discover what works best for you and to remember that time spent on discovery is not time wasted, even if the chosen 15 minutes does not produce a subject neatly wrapped and ready for delivery. Time spent at this stage of writing may for a while serve only to eliminate subjects you aren't ready for, but this, too, is a valuable discovery. You may for a while be doing little more than making yourself into what the poet John Milton called, "a fit vessel," a worthy container, ready for the ideas when they *do* come. At the very least, you are a writer with writing on your mind.

As short-story writer Eudora Welty explains:

> I don't feel that anything flies in the window and comes into your mind and you write it down. I think the final thing may fly in through the window, but only if you've received it by a constant brooding on something. I think it's a much longer process.

PRACTICE

1. Read the following "brainstorming" list, typed from handwritten notes, to see if you can discover any possible subjects there. What possible groupings emerge? Do you see any points that might be made? In short, what seems to be on this writer's mind?

   —school, school, school
   —how to forget school
   —sitting here bored
   —do I want to
   —not comfortable
   —why, why
   —working with Jack
   —summer job
   —lots of hours, lots of money
   —don't want this, too heavy, too many stairs
   —moving boxes, tables, chairs, mirrors, heavy couch-beds
   —weekends
   —sun

—no summer, too much work
—major in business—dad's idea
—dad's job, I can take over without the degree
—camping, tent, Canada
—would like to buy a new van
—too much money for textbooks
—school
—change major to phys. ed.?

FOR YOUR OWN PAPER

1. If your subject is totally open, try brainstorming to come up with a list by "free writing" for 15 minutes. If you can't think of anything to say, write about that or describe the room in which you are sitting. See where your thoughts take you. See if ideas group around any particular subject or any particular feeling that you might like to express.

2. Try writing further, perhaps on one of the subjects that began to emerge in the previous exercise.

3. If a specific assignment has been given to you or if you have chosen one of yourself, write as much as you can on it for at least 15 minutes. Do your thoughts continue to grow? Does the subject remain interesting and rich to you? Can you go on with this? Where do you think you should go from here?

4. Read through other things you have written—journals, diaries, letters—all the while looking for a subject that may allow, even urge, you to write. Talk to a friend and take note of what is really on your mind.

Clarifying the Point

If the process of writing has proceeded neatly, you have by now carefully considered your options and written your way to a subject that interests you and that you are ready to write about. You even have some idea of what you want to *say* about it. Your thesis, your one-sentence judgment about your subject, is clear. You may, however, be nowhere near this kind of clarity. You may have only a possible subject in mind, with little idea of what you want to do with it. You may know that you want to write *about* your school, but you don't know if you want to argue in favor of new requirements in the curriculum or if you want to explain *why* most freshmen flunk certain courses. Your thesis may be far from sure. Neither situation is unusual, nor is it a problem. Each piece of writing moves in its own way, at its own pace.

It is unnecessary to create false difficulties for a subject that practically falls into place, just as it is impossible to expect easy solutions for a complex or elusive subject that does not so easily reveal its meaning. John Baron's paper on collecting autographs, for example (see pages 101–105), made its main point and organized itself in his head: "These are the major steps for collecting autographs." For her piece, "Seventh of the Litter" (see pages 15–17), however, Sharyn Carbone wrote through several different thesis statements, *after* she had settled on her family as her subject: "Being the youngest child is a mixed blessing" (there are some advantages and some disadvantages); "I like being a member of a large family" (several advantages); "I'd like to be the oldest in my family" (reasons why she envies the oldest). When she finally realized that it was irritating to be the youngest, she found a thesis that she wanted to develop: "People don't realize how difficult being the baby can be" (several disadvantages).

For his piece on the Strand (see pages 134–136), Chris Stephens mined his journals and wrote drafts comparing old theaters and new ones, drafts registering complaints about the colorization of black-and-white films, a draft on the connection between videos and film, and finally a combination of these drafts in a personal-experience piece that seemed to have no main point at all. He submitted this "all-purpose" draft to a workshop class and got the following comments:

—"Chris, I'm not really sure what the main point of your paper is. It could be the major effect the Strand had on your life, or it could be how you grew up and now you're wondering what happened to your dreams."

—"I love the details, but I think the connection between the Strand and your own life is confusing."

—"I enjoyed much of this, but isn't the commentary on local movie houses a side issue?"
—"Is life a movie? Is *your* life a movie? At times, you lose the Strand completely."
—"Couldn't you drop the whole paragraph on videos and Amadeus?"

(Notice that these comments reflect the writer's own confusion at this point and his own difficulty with choosing a point for his writing. With some guidance from his readers, Chris finally chose to focus on the reasons why he felt so attached to the demolished theater. It became a "cause-and-effect" paper with many personal details.)

As you rummage through the old notes created while you searched for a subject and through the new notes written as your subject became more clear; as you scribble your way in and out of ideas; as you consider what your readers or listeners might say, be on the alert for the point you really want to make. If you can, try working your thoughts into a one-sentence thesis or continue to write until you discover an idea that seems to move toward some conclusion. Follow the track of your greatest interest and develop the aspect that leads you to the most detail.

Remember, however, that as efficient as it may sound to move from notes, to subject, to thesis, to plan, to first draft, to revisions, and to final draft, you may need to skip ahead to an entire first draft before your own thoughts become clear to you. Some writers, like Eudora Welty, compose with a goal in mind: "I think the end is implicit in the beginning. It must be. If that isn't there in the beginning, you don't know what you're working toward." Others continue to write for quite some time without fixed direction, without judgments, outlines, or plans. As novelist John Updike explains, "Writing and rewriting are a constant search for what one is saying."

Even among professional writers, there is nothing sacred about the order of steps in the process. The important thing is that somewhere, sometime, things are thought about. Sooner or later, a judgment must be made.

Also important at this time, as you begin to work toward a thesis that you can develop, is to pay some attention to what you *can* bring yourself to say about your subject. You must consider not only your subject, your thesis, and your readers but also yourself and how much you *want* to tell. This selection of material becomes even more of a concern in personal-experience essays. Try to avoid subjects that require more revelations or more intimacy than you are ready to share. Don't invite the reader into your house and then slam the door on his foot. Here is an example: After choosing her boyfriend as her subject, a student decided to focus on his "overprotectiveness" and to give many examples of this behavior to back up her judgment—he follows her to parties, he calls up wherever she is visiting, he trails her when she goes to the movies. About halfway through the paper, however, she shifted to praising his good nature and his generosity, and she concluded with a romantic description of a seaside restaurant where he recently took her. Her explanation of this curious deviation from her thesis was that she began to feel guilty and couldn't go on with it. No reader, except the most intrusive, would expect her to, and it's certainly always the writer's option to give up on a topic that is too intimate or painful.

As essayist M. F. K. Fisher says, "Not everything can be told, nor need it be." The problem is that the essay that *does* get written needs to work as an essay, regardless of the writer's scruples or second thoughts. It is important to write honestly. If you find yourself getting "cagey," keeping secrets as you write, you may end up sacrificing the best details and the emotional commitment you need to be interesting. If you can't tell it, don't write it. Search out something less threatening.

You must not only know your point, you must be willing to make it.

PRACTICE

1. Evaluate the following statements. Identify which ones could be used as thesis statements for successful papers and which ones may well lead to problems in writing. How might the workable ones be developed? What are the potential problems in the weak ones?

   a. My worst fault, of which I have many examples, is that I am a procrastinator.
   b. My dog, Chippy.
   c. My camping trip to New Hampshire.
   d. My camping trip to New Hampshire was a disaster from beginning to end.
   e. Learning from your mistakes.
   f. I learned several lessons this summer—the hard way.
   g. I spent the summer getting into trouble practically every place I went.
   h. Coffee is one of Brazil's major exports.
   i. If the college closed tomorrow, I'd call my mother.
   j. If the college closed tomorrow, I'd be miserable, but I'd probably take several practical steps.
   k. My subject is Professor Johnson.
   l. Professor Johnson is a great teacher.
   m. Advertising creates desires and needs that we might otherwise not have.

n. J.F.K., President of the United States, was assassinated.
o. The ethical standards for politicians seem to change with the times.
p. Minority communities need to be educated on issues of "empowerment."
q. Here's how to make a terrarium.
r. My ten-day stay in Italy was very nice.
s. This is a ridiculous subject, and I don't want to write about it.
t. Miss America.
u. Miss America is very attractive.
v. Miss America is more than a swimsuit.
w. The Miss America pageant is an expression of American values.
x. The Miss America pagent is not appealing to many women; consider some of these comments from feminists.
y. The private life of a contestant or a winner should have nothing to do with wearing the Miss America crown.
z. The Miss America pageant is more appealing than the Miss Universe Pageant.

2. Choose five subjects from the following list. Make up at least one workable thesis for each one. Think of some questions: What is it? What does it do? How does it work? How did it get this way? What is the worth? How do you feel about it? How do you want your reader to feel? Consider automobiles, for example: "There are many reasons for the popularity of muscle cars" (see the piece on pages 125–126).

a. Beverages.
b. Handicaps.
c. Crime.
d. Food.
e. Entertainment.
f. Celebrities.
g. Religion.
h. Feasts and festivals.
i. Advertising.
j. Politics.
k. Music.
l. Customs.
m. Habits.
n. Animals.
o. Dreams.
p. Family.
q. Places to live.
r. Behavior.
s. Health.
t. Hobbies.
u. Transportation.
v. Teachers.
w. Television.
x. Sports.
y. Travel.
z. Clothing.

Determining the Purpose (What and to Whom?)

Let me begin this discussion with a personal experience. I was once asked by the editor of the Massachusetts Audubon Society's journal, *Sanctuary,* to write a piece on bird-watchers (see pages 171–176). "Fun," I thought to myself, as names of famous bird-watchers raced through my mind, and as I recalled things I had read about them. But that was before I sat down to write. The "fun" of writing eluded me with more agility than the fastest spring warbler. I had to write, and write, and write my way to what I was trying to say. I couldn't figure out what to *do* with the subject.

So I "brainstormed." I made bad drawings of birds. I drank lots of coffee. I called friends. I played with the baby. And I came up with absolutely nothing I liked. I worried. What *could* I say to the collective Audubon membership, bird-watchers all, and far better bird-watchers than I? I knew I wanted to write a positive piece about different types of bird-watchers, something that would suggest the variety among them, but I was writing *to* the bird-watchers themselves. Everything in my notes sounded stupid, unworthy of their time.

I decided I didn't know enough. I had to read some more before writing more. I read Roger Tory Peterson, Faith McNulty, Olin Sewall Pettingill, Edward Howe Forbush, John Burroughs, Florence Page Jaques, and Gilbert White, among others. I learned much more about birds and the professional watchers. Then I tried to write again. First I made lists, then I tried a draft in which I diligently catalogued all the different kinds of bird-watchers I discovered in my books and articles (few of whom I had ever met firsthand). I was going to call it "Fifteen Ways of Looking at Bird-watchers"; it was about as much "fun" to write, or to read, as the Audubon Society's mailing list.

Only after additional tedious drafts and a flight to Naples (for a planned vacation) with a suitcase stuffed with bird books, duplicated articles, and poems, did I discover what I was doing wrong. I remember sitting at Lake Avernus (with American rock music on the jukebox at the Cafe Charon), when I thought of a very large, football-tackle-type bird-watcher who was completely happy about sighting some Wilson's warblers one spring afternoon. I smiled to myself and jotted down the following note on a pad in my wallet:

Warbler wave
days you'd <u>kill</u> for a Wilson's
Hey — that's the best Nashville I've

Extra seen: X this year!
I'm still after that elusive
Blackburnian
— had to take a day off —
— everything that moved looked
like a warbler ——

(Maybe I needed some distance?)

Cowed by the superior knowledge of my readers, I had been posing as an expert, knowing all the time that I wasn't. I was trying to hide my ignorance in the authority of others. I was avoiding being me—a relatively new, very inexperienced, and often befuddled bird-watcher. Once I heard the falsity in this fake expert's voice, however, I decided to write in my own voice, sharing what I had learned and describing the people whom I had met, like my warbler watcher. My point and my purpose were finally in sync. My point was still to suggest the many types of bird-watchers, but my purpose became simply to share some of my own feelings with the more qualified readers and, indirectly, to enlighten those who might learn from my experiences. To allow for the necessary self-mockery, I decided to keep the tone light.

I tell this long story because it describes the all-too-familiar experience of struggling with purpose, even with the subject already assigned, and because it brings up another important issue intimately tied to purpose—the writer's relationship to the reader. I had to discover what I already knew about bird-watchers. I had to sift, gather additional information, and focus on what I actually *could* say. And I had to adapt all of this to my bird-watcher readers. Many lists, lots of rewriting, and a rather extreme change in perspective helped me to discover just what I was trying to do. With other subjects and with other audiences, I might have gotten through this stage much more easily.

Ironically, determining purpose requires almost a split personality, one of which still "plays" with ideas and is still in the process of discovering new meaning *and* the other of which thinks seriously about the aim of the writing. It is a stage that requires continued, unguided exploration and, simultaneously, a conscious mapping of new roads, giving some thought to where they should lead (and who might be using them).

At this stage, too, you need to consider *why* you are writing in the first place. Your most immediate purpose may be to earn an "A" from an instructor, but beyond the practical goal of the moment, you need to ask what you are trying to say to your readers and what you have in mind for them as you write:

to entertain (as in an account of a funny incident), to enlighten (as in a research report), to demonstrate knowledge (as in an examination), to express yourself (as in a lyric essay), or to stir them to action (as in a letter to the editor). Are you thinking of doing several of these things at the same time?

You need to ask yourself the big question, "So what?": Why am I telling this to someone? Why am I taking the reader's time? What do I want the reader to feel or to do when I am finished? After Chris Stephens decided to focus on his own feelings about the Strand, he hoped to share this nostalgia with his readers and, in the process, possibly to win some appreciation for the less glossy days at the movies. After Sharyn Carbone decided to complain about being the last born in a big family, she also planned to enlighten readers who may think it is an advantage to be the "baby."

As you can see, it is impossible to identify purpose without giving some attention to readers as well, to those who will eventually hold your manuscript in their hands. All too often, prose is composed "reader-less" (and may well remain that way). Writing composed in a vacuum with only the writer in mind is often empty ("Shakespeare was a great writer"), silly ("My life as a student is a perfect dream come true"), tedious ("My skiing vacation was really interesting"), or pompous ("My intention is to provide a portrait of a consummate didacticist").

Although it is important to remember that you may need to write *through* this stage before you can discover either your main point or your audience, one nagging question you should always ask is, "Is somebody out there listening?" followed by a quick, "And if so, who?" Try not to be intimidated by your readers (as I was in the bird-watching piece), but, somewhere along the line, do spend some time thinking of at least some tentative readers. Even the famous "general" readers tend to be like the rest of us—busy, distracted, cantankerous, confused, and sometimes tolerant human beings who may actually get to look at our words on the page and who more than likely do not like being bored. As E. B. White warns, "Most readers are in trouble half the time." Anticipate their troubles; give them something worth reading.

All good writing, finally, is not simply writing round and about a subject, but writing with a purpose. Various writers may take exactly the same information, the same "raw material" of life, and do something entirely different with it, with entirely different purposes for the reader. Langston Hughes, for example, failed in his efforts to be "saved" when he was a child (pages 305–307), yet out of this difficult experience, he writes a remarkably tolerant, even warm, essay. The reader sympathizes with the boy's plight and understands the adult writer's decisions. Another writer who might be more resentful, or even Hughes himself in a nastier mood, might well have turned those same experiences into a bitter indictment of "old time religion" and its perpetrators. The reader then would be asked to share in the bitterness.

The chapter divisions in this book will help you to understand what writers are able to *do* with their writing: explain, argue, persuade, describe, or tell a story, but, as Frank Conroy suggests in his essay, "Think about It," the writer needs also to think about the meaning of what is being done about the "why" as well as the "what" of writing: "The light bulb may appear over your head, is what I'm saying, but it may be a while before it actually goes on."

PRACTICE

1. Identify the purpose and the intended audience of the following statement. Ask yourself who is the writer, why is the statement written, and what is the writer's purpose for the reader?

> I was proceeding on Raymond Road at approximately 30 m.p.h. (in a 35 m.p.h. zone) when a red '68 Olds, driven by Mr. Peter O'Leary, went through a blinking red light at the intersection of Raymond and Pearl and collided broadside with my car. The impact turned my car 180 degrees and smashed the door permanently shut on the driver's side. Neither I, nor my boyfriend, riding in the passenger seat were injured, but the damage to my car is considerable. At the time of the accident, Mr. O'Leary accepted responsibility in front of Officer John Govoni, and apologized to us.

2. Assume that Mr. O'Leary has just learned that his insurance company will put him in a "bad risk" pool and double his insurance rates as a result of this accident, if he is at fault. Write *his* description of the same incident.

3. What is the purpose for the reader of the following letter? Ask yourself why it has been written and what the writer hopes as a result. Is it effective?

Dear Lisa,

It would be easier to just go to the shop and buy an "I'm sorry" card, but I think it would be a cop-out. I really didn't mean to hurt you the other night when I took off with Karen. You know how it is at these end-of-the-school-year parties. People don't always think clearly. Especially me. I really do want to go on seeing you, if you can forgive me. I hope you got home all right. I wouldn't blame you if you couldn't bring yourself to see me again. All I can do is apologize and ask if you are free for Saturday night. How about dinner at the Seashore Grille? I know how much you like it there.

With high hopes,
Mike

4. Write Lisa's response. Be sure to decide what her point is and what message she intends for *her* reader.

5. What is the purpose for the reader of the following letter? How does she *want* Mrs. Johnson to feel? What does she want her to do? Has the writer successfully fulfilled her purpose?

Dear Mrs. Johnson,

This is just to let you know how ridiculous it is that you won't let Shelley travel with us to Europe this summer. After all, there'll be four us, and two of us, Bob and I, have been there before. We are quite sure of ourselves and I'm positive we could take good care of your precious little girl. She's not a baby anymore, you know. I can't imagine why you're so worried about money either. It's actually quite cheap if you stay in the hostels with all the other kids and besides, we can hitchhike to save more money on transportation. As for tuition, she can probably get an on-campus job in September. I really don't see the problem. Anyway, I'm glad I told you what I think and I hope you'll have the sense to think this over.

Sincerely,
Ginnie

6. Write a response from Mrs. Johnson to Ginnie. Be sure to consider point and purpose.

7. Rewrite this letter to Mrs. Johnson, making it a more effective appeal from Ginnie to Mrs. Johnson.

8. Read the various essays written on steroids (pages 144–146, 165–167, and 292–294) and evaluate the purpose of each. What effect does the purpose have on the writing itself?

9. In the "Working with . . ." sections of the chapter introductions in Part I are sample paragraphs, all written on the same topic—student housing. Read through them and notice how each one changes as the approach and purpose change.

FOR YOUR OWN PAPER

1. Try to think of a thesis you might like to develop into a longer paper. Consider your main purpose—to entertain, to persuade, to inform, to argue a point, to express your own feelings, or to illustrate what you know.

2. Identify your audience—a general one, like a magazine or a newspaper readership, or a specific one, like your English teacher, your workshop class, or someone who needs to hear what's on your mind.

3. Consider what effect any changes in purpose or readership might have on your approach to the subject. Experiment a bit. Try adapting the same subject to two different purposes and to two different audiences. (It isn't necessary to write the *whole piece* twice unless you are discovering new possibilities as you proceed.) Always ask yourself, "Will this approach *work* for my purposes and my audience?"

Making a Plan

Based on the definition of Montaigne, called the father of the essay, an "essay" is an "attempt," an exploration of a subject, often unplanned, often arriving at no firm conclusion. One idea sets off another, and trips down the byways are frequent. To read these wandering thoughts of sophisticated and skilled writers is among the most satisfying of literary pleasures. Essayist Gilbert Highet compares these pieces to "light caught in many broken reflections from the surface of a pool." With minds "intense and deeply penetrated with harmonious impulses," these explorers create a "spiritual unity" that holds the reader's attention.

Without this kind of intensity, however, without this inner sense of unity and purpose, unplanned and pointless writing is no pleasure at all. The reader feels that the writing is out of control, that ideas are randomly expressed, and that the purpose of the entire piece is unknown to anyone, including the writer. Frustrated, confused, often irritated, the reader scrambles around in what Highet describes as "a heap of clothespins in a basket." As wise as individual thoughts may be, as clever as the writer may be, the reader feels abandoned, lost.

This is the reason why most essays, somewhere in the process, need some planning, some sense of shape that allows the reader to move *through* the writing without stopping, exhausted, to untangle where the writer has been and where the writer is going. A pause for reflection is a pleasure for the reader; a pause for oxygen is not. As E. B. White says, "The first principle of composition ... is to foresee or determine the shape of what is to come, and pursue that shape." As Gilbert Highet says, with some humor,

> Before you start you must have a form in your mind; and it ought to be a form felt in paragraphs or sections, not in words or sentences—so that, if necessary, you could summarize each paragraph in a single line and put the entire essay on a postcard.

Where do you find this shape, this "form felt in paragraphs or sections?" Where do you discover a plan for your writing?

Put simply, it most often grows out of what you are trying to do. If, for example, you have come to some clear idea of point and purpose, some thoughts about *how* you want to make your point, then a plan, at least a tentative one, may already be apparent to you. If you are still exploring, you may need to look more deliberately for a possible shape for what you are trying to do.

You may want to search through your "free writing" and your notes. Just as you may discover subject, thesis, and purpose there, so you may find a possible plan. For her essay on "Doubting My Major" (page 131), for example, Tracey Brown wrote the following random thoughts:

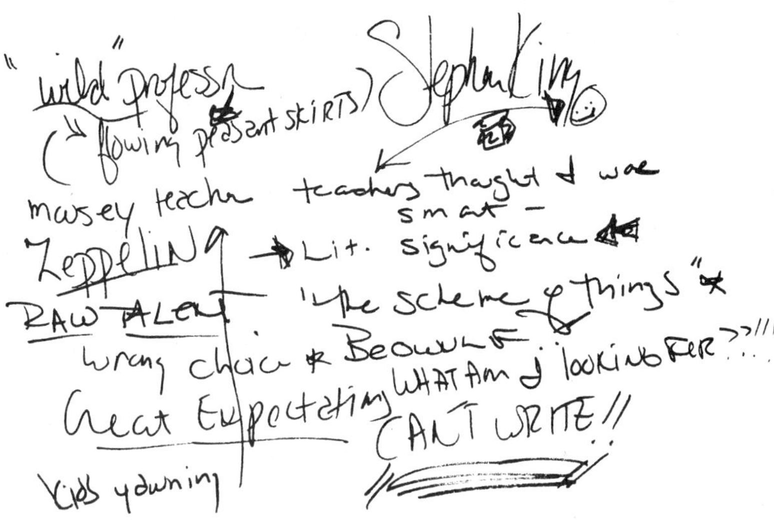

(As you can see, she also underlined thoughts that could possibly work as topics for paragraphs. She was already thinking about focusing on *causes* for her doubts.)

After this searching, she arrived at the following tentative outline for her paper:

I DISCOURAGED — I DON'T THINK I HAVE WHAT IT TAKES

II CAN'T WRITE

III CAN'T INT. LIT.

IV TEACH?

V SPECULATION?

(Notice that this list is simply an early "verbal sketch" or rough paragraph plan for the paper she was about to write. At this point, it simply provided her with some division of topics and some sense of where the paper might be heading. As it turned out, this paper continued through to the final draft with this same basic plan but only because it continued to work for the writer.)

Plans may also be suggested by the controlling idea within the thesis. Tien Truong's thesis, "I came to hate almost everything about my job at the Chinese Restaurant" (pages 12–14), led inevitably to paragraphs on *things* she did not like about her job: boredom, customers, co-workers, chefs. Roger Froilan's thesis, suggesting that "Super Beings may be categorized according to the ways they got their power" (pages 69–71), had to lead to paragraphs on these ways, as Roger's first scratch outline shows:

—Mutant—
—X-factor
—Magical
—Outside forces
—Humans pushed to extremes

(Like Tracey Brown's outline, this outline is sketchy, simply hinting to the writer about where the paper might go. As you may see in the printed draft, Roger later distinguished further among these categories and gave each type a name that made the discussion easier to read. Very early in the writing he had a sense of what he was trying to do, but it took several drafts to clarify the categories and give them appropriate names.)

Linda Alves, on the other hand, prepared a much more formal outline for her research paper, "Some Major Effects of Divorce on Children (pages 138–141). Her thesis, "Research shows that the effects are many and long-lasting," also suggested a clear controlling idea, in this case, *effects:*

—Paragraph 1—background on divorce
—Paragraph 2—effect #1 (denial)
—Paragraph 3—effect #2 (guilt)
—Paragraph 4—effect #3 (grief)
—paragraph 5—effect #4 (depression)
—paragraph 6—effect #5 (feelings of rejection)
—Paragraph 7—effect #6 (anger)
—Paragraph 8—effect #7 (embarrassment)
—Paragraph 9—transition from short- to long-term effects
—Paragraph 10—effects after five and ten years
—Paragraph 11—sleeper effects
—Paragraph 12—conclusion

(This outline grew out of research done with a specific topic and approach already in mind, a narrowing down of the "family" subject listed on page 367. She went to the library *looking* for *effects* of divorce. In fact, she planned the paper after her research but *before* she wrote a single paragraph of her own. Her clear idea of her subject and its controlling idea, plus her focused research provided her with a reasonable plan.)

The *kind* of writing you are doing may also help you to set up a plan. In fact, one of the major advantages of learning about writing according to the major categories—exposition, argumentation, description, and narration—is that with an understanding of what each one *does* come some recognition of *how* each one may be effectively structured. Exposition, for example, is an attempt to explain and therefore presents information logically, always in the direction of clarity, while the various major types of exposition—exemplification, comparison–contrast, classification, process, cause–effect, and definition—suggest their own possibilities for planning (see relevant discussions in Part I). Argumentation seeks to gain assent and therefore usually moves toward the *most convincing* point. In descriptive writing, the order is suggested by the approach to the thing being described—from far to near, from top to bottom, from left to right. Narration, based on events in time, is often set up in a time sequence (with possible flashbacks and foreshadowings, of course).

For further thoughts on organizing ideas as they relate to specific kinds of writing, please see the many paragraph plans in the chapter introductions in Part I and the more detailed discussions in the "Working with . . ." sections. It is also possible to mix these various kinds of writing, for example, to open an argument with a narrative or to elaborate on a particular effect with a detailed description, but it is important for the writer to know *how* such variations fit into the overall purpose and how they may be adapted to the overall plan, for it is not only the breakdown of topics but also the order or the relationships among the parts that make successful essays.

It is necessary to think about which topics lead into and out of one another, which topics stand alone, which topics are the strongest, and which ones are less significant. It is necessary to think about *when* these topics should be developed. During the reading of your essay, even if it is well written, the attention and the energy of the reader may begin to falter. Save some strong points for the climax, near the end. Build *up* toward interest; don't slide toward a tedious finish. In her analysis of her job, Tien Truong saved describing the "chefs" for last because they were the most difficult to tolerate. Tracey Brown, thinking that her potential failure as a teacher was the worst of her reasons to doubt her English major, saved that topic for the last. Good timing is indispensable—giving the right information at the right moment, sensing what topics the reader must understand early, and sensing what should be held back for greater effect. In planning, think not only of the *what* but of the *when.*

As we have already seen, some writers are able to compose successfully without a specific aim in mind. Others prefer to hold the organization in suspense until they discover in their drafts what they are trying to say. Writers must do what works for them. It is important, however, to recognize what is actually *happening* as you write. Are you allowing yourself the luxury of rambling, disconnected, and aimless prose, with the intention of imposing order upon it later, or are you simply forcing yourself through pages of writing, paragraphing when it seems "about time," and inserting ideas whenever they occur to you? Are you rambling far beyond reasonable time limits, continually stopping, changing direction, losing sight of a goal, or, worse, forgetting that you need one? Is your writing producing nothing but a bigger headache as the deadline draws near? Has the writing become truly random, not by design, but by default?

If you are among the "discoverers," keep on writing and stay alert. If you are among the latter, the "aimless wanderers," you may need to stop and rethink. You may need to go back as far as your selection of the subject, to your thesis, to your sense of purpose, or possibly to your thoughts about your audience.

You may also need to stop and think about a plan, even a rough sketch of where you might want to take your subject. However and whenever it is achieved, whether it is early in the planning or late in the shaping of the final draft, writing that suggests that you know where you have been and where you are going gives the reader greater confidence in your guidance and your judgment. A plan provides a firm foundation for what you want to say.

PRACTICE

1. For each example, arrange the following thoughts in what seems to you the best order. Be able to explain why you chose the plan. If appropriate, combine topics, add to them, and eliminate ones you don't want to use.

   a. For an argumentative paper that is trying to prove that time off after high school is a mistake (for argument, see pages 180–183):

      1. May lose momentum for studying
      2. Waste of time at a job you do not want to keep
      3. Earn money on a full-time job now
      4. Buy a new car as soon as possible
      5. Loss of focus on school and future goals
      6. Possibility of never going to college
      7. Timing (when most students are your own age)

   b. For a process paper on how to change a tire (for process, see pages 92–95):

      1. Jack car up
      2. Get spare tire out of trunk

3. Loosen lug nuts on wheel
4. Replace with spare tire
5. Remove flat tire
6. Put flat tire in trunk
7. Drive to nearest station to have flat tire repaired

c. For a description of a high-school basketball pregame warm-up (for description, see pages 253–258):

1. The school tiger logo painted at center court
2. The Tigers' practice
3. The foul lines and out-of-bounds lines
4. The Tanners' warm-up
5. The entrance
6. The hot-dog stand
7. The popcorn vendor
8. The mustard yellow seats
9. The coaches
10. The trainers
11. The benches

2. In the following scratch notes about travel, identify what seem to be connected and relevant pieces of information, list them, consider a possible thesis, and arrange them in some reasonable and convincing order (add, combine, or eliminate, as you see fit):

—The "Grand Tour"
—Last year
—England to Greece back to Europe through Italy, Switzerland, Germany, and France
—clothing
—Tower of London
—tickets
—student fares
—food
—books
—fish and chips
—medicine
—hostels
—meeting people
—Eurail pass
—backpacking
—decks of Greek ships at night
—crepes
—fondue
—major monuments

—nature
—languages
—moussaka
—Michelangelo's *David*
—Parthenon
—Alps
—overrated?

FOR YOUR OWN PAPER

1. Group related ideas into what may eventually become paragraphs. Consider your thesis and write a tentative paragraph plan, jotting down relevant supporting thoughts with each topic (if it seems helpful at this point). Think of what *kind* of paper you are writing and of how this kind of writing is best organized. (Read appropriate introductions and "Working with . . ." sections, if you need further guidance.) Ask yourself, "What does my reader need to know early?" "What information is best held until near the end, at the climax of the paper, when interest may be declining?" Be able to give reasons for your plan at this point, and remember, you may change it dramatically before your final draft is done.

2. If you are having problems with discovering a sense of direction in your writing, go back to the earlier stages of the process. Ask yourself again, "Just what am I trying to prove?" "Why am I saying this?" and "To whom?" Read through earlier notes and drafts or see if the thesis can be refined to lead to better paragraphs (not "I want to write about Super Beings" but "Super Beings may be divided into categories, according to the sources of their power."). Remember: A thesis is a judgment. Look more closely at the *kind* of writing you are trying to do. Are you comparing two ideas, or are you looking at causes? Are you arguing or simply telling a story? Are you mixing up your approaches on purpose? In short, try to discover the plan within your own work, but if all of these procedures continue to fail, if you are still writing with no sense of satisfaction, take some time away if you can or consider changing your subject as soon as possible.

3. Here is a hint for drafting *after* you have made a paragraph plan or an outline: Begin a new page for each new topic. Separate sheets for separate topics help to keep your ideas separate as you write, and they are easier to rearrange, if you should decide to change their order.

Writing

This is the stage in the writing process when the "prewriting"—the study of options, the free rambling, the lists, the search for subjects, purposes, and audiences, the breaking of subjects into topics, and the tentative plans—begins to come together. It is when thoughts and words start to become paragraphs and when paragraphs start to become essays. It may also be time again for "play."

If the process of writing were orderly and predictable, you would only now, for the first time, be entering this first-draft stage of your paper. You may, however, have already ventured many times over the line from prewriting to drafting as you searched out subjects, topics, and logical plans for discussing them. You may already have written some sentences and paragraphs that will survive all revisions. As in the steps of prewriting, the drafting of longer, more thought-out passages or even entire essays occurs at different times for different writers in different situations.

For some writers, especially for those who spend a long time thinking, sketching, and planning, this first complete draft may be very close to the final version. These writers may be almost ready to move to the "polishing," to the close reading and correction of the later stages of the process. But for others, perhaps most, this first complete draft is really the beginning, the first of many, maybe dozens, of drafts. For them, this is a "discovery draft," a tryout to see where the work so far has been taking them. It is this draft and its revisions that will finally evolve into the finished product.

Putting the First Draft Down on Paper

"Don't stop to polish the stone in its descent," advises Henry David Thoreau in a letter to a younger writer. In other words, if you are getting those big ideas down for the *first time,* don't strive for perfection. Strive to get something down.

This stage of writing can be the most enjoyable, because your paper is finally beginning to take shape and you are still able to feel the excitement of learning as you write. New ideas have not become old ideas yet. Sentences are not so familiar that you can quote them to yourself in your sleep. No words, no images, have had time to become dull. And the critic may still be kept silent.

The word for this stage of the process is "fast." It can be profitable to write or type as fast as you can, to see where your subject, your thoughts about purpose and audience, and your tentative plans take you. Your hand may ache and your word processor may scramble to keep up with you, but try to put *all* your ideas down the moment they occur to you. Save nothing. Hold nothing back, for you may forever lose some of your best passing thoughts. As Annie Dillard says,

> The impulse to save something good for a better place later is the signal to spend it now. Something more will arise for later, something better. These things fill from behind, from beneath, like well water.

You will have plenty of time for creating new ideas and for rearranging old ones. Remember, the critic can stay quiet only so long.

If your writing is flowing, temporarily forget spelling, grammar, vocabulary, and punctuation. Forget statistics buried in your folder or your notecards. Leave blanks where words won't come. Type over words. Cross out. Just as for early "free writing," this draft is only for you. Put question marks in the margins, but don't dally for an answer. Give yourself stars (or smiley faces, if you happen to like them) where you are really pleased.

If you can, you might try to write all the way to the end. Don't interrupt yourself. Don't stop to worry too much. Make the connections freely. Imagine the simile to describe what it was like, the conversation that brings the scene to life, the quotation that says it all, or the perfect word that seems to come from nowhere. Here you may discover whether or not you *have* a paper. If you feel good as you are writing, if the thoughts keep on coming, and if you are making sense to yourself, then you probably are.

In fact, you may have more than one paper. Keep a separate sheet beside you for jotting stray thoughts on entirely different subjects—valuable thoughts that may lure you off your chosen subject at just the wrong time. (While writing an earlier discussion of comparison and contrast, I, for some reason, remembered the preceding quotation from Annie Dillard and reminded myself on a note card to use it here. While writing this section, I remembered and listed a quotation by Russell Baker on writer's block that I should have used earlier in the "Discovering a Subject," section. I also jotted down appointment times with three students and wrote the words, "World on Ice," so I'd remember to get tickets.)

As you muddy the waters, you may also stir up from the depths some other subjects you weren't planning for, some of them which might be totally irrelevant for your purposes and some of which might be worthy of notice later but not just yet. One of these "side-subjects" may, in fact, work into your paper, or even *become* your paper, but try to put it aside until you have given undivided attention to the draft at hand.

If you try this extended and fast writing, the end of your draft may consist of several pages of almost unreadable prose and you may feel great relief. The paper isn't done, but *something* is. You finally have more than inspiration, notes, lists, and random paragraphs down on paper. You have not created a sacred text; this is not the precise and timeless chiseling of the Rosetta stone. However, it is a beginning, a draft in the direction of a final document. You have reason to be pleased.

But, if you can, try not to be so pleased that you leave the desk right away. Now, while it is still fresh in your mind, you may benefit from reading the entire piece quickly from beginning to end. Make notes along the way, put question marks in the margin, print out unreadable words, and underline sentences that sound wrong, but don't necessarily stop to fix them. Put in arrows where more information seems to be needed. Push yourself, as a reader, as far as you can.

If you write by hand (as I always do, with needle-sharp pencils), it may look something like the following draft for my piece on bird-watchers (see pages 171–176):

troubadours', minnesingers'

As near as I can tell, it has been lit — not only this unidentified speck over V's Avenue but lit. birds — — — — Dante's, Chaucer's and more locally, Poe's ~~guilt~~ — Eliot's Catalog of birds at Cape Ann?) or Frost's oven-bird: ~~that inspired me to b.w.~~

No special to whet. S. Tanager

No partic spark of recog. that ignited the flame of interest only a growing delight in passages like those in W where T. follows the devious progress of a loon across a Pond or listens to the owl's ——. "I rejoice that there are o's." (?) In fact, lit. + b's are so often allied a grad stu. recently asked if a life list should be required ~~were necess.~~ for an M.A. in Eng. (not a bad idea).

(Notice the abbreviations, the randomness of the thoughts, the blanks left for literary quotations, and the arrows for additional information. Probably only the writer could make sense of such crammed and cryptic prose.)

If you type, your first-draft pages may look something like the one by E. B. White (shown on page 385), which is a development from his earlier notes (pages 359–360).

(Notice the crowded mix of single and double spacing, the convergence of the personal notes about thermostats (page 359), and the notes taken at the meeting on nuclear power. White is typing quickly, revising *as* he types and *after* he types.)

After your first draft and rereading, you may benefit from some time away from it. For a poem, Horace recommended putting drafts away for nine years, rather a long incubation for the average student's paper. It is true, however, that time away from your own writing allows you more critical distance when you read it again. You will not be as able to anticipate your own lines and passages. They will seem slightly alien, almost written by someone else. You will be more ready to correct this "other writer," and you will be less protective of any mistakes. You might try to set your paper aside for at least a couple of days. "Out of sight" will probably not mean "out of mind."

Whenever you do return to it (in fact, *every* time you return to it), read the whole piece through. Like a landscape painter coloring in the tints of a tulip petal, it is important to stand back often, in order to take in the whole picture.

4

Almost everyone makes a token attempt to save fuel---we nudge down the thermostat, turn off the unnecessary lamp, and drive only when we think we must. (Except, of ourse, the snowmobilers---who organize races and go round and round.)

dined at a friend's house recently and they tasted great---delicate, like a brook trout. I'm a believer in mercury anyway. Am curing my ~~xxxxxxx~~ arthritis with a diet of fish and rice. All fish contain mercury, and I'm going on the assumption that it is ~~the mercury~~ not the fish that knocks the arthritis. A man has to ~~xxxxxxx xxxx~~ have a few firm beliefs to cling to. A waiter once told me I should eat the skins of fishes in order ~~xxxxxxxxxx~~ if I were o stay healthy, and he may have been right.

Energy, of course, is the leading topic and the toughest nut to crack. ~~xxxxxxxxxxxxx~~ Just the mere attempt business of to solve the energy oil crisis is itself a great drain on energy: lights burn half the night in the rooms where the planners do their planning and the ~~politicians~~ debaters hold their debates ~~xxxxxxxxxxx hearings~~. I ~~xxxx~~ drove over to South Brooksville not long ago ~~on a recent night~~ to attend a evening forum ~~session~~ on nuclear power, ~~organized by a group called xxxxxxxxxxxxxxx~~ Sponsored by the Brooksville Public Library. To get there, and back I had to make a round trip of over about twenty-five miles, which must have burned up a gallon or more of gas. And the hall had to be lighted. And the representative of the Central Maine Power Company had to use up ~~xx~~ quite a lot of a great deal more gas than I did, because he came a long distance for the pow-wow. Furthermore, people in this age are adjusted to the abundance of power. On my way home, after the meeting, I noticed that most of the houses I passed were ~~xxx~~ brightly lit---people sitting up to watch television. ~~while~~ the oil-burner ~~ground~~ grinding away in the basement and the water pump ~~responded~~ to its pressure valve. A hundred years ago, ~~xxxxxxxxxxxxxxxxxxxxxxxxxxxxxxxxxxxxxx~~ A hundred years ago, the same denizens of these houses would have been abed long since. They would have had neither power nor a power shortage---merely a long good night's sleep. ~~Maybe~~ We don't really know yet whether you can't have Johnny Carson ~~xxxxx a power xxxxxxx~~ ~~--who knows?~~ we can have energy all day and Johnny Carson all night. It just isn't clear yet.

leaping into action at the bidding of str

Close-up work, the work that remains to be done, must be in harmony with the whole. If, on this reading, you can readily identify a subject, a thesis, an audience, a purpose, or an effective arrangement and if you are satisfied that you have said what you were trying to say, then you are ready for more detailed work and to release the critic. The "stone" has "descended." It's time to get out the polisher.

PRACTICE

1. Evaluate the following first draft of Lyn Capodanno's paragraph, "Anger at First Sight" (pages 7–8). Do you like it? Where does it seem to be going? Mark where it seems to need further work. What kind of work does it need? Then compare this version with the finished paragraph to see what *she* did with it. Specifically, what improvements did she make?

   As we drove down route IA, the tears streamed down my cheeks. I ~~constantly~~ eagerly ~~asked~~ coaxed my father to turn around and take me back to my comfortable surroundings. I wanted to go back to highschool., I wasn't ready to grow up. My parents nearly pushed me out of the car when I arrived at my new home, or Peabody Hall. "How could that be home?" I asked myself miserably as I unloaded the crates full of pictures and cards from ~~my~~ the only friends I could ever ~~need~~ want. I didn't need these two people that were my so-called roommates. And as my parents sped away, I ran to the pay phone to call my highschool boyfriend. ~~Life~~ My life ~~was changed,~~ had changed so drastically in 24 hours and I was unprepared to accept my new challenge: making friends.

2. For E. B. White's paragraph on "energy," read the scratch notes on pages 359–360, then read the rough draft on page 385 of this section. Analyze as well as you can the relationships between the notes and the draft and the written corrections on the draft itself. As far as you can see, what point is White making through his notes and this corrected draft? What ***kinds*** of corrections does he make on this early rereading?

FOR YOUR OWN PAPER

1. Write a complete first draft of your paper without "stopping to polish the stone in its descent." Examine how you felt as you wrote it. Was the writing satisfying? Did you know what you were trying to get at, or were you writing to discover a clear central point? Is the point clear now? Did details and examples occur to you readily? Did new and better ways of saying things occur to you as you wrote? Did you experience some of the "joy in it," described by Seamus Heaney? If you feel content at this point, you are probably ready to move on to more detailed, polished work.

2. Read the first draft over, soon after you have finished it. Fix obvious errors, ask yourself questions, and write notes to yourself in the margins. Then, if

you can, take some time away from the draft before you read it from beginning to end, again.

3. If, however, your experience writing this draft was not satisfying, if you felt no sense of urgency or even mild pleasure, or if you found yourself getting bored or confused as you read through it, you may need to return to the drawing board. You may need to give yourself more time to think of the earlier stages of evaluation and planning. Then try again. (You may also need a nap or some peace and quiet; it is difficult to *compose* when your mind is in the state so accurately described by Gilbert Highet on page 266.)

Rewriting

Hoping that the first draft will "do," or "get by," many writers, unfortunately, give up before they work through this rewriting stage. They take an "I-don't-want-to-think-about-it-anymore" attitude at a time when important, often detailed, thinking remains to be done. But the fact is that, for most professional writers, this rewriting stage is the *real* beginning; all the rest is just a warm-up.

Thoreau, for example, warned of the possible numbers of drafts: "Don't suppose that you can tell it precisely the first dozen times you try, but at 'em again. . . ." Vladimir Nabokov told of constant trial and error: 'I have re-written—often several times—every work I have ever published. My pencils outlast their erasures." Russian short-story writer Anton Chekhov described some of the emotions associated with rewriting: "I write the beginning serenely, let my self go, but in the middle I have already begun cowering and fearing." And E. B. White, quoting Mrs. Gene Stratton Porter's contribution to Forbush's bird encyclopedia, hinted further at the nature of this detailed rewriting stage:

> Examined food remains in nest of kingfishers found one-tenth of them to be nearly equally divided between berry seeds and the hard parts of grasshoppers. Exacting work but easier than writing.

Perhaps the reason many writers see it as so exacting is that rewriting covers so many different activities and so many different *kinds* of attention to the writing. It requires a constant moving in to focus on specifics, from selecting the type of introduction and the details, to deciding which word best conveys the message and even where that word may best be placed in the sentence. It also requires a constant standing back to see the writing whole again, so that the specifics will be right for the larger purposes. It also requires sometimes making difficult decisions, such as whether or not to go to across town to a library that has an important source, whether or not to try to write yet another kind of introduction, or whether or not to cut a paragraph, a page, or many pages (especially if they seem to be well written).

Rewriting covers *all* of the things that need to be done between the first, rough draft written for the writer alone and the final, polished draft written for others to read. Given the range and the depth of these possibilities, given the thousands of decisions that must be made, it is no wonder that drafts may number 12 or more, that erasers may wear off pencils, that cowering and fearing may set in, or even that counting berry seeds and the hard parts of grasshoppers may be preferable.

If you are satisfied with what you have been able to achieve in your first draft, however, you are ready for the finer work that rewriting requires.

Reading with a Critical Eye

I include this discussion first among the steps for rewriting because it is so continually a part of the entire process of producing a final draft—from beginning to end. It needs to be known now but cannot be left behind as the writing proceeds. Reading critically is perhaps the one thing most writers do most often as they write (probably more than writing itself). They constantly go over and over what they have done, reviewing words, phrases, sentences, and paragraphs as they are written and reviewing the entire paper for overall effect. They read the whole thing before they go to bed. They read it over their breakfast cereal. They carry a copy when they go out, "just in case" they have a spare moment in a traffic jam. Writers are compulsive "tinkerers," constantly taking things apart and putting them back together again. No sentence is safe.

If you are working carefully on your own rewriting, you too will probably return to this step repeatedly, reading and rereading, giving up only when the final draft is safely out of your hands. (Even then, you will possibly find yourself "improving it," thinking of things you could have said better, and wishing you could eliminate things you shouldn't have said at all.)

How might you go about this task of critical reading? First of all, it is important to read the manuscript often, from beginning to end, and it is equally important to allow yourself some distance on what you have already written. Give yourself time to become more objective, more honest: Horace's nine years, your own two days, or even two hours away from the paper. You might also consider changing location. Get up and take your paper from your desk to the easy chair in the living room. Go from the library to the car. One poet I know writes first drafts at his big mahogany desk, "middle" drafts at his professional drafting table, and final drafts back at his desk. I found rewriting my paper (pages 171–176) on bird-watchers (most of whom I had met in New England) to be much easier in Italy than in Massachusetts! Distance is sometimes more than just a metaphor.

You might also try reading aloud to yourself; it sometimes is a good way to "hear" the text more objectively. I have also been told that a tape recorder can help in this process, because it allows you to be the audience for your own reading. A similar effect can be achieved by having someone read your paper aloud to you, not yet for critical reaction but simply to allow you to change your perspective; you become the listener rather than the writer. In all of these procedures, the idea is for you to notice places that are working well, and more importantly, places that need more work. Stumbles in the reading, confusion, repetitions, a tendency for the mind to wander, or a longing for the conclusion are all likely signs that something is going wrong. Take notice of the places where these reactions occur and then set out to discover just what that "something" is.

Probably because the possible explanations for these difficulties are so numerous, it is much easier to suggest procedures for *how* to go about this critical reading than it is to specify exactly *what* your are looking for in the first place. Also, different stages of writing and revising require different kinds of attention and different levels of concentration. Early in the process you may be looking for a clear thesis and for an organization that makes your point best, which are the concerns of your first draft. You may not be *ready* to worry about the rhythm of your conclusion. If the whole paper makes little sense to you on this early reading, diligent searching for just the right words in the thesaurus could waste precious time.

Later on, however, after the larger concerns have been addressed, all of the subjects discussed hereafter in this section of the book take on increasingly greater significance. Particulars like the strong lead, the well-chosen details, the well-crafted sentences, the correct words, and the perfect images finally are the things that separate excellent writing from the average or the average from the incompetent.

As much as these constant rereadings may seem to slow down progress—one step forward, two steps back—they are, in fact, real steps toward the final draft. Each sure step brings you a little closer to the goal and allows for greater and greater concentration on the details of the route. In the early stages of the process, you simply inspect the topography, planning possible routes and avoiding the pitfalls. Later, as a more informed explorer, you know the intricacies of the territory and invite your reader to appreciate them. Rereading, like rewriting, is a constant process of refinement.

PRACTICE

1. Read the following first draft out loud. Determine the subject, the thesis, the audience, and the purpose. Has the writer determined these things? As a first draft, what is wrong with this selection? What would you suggest to the writer? Now try rewriting at least one paragraph as *you* might do it, after asking yourself how it might succeed as a first draft. Think of possible ways to bring this writing to life.

My Summer Vacation

My summer vacation was one in which I was restricted in a certain way, but I enjoyed myself anyway. I was in severe debt to my parents and I had to work a lot. Sometimes I could do what I wanted, though. 1

Having some experience as a painter, I talked with some friends and we made it known that we would be able to do some painting. I didn't 2 like the responsibility, but it was a necessary evil. I could earn more money, although it wasn't great. I had stopped working in January so my debts were great. I had to continue what I was doing.

After work, I didn't have much money because I had to pay off old debts, but I did get some fun in. Most of the time we just hung around, but it was a lot better than work. At least I enjoyed it. 3

My parents are very understanding and they didn't mind waiting for me to pay them back, but I'm really happy I could do it this summer. I didn't do all that well in high school and I didn't put much effort into my studies, so at least I got a chance to do something right. They still want me to pay some college bills, but I have some left over. I can see why they want me to, though. 4

All in all, it was a fairly successful summer. It wasn't really that bad. I did make some money, I held a job for a certain period of time and I showed my parents a thing or two for once. 5

2. This practice assignment might be better done later in the course, at a later stage of rereading, when you are more familiar with the more detailed discussions that follow this section. The first practice assignment asked you to read and rewrite a draft at an early stage in the process (looking back to the concerns of prewriting), while at the same time bringing up the issue of giving it "life," which is the concern of the following sections. Possibly after you have read through these sections, read and evaluate the following rewritten paragraph, focusing on the specifics that seem to be working here and on possible further improvements. Again, try to rewrite it yourself. Here is a rewriting of the second paragraph of "My Summer Vacation."

Having painted houses for two summers with my uncle, I thought I knew all there was to know about painting houses. I was wrong. My two friends and I advertised and got a job painting a woman's house she was elderly and wealthy and she wanted a bargain. My friends didn't know anything about painting houses. I didn't know much either, because I found out that it took more than I thought. I didn't like the indispensable responsibility, or the excessive reliance upon me by my companions. We had a contract, though, so we had to go on and try. We made so many mistakes I had to give a ring to my uncle to see if he could give us a hand and bail us out of our dilemma. I didn't want to cut my losses just yet. I felt luckier than a puppy with a bone when he came over and took the reins. Of course, he took the dough too, and we still owed him for the extra supplies at the end of the summer. This part of my summer didn't pan out at all.

FOR YOUR OWN PAPER

1. Reread your entire first draft and evaluate its overall quality and effectiveness. Do you have a workable subject? Do you know what you want to say about it? Have you thought about your potential audience? What would you like your audience to take with them from your writing? Are you satisfied enough at this point to move on to more detailed improvements?

2. For your first draft and subsequent drafts, try reading aloud, from beginning to end. Mark places where you think further work is necessary. Is the introduction flat or off the point (page 394)? Are there expanses of general statements; where do you need more details (page 400)? Are there places where you get lost in a maze of words; where could words be cut (page 406)? Are there places where the connections seem vague; did you find yourself wondering what ideas, paragraphs, or sentences had to do with one another (page 415)? Is your attitude ever inconsistent with what you are trying to say? Are you overly serious with a subject that might be amusing or amusing with a subject that should be treated seriously (page 421)? Do some words seem wrong for your purposes (page 422)? Do the sentences run on and break up in grammatically incorrect ways; do you ramble on with too many long sentences in a row or too many short ones (page 426)? Is the paper entirely lacking in original, appropriate images; where could a good comparison enhance the meaning (page 431)? And, finally, does your conclusion simply stop, as if you had to get to supper (page 435)? If you have identified and located any of these problems, turn to the appropriate discussions following this section and try rewriting and, of course, rereading.

Getting the Reader's Attention

Consider how most readers, including teachers, spend their time. They are active, preoccupied, and busy with their own affairs. Many of them have stacks of newspapers, magazines, journals, and books not yet read, plus mounds of new mail at the doorstep almost every day. Consider other competition for whatever you may write—television, videos, radio, movies, telephones, plays, concerts, ballet, opera, jogging, basketball, bike rides, visits with friends, shopping, repairing the car, caring for kids, cooking, going out to dinner, napping. Make up your own list.

It is not by mistake that journalists call their first line the "hook," for introductions need to do more than introduce. They need to pull readers away from the stacks of reading, from the television, from the nap and, at the same time, turn their attention to the subject *you* want to discuss. You are tapping them on the shoulder and saying, "Look! I have something interesting to say to you." As essayist John McPhee says, "A lead ought to shine like a flashlight, down into the whole piece, if possible."

Actually, good introductions can begin one step back from the first line—in the title. The "hooking" can take hold there. Ask yourself what titles might get your attention as you glance through a bibliography, down a table of contents, or through the pages of a newspaper or magazine. Readers do, at first, judge books by their covers and essays by their titles. Think about them.

In academic articles, titles that directly reflect content are preferable: "Some Major Effects of Divorce on Children" (page 138), "What Are Steroids?" (page 165), "The Meeting with the Old Proletarian in *Nineteen Eighty-Four*" (page 199). Inaccurate or overly clever titles for pieces that might be listed in professional bibliographies can waste time for unsuspecting readers, as they search out the totally irrelevant article or overlook the one that should be read.

But more personal writing or writing intended for a wider audience can have a more suggestive title. As always, think of what kind of writing you are doing, for what audience, and for what purpose. Try to make your own titles appropriate and attractive. Give some hint of the interest and value of what you have to say.

Look at some of the nonacademic titles of essays in this book: "Anger at First Sight," "Seventh of the Litter," "What's Wrong with 'Me, Me, Me'?" "How to Correspond with the Stars," "Bigger and Better?" They may easily have been called, "My Strongest Feeling in September," "Being the Youngest," "Egotism," "How to Collect Autographs," and "My Friend, Rob," but these titles might not stir the same curiosity about the content. As you can see, reversals of common usage ("anger" instead of "love"), ambiguous titles (which "litter"?), rhetorical questions ("What's wrong . . ."), plays on words ("correspond" with its vaguely mystical aura and its literal meaning of "to write to"), and alliteration ("b" and "b"), are easily adaptable to titles and are commonplace among them. Be careful to avoid clichés in your titles. Straightforwardness is preferable.

Introductions themselves also turn to certain commonplace methods of opening that often succeed. It is, however, painfully easy to write unsuccessful introductions, openers that are almost certain to send the reader to the next essay. They can be tedious, draining the energy out of even a powerful topic:

> The reason I am writing this is to give you some information about rent control.

They can be naïve, breaking the confidence of the reader immediately:

> I really don't know much about this subject, but I'll do what I can with it.

They can also be windy, puffing up a complete lack of thought with airy words:

> Every year I have a very interesting vacation. Going to a lake is always fun for me. I really like to swim and I hope to be able to do the same thing every year. My family also likes to go to a lake, so I think I'll be able to keep this up for many years to come. And it's a good thing, because I always find this type of vacation really fun.

Even well-written introductions can go on so long that the reader loses interest.

Why not try one of the following types of introductions, which might work better for your purposes? Why not tell a story or an anecdote, quote someone else, ask a question, contradict your own main point, draw a picture by using the senses, make your subject significant by building it up, or use a surprising opening statement? Why not try combining some of these methods?

Consider these classroom examples, all of which were openers to papers on the same subject, written by small groups on the first day of school (then rewritten later in the semester). The topic was: "What would you do if the college closed tomorrow?"

1. Tell a story or an anecdote.

> It's the first day of school, the day when I used to walk down the road in a brand-new dress and brand-new shoes. Now I sit in my beat-up clothes and my ancient car waiting for traffic to creep around the downtown Rotary. My tape deck is broken. I wonder why I'm sitting here in the first place. I don't even want to come to college. This whole mess is my father's idea. Finally within walking distance of my first class, I wonder even more. I know where my 10:00 class is, and I even have a notebook and a pen, but I can't get out of my car! Every parking

space, legal or illegal, is taken. "No parking this side," yell the army of signs into the far distance. "Violators will be towed," warn the ones on the other side. I drive around campus three times. I try the library lot—closed to students. I try the main lot—filled. I cruise through the Sports Complex Lot—no room for a motor scooter. Desperate, I finally pull up on the slanted yellow lines near the exit lane. I almost knock over the "TOW ZONE" sign as I dash to my "Composition I" class where the teacher is assigning our first college paper, "What would I do if the college closed tomorrow?" I can feel myself beginning to sneer as I write this one, especially since I expect a $20.00 towing fee when I finally find my car. I don't have any problem at all with my very first English assignment.

2. Quote someone else.

I have always liked Mark Twain's comment, "The cauliflower is nothing but a cabbage with a college education." I have given up hours of study, hours of examinations, hours of applying, hours of mailing, hours of waiting, so I could have a chance to become a prize-winning "cauliflower." Because this cabbage wants a good job in management, probably in an investment firm, and because this school has one of the best programs in the business garden, I decided to come here. But just as my roots are taking hold, what do I get from my English teacher? An assignment asking me what I would do if the college closed tomorrow! I don't even want to think about it, but I suppose if I had to uproot myself, I'd have to come up with some other ways to make myself into a cauliflower.

3. Ask a question.

What would I, a healthy, nineteen-year-old American high school graduate, class of June '90, do when September, '90 finally rolled around? Go to the local college, of course! I've lived down the street for as long as I can remember, and I always knew that's where I'd be getting my degree. At least that's what I thought, until I got to my English class this morning and the teacher announced, "Students are advised that the Board of Regents has closed the college permanently as of September 6, 1990. No reasons will be given at this time." I knew it was only part of our first assignment, to write on what we'd do if the college closed tomorrow, but I still got worried. I've always taken this college as part of my landscape, sort of like the Atlantic Ocean. It never even occurred to me that it could not be there some day. I have no idea what I'd do if it closed.

4. Contradict your own main point.

When my freshman English teacher asked us to write our first paper on what we would do if the college closed, many students reacted with glee. Just the thought of locked doors seemed to make them happy. I was surprised at how many of them planned fantasy trips to far-away places, and started thinking about all-night parties, week-long naps, and months at sunny beaches. Many of them welcomed the chance to skip school, even if it was just in a paper. My reaction is entirely different. Not only do I hate the question, I hate writing about it. I'm looking forward to school, and I'm not yearning for great escapes. I don't want to make other plans, so it's going to be hard to come up with even a few alternatives.

5. Draw a picture by using the senses.

Four more years of pencils, books, and dirty looks. Late nights memorizing the reasons for the fall of the Roman Empire again. Early mornings dozing through bicameral legislature definitions. Endless hours of lecture and lab on cloud formations and frog parts. Biting fingernails and sweating through exams that I haven't studied for yet. The stale smell of cafeteria food. Roommates screaming, telephones ringing late into the night, heavy metal pounding, televisions blaring. The English teacher assigning a "short composition"—this one on what I would do if the college closed. I can think of a few things I'd do—as fast as I could say, "See you later!"

6. Make your subject significant.

I can't remember a time when I didn't expect to go to college. I think my parents started discussing it with me in the hospital nursery. Over the years, it has never been a question of "whether," but only of "where" I would be getting my degree. So, needless to say, my choice of this college was no light decision at my house. President Bush probably gave less time to debating the budget than I did to debating the pros and cons of enrollments, locations, tuitions, and programs before I finally settled on this college. Can you imagine the shock I would feel if I *really* had to face the fact that the college was about to close? I find it hard even to imagine it. But if it did happen, just how long could I stand on the doorstep waiting for the door to open? I'd have to come up with something else.

7. Use a surprising statement.

I hate college. I also hated nursery school, kindergarten, elementary school, middle school, and high school, so I don't know why I should feel any different now on my first day of "higher education." School has never been a high for me. In fact, I can't imagine anything I'd rather hear than the president's announcement that the college is closing tomorrow. That's one day too late as far as I'm concerned.

These are just some of the many ways to get yourself and your readers into your essays. Introductions do demand careful attention, but it is also important not to get stalled in writing them. Don't overwork something that needs to be lively and interesting. You may need to work further on the body of your paper before the best introduction occurs to you. (Sometimes it turns out to be paragraph two!) Or you may try writing quick versions of more than one possible type of introduction, selecting the one that seems to work.

First impressions do count. Introductions don't have to be long, complex, or overly clever; they just have to keep the reader reading.

PRACTICE

1. Consider the following titles. What might you expect in the essay that follows? Think of possible content, approach, formality, informality, and your own potential interest.

   a. "What Is a TV Talk-Show Host?" (a media subject, exposition by definition, probably informal, most likely for readers of television magazines or television sections of newspapers. Depending on the quality of the insights and the writing, I *might* be interested.)
   b. "How to Cook with Leftovers!"
   c. "The Crisis in Secondary Education: Why We Need to Pay More Taxes"
   d. "The Varieties of Religious Experience"
   e. "My Afternoon on Mount Vesuvius"
   f. "Things to Take When Traveling with Kids"
   g. "Epic Motifs in Chaucer's *Tale of Ceyx and Alcyone*"
   h. " 'Dumbing Down' at the Movies: a Review of 'The Whiz Kid' "
   i. "The Beauties of Vesuvius"
   j. "Private vs. Public School: The Parents' Dilemma"

2. See the introductions on pages 12, 40, 72, 101, 168, 171, 224, 227, 245, 296, 305, 310, 316, 319, and 328 of this text and describe what kind of introduction each one is. Write an imitation of one of them.

3. Evaluate the following introductions by asking: "Is this an interesting opening?" "Do you feel drawn to read on?" "What do you think of the writer?" "What is the main fault?" Then try to write more successful versions of each (or at least identify what you would do to make each one better).

   a. When I think of my perfect job, lots of things come to mind, but I'm not sure what it will really involve. I think I'd like to work in an office, but I guess I'll just have to wait and find out what I really want to do.
   b. I have read that Andrew Jackson was a really great President. I also heard that he became involved in a duel to defend his wife's honor, but I don't know that much about it.
   c. My summer vacation was one in which I enjoyed myself to a very high degree. I was somewhat restricted or confined in my movements, but I had some very severe debts that I had to pay off before the beginning of the school year. Taking into account the quality

of my labor and my extensive experience, I didn't make the money I was worth, so my parents had to give me some monetary supplements. I got a tremendous amount of job satisfaction from my job though, in spite of the anticipation of the astronomical tuitions that were facing me.

d. I'm one of those people who finds it hard to say no. This is only my first year at college, and I feel that I haven't yet developed into the kind of student that I thought I would be. Many things have hindered me, but I have overcome these hindrances fairly well. Too much socializing has been the most damaging factor to me academically. The most obvious detrimental factor of my hyper-socializing is time.

e. In today's society, there is an abundance of social problems. Suicide can only be reversed if someone notices the symptoms in time.

4. Look up and copy introductions that you found particularly good. Explain what kind they are, why you like them, and whether or not the writing that follows fulfills the expectations created in the introductions. (For future reference, you might consider saving the whole piece and especially the conclusion.)

FOR YOUR OWN WRITING

1. Read your own introduction and ask yourself the same questions that you asked about the introductions printed previously. What kind of introduction have you written? Do you like it? Does it "shine like a flashlight" through the rest of the paper? If you can improve this draft, try it now.

2. Write two alternative introductions for the same paper already drafted. Identify what kind they are and choose the one that works best for your paper—the original or one of the alternates.

Using Details

If a friend, flushed from hurrying, runs up to you and says, "Boy, do I have some news for you!" how do you react? Are you satisfied with the general word *news?* Are you only interested in picking up your books and walking away, or does your mind immediately race to possible images of what that *news* is—she has been accepted to graduate school in California, her father won $1 million in the lottery, she got an "A" in Biology when she was expecting a "C," or her boyfriend went out Saturday night behind her back. If this friend does not go on to fill in the details, the individual aspects of her larger subject (news), you are left with your own imaginings—creative, but possibly having nothing at all to do with her real news. If she does fill in details—she is going to marry Jason in January—you understand her excitement and react to *her* message, not to your own guesses about her message.

Details in essays work the same way. They stimulate interest; they fill in the blanks; they steer the reader from private speculations; and they give some direction for a response. As novelist Vladimir Nabokov advises, "Caress the detail, the divine detail."

Compare the following two paragraphs:

> I really enjoyed my vacation in Italy. I saw lots of beautiful things every single day, especially in Florence.

and

> Florence is like a geode, a stoney surface with treasure hidden within. Every morning for two delightful weeks, I set out to discover more and more of these crystals: at the Uffizi, I saw Botticelli's flower-bedecked Primavera, a season on canvas; in a tiny chapel of the Medici Palace, Gozzoli's wall paintings breathing life into major figures of Lorenzo's time; high above the nave of the Duomo, Brunelleschi's interior maze of double domes, and underground beneath the rougher surface of the main aisle, the gleaming black and white marble pavement. At the Accademia, Michelangelo's David flanked by his slaves still emerging from their stone, and in the stark dormitory of San Marco, the elegant frescoes of Giotto. Hidden in back rooms of countless galleries, I discovered the minute carvings in ivory, the inlaid wooden ceilings, the precious jewels, the transparent alabaster, the cut-glass chandeliers, the sculptures in bronze often missed by the tour groups. Florence may at first appear stoney, even dull, but within, it is bright with countless treasures.

Both paragraphs express the same feeling—appreciation for the beauties of Italy, but obviously the first one is sketchy, merely sentences that *tell* the reader that Italy was enjoyable. The second is detailed, full of visual evidence that *shows* what was so enjoyable, specifically, *within* Florence.

Readers are easily distracted, necessarily preoccupied with their own lives, their own pleasures, or their own vacations. If the writer does not provide enough detail, the reader will fill in the blanks and will take a private vacation. The writer's "beautiful things" will be taken over by the reader's "beautiful things," and the sharing will be over.

Details, that "gleaming pavement" at the Duomo versus the "beautiful things" in all of Italy, are the "thumbprints" of writing. They are what make your writing truly your own and no one else's. Anyone, even a committee, could "enjoy" Italy, but no one, not even someone writing on the treasures of Florence, would choose exactly the same treasures to write about as those in the more detailed paragraph. For better or for worse, those details are the writer's own, chosen to illustrate a point (that many of Florence's treasures are like crystals in a geode).

Good writing is not made entirely of details, however. It is usually the movement between a general statement (high on a diving board) and then a plunge deep into the pool for the specific details that illustrate the point—from the general "news" down to the wedding announcement, from the general delights of Florence down to the paintings, sculptures, jewels, and pavements. Study the following diagrams, as they move downward toward the specific:

1. News

   Good news

   Good news about the future

   Good news about the future with my boyfriend

   Marriage to Jason in January

2. Movies

   I liked the movie.

   I liked *Batman.*

   I liked Jack Nicholson in *Batman.*

   I liked the scene in which the Joker sponsors a parade.

The judgments are near the top; the evidence is at the bottom.

For writing to be effective, general statements are necessary. They are the thoughts before the dive—the thesis statements, terms, and "big ideas" for the whole paper, the topic sentences for the paragraphs, the more inclusive words when the specifics begin to bore. Details, too, are necessary. They are the plunge into the specifics that bring the general statements to life. Neither lives without the other. Actually, good writing moves down and up and down again—off the board, into the pool, around and back to the board again for another dive.

It is possible to stay too general—to stretch the muscles, flex the knees, bounce at the edge, and pose—for too long. But such hesitation is, in fact, one of the major sources of tedium in writing. It is too much telling and not enough showing. In her first draft of a paragraph in her paper about being the youngest in a large family (pages 15–17), Sharyn Carbone wrote the following about eating at home:

> Dinners were always the toughest part of the day for me. As soon as the plates of food appeared on the table they disappeared. The older children always had the advantage of reach in my family. Six older than myself I often found myself inhaling my food. As a result of such an act over the years I formed animalistic eating habits that my boyfriend just can't understand.

(This paragraph desperately needs to take the plunge, to dive into the details that will show just what happened here. In a workshop class discussing this paper, students made the following comments: "I can't really *see* these dinners. What happened?" "How did the food get there?" "How do you 'inhale' food?" "What are your animalistic habits?" "Why were the dinners so tough?" "Were you hungry?" In rewriting, Sharyn focused on the details that eventually appeared in her final draft (page 15): mother, competition, arms flying, mouths chomping, first bite, grabbing, nothing to steal, today, fair share.)

As often as you can, say things *through* specifics, rather than talk, talk, talk *about* what you are trying to get at. The reader's imagination seeks out the details, just as the student sought out her friend's real "news."

Ironically, however, it is also possible to spend too much time in the water, never coming up for a breath, never telling the reader what all this detail is supposed to mean:

> Beside the thirty-foot-long and twenty-foot-wide pool, I stretched out on a brown wooden lounge chair with yellow cushions. The temperature was 82 degrees and the barometric pressure was 30.10 and falling. My friend served Pepperidge Farm cookies, and I ate one Milano, one Capri, and one Bordeaux. I then went in for a five-minute swim. The water was, I guess, about 75 degrees. I felt a little chilly, particularly in my left foot, so. . . .

(Do you want to read more? This writer clearly needs to select the details. The reader feels buried (drowned?) in specifics and is not quite sure what they all mean.)

In early drafts, an excess of details may be a virtue because it is then easier to select or possibly to discover meaning among them, but sooner or later the details *must* add up to something—a judgment, a mood, a point to be made. It is the difference between the straight recording of the diary:

> Today I got up at 10:00, took a laundry to the coin-op where the machines were out of order, and slept the entire afternoon.

and the judgment of the essay:

> Today was an exercise in waste. For example, I. . . .

Let's rewrite the "pool" paragraph:

> Yesterday, I spent an entire afternoon doing what a friend likes to call "lizarding," that is, lying flat out in the hot sun, baking, practicing being inert. Occasionally, I did stir to cool down in the pool or to eat another Pepperidge Farm cookie, but mostly I just stretched out on my soft yellow cushions, absorbing heat rays and waiting for the sun to go down. Lizards sure know how to live.

While writing, you need to keep your tedium detector operating. Too many general statements without the details to show what you mean will put the reader to sleep. Too many details without any indication of what they mean will have the same effect. Tell the reader what you mean to say, but always be ready to take the dive—always keep the details in sight. That's where the life is. Divers get wet. Ask yourself, "What makes me think so?" "What would help the reader to *see* this point?" "What does all this 'stuff' mean?" If *you* ask first, you'll be ready for the reader's questions, and the reader won't have to make up the answers.

PRACTICE

1. Work your way gradually down from the following general ideas to the specifics:

   a. I had a good time.

   ____

   ____

   ↓

   b. School.
   Opening of school.
   I disliked lots of things about my first week of school.

   ____

   ____

   ↓

c. Room.

____

↓_______________________

d. Entertainment.

____

↓_______________________

2. Rewrite the following paragraphs:

   a. One friend when I was small wasn't very nice to me. It was hard for us to get along. Our parents didn't either. We used to play together for a short period of time and then we'd have to stop playing because he'd make me mad about something.

      My other friend was different, though. We got along very well and treated one another nicely. We could play a long time and I would never get mad at him. We had so many things we liked to do together.

   (See "Three Boys," by John Updike, for an example of what might be done with such a topic.)

   b. I went shopping today and looked at televisions, VCR's, video cameras, CD players, lots of furniture, big appliances, dishes, silverware, table settings, lamps, rugs, pots, pans, cooking utensils, clothes, boots, shoes, and lots of other things.

   (Remember, there needs to be some reason for details, not just a dumping of all that crosses the mind.)

3. Read the following paragraphs and explain the meaning and the purpose of the details: "The Bowerbird" (page 10), "Letter to My Father" (pages 128–129), "Getting Through to Students" (pages 266–267), "Beating for the Hunt" (page 287).

FOR YOUR OWN PAPER

1. Read slowly through sentence after sentence of your draft. Underline sharp details. Evaluate what you see. Does the paper stay mostly general? Does it only occasionally dip down into the specific? Does it include mostly details, with very little suggestion about what to do with them? Does the writing move up to the general, then down to the specific, then back up again (in a sort of Greek meander pattern)?

2. Try adding relevant detail where you feel it is lacking or try putting in general statements where the meaning of the details is not clear.

3. Notice the "rhythm" of your paper. Does it alternate between general and specific statements, so that the reader gets the right *kind* of information at the right time?

Cutting Words

For a variety of reasons, "wordiness," or the use of extra words that serve no valuable purpose, is one of the major problems in writing. With numbing persistence, it may simply make the reading less enjoyable and certainly less exhilarating. But, at its worse, it may produce confusion, boredom, frustration, and even anger. It can drive a reader away—forever. Consider the following paragraphs:

> There is one thing I don't really like and that thing is going to school. It has never been much of a pleasure for me. I don't like anything about school. I don't like to study. Also, I don't get very good grades. On the other hand, I have some real problems associated with school right now and I'd better get to taking care of these problems real soon, or otherwise they'll make things a lot worse for me later on. I'd like to get a college degree, but to all intents and purposes, I'll be back at my very bad place of employment where I worked this summer, if I don't start doing something about my school problems.
>
> I've never liked anything about school. Sitting up 'till 2 A.M. figuring out the plot to *The Merchant of Venice,* which I have yet to read, or memorizing the major achievements of the Carolingian Renaissance are not my idea of a good time. I also hate to go to classes, I hate to listen to lectures, I hate to take tests (which I usually fail). I have a problem, though. I have expensive tastes, and I want to make some big bucks over the next sixty or so years. For this, especially in business management, I probably need a degree. Maybe the thought of my summer job humping convertible couches up narrow three-decker staircases will do something for my attitude.

(As you can see, the first paragraph simply pads out the sentences and allows them to remain dull, almost devoid of detail. The first three sentences say practically the same thing; they don't all need to be said. The "problems" are not defined. The style is repetitive ("problems"), and redundant ("place of employment . . . where I worked"). It is tedious and unrewarding to read. After the "word operation," cutting away dead words and adding details, the second paragraph says more in fewer words (110 words) than the first paragraph (126 words). The second paragraph moves immediately to detail and transforms "one thing . . . that thing," "much of a pleasure," "very good grades," "on the other hand," "real problems . . . these problems," "to all intents and purposes," "very bad place of employment . . where I worked this summer," into *"The Merchant of Venice,"* "Carolingian Renaissance," the hated classes, lectures, and tests, "some big bucks," "convertible couches," and "three-decker staircases." You now ***know*** what this student dislikes, what he wants, and what he fears.)

Adding details (the subject of the previous section) is, surprisingly, one of the best ways to get rid of extra, unwanted words. They have a way of crowding out vague, flat expanses of empty prose almost automatically. In fact, if you habitually move down to sharp details, vivid images, and real conversation, to whatever is necessary to bring your paper to life, it almost takes a special commitment to keep the paper overstuffed. So, as a general rule, work on adding well-chosen details *before* you work on cutting extra words.

Focusing on wordiness is not, however, just a matter of getting things said faster or of saving paper. It is ultimately a matter of interest, of saving the entire piece. A wordy style allows, and almost forces, busy readers to wander from what you are saying. Given little to capture their imaginations and lost in the cottony softness of words, words, words, they feel driven to escape—to thinking their own thoughts, to dozing at their desk. They may also not appreciate the writer who seems more interested in filling up a page than in getting their attention.

Fortunately, many problems associated with wordiness can be cured with relative ease by following some simple suggestions. It is important first, however, to recognize that wordiness is often a symptom of other, more serious problems that are not so easily erased: fear, lack of information, and, ironically, a misplaced desire to impress.

For the fearful, wordy writing is the "midnight-before-the-paper-is-due" writing. It is a desperate and tortured effort to fill up two, three, or ten pages with *something*. It is the miserable puffing up of basically nothing, which many writers see as a necessary misery of composition. Although quite possibly well informed but afraid to stop, think, and move down into the subject, the fearful word churners drag themselves and their readers across a surface of empty prose. Afraid they'll have nothing to say, and too afraid to discover what they *do* have to say, they say absolutely nothing—line after line, page after page. Here is a paragraph from a paper called "Problems":

> One of my really big problems right now is babysitting. I have been babysitting for families in my neighborhood for many, many years, but I don't want to do it at all anymore. They think I still do, though, and they keep calling me up on the telephone to ask me to sit with their kids. I find it really hard to refuse them, so I usually say yes and then I spend a lot of time wishing I had the nerve to refuse them. The kids really aren't fun or very enjoyable to sit for at all, and the money isn't very good either, given the very high college expenses. I often think in my mind that I have to start refusing to sit for them very soon.

(This writer needs to start earlier on the paper, allowing time for a more energetic and detailed thinking about the subject.)

Here is a paragraph from the rewritten paper:

> Besides my big college bills and my difficult parents, I have this problem with babysitting. When I was 14, 15, and 16, I really loved it. I enjoyed playing tag

> with the kids, I liked taking them for walks to the park, I even thought it was fun to bake cookies with them, messy as it was. I've outgrown it, though. My problem is that I haven't grown up enough to say no when the old families ask me to come over. I end up going, even when I have studying to do or plans with my friends. I don't enjoy the kids anymore. Jackie and Jennifer no longer play tag; all they want to do is watch TV (dumb sitcoms.). Paul is too big to take for a walk. He whines to go to Michael's house (where his parents don't let him go because they aren't speaking to Michael's father). Baking cookies with any of them is out of the question. And besides, given my $600.00 semester's tuition, my $150.00 for books, and my need to eat occasionally, the $2.50 an hour doesn't count for much. Maybe it's time to break the news to the neighborhood.

(At least we know what makes this writer want to be a "former" babysitter.)

For the uninformed, wordiness is a way of covering up a lack of information. It is the "twenty-minute-examination-answer-on-the-poem-you-haven't-read-yet" ' writing. "Snow" is one of the more genteel descriptions of this puffery. As in the overblown prose of the fearful, interest is minimal, and the reader's attention is gone by the second sentence.

Question: Discuss some of Virgil's major contributions to the epic tradition (20 minutes).

Answer 1: Epic poetry is really great poetry. Most epic poems are long, like Virgil's. Virgil was a great writer of epic poetry and among the ancient Romans he was one of the very best poets of all. In his epic poem, he contributed many things to the tradition. Lots of later writers learned from him—Milton, for instance. He was also a great epic poet . . . etc., etc. (for fifteen more agonizing minutes).

(This writer needs to repeat "Classics I," come to class, and read the *Aeneid*. Maybe then the answer would have some content to back up the words.)

Answer 2: Although the Roman Virgil was greatly influenced by Homer, adapting his epic meter and many of his characters and scenes to his own purposes, Virgil was an important contributor to the tradition of epic poetry. In the temporary attraction of his hero, Aeneas, for the beautiful Queen of Carthage, Dido, he introduced the element of romantic, yet tragic love. Consider the "cave" scene and Dido's agonizing suicide (idea developed). He also portrayed the Roman concern for origins and identity and their constant concern with futurity and the legacy they would be leaving. Evander and his son Pallas are part of this larger theme (idea developed). In Aeneas too may be seen the Roman preoccupation with political as well as military leadership. Take, for example, the famous scene where Neptune calms the raging sea (idea developed). This answer could easily go on for another 18 minutes.

(This answer is at least on the right track and seems to have been written by someone who may have read the poem.)

For the writer who is seeking to impress, wordiness is meant to be a sign of wisdom, an indication of a profound mind at work. This is the "If-you-don't-get-what-I'm-saying-I-must-be-brilliant" wordiness of some politicians, educators, textbook writers, and, alas, literary critics. This is the "words equal wisdom" fallacy. Excluding the reader is not an accident; it is a goal. Consider this committee report on an elementary school textbook survey:

> After extensive dialogue with and input from concerned constituents, it has been concluded by this duly-appointed committee that elementary pedagogical resources, particularly those of the print medium, have been time-factored out of current relevancy to education contingencies. It is therefore the conclusion and recommendation of this committee that this negative reading of the present state receive appropriate attention for accomplishment of the desired updating in an accelerated time frame.

(Advice for these writers who, unlike the fearful or the uninformed, are sometimes all too aware, even cynical, about what they're doing, is not so easy. In the best of all possible worlds, they would be recognized for the pretenders they are and forced to learn the hard way. It is a sad fact, though, that this kind of writing sometimes brings success: votes from the impressed and rewards from the naïve. These writers need to rethink their attitude toward their readers; the readers need to rethink their attitude toward them.)

Could the textbook committee simply say,

> After talking to principals, teachers, pupils, and parents, the committee concluded that most of the textbooks in the elementary schools are worn out and, worse, 20 years out of date. We need some new ones, fast!

and be chosen to do the next survey? I would like to think so.

Now, assuming that you are not permanently committed to padding out your prose, consider the following practical methods for eliminating wordiness.

1. One of the best ways to get rid of wordiness is to sharpen the details. Where it makes sense, try "5 A.M." instead of "early," "maple" instead of "tree," and "procrastination" instead of "bad habit."

2. Make all doubles, triples, and so on, earn their keep. Do not say, "I like to write and compose papers." The *write* and the *compose* are not different enough from one another to justify your using both. Duplication does *not* make writing more exact. Ironically, it helps to keep it vague. It would be far better to say, "I like to write, especially about my childhood on a Minnesota farm." Do not say, "One of the quickest ways to become wordy is to embroider, embellish, and decorate your papers too much." Distinguishing among the meanings in this series of words takes the reader's time and attention. The effort must be worth it, a true extension of meaning, not just a random flurry of synonyms for the self-indulgent writer. Caesar said, "Veni, vidi, vici," not, "I arrived and came; I took a look around and saw; I took over the place; that is, I conquered."

3. Avoid the passive voice unless you need it. "The door was closed" can easily become "John closed the door" if, of course, the writer *wants* to identify the person who is closing the door. The devious politician's statement, "The bridge has been rendered nonfunctional," covers up his vote against fixing it, "I voted to have the bridge closed rather than spend $10,000.00 on repairs." The slippery bank notice, "You have been provided with a new opportunity for efficiency in savings through the new $3,000.00 minimum balance account," rather than, "We are raising the minimum balance from $1,000.00 to $3,000.00; please deposit $2,000.00 or pay for your checks," pays no compliment to your intelligence or to your wallet. Recognize both wordy and "slippery" passives and avoid them in your own writing. Use them when they work best for you: "That vase was broken by *John!*"

4. Avoid starting sentences with "There is" or "There are." They can usually be cut simply by making the sentence more direct. Change "There are four courses that I want to take next term" to "I want to take four courses next term," or "There is too much money spent on sports" to "This school spends too much money on sports." (Sometimes, "there is" and "there are," like the passive voice, are meant to hide the subject—"There is something fishy in this office" rather than "The secretary stole the cashbox").

5. Combine closely related sentences. The following set of sentences is wordy: "Mark has three different jobs. They are bagging at the supermarket, moving furniture, and coaching basketball." It would be better to say: "Mark has three different jobs: bagging at the supermarket, moving furniture, and coaching basketball" because it gets rid of the unnecessary "They are." After sentences that have already identified the subject, "It is," "She was," "He is," and so forth may often be cut.

6. Use some short, subject-verb-object sentences. They clarify ideas and provide the reader with "resting spots": "The toad eyed the worm" or "The worm was upset." Use short statements, particularly if you have been "rambling on" with many long sentences or if your ideas have been complex. Restate as simply as you can.

7. Avoid redundancy—excessive, repetitive words unnecessary to the meaning: "She looked at me with a startled face," "When people talk about the mysteries of human nature, they're usually talking about the unique emotions that are characteristic of human beings" (What is the meaning? I have no idea), or "I thought that being nice and possessing an optimistic trait was the best quality a human being could have, but I was mistaken, very mistaken."

8. Avoid adverbial intensifiers: "I felt *terribly* sad" or "I was *very* happy."

Sharpen the verb or the adjective. Eliminate the intensifier—for example, "I wept" or "I was miserable"; "I laughed with joy" or "I was delighted."

9. Avoid ready-made phrases: "As it turns out," "In any event," "To all intents and purposes." Reduce padded phrases like "at the present time" (now), "for the purpose of" (for), or "due to the fact that" (because).

10. Try not to be artificially formal. "I want to express myself in a written format" could be simply "I want to write." "My endeavor is to acquire sufficient learning in business to augment my financial opportunities for the future" could be "I want a degree in business so I can make more money." Another source of artificiality is a long series of Latinate words—"My primary intention is to elucidate the ramifications of the dilemma" could just as well be "I want to study the problem." Short, Anglo-Saxon words help.

11. Check "that's" and "which's," not only for correct usage, but also for cutting, if possible. "The tree that is growing in my backyard needs to be cut down" could be "The tree in my backyard needs to be cut down." "That" is "restrictive," part of the meaning of the previous word, and should not be set off by commas when used in this way. "The tree *that* is growing . . ." is correct, but *that is growing* can also be dropped (and maybe turned into a maple or an oak in the process). In the sentence, "My job, which I sometimes find almost impossible, is paying my tuition," "which" is usually "nonrestrictive," that is, it is able to be separated from the previous noun, so it is set off by commas. The sentence could read, "My almost impossible job is paying my tuition." Cutting the dead phrase also leaves some room for new detail—"My almost impossible job delivering pizza is paying my tuition."

When you are focusing on problems with wordiness, move toward achieving your reader's understanding. Ask yourself, "Just what am I trying to say here?" and then say it, just as you would to a person sitting right in front of you. Wordiness often comes from jumbled thinking; you should be the first to know what you're talking about.

PRACTICE

1. Remove the wordiness in the following sentences. (Look for unnecessary repetitions, unnecessary duplications, passive voice, stuffy circumlocutions, extra phrases, modifiers, etc.)

   a. I am desirous of sharing my opinions, reflections, and ideas.
   b. It was a very grueling and well-rewarding experience.
   c. My summer was definitely interesting.
   d. I just want to round out my character to a more balanced state of mind.

e. I was questioning in my mind why I was doing this.
f. I am definitely intending to attend and be present at the conference due to the fact that I need what it has to offer me.
g. Joan is my younger sister. She is prettier than I am. She is not as smart.
h. The toad, having assessed the situation with the utmost attention, determined that it would be very appropriate at this point in time to devour the worm.
i. Our gas provider has "determined to offer a new value-enhanced option by which fuel will be provided in two major types or forms—super and regular unleaded."
j. There are many reasons why camping at Algonquin National Park was found to be a very rewarding experience.
k. The watch that is on my wrist has been rendered nonfunctional by a blow or hit to the face of it.
l. In today's modern world, in the last decade of the twentieth century, many problems still remain to be solved.
m. He was always kept very busy repairing garbage disposals that were electrical.
n. When she comes to town she'll be promoting the large in size book that many people say is not a very good book.
o. We planned to go out at dusk just after sunset.
p. I want to learn to write in such a way that it would hold someone's attention and make them identify with the point of view I am trying to get across.

2. Rewrite the following essay, cutting words and adding details for interest.

My Sister, Joanne

My family is four in number—my mother, my stepfather, my sister, and myself. As a family, we really get along very well together, even though we all have a particular personality trait or characteristic that really bugs or bothers everyone else in the family sometimes. One member of the family, my stepfather, for example, is moody. We never know what kind of a mood he's going to be in, so we try not to come into contact with him at all until we can check out his mood and see if he seems to be in a good mood. If his mood seems good, we might speak to him then. My mother, unlike my stepfather, usually does not talk very much, not that not talking very much is a bad thing to do, but she's too quiet sometimes, so we can't really tell why she's quiet. She may be quiet for a day or so and then burst out crying when she is eating supper. We never know for sure why she's crying, or who made her sad, but all of a sudden we find out. To make a long story short, it's usually something that happened 1 days ago and often something I did. Too bad for me, but my main irritating personality trait or characteristic is that I lose my temper easily. It's very easy to be angry at my sister, because she has a trait that it's really hard to live with, especially me. I'm not very neat, but she's the neatest person I've ever come into contact with in my life.

For example, the room where she sleeps looks like it should be in the magazines *Better Homes and Gardens* or *House Beautiful,* or some other magazines that show beautiful rooms in them, because she's so neat all of the time. Every day in the morning, she uses the vacuum cleaner on her floor and shakes out the rugs that are scattered all around her room out of the window of her room. Then she dusts her bureau with a feather duster and then makes her bed after she shakes out the down cover for her bed. There are never any clothes at all lying around her bedroom because she puts them on hangers or puts them right into the laundry each and every night when she is getting ready to hit the sack. Her shoes are always neatly placed on the shoe rack hanging on her closet door, but her boots are never near her closet door because of the fact that she leaves them carefully placed on newspapers in the entry hall of the house near the outside door. I sometimes wonder if she really lives in her room because it's always so neat, but I guess that's just the way she wants it to be to give her a charge. 2

She is also really neat around the rest of the house. There is no one, including my mother, who makes the house clean enough for her. At the present time, almost every night, I watch television with the hum of the vacuum cleaner humming in the background. Sometimes I have to pick up my feet off the rug so she can run the vacuum cleaner under my feet. There is also a place for everything and everything in its place for her, especially in the living room. Nothing can be left anywhere around the house where she thinks it shouldn't be. She also complains if I wear my shoes in the house. "Why don't you leave them outside?" she says. She also doesn't appear very happy if I don't take my boots off in the winter. My mother doesn't mind much, but Joanne does mind. In the kitchen too she gets all bent out of shape if the stove gets greasy, but it's not easy to cook without having a little grease spatter on the stove. She also doesn't like to see a dirty dish or a glass that has been used left in the sink and tells us to wash them as soon as we're finished using them. She is really neat around the house. 3

But even though she may be super neat about her own room and around the house, she is also neat about herself. Her clothes are always perfect; they are clean and neat and very well pressed. You would never be able to find any dirt at all on her clothes, and you couldn't find a wrinkle on her clothes either. As a true fact, she always looks as if she just came out of the hairdresser's too, on account of the fact that not a single hair is ever out of place. Everything she wears always matches. Colors always go with one another and her shoes always go with her clothes. She spends many hours shopping in the stores for just the right things to wear and she also spends a very large amount of money on her 4 expensive clothes too. When she's around the house, when she's doing the vacuuming, she covers her face with cold cream, and after she's finished, she does her fingernails. The resulting effect of all this time and attention is that she always looks really neat all the time.

As you can easily see, to all intents and purposes, my sister is one of 5
the neatest people who ever existed. Actually, I don't really mind a lot if she wants to be this neat, but I just don't like it when she makes me feel like I'm being such a slob. In addition, I would also like to be able to move a book or something else in the living room without having her get upset about making things messed up. I also would like to be able to watch a television program in the evening without having her running the vacuum cleaner around under my feet. It's easy for me to get angry at her though, because she says she's just trying to keep things nice for us, so I usually don't take the time to say much to her about these things. I guess we all have our own personal personality traits—especially the ones in my family. It's just as well that we make our best effort to cooperate together.

3. Read the paragraph by Scott Russell Sanders on page 287 and make it as wordy as possible. How do the extra words affect the meaning?

FOR YOUR OWN PAPER

1. Read through your paper and identify places where adding details could possibly help you to cut empty words, and then add them in. (See pages 400–403 for a further discussion of details.)

2. Test your own writing honestly for extra words that add nothing extra to the *quality* of your prose. Are you, for example, fearfully trying to meet a deadline by padding out pages? Are you trying to cover up the fact that you don't really know what you are talking about? Or are you trying to impress the reader with complex constructions and "impressive" vocabulary? Do you have any of the smaller bad habits, the ones discussed above? If you discover that you do have problems with wordiness, identify the reasons why and then work either on the larger issues of communication (learn more about your subject, abandon the "false" style) or the smaller "repairs" that can make such a big difference.

3. Take one of your paragraphs (or more than one, if this exercise works for you) and write the sentences down sequentially, numbered one after another, as if you were doing an exercise. Make each sentence as sharp as possible and then return the whole set to paragraph form. (This new paragraph may now need some work on making connections, which is the subject of the next section.)

Making Connections

The word *coherence* comes from the Latin *con* ("with") and *haerere* ("to stick"). Coherent writing means writing that "sticks together," writing in which the various parts connect. *Unified* writing is consistent within itself. The paper does not stray from its subject; paragraphs do not stray from their topic. Unified writing does not build a snowman in a desert. *Coherent* writing is not only unified but also keeps the sun, the shadows, the sand dunes, the gravel fans, and the cacti of the desert scene in harmony with one another—in the right places and in the right proportions. Thinking about coherence is thinking about relationships.

Read the following paragraph about returning to an old elementary school:

> When I returned to the old Shamrock School so that I could write this paper, I was surprised at how different everything looked. The hallways looked shorter; the rooms looked smaller. I couldn't believe I used to sit at those little desks, or drink at those lowly bubblers. Mrs. Kirk's room looked the same to me. I really liked her classes, especially the Friday afternoon science classes when we used to experiment with water, and air, and bubbles, and gas. She was really a good teacher. I'm glad I went back to the school.

(This writer has a problem with unity and, therefore, of necessity, with coherence. The topic of the paragraph is the "difference" she perceived when she returned to the school, but halfway through, she turns her attention not only to a classroom that does *not* look different but also to a teacher whom she used to enjoy. Such a jumble of topics makes coherence impossible. A revision would require that the writer separate the topics into separate paragraphs or possibly that the writer think of an "umbrella" topic sentence that would allow her to connect all of these details.)

Now consider the following paragraph, which is about going to college:

> I'm the youngest in my family of four kids. My brothers and sister went to college. I'm going to college. I should get a degree. I'm not a good student. My parents want business. My sister wants me to try nursing. Accounting is my major. I'll try nursing. Maybe I'll try a Criminal Justice or Cartography. I might quit and get a job. Laurie is happier.

(This paragraph has a certain kind of unity; it is entirely devoted to the problem of going to college. But it suffers from one of the worst faults of unrevised prose—no glue. The writer simply makes a series of statements and leaves the reader to find the links. Is she going to college because her brothers and sisters went? What does not being a good student have to do with her parents' choice? How does her sister's choice fit in? Does she like accounting? Why is she trying nursing or some other major? Why is she thinking of quitting? Who is Laurie?)

The writer of the preceding paragraph may have had some connections in mind, but the reader must do the work of creating them. Rarely will readers choose such exhausting prose, especially when they could read the same information with far less effort. The following paragraph is a revision by a workshop class. The sentences are numbered, because I will refer to them in the discussion that follows.

> [1]My two brothers and my sister all went to college before me, so it was only logical that I go too. [2]"Get a degree!" they all ordered in unison. [3]The problem is I'm not a very good student and I have no idea of what I want to do with my life. [4]Figuring that women have a better chance for big money these days, my parents recommended business. [5]So right now, I'm in Accounting. [6]I wish I weren't, though, because I don't like working with numbers and I have no interest in business. [7]My sister, a nurse, thinks I should follow her footsteps down the hospital corridors and major in nursing. [8]Next semester, I might give that idea a try, if I can get in. [9]Or then again, maybe I'll test out an idea of my own—like Criminal Justice or Cartography. [10]Before I came to college, I didn't even know these majors existed. [11]Or maybe I'll just quit school for a while and take a job at a bank with my cousin Laurie. [12]She seems a lot happier than I am right now.

(The meaning of this paragraph is clearer. The writer is in college because of family pressure. She doesn't really want to be there. She doesn't like her parents' choice and may try nursing to please her sister. She may also try her own choice of major or possibly go to work, as her cousin did. The reader's questions are answered. The paragraph needs connectors.)

A closer look at the relationships among the sentences within the paragraph should give you some idea of how they *work* to clarify meaning.

—Sentences 1 and 2—pronoun connection between "two brothers" and "sister" (1) and "they" (2)

—Sentences 2 and 3—idea connection, suggesting contrast; they all agree (2), the writer has a "problem" (3)

—Sentences 3 and 4—idea connection, "no idea" about what to do (3); parents have one, "business" (4)

—Sentences 4 and 5—a result of parents' preference (4), indicated by "So" (5) and greater detail, from "business" (4) to "Accounting" (5)

—Sentences 5 and 6—elaboration of feelings about "Accounting" (5), indicated by "weren't" (6) and a contrast suggested by "though" (6), a finishing of the "Accounting" discussion by reference to "numbers" and "business" (6)

—Sentences 6 and 7—idea connection, probably a result of dislike for "numbers" and "business" (6), sister's new suggestion for "nursing" (7)
—Sentences 7 and 8—time transition, "next semester" (7), no longer the "now" of (5), and reference back to "nursing" (7) with "that idea" (8)
—Sentences 8 and 9—idea connection, "Or then again" suggesting another alternative to parents and sister (4 and 7) by reference to "idea of my own" (9) and also alternative to their suggestions for majors in business (4) and nursing (7 and 8), namely, "Criminal Justice or Cartography" (9)
—Sentences 9 and 10—time relationship, "before" (10) the "now" of (5) and verbal relationship between "Criminal Justice or Cartography" (9) and "these majors" (10)
—Sentences 10 and 11—further development of alternatives, "Or" (11), related to the suggestions of parents, sister, and the "Or then again" of (9), with new alternative, "quit" and "take a job . . . with cousin Laurie" (11)
—Sentences 11 and 12—pronoun connection between "Laurie" (11) and "She" (12), plus concluding statement (12)

(As tedious as it may be to discover the detailed connections within this paragraph, and as difficult as it may be to believe that writers think of such minute details, an important lesson may be learned here. Transitions *are* subtle and often apparently insignificant, and yes, writers *do* and *must* constantly pay attention to these connections. The writer must constantly anticipate the reader's needs, weaving pieces together so that the whole becomes understandable. Sometimes they are natural and simple, and as easy as they would be in conversation. At other times, they require deliberate attention to difficult and complex relationships. But they are always on the writer's mind.)

Coherence is a concern with every "if," "and," and "but" of writing, a focus on thoughts that are related to one another, and a focus on the connecting details that earlier drafts may not have allowed. The word *transition* comes from the Latin *trans* ("across") and *ire* ("to go") and thus means going across from one idea to the next, as a bridge stretches across a chasm. The reader should never be forced to leap and should never feel deserted by the writer, whose job it is to lead through unfamiliar territory.

A transition is the well-timed "however," "nevertheless," "in addition," "on the other hand," "in contrast," or "finally" *within* and *between* paragraphs. It is the repetition of a key word or idea from a previous sentence. It is the entire sentence or the entire paragraph devoted to making a connection for the reader.

A problem with these connectors, a sense that the whole piece is not "hanging together," may require something as basic as returning to the planning board, or the larger concerns of the prewriting stage (pages 349–379). It may require rethinking the subject, the point, and the purpose. It may require further thought about the plan, and about more important and less important pieces of information and how they relate to one another. Possibly the writing needs restructuring, based on the *type* of writing you are trying to do—according to space, time, a pattern of contrasts, or an order of increasing interest—both within paragraphs and within the entire paper. A problem with coherence may also require thinking more generously about the reader's needs.

Sometimes, however, the problem is even larger. The "shot-gun style" may, in fact, be a sign of the writer's confusion, a hint that the connections have yet to be *discovered.* The reader must do what the writer was *unable* to do—make sense of it all. But, no matter how much information is presented, no matter how much research or thinking has been done, making the connections is the writer's problem, not the reader's.

"Only connect," says E. M. Forster in his novel, *Howard's End,* in which he argues the importance of getting to know the hearts and minds of others, if we are ever to communicate honestly. Coherence is also a concern with this kind of connection among human beings, not just with the occasional "if," "and," or "but." It is a sign of logical thinking, an honest effort on the writer's part to help the reader *through* the writing from beginning to end. Coherence provides the destination markers, the distance tables, the "no exit" or "detour" signs, the bridges, tunnels, and ferries to get the reader safely to the desired goal. Remember E. B. White's warning that "Readers are in trouble half the time." Troubled drivers curse bad directions; troubled readers do, too.

PRACTICE

1. Rewrite the student's paragraph on returning to her elementary school (page 415). Be able to explain your method for making the paragraph unified and the connections among your sentences.

2. Underline and explain the connectors in paragraph 4 of Tien Truong's essay, "The Woes of a Waitress" (pages 12–14).

3. In a very early draft of his paper on superbeings, Roger Froilan wrote the following paragraph. Identify the problems he has with making transitions and try to rewrite the paragraph for him. (Afterwards, read his final draft on pages 69–71 to see if you were able to figure out his meaning. Then explain the connectors that he finally used.)

> The first type of super being is a Mutant. A Mutant is any being who is born with super powers which sets them apart from the rest of humanity. All beings contain an X-factor in their genes which gives them the potential to become a

super-powered being. Mutants' X-factors are active, and unleash the powers within them, usually at puberty. Some beings (to be described later) activate this X-factor through an outside force. The main cause of mutations is a result of the increase in the Earth's background radiation. Mutants are considered the next step in evolution, and are technically referrred to as Homo Superior. The difference between Mutants and other super beings is that Mutants are considered a separate race, and so are stereotyped.

4. Identify and explain the transitions from paragraph to paragraph in Tien Truong's. "The Woes of a Waitress." What kinds of connections does she make? Are they additions, contrasts, examples, concessions, or subtopics?

5. Rearrange the following sentences into coherent paragraphs.

(1) I am disappointed that there are no birds, none but the ones I'm conjuring up from his essays. (2) No, I don't think a congenial Mr. Chipmunk is sharing a nostalgic moment with me, certainly not at this particular location. (3) Sitting alone on Burroughs' Boyhood Rock just above his birthplace in Roxbury, the same spot he so often used as a vantage point, I jot down squeaky, fake-profound notes with my fading red-felt-tipped pen. (4) When it spots me on the rock, it freezes, but finally sits back on its haunches, also looking towards the hills. (5) But I put down my pen and I watch, glad he's there, if only for a quick chipmunk-rest. (6) Frustrated, I look out across his grave to the old, worn Catskills rolling gently across the horizon. (7) Then a chipmunk scrambles about the flat stone wall surrounding the grave.

(1) That time would never come back; the progress was inevitable and relentless, I thought. (2) On another occasion, I was standing alone waiting for an overdue trolley in a Boston subway station. (3) Would I ever be happy again? (4) It was around the time of my twenty-first birthday, and never had I felt so aging, so old, so vulnerable. (5) To my relief, the trolley clattered in and sped me to my appointment. (6) I remember fearing that I would never be free from that taunting awareness of time's slipping away from me. (7) Without humor, I thought of myself growing older as I stood there and of the grim fact that I would never be as young as I was the moment before.

FOR YOUR OWN PAPER

1. Think again about your thesis and your plan for the content of your paragraphs. Are your paragraphs unified around your chosen topics?

2. Do a practice analysis of one of your own paragraphs, explaining the links, as for the workshop paragraph on page 416.

3. Within your paragraphs, underline words and phrases that work as connectors from sentence to sentence. If specific connectors are missing, is the

progress of ideas clear enough for the reader to follow? If not, you may need to think about the relationships yourself. Never leave such thinking to the reader.

4. Check the connections between paragraphs. Is there any place where the reader would be required to jump from topic to topic, without a sure sense of where the paper is going? Be sure to guide the reader, not only through your paragraphs, but also through your whole paper.

Adapting Tone and Diction

Consider how many ways the following statement may be spoken:

—(With a sigh) "Oh yes, I had a great time at the party."
—(With enthusiasm) "Oh yes! I had a great time at the party!"
—(With a sneer) "Oh yes, I had a *great* time at the party."
—(With hesitation) "Oh, yes, . . . I had a great time at the party."

All of these variations are matters of tone, the speaker's attitude toward the subject and the listener. Writers, too, reveal their feelings as they write—amused, angry, flippant, ironic, bitter, serious—and readers are sensitive to these feelings as they read. They may even be able to conjure up an image of what the writer might be like should he or she walk into the room. They may be able to imagine a tone of voice, if the paper were to be spoken rather than written. Readers do not read in a vacuum; they are constantly forming opinions about the writer and the writer's attitude.

It is therefore important for a writer to think carefully about tone, to choose a stance that is appropriate for the subject and the intended readers. A guest who is hoping for an invitation to the next party had better not answer with an ironic sneer. A friend who is writing a sympathy note had better not sink to adding jokes and giggles. A student hoping for an "A" from an English teacher would be wise not to write about Shakespeare in gushy, greeting card prose. Think of getting your message across and respect your reader, without expressing condescension or false intimacy.

In fact, one of the most common problems in tone is the adoption of a "chatty" or "intimate" tone with a reader who is unfamiliar with the writer. The writer may make false assumptions, possibly even insulting the reader. Consider the following note written by a student to his *new* advisor:

Hi!

Can you imagine that Curriculum Committee meeting the other day? Wasn't it the pits? I was glad to see you there, though. I know we were both wondering what the bozo in the first row was talking about. More requirements? Are you kidding? I'm barely getting by as it is! I'd like to graduate before I get to be the same age as my professors! Could we meet soon to discuss how much I have to do before I get out of here? I'm free on Monday between 12 and 1.

Your advisee,
Brad

(The tone here is inappropriate, unless it is from a student who knows his advisor well and is sure of her attitudes toward curriculum. Being unfamiliar with the advisor, he makes too many assumptions about how she is likely to feel and about her willingness to become an ally. The comment on age is insensitive, possibly insulting, and the hours suggested (for *his* convenience) show little concern for the demands on the advisor's time.)

The following letter of application from a second-semester senior also contains problems with tone:

6 Raines Road
Big Town, Kansas
January 3, 1991

Mr. Peter Carlson, Head Librarian
Big Town Library
1600 Main Street
Big Town, Kansas

Dear Mr. Carlson:

This letter is in response to your advertisement for an assistant librarian at your library. I feel that I am fully qualified for this job. I have worked at the college library for a year, and I plan to study library science after I get my degree in Accounting. I've done lots of different things on this job, so I'm sure your job as assistant would be perfectly appropriate for me. I'd be willing to talk to you as soon as possible about this. You can reach me at the above address or by phone (555–7835). Expecting to hear from you soon, I thank you in advance.

Sincerely,
Joan Cross

(Confident and qualified as she may be, this writer is too aggressive in this first contact with the head librarian. When he learns what her real qualifications are and after he interviews her, *he* will be able to judge if she is "perfectly qualified" for the job. Also, the *pressure* for an interview, the near demand for contact, and the thank you when there is as yet no cause for one are rude.)

In short, the problem in both of these examples is not necessarily with the content but with the tone.

Diction too, the actual *words* we choose, also contribute to meaning and mood and to the overall effect of what we have to say. Diction may be formal or informal:

—"I found the concert most enjoyable."
—"The gig was wicked awesome!"

It may be general or particular:

—"Yes, I had a good time at the gathering."
—"Yes, I loved the food, the wine, and the conversation at my high-school reunion" (or better, ". . . the lasagna, the chianti, and the long talk with Lisa.")

As with tone, choosing vocabulary for what you write is directly related to your attitude toward what you are saying and toward your readers. Many beginning writers identify lack of vocabulary as a major problem, but this rarely is the case. For clear, honest communication, vocabulary does not have to be "fancy," nor should it call attention to itself; it just has to be right for the purposes. It needs to be exact in meaning (e.g., not "sandwiched around" when you want to say "sandwiched between"). As Mark Twain said, ". . . the difference between the *almost right* word and the *right* word is really a large matter—'tis the difference between the lightning-bug and the lightning."

Vocabulary also needs to avoid the tedium of overuse, the "triteness" or worn-down quality of "tried and true," "to each his own," "broadening my horizons"—words and phrases that all too easily come to mind. It needs to avoid pretentiousness—the "consummate didacticist," instead of the "fine teacher." And it needs to be consistent within the piece being written (e.g., not "She's an entirely out-of-sight business associate"). Mixtures in either tone or diction are confusing to the reader.

Most college writing should be in straightforward, readable English and should be serious for the most part. The diction will probably be more formal than informal, and, ideally, there will be a mixture of general and particular—the details supporting the general statements. More elaborate and subtle diction will develop naturally as the writer's more subtle knowledge of the subject demands. Think about your reader first.

Tone and diction then, like so many other aspects of writing, are not only expressions of the writer's personality, skill, and interest but also an expression of the writer's awareness of the audience. Write in a "tone of voice" that is appropriate to you, choose diction that feels natural to you, but always keep in mind your subject, your readers, and your overall purposes.

I once knew a student who wrote all of her papers in "normal" English and then used a *Thesaurus* to make the vocabulary more formal. Be careful of this practice, which often is a source of misuse and misunderstanding for both writer and reader. Another student wrote on all subjects in the slang of her hometown, defending it as her own "real voice." The problem with this is that no matter how vivid the language is, no matter how effective it is in her neighborhood, a "private" diction may end up excluding a wider audience, made up mostly of outsiders, or strangers. Private writing may go unread. The trick of all good writing is to remain true to yourself *and* to your readers.

PRACTICE

1. Analyze and explain the tone of the following paragraph. Do you see any problems in tone here? Rewrite the paragraph, making the tone more clear: ironic, angry, mocking, or sincere.

   Dear Kerri,

   This is just to thank you for the lovely time at your party the other night. It was really fun to see the other kids after so many years of not hearing from them. It isn't your fault that Candy still holds a grudge and that Mark wasn't in the mood for a party. And the pizza *did* eventually get there. I hope you'll keep me in mind next time you plan a reunion. Again, thanks.

   Best,
   Darlene

2. Rewrite the two student paragraphs—the one to the advisor on page 421 and the one to the head librarian on page 422. Be sure to think of audience and purpose.
3. Rewrite Edward Abbey's paragraph on page 222 as if he were not an admirer of the wilderness.
4. Compare the tone, diction, and purpose of the three pieces on housing: Hession (pages 38–39), Moore (pages 75–78), and Glezer (pages 268–271).
5. In a workshop class, some students had problems with the tone of two student pieces, "Seventh of the Litter" (pages 15–17) and "Portrait of a Credit Card Junkie" (pages 168–170). Can you identify possible problems and suggest some remedies?
6. By rewriting, make the tone of the following statements consistent within themselves.

   a. We slam banged up the stairs and smack dab into the teacher prepared to discipline us for our infractions.
   b. I had a marvelous time on the occasion of my venture to Disneyworld, but the lines almost drove me bonkers.
   c. Andrew Jackson was a daring President who wasn't about to take any garbage from a guy who spoke ill of his wife.

7. Make the diction of the following statements either more or less formal.

   a. He's up for time in the slammer.
   b. It's best to convey how you feel rather than suffer internally.

c. (From a woman named Queenie, who is on the telephone): No, we ain't comin' back for your trash, and let me tell you, my boss has been in trash since he was nine years old. If he found a trash bag in the middle of the street, he'd know it was yours. *Your* trash wasn't out in time!
d. My major intention is to elucidate the ramifications of the dilemma.

8. Replace the inappropriate diction.

   a. I was chock full to the brim with an overwhelming sense of happiness.
   b. It wasn't a very fun time.
   c. I like the lazy, hazy, crazy days of summer, but I love the hustle and bustle of Christmas.
   d. I'm taking the tried and true path of getting a degree because of what I might encounter down the road on life's long journey.
   e. When I write a paper, I'm seeking out input on an endeavor which I hope to turn to my advantage in pursuing my career goals.
   f. My major pursuit is to distance myself from the thought mode.
   g. Many women vision this image of the TV woman and obtain a sense of exhaustion.

9. Rewrite the following paragraph, first to create a positive effect, and then to create a negative one. Example: "The young child. . . ." (positive: "tiny tot"; negative: "little brat").

   The young child went into the toy store and removed many things from the shelves. After a time, he showed his father a game that he had chosen and asked if he could have it. His tired father refused and led the child to the exit.

FOR YOUR OWN PAPER

1. Ask yourself how you felt as you composed the essay you are working on. Did you feel angry, calm, objective, humorous, bored, ironic? Read your paper to see if the attitude of the paper is an accurate reflection of this feeling. Is the attitude consistent throughout? Also, ask yourself about your audience. Who are your readers? What tone of voice are you taking with them? What tone might they welcome or expect from you?

2. Check the diction carefully. Is it formal or informal? What impression are you trying to create through the diction? does the selection of words support the tone of your message? Are the words appropriate for your audience?

Forming Sentences

In writing, most sentences should be based on the simple "subject-verb-object" sequence ("I slammed the door" or "I love English grammar") and its developments ("When he refused to help me, I slammed the door" or "I loved English grammar, until I started studying sentences"). This is because, more than anything else, sentences need to communicate meaning. Think first of what you have to say, and you will already have taken a big step to writing them well.

But to communicate even better, it is advisable sometimes to break from the most basic form, for just as variety spices up life, so does it spice up prose. It keeps it from being flat and predictable. Being able to vary sentences in writing comes partly from an understanding of grammar. What is a complete sentence? What is a fragment? What is the difference between a simple and a complex sentence? What is a subordinate clause? It also comes from developing an "ear" as you reread sentences—an ability to "hear" when it is time for a change.

Read the following paragraph on vocabulary:

> One good way to improve vocabulary (and spelling) is to read good writers as often as possible and to look up unfamiliar words if you can't figure them out from context. This way, you unconsciously develop an ear and an eye for words and the more you read the more familiar they become to you, the more they become part of your own treasury of words. Memorizing vocabulary lists of important words may also help to improve vocabulary, but always remember to use diction that seems natural to you so that you won't mis-use words or give false meanings in the wrong places. Be aware of words and love words and their personal history of meaning, but don't let worrying about "bad vocabulary" keep you from writing, because you will be wasting important time.

(This paragraph was written by someone with a tin ear, someone who did not avoid flatness. Generally, the sentences are too long, and they are also mostly the *same* length, giving the paragraph a dragged-out sound, like a record played at a slow speed.)

Rewritten, this time entirely with short sentences, the paragraph's effect is slightly better, but not much:

> One way to improve vocabulary (and spelling) is to read good writers. Read them as often as possible. Look up unfamiliar words. But try to figure them out from context first. This way, you unconsciously develop an ear and an eye for words. The more you read, the more familiar they become to you. The more they become part of your own treasury of words. Memorizing vocabulary lists of

> important words may also help to improve vocabulary. Always remember to use diction that seems natural to you so that you won't misuse words. You also won't give false meanings in the wrong places. Be aware of words. Know their personal history of meaning. But don't let worrying about a "bad vocabulary" keep you from writing. You will be wasting important time.

(Here, again, the problem is not with meaning, coherence, or audience but with the lack of variety in the sentences. The writer has "the fidgets." The reader feels poked at.)

Read the third version of this paragraph to see if it is better:

> One way to improve vocabulary (and spelling) is to read good writers as often as possible. If you can't figure certain words out from context, look them up. This way, you develop both an ear and an eye for words. The more you read, the more familiar words become to you, the more they become part of your personal treasury. Memorizing lists may also help to improve vocabulary, but to avoid misuse, remember to use only words that seem natural to you. Be aware of words; know their history of meaning. But don't let worry about a "bad vocabulary" keep you from writing, or you'll be wasting important time.

(The variety of sentences in this paragraph is better, and, in the process, some wordiness has been eliminated.)

According to the demands of the message, good prose takes advantage of the many options for writing sentences. Let the short, simple sentences hurry along when you want the reader to hurry. Slow the action down with longer, more complex sentences when you want slower, more contemplative reading. Make the style fit the immediate purpose, but keep variety in mind as you move throughout the various stages of your whole essay.

One of the most obvious and most direct ways of improving the sound of prose is to use short, direct sentences regularly, not as often as in the second example just given, but often enough to provide "resting spots" for the reader. They emphasize important points. Short subject-verb-object sentences break the sometimes tedious rhythm of too many long, complex sentences. Well used, they clarify meaning for both the reader and the writer. It is hard to nitpick and to overdo the distinctions when you allow yourself only a few words before the sentence is over. As Thoreau said, "Simplify, simplify, simplify."

Another way of providing variety in sentence forms is by using various types of sentences—simple, compound, and complex. This is not, however, simply an exercise in grammar. Each type of sentence provides for a different kind of thinking; each allows for different relationships among its various parts. The simple sentence allows for the most straightforward statement ("Christmas vacation starts tomorrow"); the compound sentence allows for parallel and balancing thoughts within a single statement ("The Christmas vacation starts tomorrow, and I'm dying to get home"); and the complex sentence allows for making some parts of the statement more important than other parts, or subordinating some of them ("Although Christmas vacation may start tomorrow, I'm finishing my research paper tonight").

It is also possible to vary the way sentences are "set up." A loose sentence, for example, allows the accumulation of information *after* the main statement ("My Christmas vacation starts tomorrow, with school closed, examinations finished, plane ticket bought, presents and cards in the mail"). A periodic sentence *delays* the main statement to the end, building to it (School closed, examinations finished, plane ticket bought, presents and cards in the mail, my Christmas vacation starts tomorrow").

Writing good sentences, however, is not entirely a matter of creating variety. It is also a particular concern with smaller matters, like word order and parallelism. Generally, written sentences should follow standard English order—subject, verb, and object. And, generally, as in overall planning and coherence, word order, too, should take climax into account. However this effect is achieved, as for whole papers and paragraphs, sentences should rise in interest. Because the reader needs an incentive to go on, sentences should not be drained of energy at the end (not "I want good grades first, but sports also hold some interest for me too sometimes," but "Although I'm interested in sports, good grades come first"). The words at the ends of sentences, for better or for worse, get the reader's attention. Plan for them.

Parallelism too, making the parts of the sentence balance, is important (not "I like to walk, to run, and swimming," but "I like walking, running, and swimming" or "I like to walk, to run, and to swim"). Consider the larger patterns of this balanced sentence: "Last year, Christmas was simply the closing of school and the finishing of examinations, but this year it is buying the plane ticket home and getting the presents and cards in the mail." When you create patterns in your writing, the reader comes to expect them and often unconsciously relies upon them for discovering meaning. Faulty parallelism—a breaking of the pattern—not only breaks the rhythm of your writing but also breaks the sense of what you are trying to say.

Most important, sentences must convey meaning. If you find *yourself* getting entangled in your own words, lost in your own compound-complex sentence mazes, tripped up by your own quirky constructions, and veering off your own parallel lines, think of your *reader's* predicament. Return to the simple construction. Break up your ideas. Above all, make your sentences make sense.

Great symphonies are written in movements, selecting and restating the major themes, varying the rhythm and pace. You may not be composing a Fifth Symphony but only a fifth essay in Composition 101, yet your audience, too, needs variety and timely repetition: drums for the dramatic moments; silences for contemplation.

PRACTICE

1. Rewrite the following sentences. Be sure to focus on their meaning, on just what these sentences are saying.

    a. The sand clung to the insides of our toes.
    b. This is from a town newspaper: "Local man found guilty of taking taxi."
    c. There was a great smell of aroma in the air.
    d. The ambiance strikes you like a place you want to stay.
    e. I want some cold water on a parched throat just in from mowing the lawn.
    f. Chocolate mouse was our favorite desert.
    g. I had an average student's summer fooling around with girlfriends and your friends.
    h. Everyone loves an early morning ski down the icy slopes.
    i. I also hope to develop some clarity, which is a problem.
    j. When I graduate, I'm going to need some sort of writing habits to start.
    k. Maybe I live in a dream world, but as a lawyer I will be able to aid people with all the unfairness in our bureaucratic system.

2. Rewrite the following groups of sentences, making them work better together. Consider combining, cutting, adding, balancing, building up to a point, or delaying the point—whatever improves the delivery of the message. (Remember to think about meaning.)

Christmas vacation is here. I still have an important paper to write. I also have examinations. I want to get home. I've already mailed my presents. I must get my plane ticket before they are sold out.

This year, he went to hockey practice. It was important to him. He bought knee pads, a hockey stick, a face mask, whatever. He went to all the practices. His main purpose was to score at least one goal per game. The coach really wanted him to improve.

Into the room she walked. Dressed and eager for a good time she was. She could feel the tension, after she got there, though. Fidgeting and getting red, her boyfriend looked uncomfortable across the room. Sheila did also, a person she thought was her friend in the past. Wanting to talk to them, across the room she went, but he looked the other way as Sheila did also. She walked out.

This summer I want to work for my father. He runs a small grocery store. I used to think it was boring. I think I might like it. Maybe it's because I've grown up. College has made me understand more. I appreciate his hard work. I also like the customers. They are neighbors. They are friends. They always come in every day. Maybe I'll take over the store some day. I might make it bigger.

I really enjoyed my "Classical Backgrounds to Literature" course, although I almost never read any classical literature before I took this course. Although the teacher was hard, making us do lots of short papers and one long one and making us take two difficult examinations that involved practically memorizing the texts, I am very grateful I took this course. Because I had so little understanding of where our own literary traditions came from, I couldn't read our own American literature as well as I can now, since I took this course. It gave me a context in which to read and to think, but now I think I want to take all my other literature courses over again, because I think I would get so much more out of them now. I also think the school should make this course a required one so that other students will understand better what modern writers are doing, because they also know this tradition.

3. Read the following paragraph aloud and identify places where you become confused or where you find yourself asking "What?" Try to figure out the sense of the paragraph and then rewrite it to make the meaning more clear.

On summer evenings things all went basically the same with slight variations. After work, the evenings provided either more work or I went out with friends if I wasn't too tired. I got entertainment by entertaining myself with a few drinks with my friends. It was always a pleasure, for instance, margaritas. Sometimes I went to a movie, or a concert or to have a nice relaxing evening with a book. Summer evenings were better than my days, though, because I had more freedom than I did in the daytime, although even then it wasn't much.

FOR YOUR OWN PAPER

1. Sometimes badly written sentences are an unintentional "cover-up" for unclear thinking. They sometimes mark spots where you yourself are not sure of what you are trying to say. Where your sentences wander, your mind may be wandering too. Read your paper aloud, listening for spots where you stumble or become confused. Mark them as you read. As you review your "trouble spots," see first if you understand your own meaning. Stand back and ask, "How can I say this more simply and more clearly?" Then rewrite.

2. Always remembering that communication is your most important goal, examine your sentences closely for variety. Is there a reasonable and effective mixture of short and long sentences? Do sentences rise in interest, with the most important information placed near the end? Do you give your reader some "rest stops," occasional short, subject-verb-object sentences? Are patterns within sentences parallel? If you use a fragment, or a piece of a sentence, is it intentional and for a particular purpose? Be aware of any habits that call attention to themselves (constant use of parentheses or fragments, for example), because they distract from your *meaning.*

Creating Comparisons

In his *Iliad,* just after the death of Zeus' son, Sarpedon, Homer includes an extended simile, a comparison between the battlefield and the barnyard:

> No longer
> could a man, even a knowing one, have made out the godlike
> Sarpedon, since he was piled from head to ends of feet under
> a mass of weapons, the blood and the dust, while others about him
> kept forever swarming over his dead body, as flies
> through a sheepfold thunder about the pails overspilling
> milk, in the season of spring when the milk splashes in the buckets.
> So they swarmed over the dead man....

(Through this extended comparison, the master of simile not only helps the audience to understand what the battlefield looked like but also allows a brief respite from the world of war, a temporary pause in the action before the fighting resumes to the death. He sends his audience on a verbal escape into the normal domestic world of cows, milk pails, and little boys getting into trouble and thus emphasizes, by contrast, the greater horror of losing such simplicity, possibly forever. The comparison thus works on many levels, challenging and rewarding the reader's imagination.)

With less resonance, and usually in a briefer form, all comparisons provide both challenge and reward, for such connections are departures from the straightforward, usual way of saying things. They are steps into the world of suggestion. Shakespeare's simile (a cloud that looks "very like a whale"), Flaubert's metaphorical image of Madame Bovary's subtlety ("Her mind was a sidewalk on which passed the ideas of everyman"), or E. B. White's personified chickens on a cold winter morning "standing around with their collars turned up" all suggest additional meaning, or feeling, through comparison.

For the reader, the comprehension of an apt image is a discovery, an actual sharing in the writer's creativity. When the image works well, the reader senses the "rightness," understands the implied meaning, and feels somewhat wise and satisfied. In a journal account of a night of camping, for example, the poet Wallace Stevens says, "Wrapped in my White Hudson Bay blanket, I look like a loaf of bread by the fire." The suggestions of warmth, even homeyness, associated with bread make him seem all the more cozy in his blanket, and the reader enjoys imagining him there.

It is this pleasure in the particulars of a comparison that gives the writer all the more reason to be precise. If the image is just slightly off, for example, if Homer had not mentioned the springtime milk, the sense of loss would have been diminished. If Wallace Stevens had compared himself to a burned bagel, the effect would have been far less cozy. Comparisons must be chosen with great care.

Also, if the images are used to clarify, as they so often are in scientific writing, the comparison is not only a matter of aesthetics but also of meaning. Consider the following comparison by Dr. Lewis Thomas, in which he humorously compares the behavior of beans to human social behavior:

> Beans carry self-labels, and are marked by these as distinctly as a mouse by his special smell. The labels are glycoproteins, the lectins, and may have something to do with negotiating the intimate and essential attachment between the bean and the nitrogen-fixing bacteria which live as part of the plant's flesh, embedded in root nodules. The lectin from one line of legume has a special affinity for the surfaces of the particular bacteria which colonize that line, but not for bacteria from other types of bean. The system seems designed for the maintenance of exclusive partnerships. Nature is pieced together by little snobberies like this.

(Notice the scientific terms ("glycoproteins," "lectins") and the indirect references to human relationships that make the meaning clearer ("intimate and essential attachment," "special affinity," "exclusive partnerships," "little snobberies").)

Delightful as images may be, however, aptness is not the only problem in using them. For one thing, we are so enamored of making verbal pictures that some of them have become deeply embedded in our language, almost invisible, and finally clichés. We "step on the gas," "run people down" when we are angry at them, and watch with concern as "storm clouds blanket" the winter sky. What may have been lively and clever at one time ironically loses its force the more it is used. "She ran like a bat out of hell," "She's a witch," "He came on like gangbusters," and others in a list that could "go on 'till the cows come home," no longer catch the reader's attention. In fact, readers may be surprised to rediscover the meaning of the original connection. Why might a bat "run" out of hell? How long does it take cows to come home?

Often related to this problem of invisibility or of overexposure is the problem of mixing combinations like "I smell a rat in the woodpile and I'm going to nip it in the bud," "He swims like a fish, but I'm all fired up to beat him to the wire," or "These people were getting too much of the pie, so I upset their applecart," which more often make people laugh than appreciate the cleverness of the writer's connections. It is all too easy to mix comparisons when the original connection has sunk far beneath the surface, but writers must resurrect the original thought before connecting one comparison to another. Writers are supposed to know the suggesions *within* their own words.

Excessive zeal can also lead to fatal creativity in the use of images, to the "too much of a good thing" syndrome. Remember that while reading a comparison, the reader must move momentarily from your straightforward text into the world of the comparison—to the barnyard, to the bread by the fire, to the "little snobberies" of life. Ideally, this little excursion is for both the pleasure of making the connection and for the greater understanding that it provides. But too many excursions, even if the comparisons are apt and clever, can be overwhelming and may even alienate a reader. Write comparisons when they seem natural to you. Try not to force them. Try not to overdo them. In a description of an old man's face, for example, it may be clever and picturesque to compare the drooping eyelids to half-shut garage doors, but then to go on comparing the forehead to a landing strip, the nose to a ski run, the lips to candy kisses, and the cheeks to cherries, as one student did, is to go too far for this poor, "oversimilied" old man.

For both reader and writer, images are a shared pleasure, but beware of the fatal attraction to them that may leave your reader feeling abandoned.

PRACTICE

1. Make up a simile for Lyn Capodanno (pages 7–8), as her parents desert her at the college door; for Pat Hourihan (pages 43–45), as she discovers that her little boy has been "snatched"; for Mike Brangiforte (pages 220–221) as he is ordered to clean up the demolished Wishbone display.
2. Choose a particular example of figurative language by E. B. White (page 340), Murray Ross (page 46), Edwin Diamond (page 189), or Martin Luther King, Jr. (page 235), and explain how it works in the essay.
3. Complete the following with at least one original comparison:

   a. As happy as a ______________ (not "a lark," please).
   b. He was so surprised, he ______________ .
   c. He was as fit as a ______________ .
   d. Like a ______________ , the baby reached for her mother.
   e. He felt as unprepared as ______________ .
   f. The dress was as white as ______________ .

4. Consider the following situations and explain how you felt or how you *might* have felt if they had happened:

   a. You graduated from high school.
   b. You went out on your first date.
   c. You were stood up on your wedding day.
   d. You insulted a friend, unknowingly, within his hearing.
   e. You lost a loved one.

5. Rewrite the following paragraph, removing the overused comparisons and adding more original ones, if they are appropriate.

I would consider myself an overly nervous person. Much of the time I feel like I'm going to flip out. It's an out of sight experience, no matter where I am. When I'm in a big crowd, I feel totally crushed, lost, and scared, and I want to go back home. But even when I'm safe at home, I'm as nervous as a cat. I don't eat well, pecking at my food like a bird, and I never sleep, waking up regularly. Mr. Sandman doesn't put me to sleep. I know I need to get a handle on the stress in my life, but I keep waiting for some bright idea about how to pull it off. Some new ideas could sure perk me up. It'd be a real blast to get at least one full night in slumberland.

FOR YOUR OWN PAPER

1. Read through your essay, being alert for places where a comparison or a particular image might help to illuminate your meaning or help the reader better to understand your feelings. Ask yourself what something was like, what something felt like to someone else, or how you felt about something. If a comparison seems natural to you and you have not already overused your "quota" of comparisons, *and* you have not used some other comparison that could harm the effect of the new one, work it in.

2. Try to remove overly familiar or possibly mixed comparisons, substituting more original ones or making a simple statement without any comparison at all. Too much comparison itself becomes an affectation and can draw too much attention away from your meaning.

Leaving a Final Impression

An essay should not simply stop, as if the writer suddenly ran out of ink or inspiration. The reader should not be left with a futile search for the missing last page. But, unfortunately, the conclusion is often the place where the writer fades away or gives up. It is too often the place where the writer sighs, saying, "I've had enough," and escapes off to dinner or to bed.

It is normal for your energy to wane when you are so near a deadline, especially if you have been laboring over the long course of writing and rewriting the main part of a paper. All those little steps in the process, all those revisions and corrections take time, and time takes its toll. But, remember, the reader will probably *not* be worn out, especially if your labor has so far produced a good essay. The reader has not spent anywhere near the time that you have spent on your essay and may well be interested in your final comments. Your conclusion is the last chance you will have to make an impression. This impression is the one the reader will carry away, to dinner or to bed.

Allow time—not tired-out 2 A.M. time—but fresh, early morning time for writing a good conclusion. Rather than frustration, confusion, and unanswered questions, give your reader a sense of completeness. Read your whole paper over and pick up hints from your own writing; then consider the options.

You might, for example, simply summarize the main points of your paper, particularly if the discussion has been long and complex and if the reader would benefit from a recapitulation. Consider the following conclusion, taken from an article analyzing the effects of breaking up the North American forests into smaller and smaller pieces:

> Continued monitoring of bird populations, further studies of individual species, and analysis of the particular effects of breaking up the forests are necessary. But even now, action can be taken before our growing human population intrudes on all remaining woodland. Most important is maintaining some very large tracts of unbroken forest and, if necessary, leaving clusters of forested areas where fragmentation may be unavoidable. Forested corridors connecting these wooded areas and "buffer" zones surrounding forested tracts could also help protect these precious areas and their breeding species while necessary research continues. The larger the forest interiors and the less the edge, the greater the opportunity for a rich variety of breeding birds.

(Notice that this conclusion highlights important points: what *needs* to be done as time goes on and what *can* be done now "while necessary research continues." The final sentence links the goal for the forests with the other important goal—"a rich variety of breeding birds.")

Your conclusion may also return to the specific content or to an image of the introduction, thus suggesting a control of the subject and an awareness of exactly where you are. Consider the different types of introductory paragraphs on the question, "What would I do if the college closed tomorrow?" (See pages 395–397.)

For the one that opens with a narrative about the search for a parking space, for example (page 395), the student could return to the story line:

> And about that $20.00 towing fee. It was $25.00 and the garage is at the other end of town. I wish this assignment could be more than a "what if." Then I wouldn't have to worry about another $25.00 tomorrow. I'd be long gone.

For the introduction pointing out the great importance of college (page 397), the student could echo the seriousness in the conclusion:

> As you can see, college is no laughing matter for me, and I'm amazed I was able to come up with any alternatives at all. No, not trips to Bermuda, not a fantasy marriage to a millionaire, not a month-long nap, just other colleges. They may cost a little more, and they may be a little further from home, but I'd go anyway, just as soon as they let me in. I'd hope to start classes at my new school probably the day after tomorrow.

For the introduction using the image of the cauliflower (page 396), a mention of the cauliflower or the cabbage may get some "double duty" out of Mark Twain:

> I had a hard time getting into college in the first place, so I know it wouldn't be easy to move quickly to some place else, even the smaller places I discussed here. But if I am really a high school cabbage determined to get my degree as a cauliflower, I really have no choice. I have to start looking for a new garden to grow in.

Your conclusion may also speculate about the future. The following example is from an article telling of memories stirred by a return to the monastery of Capistrano after 25 years:

> Capistrano is a place I hope to see yet again, if I have the time. Maybe I'll take our children there. And every March, I'll make a point of looking for reports on the swallows' safe return, for with their coming back comes a hope—for renewal, for an ultimate sense in things, for the possibility of discovering again what may only temporarily be gone.

(This conclusion thus brings into the future a paper about memories of the past.)

The conclusion may also ask a provocative question, as in the brief conclusion of an article on Gilbert White, the English parson of Selborne who died in 1793 but who, because of his detailed study of his own environment, still seems to be alive at the parsonage:

> Did I then hear a noise like the shutting of a watch-case? Or did I simply imagine it again the way Mr. White wrote it?

(In this conclusion, the question refers back to White's own comparison of the sound of a swallow catching an insect to the sound of the shutting of a watchcase and thus acknowledges his lingering presence again. In the last line, White still has prominence.)

Particularly if your paper is argumentative, your conclusion may save the strongest point for the end, as in the conclusion in an article that tells of a utopia where good writing would get the support it deserves:

> And finally, it would be a place where the systems—schools at all levels—would support good writing, not by adding further studies or by investing in the newest magic hat, but by hiring and rewarding teachers who know and care about writing. It is distressing to read in the 1983 report *A Nation at Risk* that half of the recently hired teachers of English are unqualified for the job. For many years to come, no study of the unsteady state of the art, no magic hat (even with a magician tossed in as a bonus) will save the prose in these classes. Good writing and good teaching of writing do not come by sleight of hand. Each one is a *profession,* requiring all that is suggested by that word.

(This conclusion summarizes what is wrong, stresses it, and makes some suggestions for improvement.)

If persuasion to generate action is also a purpose of the paper, your conclusion may make some specific suggestions, as in an article discussing the dangers awaiting northern migrant birds as they return to wintering spots in Central and South America:

> We have long known about the dangers of extended migrations, those 12,000 to 20,000-mile round-trips across continents and oceans. We need to think more about the even worse dangers that await the birds after landing.

(Drawing on the grim statistics about migrant birds, this conclusion tries to persuade readers of the problems in our own backyards and suggests a subject for future work.)

All of these types of conclusions—summary, return to the introduction, speculation about the future, provocative question, a final strong point (climax), suggestion for action—may also be combined in various ways. A brief summary of major arguments, for example, could conclude with a final, strong one. Speculation about the future could lead to a suggestion for action or easily to a question.

In some ways, the conclusion is a "release point," a place to let your creativity loose. It is not the place to settle down, worn out and bored. The reader will sense your loss of interest and, unfortunately, share it.

It is important, therefore, to avoid the major problems associated with conclusions. Avoid a tedious and overexplicit summary, for example or the unnecessary recapping of a short, simply structured paper that the reader has just finished reading:

> Thus these are the three reasons I feel like quitting college. I want to make some money, I want to explore working, and I want to take some time for travel.

Repetition can lose the reader, but so also can the introduction of something that is too new, as interesting as an entirely new direction may seem to you. You will send the reader off on a wild idea chase, *away* from what you have been writing about for several paragraphs or pages. The paper on the reasons for leaving college previously mentioned should not end like this (unless this topic appeared somewhere earlier):

> I have always wanted to spend time on clothes. Fashion magazines and keeping up with the latest styles really interest me. It would be fun to cruise the malls checking out the window displays.

And, probably most important of all, it is important to avoid apology, defensiveness, and explanations in a conclusion. This is not the place to brag, to flatter, or to appeal for mercy; this is not the place for true confessions. All of these approaches destroy the reader's confidence in everything you have been saying. (Keep this in mind, especially when you are taking examinations.) Some examples of these approaches follow.

An Apology

> If only I didn't have this after-school job, I would have been able to come up with much more on what I might do if the college closed tomorrow. I really am very interested in this topic, but I'm sorry I haven't been able to put the time into thinking about it the way I would like to. I have done the best I possibly can, though.

A Defense

> You may think that writing on what I would do if the college closed tomorrow is easy, but you are sadly mistaken. I had so many ideas on this paper, I have only been able to scratch the surface, especially in the short time allowed to us. But you shouldn't take my work as superficial. I think I have come up with some

interesting ideas. Sometime, when I can think more clearly, I'll try to write on it again.

An Explanation

I'm sure you are aware that students have lots to write about this topic. I have a lot to say too, but I have had a hard time getting my ideas down on paper. I *always* have this problem when I write my first papers for my English teachers, but I expect that with your instruction, I'll be able to write much better for you as the course goes on.

At the end of your paper, don't just stop or give up; consider the options, try several different approaches, and avoid leaving the wrong impression. Leave the reader secure at the end, not besieged with doubt or the urge to escape.

PRACTICE

1. Study the conclusions in the essays by Carbone (pages 15–17), Alves (pages 138–141), Brown (pages 131–133), Beecher (pages 186–188), and Grasso (pages 292–294). Identify what type of conclusion each one is and how it relates to the introduction and to the body of the essay. After you have read the essays, write an alternative conclusion for one of them.
2. Look up and copy three conclusions that seem particularly effective to you and explain why they are effective. (You might consider analyzing them in conjunction with the introductions chosen for the practice on page 399.)
3. Evaluate the following conclusions and rewrite at least one of them.

   a. This one is for the paper beginning with introduction (A) on page 398:

   So, as you can see, an office job seems good to me right now. But I'm still not so sure.

   b. This one is for the paper beginning with introduction (B) on page 398:

   If I had more time, I'd do more reading on Jackson, and I certainly plan to this summer. But all I can say now is that he certainly was a courageous man.

c. This one is for the paper beginning with introduction (C) on page 398:

My summer was basically good because I was able to pay off my parents.

d. This one is for the paper beginning with introduction (D) on page 399:

I want to become a better student, but I have to continue to overcome the hindrances that slow me down.

e. This one is for the paper beginning with introduction (E) on page 399:

Thus, as you can see, suicide is a major social problem, as are homelessness, AIDS, and declining SAT scores.

FOR YOUR OWN PAPER

1. Read your conclusion and try to evaluate it critically. What kind of conclusion is it? Is it the best possible kind for the paper you have written? Does it leave the reader with the final impression you were aiming for? Have you given it the attention it needs?
2. Read your introduction and then immediately afterward read your conclusion. Do they seem appropriate and in harmony with one another? How do they relate to one another?
3. Try writing an alternative type of conclusion to the one you have already written. Try to make it at least as good as the original one and then determine which one you prefer to include in the final draft.

Putting It All Together

This stage of writing is in some ways practical, almost mechanical, but, ironically, it is at the same time unpredictable and subtle—a fine tuning. It's the time for you to give your essay a final, close reading before your paper is read by someone else.

On the practical level, it is the time to think about format: sometimes simply making the manuscript look good in your own eyes, sometimes responding to the particular requirements and quirks of the expected reader. Does it need a title page? Is the title on the first page? Does it need a blank correction sheet? Are sources acknowledged according to the correct system? Must the paper be folded in half?

It is the time to check the typewriter or computer to ensure that the paper will be legible. A note scribbled in the upper right-hand corner of page one—"Sorry, I need a new ribbon!"—is not encouraging to a reader. Practically, too, you need to check the overall appearance of the manuscript. Are minor corrections clearly made in black ink, rather than set off in day-glo colors? Are pages with extensive rewriting and correcting retyped? Would you want someone to hand this manuscript to you to read? At midnight?

Mechanical adjustments such as these usually involve little more than some free time before the final copy is passed in. The fine tuning, however, is less predictable, less manageable. The adjustments may be as simple as adding commas, filling in dates, or checking spelling. But they also may be time consuming and anything but simple. For style alone, they may require careful rethinking of those particular concerns already agonized over in earlier stages of the process. It will probably be necessary once again to cut what isn't needed, to redesign awkward constructions, to judge those persistent adverbs and adjectives, to replace vague verbs with more accurate ones, to deflate stuffy vocabulary, to vary sentence lengths, to shape parallel patterns, to build *up* sentences and paragraphs, and to weave in connectors.

And you may want to read aloud, with some enthusiasm, as if the reader were present. The writer must listen again for the bad notes and fix them before the reader gets an earache. The writer must hear and retune the words that sound too much alike (e.g., from "John and Carl were impressed with my expression of ideas in class," to "John and Carl admired my class comments"), the ineffective clusters of similar sounds (e.g., from "The biggest downer on our spring break was getting done doing our research papers," to "The biggest problem of our spring break was finishing our research papers"), and the empty series of prepositional phrases (e.g., from "There was a flag that danced in the breeze in tune with the music of the band of the local high school," to "A flag danced to the military music of the local high school band"). The writer must listen for rhythm, making sure that the misplaced beats do not stamp out the meaning (e.g., from "I have a very strong memory of the perfume that she used to wear and of the baked bread in the kitchen, and at Christmas of the way our home was fixed up by her," to "I remember well the perfume she wore, the bread she baked, and the decorations she put up at Christmas"). Writing is not only for the eye but also for the ear of that quiet reader curled up on the couch.

And, as the early section, "Reading with a Critical Eye," suggests, changes, even if they are only for style, may beget other changes. When an insect, however small, disturbs a spiderweb, the entire network responds. When a stone breaks through the smooth surface of a pond, the ripples, however subtle, reach the shore. A change in any part of the system may mean that changes will occur in the whole system. The same might be said of essays at this late stage of writing. A new word here may require a new image there, which may require a new sentence here (e.g., if Pat Hourihan's son has no longer been taken by "body snatchers," she cannot return to them in the conclusion; see page 45). A shift in title may mean altering the images within the paper (e.g., if Edwin Diamond's television is no longer "Social," it may not so easily be a "guest" in his house; see page 191). The removal of a line or a word will require removal of all later references back to them (e.g., if Frank Conroy removes the example of the black shoeshine men, he cannot explicate the story later; see page 311). Something as large as a shift in thesis will probably require changes in every paragraph. Each adjustment may put the whole essay out of focus, requiring you to bring it back into focus. The essay must be consistent within itself.

It is here that many writers get tired, bored by the work, bored by what the paper is saying, or bored by the whole project. It is also here that many writers fail; it is where much writing that could have been excellent remains simply good or becomes worse than it once was. The work at this stage is the difference between the hasty draft typed directly from notes (or even the rewrite that never quite got straightened out) and the carefully crafted essay by a persistent writer. This is not the time to give up, no matter how difficult the remedies may seem. As Thoreau said, "At 'em again." And again, if necessary.

Look at one student's final struggles with her title and her opening words:

Vindicated Ventures ~~Vacation~~ Vacation Vacation ~~SUMMER ODYSSEY~~ES ~~Variations~~ Vibrations Validations Vagaries (a departure from the normal, expected or logical order)

This year our vacation had two parts, one of which I looked forward to, and one of which I didn't. It was my husband's year to choose where we would go for the first week ~~This year was my husband's turn time to choose~~ ~~for the first week~~, and he chose Elderhostel, which didn't do much for me when we attended one a couple years ago.

Alice Westerhold Kahn

Before being closely read by someone else, the writer ideally needs to ignore the paper for a while, then to read and reread it many times—from beginning to end, and possibly from end to beginning. (On final reading, some writers go over each sentence independently, from the last to the first, testing each one for meaning and correctness). If a word is still not quite right, it needs to be replaced (possibly with the help of a *Thesaurus*). If a comparison is not working, it needs to be fixed. If, unhappily, the paper is still not making its point, it needs to be rewritten—from the beginning.

Be as satisfied as you can be with your own work *before* you submit it to the judgment of others. You'll be far better able to weigh their comments, far more willing to benefit from their criticisms, and far freer to enjoy their compliments.

PRACTICE

1. Read the following passages aloud and then rewrite them to make them more effective. Look for anything that makes them sound awkward or that confuses meaning.

   a. There was a grapevine that dropped down from the side of the barn in Springfield.
   b. My main problems in my reading are probably due to a difficult experience I had in the class of an instructor in the second grade.
   c. This attitude typifies a certain type of typical problem.
   d. I am feeling some certain confidence in my ability to cope with most of the many ramifications of the calamity.
   e. I usually stop and then go on to ask myself if this could possibly be some sort of character disorder that I am displaying.
   f. The kids would be playing video games all the time that I wanted them not to be going near the TV.
   g. My most serious responsibility in my job included pumping gas in the evenings.
   h. Every day began with us gathering with everyone around the long tables in the back of the cafeteria.

2. The following paragraphs are already clear and readable, but try rewriting one of them to make it even better.

   But as those halcyon days continued, I began to notice a change in our degree of enthusiasm. Like the gradual diminishing of daylight after the summer solstice, our hunger for excitement lessened. More of our time was spent at home. Afternoons consisted of lunch at Macdonald's followed by half-hearted strolls down the beach. I didn't bother getting more suntan lotion, even though I knew we were out. Our once trusty automobile was finding it difficult to lead us to a good time. (Jonathan Hart)

The 1961 Plymouth Plymouth Valiant was my first drive. It carried me from my high school prom to June of this year. Outside, the car was shiny and fun. It was white and overflowing with chrome. There was a false spare tire on the trunk and the fenders flared up to form wings. The front grill and bumper joined to give the Valiant what appeared to be a permanent smirk. Wherever I went, the dash-mounted fan blew fresh air in my face and Frank Sinatra would inevitably be singing "On the Sunny side of the Street" on the AM radio. The car made me behave like Ozzie Nelson. I didn't want to; I had to. I waved at people I didn't know, and never once broke the speed limit. I let people cross the street at every opportunity, smiling and waving in spite of myself. If I got cut off, I wouldn't even curse; I just figured that person was in a hurry. I was the car; I'm sure of it. The Plymouth was kind, fun and innocent and so was I when I drove it. (David Marsan)

3. Look closely at this final version of the writing on energy by E. B. White and the earlier draft on page 385. What can you tell about the kinds of changes he makes?

Just the day-to-day activity of the concerned citizens bent on solving the energy crisis is itself a great drain on fuel: lights burn far into the night in the halls where the planners do their planning and the debaters hold their debates. I drove over to South Brooksville not long ago to attend an evening forum on nuclear power, sponsored by the public library. To get over and back, I had to travel twenty-five miles, which must have burned up a gallon and a half of gas. And the hall had to be lighted. And the representative from the Central Maine Power Company had to burn up a great deal more gas than I did, because he came a long distance for the powwow. People in this age are adjusted to the free use of power; they do not readily change their habits, even for a power shortage. On my way home over the road after the meeting, I noticed that most of the houses I passed were brightly lit—people sitting up late to watch television, with the oil-burner grinding away in the basement and the water pump leaping into action at the bidding of the pressure tank and the hot-water heater eating up the kilowatts in answer to the thermostat. A hundred years ago, the denizens of those same houses would have been abed long since. They would have had neither power nor a power shortage—merely a long night's sleep. We don't really know yet whether we can have energy all day and Johnny Carson all night. It just isn't clear.

The Central Maine Power Company feels very good about nuclear generating plants, is not worried about radiation or accidents, and is proposing to construct a plant on Sears Island in Penobscot Bay. (It has also acquired an option on four hundred acres of land on Cape Rosier, just in case.) A group calling itself Safe Power for Maine takes the opposite position and is disturbed that nuclear plants should be built while scientists are still in disagreement and before anyone has found a way to dispose of the nuclear waste safely. A Brooksville man who keeps goats got up in meeting and asked why, if nuclear plants were so safe, he had received a letter from a research firm employed by the power company inquiring as to the whereabouts of his goats. Mr. Randazza, the C.M.P. man, replied that it was a routine inquiry. "We must know where the goats are," he said, "so corrective measures could be taken if something went wrong." Iodine can contaminate milk, he acknowledged. But he was cheerful about the prospect. You would simply put the animals on a controlled diet, he said, and after about forty days the radioactivity would be gone.

FOR YOUR OWN PAPER

1. Some writers find the following checklist convenient for working through final revisions. See if you have addressed the important matters listed here.

   a. Does this paper fulfill what is being asked of you or what you are asking of yourself?
   b. What is the main purpose of the paper?
   c. What is the thesis or main point of your paper? Write it in one *complete* sentence.
   d. Is the paper primarily exposition, argumentation, persuasion, description, or narration?
   e. Is the organization of the entire paper and the order of information in paragraphs and sentences effectively planned?
   f. What is your attitude, your tone, in this piece?
   g. For what audience is the paper written?
   h. What is the intended effect on these readers?
   i. Is the introduction engaging enough for the readers to want to go on? What kind of introduction is it?
   j. Do you back up your general statements with appropriate details?
   k. Can you justify every word that you use, or can you cut and still make your meaning clear?
   l. Are ideas connected to one another so that the readers can follow your directions?
   m. Is your attitude and your vocabulary consistent with what you are trying to say? Are they appropriate for your readers?
   n. Do you properly acknowledge information gathered from outside sources?
   o. Given your purposes, are sentences sufficiently varied in length and form?

p. Do you occasionally use a comparison to enhance meaning? Is it appropriate to your meaning? Have you avoided triteness and mixing of images?
q. Does the conclusion leave the readers still interested, still thinking?
r. Have you corrected all mechanical errors in grammar, punctuation, spelling?
s. Are verbs and nouns sharp and clear?
t. Are unnecessary adverbs and adjectives eliminated?
u. Are series written in parallel patterns?
v. Are words containing similar sounds intentional, not coincidental?
w. Have you evaluated the effect of a series of words beginning with the same sound?
x. Are prepositional phrases properly absorbed into sentences?
y. Does the rhythm of the writing support the meaning, emphasizing important words, speeding up or slowing down where haste or hesitation are needed?
z. Do you like what you have written?

2. Read your whole paper aloud as if you were delivering it in front of an audience. Place the emphasis where you feel it should be; listen to the rhythms of your own writing. Identify all spots that need further tuning up and work on getting them right. If you have time, put your paper away for at least a few days and then read it aloud again. At this point, you may also ask a benevolent critic to read it to you or to become a listener for you. (For an additional discussion of reading your own writing, reread the section, "Reading with a Critical Eye" on pages 390–393.)

Reading: Being A Reader; Being Read

*"Oh wad some power the giftie gie us
To see oursels as others see us!"*

Robert Burns

This chapter is divided into two parts—"Being a Reader" and "Being Read."

The first part involves an activity that is not only valuable but also indispensable for writers—reading other people's writing. It involves reading and learning from professionals, being pulled out of (and possibly above) yourself by focusing closely on their talents and their faults. And it involves learning with fellow students of writing, as well as sharing with them their struggle to learn what works best and what needs to be improved or abandoned.

The second part focuses on the main purpose of all this listing, drafting, revising, correcting, and polishing. It describes the often difficult experience of subjecting a paper to the scrutiny and possible criticism of others and makes some suggestions for getting the best out of this experience.

Writers have much to learn from reading the works of others. They also have much to learn from having *their* work read by others.

Being a Reader

"A good style simply does not form unless you absorb half a dozen top flight authors every year."

F. Scott Fitzgerald

One of the best ways to learn about writing is to *read* the works of other writers—professionals and amateurs. Read all the time; read cereal boxes and Shakespeare, committee reports and E. B. White. Read the way writers read, with antennae fully extended, feeling out not only *what* the writer is saying but also *how* it is being said. Learn to avoid the habits you like least in others—a tone you find offensive (flip, condescending, whimpering), a stylistic habit (using too many dashes, making all sentences the same length), or humor that you find unfunny (sneering at opponents, hurting others for the sake of the joke). Search out the writers you admire, whom you would most like to "sound" like. Read them constantly, every morning over your coffee and every night before you go to bed. Experience what they do and don't do.

The effects, which may be even unconscious, may be quite remarkable, as Mark Twain describes in some detail (notice the extended comparison to building):

> However, let us try guessing. Let us guess that whenever we read a sentence and like it, we unconsciously store it away in our model-chamber; and it goes with the myriad of its fellows to the building, brick by brick, of the eventual edifice which we call our style. And let us guess that whenever we run across other forms—bricks—whose colour, or some other defect, offends us, we unconsciously reject these, and so one never finds them in our edifice. If I have subjected myself to any training processes, and no doubt I have, it must have been in this unconscious or half-conscious fashion. I think it unlikely that deliberate and consciously methodical training is usual with the craft. I think it likely that the training most in use is of this unconscious sort, and is guided and governed and made by and by unconsciously systematic, by an automatically working taste—a taste which selects and rejects without asking you for any help, and patiently and steadily improves itself without troubling you to approve or applaud. Yes, and likely enough when the structure is at last pretty well up, and attracts attention, *you* feel complimented, whereas you didn't build it, and didn't even consciously superintend. Yes; one notices, for instance, that long, involved sentences confuse him, and that he is obliged to re-read them to get the sense. Unconsciously, then he rejects that brick. Unconsciously he accustoms himself to writing short sentences as a rule. At times he may indulge himself with a

> long one, but he will make sure that there are no folds in it, no vaguenesses, no parenthetical interruptions of its view as a whole; when he is done with it, it won't be a sea-serpent, with half of its arches under water, it will be a torch light procession.

In the above passage, Twain argues for the subtle benefits of reading, benefits unknown even to the writer, but it is also possible to learn some things deliberately from other writers. Imitate them in close detail or more casually and in spirit. Don't be at all concerned about giving up your own "creativity" or about losing your own "voice." Writers do not spin words entirely out of themselves; no writer composes in a linguistic vacuum. For better or for worse, we live surrounded by words—words on television, words on the radio, words in song lyrics, and printed words in newspapers, magazines, books, and greeting cards. Some of these words are responsibly used and carefully considered. Other words would give "trash" a bad name; sometimes words, especially spoken ones, come all too cheap. We are, however, influenced by them, no matter what their quality. You are what you eat, and in a sense, you write what you read (or hear).

Do what professional writers have done for centuries before you. Learn from your predecessors. As the twentieth-century poet T. S. Eliot points out, great literature is a combination of tradition and the individual talent. Simply studying the writing of the past is not enough, but neither is an uninformed talent. Good writing knows where it fits and where it intends to go. Consider that Virgil composed his *Aeneid* with Homer's *Iliad* and *Odyssey* close at hand. No, he did not plagiarize. He learned and wrote his own poem all the better for what Homer could teach him. The Welsh poet Dylan Thomas explains that he wrote "endless imitations, though I never thought them to be imitations, but, rather, wonderfully original things, like eggs laid by tigers." And in his long poem, "Station Island," the modern Irish poet, Seamus Heaney, acknowledges his debt to the James Joyce figure in the poem, and then receives permission from him to go on by himself:

> "I know, I know, I know, I know," he said,
> "but you have to try to make sense of what comes.
> Remember everything and keep your head."

All good writers listen well to the words of other writers, remember, and keep their heads.

Still another way to learn by reading is to read the "works-in-progress" of others—the major activity of writing workshops. This kind of reading allows you to share in the process itself and not only to study the finished product. In general, take every opportunity to read what others write and read carefully, sympathetically, with the same willingness to understand that you would want from readers of your own manuscripts. Avoid cruel attacks or rude dismissals. Do not always assume that your problem in reading is because there is a fault in the writing; simply identify where *you* had a problem reading.

More particularly, look for the parts of the paper that work and the parts that falter. Make corrections, ask questions, and, by all means, give compliments. Criticism can be expressed in the form of suggestion or of a possible remedy, not as a reduction of the efforts of the writer. You are probably unaware of what went into producing the paper. You are probably unaware of the source of the writer's problems. Be as helpful as you can. (Further suggestions for reading others' papers may be found on page 451, and some sample comments may be found on page 364.)

In this process, you may, in fact, be doing as much for your own writing as for the writer's whose work you are reading. It is much easier to face the errors in someone else's work than it is to face up to those very same errors in your own. You can set new goals for yourself by identifying what someone else did successfully. You can learn some new approaches by helping someone else out of a difficulty.

PRACTICE

1. Write an imitation of the following paragraph from an essay, "On Travel by Train," by J. B. Priestley. Begin with, "There is one type of character. . . ." (The woman portrayed here may well have her own "favorite" type; you might consider writing a paragraph in her voice.)

   > There is one type of traveller that never fails to rouse my quick hatred. She is a large, middle-aged woman, with a rasping voice and a face of brass. Above all things, she loves to invade smoking compartments that are already comfortably filled with a quiet company of smokers; she will come bustling in, shouting over her shoulder at her last victim, a prostrate porter, and, laden with packages of all maddening shapes and sizes, she will glare defiantly about her until some unfortunate has given up his seat. She is often accompanied by some sort of contemptible, whining cur that is only one degree less offensive than its mistress. From the moment that she has wedged herself in there will be no more peace in the carriage, but simmering hatred, and everywhere dark looks and muttered threats. But every one knows her. Courtesy and modesty perished in the world of travel on the day when she took her first journey; but it will not be long before she is in hourly danger of extinction, for there are strong men in our midst.

2. Find an essayist either in this book or elsewhere and write something "in the manner of." Try to identify the noteworthy characteristics and to incorporate them into your imitation.

3. Find an essayist whom you particularly admire, read at least one whole collection of essays by this writer, and write an analysis of both their content and style. Which aspects of this writing would you most like to emulate?

4. Search out a piece of nonfiction that you believe you could possibly have written. Try writing a similar piece.

5. Find a piece of nonfiction that you wish you had written and explain why you find it so appealing. Are there any aspects of the piece that you might be able to adapt to your own writing at this point?

6. About the manuscript of a fellow student of writing, answer the following questions.

   a. What is the main point?
   b. Why do you think this piece was written?
   c. What reaction do you think the writer is hoping for from you: anger, shock, agreement, action, or laughter?
   d. Were you an appropriate audience for this piece?
   e. What personality or "voice" emerges from this piece?
   f. Where is the piece "working" best? Explain why you think so.
   g. Where does this piece need more attention from the writer? (Consider where your mind wandered or where you felt "deserted" by the writer.) Do you have any specific suggestions overall or in particular?
   h. Was there any place where you wanted more information or detail?
   i. Did you make any connections that the writer failed to make? If so, suggest them to the writer.
   j. Would you want to read another similar piece by this writer? Explain.
   k. Do you see any particular stylistic faults or virtues?
   l. Did any particular details occur to you? (Try "conjuring up" the piece a few days after reading it. What stands out?)

FOR YOUR OWN WRITING

From writers you have read—both professional and amateur—make a list of things you most admire in their work. Consider what it is that you admire and what you might successfully want to adapt in your own writing. Read your own manuscript to see if there are places where your writing could benefit by learning from others.

Being Read

All of the work you have done on your essay has been for one purpose—to be read by someone else. Many writers find this stage of writing most difficult, and it is easy to understand why. For the writer who has put little energy or thought into the effort, this stage may be a cause for embarrassment; the anxiety is about being "found out." For the writer who has expended much energy and many hours of thought, this reading may also be a cause for anxiety; the concern is that the effort will not be appreciated and that the diligence has not yet produced good writing. (This writer may say, "No, I just tossed it together last night," rather than let readers know that such a "feeble" accomplishment took so much work.) Some students see the comments of the instructor and of fellow readers in a workshop as nothing short of torture ["trashing," as one student vividly put it].

Keep in mind, however, that many professional writers do not enjoy this stage of writing either, particularly at the very beginning. It is possible to become more accustomed to being read, but even for someone as accomplished as Virginia Woolf, being reviewed was a constant agony. In her *Diary,* she wrote:

> I hope this week will see me through the reviews.
>
> So all the critics split off and the wretched author who tries to keep control of them is torn asunder.
>
> I mean by that they don't see that I'm after something interesting. So that makes me suspect that I'm not.
>
> What is the use of saying one is indifferent to reviews when positive praise, though mingled with blame, gives one such a start on, that instead of feeling dried up, one feels, on the contrary, flooded with ideas?

One way to relieve some of this normal anxiety is to have a benevolent and honest friend read the paper before you give it to an instructor or to a group. But, unless you are planning to collect your essays for posthumous publication or to have them destroyed upon your demise (or possibly to take an "Incomplete" in a course), you will *need* to have your writing read. If the paper is a one-time contribution for a grade in a course, read by the instructor who assigned it, it is almost too late to worry. Hand it in and hope for the best grade you can get. If, however, this reading stage is another step in the long process of producing a polished paper, you need to anticipate some of the reactions.

"But this is all just opinion!" protested a student who was amazed that readers disagreed with one another about her paper. Yes, it *is* opinion. Some opinions are better than others. Some are more helpful than others. Some certainly are more pleasing than others. But reading is always subjective. Not all readers will read your work in the same way. Some will not understand what you are trying to say; others will not *like* what you are trying to say, even if they *do* understand. Some will disapprove of the very things you like best; others will like the parts that you thought were failures. Some will not like *you,* the personality that comes through in your writing; others will like you and everything you do, no matter what you think. Professional writers are aware of these strange and inconsistent possibilities. They often get entirely opposite reactions to a single manuscript submitted for publication: "Your manuscript is fine, but the personal-experience pieces are by far the best in this collection" may be followed by, "Except for the personal-experience pieces, this manuscript is excellent."

The task for all writers is to be able to listen—to criticism as well as to praise—and to select what seems most likely to make the writing better. As in the fable of the boy, his father, and the donkey in which, in an attempt to please every critic along the road, the donkey finally falls off a bridge and into a stream, you can't take all criticisms to heart. You can't please everyone all of the time. Listen to what others say but be sure to please yourself first and last.

PRACTICE

1. How do you react to the following comments from readers? Consider their tone and their value to the writer.

   a. This paper is really good. I like it.
   b. This is terrible! You should be ashamed of yourself!
   c. I like everything but paragraph 2, where you seem to drift away from the story and into a medical report. How do you *feel* about your father's disease? Could you make your search through medical journals part of your effort to cope with his suffering?
   d. You get a lot of mileage out of a basically simple-minded subject here.
   e. I think I'm the wrong reader for this one. I never go to movies, and I have very little interest in stars, awards, theaters, colorization, or anything else to do with movies. Don't get me wrong. I did find your paper readable, and even interesting when you started complaining about colorization of black and white classics, but the subject in general is a real "turn-off" for me.

f. See what you think of dropping your entire first paragraph. Your writing seems to get stronger in the second paragraph, so why spend so much time on unnecessary background in paragraph 1?
g. I'm sorry, but I have no idea what you're talking about here. I can't tell if I'm supposed to admire the representative because he moved in when the schools were in trouble, or if I'm supposed to see him as a busybody who should've let the teachers have their say. Have *you* made up your mind yet?
h. This account of your own recent struggles with cancer is moving and frightening, and you have my sympathy and good wishes. As a piece of writing, though, it leaves me a little confused. Why are you confiding all of these intimate details to us? What are we supposed to learn from them? Are you sure you're ready to write on this topic yet?
i. I think I liked what you were trying to say about your high-school reunion. I particularly liked your description of the "prize committee," but the run-on sentences, the missing capital letters, the misspellings, and the typos left me feeling a little irritated.
j. Keep it up! This paper is funny from beginning to end.

2. Consider the following passage, written about a job as gift shop manager at an amusement park, and the comments from a writing workshop class.

> My "easy" summer job started off simple enough. Business in the park was fairly slow during the early season, and I was allowed to spend my days reading a book in air conditioning unless, of course, the occasional customer came to the shop. However, as the days grew longer and more hectic and the summer reached its peak, I realized that my days of rest and relaxation were over. (Sue Ruhmann)

a. The quotation marks around "easy" make the writing seem affected.
b. When is the early season?
c. Cut "fairly."
d. Needs more detail for the reader to feel the relaxation that you lost.
e. Bury the "however."
f. When is the peak?
g. Any interesting customers?
h. Rest and relaxation are clichés.
i. Where is the air conditioning? Are you really *in* it?
j. It reads flat; try to liven it up.
k. Drop "I realized that."
l. Too many "my days."
m. Avoid passive: "I was allowed." Who allowed?
n. About how many days reading; reading what?

o. What did the customers want?
p. How long did it take you to realize that the rest was over?
q. What was hectic?
r. Show, don't tell!

Which of the preceding comments seem valid to you? Which seem the most helpful? Which are not detailed enough? Using the comments that seem to be the most valuable, rewrite this paragraph.

FOR YOUR OWN WRITING

1. Give your typed manuscript to a trustworthy friend and ask for comments and suggestions. You might ask him or her to answer the questions on page 451. Which comments do you find most helpful; which are disappointing or even incorrect? Which parts of your paper are you now determined to leave unchanged, no matter what anyone thinks? Rewrite where you now think it is advisable.
2. If you have the opportunity, submit the manuscript to a large group of readers. Ask yourself the same questions about their reactions.
3. How would you describe your own reactions to these "reviews in miniature?"

Reaching a Larger Audience

"*A work is never* complete . . . *but* abandoned."

Paul Valery

If, after all the drafting, revising, rethinking, reading, evaluating, and rewriting again, you are still interested in carrying on with the process, your next logical step is to try reaching a larger audience by getting published. Should you decide to move on to the outside market, you will need once again to consider options.

With the entire world of potential readers in mind and not only a course instructor or fellow students, you will have to evaluate just what it is you have created and what you might seriously be able to do with it. Does the piece fit into a category—political, natural history, science, travel, and so on? Does it espouse a particular point of view—feminist, liberal, gay, religious, family, single? A painful question to ask is—is it truly worth publishing, even though it may be well written? It may, in fact, be a worthwhile contribution to course work but not necessarily to a public audience.

Once you determine the worth of what you have in hand, you might want to set about choosing an appropriate audience for it. Go to the newsstand and the library; become familiar with the places in which people are publishing nonfiction now. Check the quarterlies and the college literary magazines. In anthologies, notice sources for the readings, particularly the readings that are similar to what you are trying to write. In guides like *Writer's Market, Literary Market Place, The International Directory of Little Magazines and Small Presses* and in publications like *The Writer* or *The Writer's Digest,* look up possible places to send what you have written. Make lists and read the specific descriptions carefully. Consider their level of sophistication, their publication history, and their preferences.

It would not be wise, for example, to choose an avowedly feminist journal for a humorous paper about picking up girls at the local bar (unless they were looking for a specimen from prehistory), but a school newspaper *may* be amused. In 1985 it would not have been productive to send a feminist article (or any other article, for that matter) to Mary Applehoff, director of a press that offered the following description of itself. Ms. Applehoff said:

> ... Although publications have included a family history ... and the *Ms. Fortune 500 Directory* ed. by Mary Applehoff, I am currently concentrating on studies about earthworms. My most recent book, *Worms Eat My Garbage*... sold 4,000 copies first year and is now in second printing. I am not seeking manuscripts...."

To save time, you should send a "query" letter, which is a description of what you have written (or propose to write) and a request that it be read. Consider the following "query" letter about an article on a "travel" subject.

Waltham, Oregon
May 12, 1990

Mr. Carlo Barretti, Editor
Italian Experiences Magazine
Via Roma 22
Rome, Italy

Dear Mr. Barretti,

I am writing to inquire about your possible interest in an article I have written on lesser-known day-trips from Florence. It seems most appropriate for your monthly column, "Off the Beaten Path," because that is just the focus of this piece.

I lived in Florence for a year and was thus able to take many short trips in the vicinity, trips that the average tourist hurrying to the major sites might miss. I focus on four of these sites: the convent at Montesenario, high above Florence, offering fine views and interesting walks among the grottoes; the Villa Demidoff, with beautiful grounds for easy springtime hikes and Giambologna's colossal statue of Appennino hovering above the gardens; the little zoo at Pistoia, with shaded walks, a lively playground, and well-tended animals from all over the world; and a bit further afield, the historical marble quarries at Carrara (where Michelangelo got his white stone for his David).

All of these sites seem appropriate for readers of your "Off the Beaten Path" column, those looking for sites beyond the Duomo and the Uffizi in Florence.

As it is now, the piece is about 2,000 words, but it could be cut or extended according to your editorial demands. (It could also be broken up into several shorter pieces, if you prefer.)

If you think you might be interested, I would be happy to send this piece immediately for your consideration.

Sincerely,
Joan Runfola

(Notice that this letter is short, states the subject early, suggests some knowledge of the magazine, and summarizes the major contents. It also expresses a willingness to accommodate the editor's needs.)

If you do send a manuscript for reading, include a self-addressed, stamped envelope (SASE) for its return, for it may well be returned. *Most* manuscripts are returned. The term "round-tripper," coined by a writer to describe the fast to-and-fro of many manuscripts is, unfortunately, all too accurate.

But try not to become defeated. (It is impossible not to become discouraged; after each return, a brief period of sulking is allowed.) Remember that literary records abound with tales of overlooked and unappreciated masterpieces, with rejections of manuscripts that eventually became best-sellers, with writers whose genius was discovered only after death. Guiseppe Tomasi di Lampedusa died thinking that his one book, *The Leopard,* would never be printed; after his death, it became well known in Europe and in America. Walt Whitman first published himself, and Thomas Hardy once commented to Virginia Woolf, "I wrote a great many poems. I used to send them about, but they were always returned.... And in those days I believed in editors." James Joyce's *Dubliners* was rejected by 22 publishers, and Beatrix Potter's *The Tale of Peter Rabbit* was rejected by at least 7 before she published it herself, which finally led to one of the 7 taking on future publication for her.

If you still believe in your manuscript, however, and you can still afford the postage, keep it in circulation. You might also retire it and return to it later, maybe much later. Meanwhile, keep writing. Keep working on new things. Keep trying to learn more about writing by *thinking* as you write and as you read. Mounds of paper will not necessarily yield a manuscript demanded by publishers before the ink is dry, but mounds of paper written by a thoughtful and determined writer just might.

PRACTICE

1. Imagine that you have just written a "seven-page discussion of alienation between a son and a father" and that you are looking for a place to send either a query letter or the manuscript. If it has been written as a "human-interest" piece, the subject may appear in a publication focusing on family life or possibly even in a women's magazine, if it has been told from a woman's point of view or from the point of view of a witness. If the focus is on the process of coping with an alienated son, it may fit into an "advice" column in the "Living" section of a newspaper, but it would have to be condensed and cut. If the approach is professional, using the experiences described as a "case-study," it may be more appropriate for a psychological journal. Tone and depth of treatment would have a great deal to do with the ultimate destination for writing on this topic.

   Using a similar approach, and if the subject seems reasonable and interesting enough for a potential reading audience, suggest appropriate locations or *types* of locations for the following manuscripts:

   a. A complaint about a college language requirement.
   b. A prayer thanking God for three healthy children.
   c. A negative account of a visit to the Taj Mahal.
   d. An appreciative account of a visit to the Taj Mahal.
   e. A discussion of seasonal entertainments in New England or some other particular location.
   f. An appreciation of a much loved elementary school teacher.
   g. How to exercise while living life in the fast lane.
   h. An interview with Larry Bird.
   i. A humorous account of climbing up a local mountain.
   j. A speech arguing for membership in the peace movement.
   k. An argument against the development of a new mall.
   l. How to prepare your garden for the spring bird migration.
   m. An inspiring portrayal of a victory over cancer.
   n. A six-page account of a miserable time at a fifth high-school reunion.
   o. An exposé on the private lives of five vice-presidents.
   p. A pro-choice essay based on personal experience.
   q. An appeal for winter housing for the homeless.
   r. An analysis of recently released letters by Ernest Hemingway.
   s. A dispute over two variant readings in a Chaucer manuscript.
   t. An article on the zen of dirt biking.
   u. A recollection of childhood vacations in Nova Scotia.
   v. A comparison between Massachusetts and Texas public high schools.

w. An argument against censorship in textbooks.
x. An appeal for more censorship in school reading.
y. A proposal for a textbook in chemistry.
z. An analysis of a current political problem, for example, a proposed new tax or a cutback in spending on education.

FOR YOUR OWN PAPER

1. Find three possible locations for a piece you might like to publish. Rank them in order of priority and explain why they seem to fit your purposes.
2. Write a query letter to all three.
3. Send a carefully prepared manuscript, if a source seems interested. Also include a SASE (Even though, of *course,* it will never be used!).

Acknowledgments

"Anger at First Sight" by Lyn Capodanno. Reprinted by permission of the author.

"The Bowerbird" [editor's title] excerpted from "Courtship Through the Ages" by James Thurber. Copyright © 1942 by James Thurber. From *My World—and Welcome to It*, published by Harcourt Brace Jovanovich, Inc. Reprinted by permission of Rosemary A. Thurber.

"The Woes of a Waitress" by Tien Truong. Copyright © 1983 by Tien Truong. Reprinted by permission of the author.

"Seventh of the Litter" by Sharyn Carbone. Reprinted by permission of the author.

"Same Train, Different Year" by David Vinopal. Reprinted by permission of the author.

"Early Impressions" [editor's title] excerpted from "Reading and Writing: Early Impressions" by Michiko Kakutani, *New York Times Book Review*, February 6, 1983. Copyright © 1983 by the New York Times Company. Reprinted by permission.

"Three Boys" by John Updike, from *Five Boyhoods*, edited by Martin Levin. Copyright © 1962, renewed 1990 by Martin Levin. Reprinted by permission.

"Playing with the Bleacher Bums" by Don Paskowski. Reprinted by permission of the author.

"A House or a Condo? A.M." by Joseph Hession. Reprinted by permission of the author.

"The Joys of Commuting?" by Deborah Pennimpede. Copyright © 1983 by Deborah Pennimpede. Reprinted by permission.

"Little Boy Lost" by Pat Hourihan. Reprinted by permission of the author.

"Football Red and Baseball Green" by Murray Ross. Copyright © 1982 by Murray Ross. Reprinted by permission of the author. An earlier version of this piece appeared in *Chicago Review*, January–February 1971.

"Museé des Beaux Arts" by W. H. Auden. From *W. H. Auden: Collected Poems*, edited by Edward Mendelson. Copyright © 1940, renewed 1968 by W. H. Auden. Reprinted by permission of Random House, Inc. and Faber and Faber Ltd.

"Landscape with the Fall of Icarus" by William Carlos Williams. From *Collected Poems, 1939–1962, Vol. II* by William Carlos Williams. Copyright © 1960 by William Carlos Williams. Reprinted by permission of New Directions Publishing Corporation.

"The Dairy Group" by Linda Erickson. Reprinted by permission of the author.

"Gifts in my Drawer" [editor's title] excerpted from "My Drawer" in *Bachelorhood: Tales of the Metropolis* by Philip Lopate. Copyright © 1981 by Philip Lopate. Reprinted by permission of The Wendy Weil Agency, Inc.

"What Makes a Being Super?" by Roger Froilan. Reprinted by permission of the author.

"Who's Who at the Modern Health Club?" by Robert Crouse. Reprinted by permission of the author.

"Homes Away from Home" by Leslie S. Moore. Reprinted by permission of the author.

"How to Detect Propaganda" by Institute for Propaganda Analysis. *Propaganda Analysis*, Vol. 1, No. 2, November 1937.

"How to Reef a Mainsail" by Erick Scheiderman. Reprinted by permission of the author.

"Getting the Film Moving Again" by Tracy Bowen. Reprinted by permission of the author.

"Bradley's Shooting Practice" [editor's title] from *A Sense of Where You Are* by John McPhee. Copyright © 1978. Reprinted by permission of Farrar Straus & Giroux.

"How to Correspond with the Stars" by John Baron. Reprinted by permission of the author.

"The Process of Writing 'Epiphany'" by Don Paskowski. Reprinted by permission of the author.

"It's Time to Play Final 'Jeopardy'" by Mark M. Lowenthal. From the *New York Times*, January 22, 1989. Copyright © 1989 by the New York Times Company. Reprinted by permission.

"How Children Learn Prejudice" [editor's title] excerpted from "People Aren't Born Prejudiced" by Ian Stevenson, M.D. *Parent's Magazine*, February 1960. Reprinted by permission of the author.

"Nutella or Guess?" by Ellen McGinn. Reprinted by permission of the author.

"Why a Muscle Car?" by Stutz Plaisted. Reprinted by permission of the author.

"Letter to My Father" from *Dearest Father* by Franz Kafka, translated by Ernst Kaiser and Eithne Williams, Copyright © 1954 by Schocken Books, Inc. Reprinted by permission of Schocken Books, published by Pantheon Books a division of Random House, Inc.

"Doubting My Major" by Tracey Brown. Reprinted by permission of the author.

"The Strand: My Own Movie" by Christopher John Stephens. Reprinted by permission of the author.

"Some Major Effects of Divorce on Children" by Linda Alves. Reprinted by permission of the author.

"The Effects of Steroids" [editor's title] by the NCAA Drug Education Committee. From *Drugs, Coach, and the Athlete* by the National Collegiate Athletic Association, Reprinted by permission of the NCAA.

"I Want a Wife" by Judy Syfers. From *Ms. Magazine*, December 1971. Reprinted by permission of the author.

"What Is Digital Video Imaging?" by Jonathan Hart. Reprinted by permission of the author.

"Finding the Missing Penny" by Garbrielle King. Reprinted by permission of the author.

"One Man's Briar Patch" by Laurel DeWolf. Reprinted by permission of the author.

"What are Steroids?" by Philip DePalma. Reprinted by permission of the author.

"Portrait of a Credit Card Junkie" by Lisa Amore. Reprinted by permission of the author.

"Watching the Watchers" by Ann Taylor. Reprinted by permission of the author.

"The Search Is Off" by Karen Connery. Reprinted by permission of the author.

"What's Wrong with Less Than Perfect?" by Tina Beecher. Reprinted by permission of the author.

"The Social Set" by Edwin Diamond. From *American Film*, February 1979. Copyright © 1979 The American Film Institute. Reprinted by permission of the author.

"The Child Before the Set" [editor's title] excerpted from *More in Anger* by Marya Mannes, J. B. Lippincott. Copyright © 1958. Reprinted by permission of David J. Blow.

"The Meeting with the Old Proletarian in *Nineteen Eighty-four*" by Eileen Drago. Reprinted by permission of the author.

"Heroic Eve" by Francis Blessington. Reprinted by permission of the author.

"One Writer's Travels in the World of Words" by Thomas D'Evelyn. *The Christian Science Monitor*. Reprinted by permission of the author.

"The Caterer Told You So!" by Nancy Gilman. Reprinted by permission of the author.

"The Not So Super Market!" by Michael Brangiforte. Reprinted by permission of the author.

"Why Wilderness?" by Edward Abbey. From *The Journey Home*, E. P. Dutton. Reprinted by permission of the author.

"The Down Side of Rock and Roll" by Robert Salerno. Reprinted by permission of the author.

"In Defense of English Majors" by Jane Jerrard. Reprinted with permission from *National Forum*, Fall 1983, special issue on "Improving America's Prose." Copyright © 1983 The Honor Society of Phi Kappa Phi.

"Running on Empty" by John Speziale. Reprinted by permission of the author.

"I Have a Dream" by Martin Luther King, Jr. Copyright © 1963 by Martin Luther King, Jr. Reprinted by permission of Joan Daves.

Three Reviews of *Batman*: From "The City Gone Psycho" by Pauline Kael, the *New Yorker*, July 10, 1989. Copyright © 1989 by Pauline Kael. Reprinted by permission. / "Batting Below Average" by John Simon from *National Review*, August 18, 1989. Copyright © 1989 by National Review, Inc. Reprinted by permission. / Review of "Batman" by Orli Low from *On Line at the Movies*, June 1989. Reprinted by permission of the author.

"The New Year's Flower Market in Canton" by Weijon Chu. Reprinted by permission of the author.

"Camping I Hate!" by Sally Atwater. Reprinted by permission of the author.

"Body Shop" by Paul Grasso. Reprinted by permission of the author.

"Getting through to Students" by Gilbert Highet. From *The Immortal Profession: The Joy of Teaching and Learning* by Gilbert Highet. Copyright © 1976 by Gilbert Highet. Reprinted by permission of Curtis Brown Ltd.

"My Room, My Prison" by Vladimir Glezer. Reprinted by permission of the author.

"The Subway to the Synagogue" [editor's title] excerpted from "From the Subway to the Synagogue" in *A Walker in the City* by Alfred Kazin. Copyright © 1951, renewed 1979 by Alfred Kazin. Reprinted by permission of Harcourt Brace Jovanovich, Inc.

"Reefing in a Brisk Wind" by Erick Scheiderman. Reprinted by permission of the author.

"I'll Take the Low Road" by John Baron. Reprinted by permission of the author.

"The Purse Test" by Anne McKay. Reprinted by permission of the author.

"Beating for the Hunt" [editor's title] excerpted from "At Play in the Paradise of Bombs" in *The Paradise of Bombs* by Scott Russell Sanders. Copyright © 1983 by Scott Russell Sanders. First appeared in *The North American Review*. Reprinted by permission of the author and the author's agent, Virginia Kidd.

"What the Dog Did" by Ian Frazier. *The New Yorker* Magazine. Reprinted by permission of the author.

"Bigger and Better?" by Paul Grasso. Reprinted by permission of the author.

"Epiphany" by Don Paskowski. Reprinted by permission of the author.

"Traveling South: Circa 1950" by Gwendolyn L. Rosemond. Reprinted by permission of the author.

"Salvation" from *The Big Sea* by Langston Hughes. Copyright © 1940 by Langston Hughes. Renewed © 1969 by Arna Bontemps and George Houston Bass. Reprinted by permission of Hill and Wang, a division of Farrar, Straus & Giroux, Inc.

"Think About It" [editor's title] excerpted from "Think About It: Ways We Know and Don't" by Frank Conroy. Copyright © 1988 by *Harper's Magazine*. All rights reserved. Reprinted from the November issue by special permission.

"What Is a Good Review?" [editor's title] excerpted from *If You Don't Mind My Saying So* by Joseph Wood Krutch. Copyright © 1964 by Joseph Wood Krutch. Reprinted by permission of William Morrow & Company, Inc.

"Can Society Banish Cruelty?" from *In the Light of History* by J. H. Plumb. Reprinted by permission of the author.

"The Ambivalence of Abortion" by Linda Bird Franke. First appeared in the *New York Times*, May 14, 1976. Copyright © 1976 by Linda Bird Franke. Reprinted by permission of the author.

"Why the Americans Are So Restless in the Midst of Their Prosperity" from *Democracy in America* by Alexis de Tocqueville, edited by Phillips Bradley, translated by Henry Reeve, revised by Francis Bowen. Copyright © 1945, renewed 1973 by Alfred A. Knopf, Inc. Reprinted by permission of the publisher.

"What's Wrong with 'Me, Me, Me'?" by Margaret Halsey from *Newsweek*, April 17, 1978. Copyright © 1978 by Margaret Halsey. Reprinted by permission of International Creative Management, Inc.

"Halloween Party" from *Takes: Stories from the Talk of the Town* by Lillian Ross. Copyright © 1983 by Lillian Ross. Reprinted by permission of Congdon & Weed.

"Japanese and American Workers" from *Theory Z* by William Ouchi. Copyright © 1981 by Addison-Wesley Publishing Co., Inc. Reprinted by permission of the publisher.

"The Family/Career Priority Problem" by Ellen Goodman. Copyright © 1979 by the Washington Post Writer's Group. Reprinted by permission.

"Aria" from *Hunger of Memory* by Richard Rodriquez. Copyright © 1982 by Richard Rodriquez. Reprinted by permission of David R. Godine, Publisher.

"Once More to the Lake" from *Essays of E. B. White* by E. B. White. Copyright © 1941 by E. B. White. Reprinted by permission of HarperCollins Publishers Inc.

Illustration Credits:

p. 91: © 1989 Volvo North America Corporation. Reprinted by permission.

p. 103: From the collection of John Baron. Used by permission.

p. 280: Drawing by M. Stevens: © 1989 The New Yorker Magazine, Inc.

p. 346: Drawing by Donald Reilly: © 1982 The New Yorker Magazine, Inc.

p. 352: Drawing by Ziegler: © 1989 The New Yorker Magazine, Inc.

pp. 359, 360, 385: Reprinted with permission of Joel White and the Cornell University Library.